INSPIRE / PLAN / DISCOVER / EXPERIENCE

THE NETHERLANDS

DK EYEWITNESS

THE NETHERLANDS

CONTENTS

The cheese market at Alkmaar

DISCOVER 6

EXPERIENCE AMSTERDAM 68

EXPERIENCE THE NETHERLANDS 176

NEED TO KNOW 392

DISCOVER

Urk Lighthouse, Flevoland

WELCOME TO
THE NETHERLANDS

Reflective waterways and tilting canal houses. Delectable wine and world-class street food. Vivid flower fields and slow-spinning windmills. Epic museums and sprawling street art. From cosmopolitan cities perched delicately on land reclaimed from the North Sea to ethereal natural wonders, this small country contains a great multitude of surprises. Whatever your dream trip to the Netherlands entails, this DK Eyewitness travel guide is the perfect companion.

1 Admiring a vast canvas in the Rijksmuseum.

2 An isolated refuge on the island of Terschelling.

3 Dutch wares on display at an Amsterdam cheese shop.

4 Gliding over a wintery Kinderdijk canal.

Lauded for its pleasingly no-nonsense and civilized way of life, this flat country reveals a surprisingly wild side. Between gorgeous cities and villages connected by canals, rugged heathland spreads across the interior, merging into marshy fenland fringed by dunes. In the country's northern reaches, a necklace of remote sandy islands is strung out across the Waddenzee, a windswept wonderland of mud flats and seal colonies.

In marvellous contrast, regimented farmland bursts into technicolour dreams in the famous bulb fields, and watersports, windmill-dotted fields, vineyard terraces and local craft beers lure visitors to postcard-pretty villages. Most of the action is to the west in the belt of cities that comprise the Randstad. Each has its own character, from the laid-back hedonism of Amsterdam to the foodie scene of Rotterdam. World-class museums await, including the Mauritshuis in Den Haag and the Rijksmuseum in Amsterdam. And of course, all have first-rate art galleries bursting with works by Vermeer, Van Gogh and Rembrandt.

The Netherlands is so full of things to see and do that it can be hard to know where to start. We've broken the country down into easily navigable sections, with detailed itineraries, expert local knowledge and comprehensive maps to help you plan the perfect visit. Whether you're staying for a weekend, a week or longer, this DK Eyewitness guide will ensure that you see the best the country has to offer. Enjoy the book, and enjoy the Netherlands.

REASONS TO LOVE
THE NETHERLANDS

Vibrant cities and abundant culture, vividly coloured bulbfields and wild dunescapes, picture-perfect windmills and freewheeling bicycles: there are endless reasons to love the Netherlands. Here are our favourites.

1 FLOWER POWER
In spring, take delight in the stunning colours of the blooming bulb fields *(p189)* and of the floating Bloemenmarkt *(p125)* in Amsterdam's canals, overflowing with flowers.

CHEESE TASTING IN GOUDA 2
Bustling with vintage weighing stations, stop-and-sample markets and wheels of sweet mellow cheese, Gouda *(p250)* is a must-visit for cheese lovers.

3 ARCHITECTURE IN ROTTERDAM
Heavy bombing during World War II turned the city *(p244)* into a blank canvas, resulting in a striking skyline of swan-like bridges, pixelated homes and upside-down skyscrapers.

TAKE A WALK ON THE WIDE SIDE 4

Ribboned with walking and cycling trails across sand dunes, heathland and woodland, Nationaal Park De Hoge Veluwe *(p346)* is the Netherlands at its wildest.

WEST FRISIAN ISLANDS 5

Get off-grid in the remote North Sea archipelago *(p273)*. Ringed by peaceful beaches, breezy dunes and wildlife-rich salt marshes, this unplugged paradise will make you want to never leave.

DUTCH MASTERS 6

Admire magnificent canvases by Dutch Old Masters depicting Dutch scenes in vivid strokes at the Mauritshuis *(p236)*. This 17th-century artistic revolution changed the art world forever.

STORMY WATERS 7

Erupting from the wild North Sea, the extraordinary Oosterscheldekering *(p260)* is an engineering marvel that protects Zeeland from the powerful waters around it.

ON TWO WHEELS 8

A trip to the Netherlands wouldn't be complete without riding city streets, coasting country trails or zooming down *fietssnelwegen* (cycle highways) on two wheels.

9 EINDHOVEN'S STRIJP-S

Shop for innovative design, seek out vintage gems, pause for coffee in quirky cafés - this sprawling industrial relic *(p370)* is now a fabulous creative city you can explore for hours.

10 THE BLOCKBUSTER RIJKSMUSEUM

Few art collections can rival the concentrated brilliance of Amsterdam's most famous museum *(p138)*. Rembrandt's masterful *The Night Watch* is not to be missed.

11 SAILING THE FRISIAN LAKES

Getting out onto the water is a quintessentially Dutch activity. Feel the spray of the surf on your face as you sail across the glassy surface of these gorgeous bodies of water.

12 PRETTY POTTERY

Richly painted in iconic blue hues, tin-glazed delftware *(p242)* is as beautiful as it is ubiquitous. Pick up pieces at vintage markets or create your own at a workshop in Delft *(p238)*.

EXPLORE
THE NETHERLANDS

This guide divides the Netherlands into 14 colour-coded sightseeing areas, as shown on this map. Find out more about each area on the following pages.

WEST FRISIAN ISLANDS
p272

Waddenzee

Den Helder

IJsselmeer

NORTH HOLLAND
p178

Enkhuizen

Hoorn

Alkmaar

Markermeer

Leylstad

FLEVOLAND
p332

Amsterdam

Almere

Haarlem

AMSTERDAM
p68

Amersfoort

North Sea

Leiden

Utrecht

UTRECHT
p208

The Hague

SOUTH HOLLAND
p222

Delft

Gouda

Hoek van Holland

Lek

Tiel

Rotterdam

Waal

Spijkenisse

Dordrecht

's Hertogenbosch

Zierikzee

NORTH BRABANT
p358

Breda

Tilburg

ZEELAND
p256

Bergen op Zoom

Middelburg

Eindhoven

Turnhout

Terneuzen

Antwerpen

Oostende

Bruges

Ghent

Mechelen

BELGIUM

Hasselt

Kortrijk

Leuven

Brussels

Oudenaarde

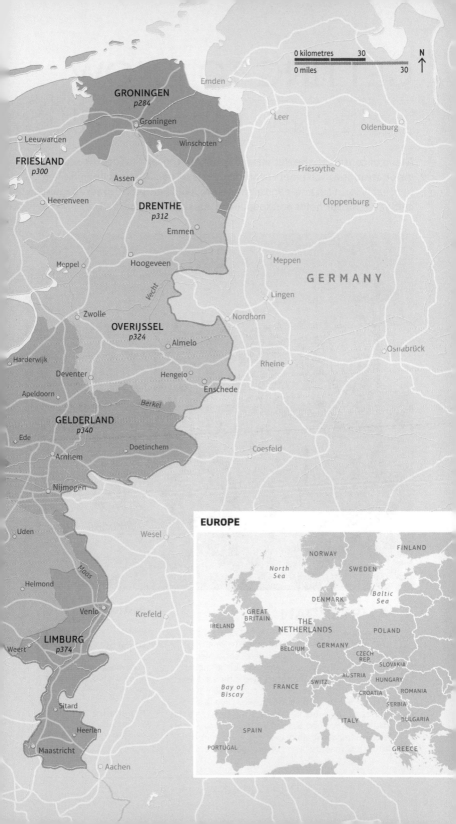

GRONINGEN
p284

Groningen

Emden

Leer

Oldenburg

Winschoten

Leeuwarden

FRIESLAND
p300

Assen

Friesoythe

Heerenveen

DRENTHE
p312

Cloppenburg

Emmen

Meppen

Meppel

Hoogeveen

GERMANY

Vecht

Lingen

Zwolle

Nordhorn

OVERIJSSEL
p324

Almelo

Osnabrück

Harderwijk

Deventer

Hengelo

Rheine

Apeldoorn

Enschede

Berkel

GELDERLAND
p340

Ede

Doetinchem

Coesfeld

Arnhem

Nijmegen

Uden

Wesel

Maas

Helmond

Venlo

Krefeld

LIMBURG
p374

Weert

Sitard

Heerlen

Maastricht

Aachen

EUROPE

NORWAY

FINLAND

North Sea

SWEDEN

DENMARK

Baltic Sea

IRELAND

GREAT BRITAIN

THE NETHERLANDS

POLAND

BELGIUM

GERMANY

CZECH REP.

SLOVAKIA

AUSTRIA

HUNGARY

Bay of Biscay

FRANCE

SWITZ.

CROATIA

ROMANIA

SERBIA

ITALY

BULGARIA

PORTUGAL

SPAIN

GREECE

GETTING TO KNOW
THE NETHERLANDS

A land of contrasts, the Netherlands is where the land meets the sea and visionary innovation meets centuries-old tradition. Quaint windmills live peaceably with cutting-edge architecture, wild heathland presses against cultivated flower fields and sparkling canals connect them all.

AMSTERDAM

PAGE 68

Ribboned with canals, picture-perfect Amsterdam is the country's bustling hub. Glorious 17th-century mansions rub shoulders with warehouses-turned-entertainment complexes, while gridded neighbourhoods fan out along the Amstel river to the art-filled Museumkwartier. The city's infamously hedonistic nightlife – so much more than the Red Light District – pulses with relentless nightclubs, world-class cafés and laid-back brown bars. Beyond the centre, history meets eccentric modernity, from evocative Anne Frank Huis to the repurposed wharves of Amsterdam Noord.

Best for
Stepped-gabled canal houses, museums, thumping nightlife

Home to
Joods Historisch Museum, Museum het Rembrandthuis, Anne Frank Huis, Rijksmuseum, Van Gogh Museum, NEMO Science Museum

Experience
Seeing the city from the water on a canal cruise

NORTH HOLLAND

PAGE 178

Anchored by Amsterdam to the south and Texel Island to the north, this postcard-pretty peninsula juts boldly into the North Sea. In the west, history comes to life in Haarlem, famous for its fringe of tulip fields. Bang in the centre, follow the Zaan River past windmills crowding the skyline at Zaanse Schans, as it snakes up to Alkmaar and its tempting cheese market. On the east coast, while away hours in tiny fishing villages – quaint jumping-off points to timeless Marken, where wooden houses teeter on stilts.

Best for
Beaches, cycling, traditional fishing towns

Home to
The bulb fields, Haarlem, Zuiderzeemuseum, Alkmaar

Experience
Cycling through technicolour bulb fields in spring

UTRECHT

PAGE 208

Petite Utrecht province, home to charming towns and ancient villages, is best known for its lively capital of the same name. The city of Utrecht is steeped in history, with Roman ruins, medieval castles and pre-Reformation cathedrals, while the exuberant Nijntje Museum and Rietveld Schröderhuis reveal a more playful side of the university town. Outside the capital, a tour through rolling countryside takes in slow-moving windmills and sprawling summerhouses along the Vecht, water sports on the Vinkeveense Plassen and 17th-century art in Amersfoort.

Best for
Castles and fortifications, encounters with Miffy

Home to
Utrecht

Experience
Discovering how water became a weapon at the Waterliniemuseum

$\rightarrow$

SOUTH HOLLAND

PAGE 222

The epicentre of Dutch culture, South Holland is dominated by two contrasting cities: the pomp and pageantry of the capital Den Haag and the modern architectural marvels and epic foodie scene of raucous Rotterdam. Elsewhere, story-book *jenever* windmills rotate in the breeze, while potters keep their wheels turning in Delft. Throughout the spring and summer, canal boats tootle through kaleidoscopic tulip fields of the bulb fields that stretch between Haarlem and Leiden. All along the coast, long sandy beaches and charming seaside resorts are ideal for family days out.

Best for
Sightseeing and floral displays

Home to
Leiden, Den Haag, Delft, Rotterdam, Gouda

Experience
Dancing until dawn at Rotterdam's annual Latino-fest, Zomercarnaval

ZEELAND

PAGE 256

Dreamy Zeeland entices visitors with the promise of lazy days on the beach and endless sea views. There are plenty of charming sights to explore. The streets of Middelburg weave a tale of Dutch East India Company trade. Seaside Domburg, surrounded by dunes and sandy beaches, is a gateway to 16th-century castles and hiker haven De Manteling nature reserve, while pleasure boats putter out from Veere's marina. Along the coast, robust dykes, historic lighthouses and heaping plates of lobster and mussels reflect an enduring relationship with the sea.

Best for
Watersports, seafood, traditional costume

Home to
Oosterscheldekering, Middelburg

Experience
Learning about the North Sea flood of 1953 at Watersnoodmuseum

PAGE 272

WEST FRISIAN ISLANDS

This wild, wind-whipped archipelago off the northwest coast of Friesland has dune-fringed beaches, tidal flats and historic villages, all tamed by the ebb and flow of the North Sea. In the north lie rugged Schiermonnikoog, the country's first national park, and laid-back Ameland, crisscrossed by scenic cycle trails. Sailing south brings seal encounters and naval history in Terschelling and Vlieland. The isolation, hard-won peace and prevailing winds that sweep these islands hold sway over anyone who sets foot on them.

Best for
Beaches, bird-watching

Home to
The Waddenzee

Experience
The horizontal alpinism of wadlopen (mud walking)

PAGE 284

GRONINGEN

Lush pastures and broad expanses of woodland and moor sweep across rural Groningen. Here the air is filled with birdsong, the buzz of bees and the scent of wild flowers. Laced with long coastal walking trails, Lauwersmeer National Park is ideal for camping under the dazzling dark skies, while isolated coves around Paterswoldemeer invite wild swimming. On the coast, you'll find marine life aplenty at Pieterburen's seal sanctuary. In contrast, university city Groningen buzzes with loud-and-proud nightlife, and its museums and markets deliver a punch of culture without the crowds.

Best for
Wide vistas, walking and cycling, history

Home to
Groningen

Experience
Wild swimming in beautiful forgotten lakes

$\rightarrow$

PAGE 300

FRIESLAND

Draped with fenland, large swathes of this picturesque province testify to Dutch land-reclaiming prowess. The resulting waterways and lakes promise hop-on hop-off cruises between villages and – most intriguingly – the chance for *skûtsjesilen* (barge sailing). Inland lies postcard-pretty Leeuwarden with its candy-coloured houses and unbeatable foodie experiences. For sports fans, an unmissable event is the Elfstedentocht, a historic 11-city winter ice-skating marathon – watch it or join in the fun by hiking, biking or skating the route when its interconnecting canals freeze.

Best for
Sailing, Frisian culture

Home to
The Thialfstadion

Experience
Sailing on a traditional skûtsje *(barge)*

PAGE 312

DRENTHE

A product of the last Ice Age and inhabited for millennia, this little-visited hidden gem may be the country's most alluring region. Cresting the Hondsrug ridge, the peat moors of the UNESCO Global Geopark are dotted with 5,000-year-old *hunebedden* (megaliths), while Orvelte, with its 19th-century farmhouses and horse-drawn trams, is a reminder of more recent times. Most trips are bookended with a stop in Assen or Emmen, but the real allure are the 1,400 km (870 miles) of cycle paths and the endless hiking trails through heathland and forest.

Best for
Prehistory, heathlands

Home to
Assen, Hondsrug UNESCO Global Geopark

Experience
Cycling between megaliths

PAGE 324

OVERIJSSEL

Historic towns compete for attention with ancient wild spaces in this diverse eastern provice. Buttressing the western edge, the port town of Zwolle is a cultural hothouse, with light-filled art galleries and impressive museums. Further up the IJseel river, the towns of Deventer and Kampen, with their medieval houses and bustling markets, recall their prosperous Hanseatic pasts. However, the best way to experience Overijssel is in the great outdoors – canoeing the Weerribben-Wieden wetlands or cycling through the Sallandse Heuvelrug reveals a land bursting with wildlife.

Best for
History, Hanseatic towns, rivers and wetlands

Home to
Deventer, Sallandse Heuvelrug Nationaal Park, Giethoorn

Experience
Canoeing in the Weerribben

→

FLEVOLAND

Reclaimed from the Zuiderzee, the Netherlands' youngest province is distinguished by its flat polder landscape and verdant farmland, all ringed by sandy beaches. The complicated relationship between land and sea has given rise to a string of enormous "landscape art", made in the forests and deltas around Zeewolde and Lelystad. Vibrant modern cities like Almere and Lelystad provide a dynamic alternative to storied fishing villages such as Urk and Oostelijk. Wrapping around them are the wide open marshlands of Knardijk and the Oostvaardersplassen.

Best for
Man-made nature, "landscape art", fishing villages

Home to
Urk, Almere, Nagele

Experience
Paragliding over the countryside for a bird's-eye view of large-scale "landscape art"

GELDERLAND

Hugged by the German border, the Netherlands' largest province feels a world away from the windmills and bulb fields of the west. Explore the ancient foundations of Arnhem and Nijmegen, then join history buffs at quiet Apeldoorn and its landmark castle, the 17th-century Paleis Het Loo. Upping the adventure, follow hiking trails past herds of deer in Nationaal Park De Hoge Veluwe, while in the centre of the park is the modern art mecca of the Kröller-Müller Museum, which offers insights into the mind of Vincent van Gogh.

Best for
Nature, history, regional produce

Home to
Paleis Het Loo, Nationaal Park De Hoge Veluwe, Kröller-Müller Museum

Experience
Cherry sampling in De Betuwe

PAGE 358

NORTH BRABANT

Along the coast, rippling dunes create a vision of sandy wilderness backed by rolling hills. Strabrechtse Heide is a natural heathland for rambles and ambles, while the stirring monuments, soaring cathedrals and centuries-old canals in Den Bosch bask in medieval magic. Just when you think you know the province as a delightful backwater, Eindhoven presents a portrait of cutting-edge design. Home to a multitude of creatives and start-ups, its Strijp-S district has made it one of Europe's design capitals.

Best for
Dutch design, local cuisine, walking

Home to
's-Hertogenbosch

Experience
A glimpse of the future at Dutch Design Week in Eindhoven

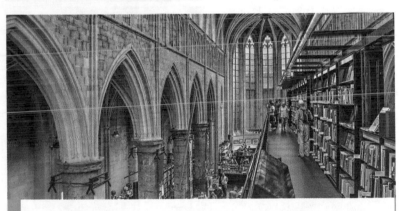

PAGE 374

LIMBURG

This slice of hilly land to Brabant's southeast is dotted with excellent vineyards. Oenophiles flock here to sample wine cellar offerings, while foodies are in for a treat with white asparagus, *vlaai* (fruit pies) and pastries oozing with Limburger and Herve cheese. Beyond the vineyards, buzzy Maastrict, home to meandering canals, Roman ruins and the glorious Bonnefantenmuseum, bursts into colourful disarray during carnival. In Arcen, a romantic castle and lavish gardens vie for attention with mineral-rich natural spas, drawn from 900 m (3,000 ft) underground.

Best for
Hills, local wineries, castles

Home to
Maastricht

Experience
Wandering around vineyards, a glass of local bubbly in hand

←

1 A *rondvaartboot* cruising down a canal.

2 A performer in Leidseplein.

3 The Art Deco interior of Café Americain.

4 Flowers, bulbs and seeds for sale at the Bloemenmarkt.

Beautiful and varied, the Netherlands brims with travel possibilities. To help you plan your time in this fascinating country, these suggested itineraries pick out the highlights of each of its regions and of the capital city, Amsterdam.

5 HOURS
in Amsterdam

Morning

Whether arriving in the city centre from the airport or by train, Centraal Station is the perfect gateway to the heart of this vibrant city. Historically, Amsterdam has been shaped by the water, so choose to explore the city for the first time by boat, rather than on foot. The Open Haven, in front of the station, is the best place to hop on a canal boat. There are lots of options to choose from, including multi-stop boats that connect all the major museums for those who want to cover a lot of sights in a short space of time. For a more relaxed introduction to the city, glass-topped *rondvaartboten* (tour boats) offer trips that last anywhere from one hour to 90 minutes, with multi-lingual commentary that highlights the opulent 17th-century architecture of the Herengracht, Prinsegracht and Keizersgracht canals, the splendour of the Golden Bend *(p119)* and canalside landmarks. You'll cruise past the striking spires of the Westerkerk *(p117)*, and Munttoren *(p125)*, as well as the pretty floating Bloemenmarkt *(p125)*.

Afternoon

After leisurely taking in the city, hop off your boat at Leidseplein *(p121)* – a square filled with street performers eager for applause – where you'll find plenty of pleasant places for a lunch break. Sit back at one of the open-air cafés and watch the free entertainment. The nearby Café Americain *(p121)*, with its fountain and striped awnings, is a good choice. If the weather is problematic, the interior, with its vibrant stained glass, will not disappoint. After savouring your meal, you'll be ready to continue discovering the city's highlights. Many canal cruise companies offer combination tickets that give you fast-track access to the vast Rijksmuseum *(p138)*. Rembrandt's *The Night Watch* has pride of place in the museum's Gallery of Honour, but book a guided Highlights of the Rijksmuseum tour to take in other masterpieces, such as Rembrandt's *The Jewish Bride*, Frans Hals's *The Wedding Portrait* and *The Merry Drinker*, and Jan Vermeer's serenely luminous *The Kitchen Maid* and *Woman Reading a Letter*. The perfect end to your day in the city.

←

1 Discovering the past at the Joods Historisch Museum.

2 The Nationaal Monument dominating Dam Square.

3 Café de Sluyswacht's outdoor seating.

4 Cantonese cuisine at Oriental City.

2 DAYS
in Amsterdam

Day 1

Morning The Dam is the natural starting point for your voyage of discovery around Amsterdam. Pay your respects to Dutch victims of World War II at the Nationaal Monument *(p104)*, then stroll down Rokin to the Amsterdam Museum *(p96)*. For a quick glimpse of the diverse collection, head straight for the Amsterdam Gallery, which is free to enter. After admiring the Old Masters here, say hello to *'T Lieverdje*, a cheeky bronze personification of Amsterdam, on the Spui. Next, take a peek into the tranquil Begijnhof *(p103)*, where Het Houten Huis is one of the oldest houses in Amsterdam.

Afternoon Pause for lunch on the Spui at Café Luxembourg *(p101)*, a classic brasserie. Order prawn croquettes and *bitterballen* (fried meatballs). Make your way along the canal-lined streets to the Museum Quarter in time for the 3:30pm guided tour of the Van Gogh Museum *(p142)*. Discover more about one of the world's most famous artists while exploring one of the largest collections of his works.

Evening For tasty street dining, amble a couple of blocks along Stadhouderskade, turning right into Ferdinand Bolstraat. Here, and in the Albert Cuypmarkt *(p174)*, you'll be spoiled for choice.

Day 2

Morning A visit to the Joods Historisch Museum *(p82)* is a humbling reminder of how much the city owes to the Sephardic and Ashkenazi Jews who found a tolerant refuge here as early as the 15th century. In sharp contrast, the Waterlooplein market *(p90)* around the corner is a worldly clutter of flea-market stalls. Browsers can find everything here: vintage clothing, ethnic jewellery, antiques, curios and even pornography.

Afternoon The waterside Café de Sluyswacht *(p89)* is the perfect place for a snack before strolling to the Museum Het Rembrandhuis *(p84)*. Take your time gaining an insight into the home life of Amsterdam's greatest painter, before embarking on a leisurely walk along Sint Antoniesbreestraat to the Nieuwmarkt *(p86)*. Pause at In de Waag *(p87)* for a coffee before walking along Zeedijk – the main thoroughfare of Chinatown.

Evening This area is dotted with Chinese, Indonesian and Thai eateries. Oriental City *(p87)* is favoured by locals and specializes in Cantonese and Szechuan food. Feast on the fabulous dim sum, with deliciously warming fillings. After dinner, wind up at In de Wildeman *(p101)*, one of the city's finest *proeflokalen*, for an after-dinner glass of *jenever*.

←

1 Soaring Domtoren rising above downtown shops.

2 The atmospheric Olivier Biercafé, set in a former church dating from 1860.

3 Peaceful Wilhelminapark.

4 Vintage trams at the curious Spoorwegmusem.

2 DAYS
in Utrecht

Day 1

Morning Start by exploring the medieval centre on foot. First stop: the striking Domkerk *(p212)* and its soaring tower. Climb the 465 steps all the way to the top for unbeatable city views. An array of lamplit coffee shops line the leafy canals – pop into bean-to-brew specialist 't Koffieboontje *(www.tkoffieboontje.nl)* and join its almost religious following over an *appelflap* (apple turnover). The caffeine hit will power you south to meet Miffy at the Nijntje Museum *(p213)*, for a dive into the country's whimsical side.

Afternoon Take a picnic lunch in the Oude Hortus, the serene botanical gardens tucked within the grounds of Utrecht University. After, enjoy a bridge-hopping browse of the boutiques that line Oudegracht and Nieuwegracht canals.

Evening Craft beer flows through Utrecht. Grab a prandial IPA at Olivier Biercafé *(utrecht.cafe-olivier.be)*, set in a wonderfully preserved old church. Then sample French-inspired dishes at Restaurant Bis *(www.bis-utrecht.nl)* on de Lijnmarkt, one of Utrecht's quaintest streets. As sleep beckons, wend your way along Oudegracht all the way up to a green night's sleep at Mary K Hotel *(www.marykhotel.com)*, an arty, eco-friendly oasis.

Day 2

Morning Rise early for a tasty organic breakfast at the hotel. Borrow a bicycle and coast over to Rietveld Schröderhuis *(p214)*. This extraordinary house, brainchild of Dutch architect Gerrit Rietveld, is as visionary as it is stunning. Book a tour around the eccentric interiors to learn about the De Stijl movement that Rietveld spearheaded. Afterwards, let your imagination take flight with a stroll around Wilhelminapark *(www.wilhelminapark.nl)*. This tranquil green space was inaugurated in 1898 to coincide with Wilhelmina becoming queen of the Netherlands. Lunch at Parkcafé Buiten *(www.parkcafe utrecht.nl)* across the road – locals recommend the salads and homemade cakes.

Afternoon After lunch awaken your inner steampunk at the Spoorwegmuseum *(p213)*, a surprising museum dedicated to the golden age of steam. Wander up Maliebaan to Wittevrouwen, a district renowned for boutiques and a canny ability to lure in window-shoppers.

Evening As the sun sets, sit at a table for dinner at Goesting *(www.restaurant goesting.nl)*, a candlelit affair with a menu that's all about local provenance: Zeeland oysters, stuffed zucchini flowers and Dutch halibut – and great wine.

5 DAYS
in the Western Netherlands

Day 1

Morning Arrive early in Dordrecht *(p255)* to explore Holland's oldest city on foot. Dip into the merchant streets and inner harbour on your way to 13th-century Augustine monastery Het Hof and the Grote Kerk. Seek out Nobel's Brood *(www. nobelsdordrecht.nl)*, between Grote Kerk and the town hall, for fresh sandwiches and giant *eierkoeken* (egg cakes).

Afternoon Dust off any crumbs then carry on to UNESCO-worthy Kinderdijk *(p251)*, an open-air park of traditional windmills. Catch a boat to Rotterdam *(p244)*, the country's second city, and you'll see dozens of these 17th-century structures dotting the landscape.

Evening Stay at STROOM *(www.stroom rotterdam.nl)*, set in a converted power station Before bed, unwind with a cocktail and broad views from the rooftop terrace.

Day 2

Morning Start by fuelling up with coffee and a caramel *stroopwafel* before joining Architour *(www.architour.nl)* for a wander past the city's architectural marvels, led

by expert guides. The tour will take you past the striking and photogenic "cube houses", or Kubuswoningen, which typify up Rotterdam's playful architecture.

Afternoon Lunch at trendsetting FG Food Labs *(www.fgfoodlabs.nl)*, where Michelin-starred chef François Geurds perfects new dishes before serving them at his main restaurant. Hire a bicycle and cycle the hour-long route out to the iconic Kinderdijks. Remember to take your camera to capture the majesty of the windmill sails turning slowly on the horizon. As the afternoon wanes, hop onto a water bus to take you all the way back to the centre along the Maas River.

Evening Pop into the buzzy Fenix Food Factory *(www.fenixfoodfactory.nl)* in Katendrecht for global eats and locally produced craft beers.

Day 3

Morning Breakfast on a Dutch classic, *ontbijtkoek* (spiced breakfast cake), then leave for nearby Delft *(p238)*. Arrive in time to try your hand at crafting your own Delft blue designs at De Delftse Pauw

1 Windmills at Kinderdijk.
2 FG Food Labs experiments.
3 Floating moorings in The Hague's canals.
4 Scheveningen beach.
5 Balmy Hortus Botanicus.

(www.delftpottery.com). Arrange to ship your final fired piece anywhere in the world as a one-of-a kind souvenir.

Afternoon For lunch, sandwiches and smoothies at Kek (www.kekdelft.nl) are a tasty treat. Spend the rest of the afternoon discovering one of the city's most famous sons, Johannes Vermeer, at the Vermeer Centrum Delft (p241), a fabulous collection of Dutch art.

Evening Make your way to Den Haag (p230) for dinner at neighbourhood restaurant Oogst (www.restaurantoogst. nl). Afterwards, a cosy night at 't Goude Hooft (www.tgoudehooft.nl) beckons.

Day 4

Morning Tuck into an early breakfast of uitsmijter, a Dutch fry-up, and beat the crowds to the Maritshuis (p236). There's no better place to spend some time with a Rembrandt oil on canvas to yourself. Continue your culture fix at nearby Escher in Het Paleis (p232) to see mind-bending works from the Dutch graphic artist.

Afternoon Enjoy the rest of the day at Scheveningen (p252) beach – wander the

pier, snap selfies at the lighthouse, grab an ice cream waffle – then head back into the capital.

Evening Feast on Javanese classics at Warung Bude Kati (Wagenstraat 190) – the lontong with gado-gado is worth the wait.

Day 5

Morning Save breakfast until you get to Leiden (p226), 30 minutes away by train. Fuelled on smoothie bowls and single-estate coffee at Roos (www.roosleiden.nl), head to the brilliantly curated Young Rembrandt Studio (Langebrug 89), an essential stop for art lovers.

Afternoon Join artists and students seeking inspiration in Hortus Botanicus (p228) gardens, a pleasant place to picnic. Nearby, the imposing remains of Burcht van Leiden, an abandoned castle, has glorious views of Hooglandse Kerk.

Evening Stop in foodie haven, the Bishop (www.thebishop.nl), for a classic Dutch steak and scrumptious veggie options. Round off the trip with live jazz and a nightcap at Twee Spieghels (www.detweespieghels.nl).

7 DAYS
in The South

▌ Day 1

Start your trip with breakfast at Bij Betty *(www.bijbettyboz.nl)* in compact Bergen op Zoom *(p372)*. Hire a bicycle to zip past the 15th-century Het Markiezenhof palace, Lievevrouwepoort (Prisoners' Gate) and historic Grote Markt. Climb the Peperbus ("pepper-box" tower) for lovely views. Pop into Old Bakery *(www.theold bakery.nl)* for sandwiches before getting on the road. Pause in port town Willemstad *(p369)* to snap its photogenic windmills and boat-brimming harbour. Then continue to 's-Hertogenbosch *(p362)* to overnight.

▌ Day 2

Best known for its epic carnival *(p366)*, 's-Hertogenbosch is a pleasingly walkable city with a well-preserved medieval core. Wander pretty Uilenburg, glimpsing the Binnedieze canal on your way to Gothic Sint Jan *(p364)*. After lunch on Korte Putstraat, the city's self-proclaimed "eat street", indulge in *Bossche bol* (chocolate-covered cream puffs) at Banketbakkerij Jan de Groot *(p363)* – their version of the sweet treat is legendary. Afterwards, swing by the Jheronimus Bosch Art Center *(www.jheronimusbosch-artcenter.nl)* to see era-defining works from the Dutch Master. Come evening, sample the chef's "surprise menu" at Restaurant Fabuleux *(p363)*, then rub shoulders with the locals at Stadherberg 't Pumpke *(www.hetpumpke. nl)*, a lively brown bar (traditional café).

▌ Day 3

Enjoy a leisurely breakfast of *uitsmijter* (cheesy eggs on toast), pick up all you need for a picnic and hit the road for a day in the great outdoors. An hour south-east, Nationaal Park De Groote Peel *(www. natuurparkenlimburg.nl)* is laced with excellent hiking and biking trails. Don't forget your binoculars – it's ideal bird-watching country. Have a trailside picnic, ramble into the late afternoon, then head to La Vie en Rose *(p387)*, a cosy spot to lay your head.

▌ Day 4

Rise with the birds for an early morning stroll through sprawling Kasteeltuinen *(p385)*, the exquisite rose-filled gardens of stately Arcen castle. Nip south to Venlo

① Prisoners' Gate,-Bergen op Zoom.
② National Park de Groote Peel.
③ Thorn's whitewashed houses.
④ A slab of local specialty, Vlaai pie.
⑤ The famous maze of Vaals.

(p384) to sample Limburg cheeses at Kaas & Kaasjes (www.kaasenkaasjes.nl). Spend the rest of the afternoon brushing up on Dutch modern art at Museum Van Bommel-Van Dam. As the evening approaches, drop into In den Dorstigen Haen (p385) for a drink overlooking the town hall, before returning to the hotel.

Day 5

Carry on to Thorn (p386), a delightful little town, all cobbled streets and whitewashed buildings, for a lazy morning stroll. Start at the Abdijkerk, where once only royal women and girls were allowed to live. The Gemeentemuseum Land van Thorn explores the 800-year history of the town with well-curated displays. After, dive into wild swimming at nearby De Grote Hegge lake, on the way to to buzzy Maastricht (p378). Join a walking tour (p380) to discover the city's hidden gems. At dinner, head to one of them, 't Klääoske (p379), to feast on super-fresh seafood. Later, learn the tricks of the trade from master mixologists at Hotel Beez No 106 (www.beezmaastricht.nl), then fall into bed in one of its comfortable rooms.

Day 6

For breakfast buy a fruit-filled vlaai pie from De Bisschopsmolen (p378) – it's ideal fuel for exploring Maastricht's walkable centre. Grab lunch at one of the cafés lining het Vrijthof, which lights up during Lent. In the afternoon, follow Explore Maastricht (www.exploremaastricht.nl) into a network of 1,000-year-old caves which have been used as a refuge whenever Maastricht has been under siege. Emerge in time for a crisp glass of local Limburg wine at Via Mucca (www.viamucca.nl), then move on to Mes Amis (p379) for home-cooking with a twist.

Day 7

Keep your camera ready on a morning drive around picture-perfect Heuvelland (p390), near the Belgian border. The undulating landscape is littered with vineyards, breweries and ancient castles. Take the Valkenburg (p388) cable car to see it all from above. Back on the ground, finish your tour at the Domein Holset vineyards (www.domeinholset.nl), not far from the Vaals (p387) maze, and raise a glass to the week gone by.

7 DAYS

in The North and The Islands

Day 1

Start your tour in Sloten *(p309)* and get to know the town with a stroll around the canalside streets. Dip your toes into the water at Slotermeer, a short bike ride from the centre. Come afternoon, snag a table at Pannenkoekhuis De Koepoort *(Koestraat 42)* for a stack of Dutch pancakes. Drive past the landmark water gates on the way to Sneek *(p310)* for an evening cruise on the Houkesleat canal onboard a *skûtsje* (traditional barge).

Day 2

Tuck into a plate of *rollmops* (pickled fish) then set off to explore the city's waterways. Visit the Fries Scheepvaart Museum *(www.friesscheepvaartmuseum.nl)*, the enthralling seafaring museum, then walk along the canals. Stop at Lewinkel *(www. lewinkel.nl)* for sandwiches and smoothies. Recharged, drive on to Franeker *(p307)* to see the incomparable Royal Eise Eisinga Planetarium *(www.planetarium-friesland. nl)* – be sure to look up to best admire the scale model of the solar system on the ceiling. Before twilight, roll up in Leeuwarden *(p306)* in time for dinner in

the Post Plaza Hotel's Art Deco brasserie, before snuggling into bed in one of its stylish rooms.

Day 3

Spend the morning at the Fries Museum *(www.friesmuseum.nl)*, a trove of artifacts from province's cultural life. From the upper galleries, look out for De Oldehove, a crooked medieval tower. Lunch at quirky Proefverlof *(www.proefverlof.frl)*, housed in the former Gothic Blokhuispoort prison – tables come with steel-barred windows. Hire a bike at Fietsstation 058 *(www. fietsstation058.nl)* to tour the canal paths and city parks. Stop for a boozy refuel at Boomsma Beerenburger *(www.boomsma. frl)*, a micro-distillery and tasting room for herbal bitters. As the evening draws in, settle down to dine on big-bowl salads and slow-cooked meats at Roast *(p309)*.

Day 4

Breakfast on smoothie bowls and tasty granola at Fruitbar Sis *(www.fruitbarsis.nl)* all you need for the journey to Dokkum *(p307)*, the region's oldest city. Brimming

1 Sneek's landmark water gate.

2 Perfect presentation at Leeuwarden's Proefverlof.

3 Fries Museum, Leeuwarden.

4 Idyllic Menkemaborg castle.

5 Martinitoren, Pieterburen.

with sights, it has over 140 national monuments within its fortified city walls. Admire the mesmerizing stepped-gable houses and handsome St Boniface Chapel. Sample *Dokkumer koffie* (coffee with Beerenburg bitter and cream) before driving onto Lauwersoog *(p296)*. Leave your car and take the ferry across to the island of Schiermonnikoog *(p282)*. Indulge in delicious ice cream at Ambrosijn ice-cream parlour *(www.ambrosijn.nl)*, then check in to one of its country-style rooms.

Day 5

Wear plenty of layers and your sturdiest shoes for a ramble over the dunes and mudflats of Netherlands' first national park. The moods of the car-free island are dictated by the North Sea. Take binoculars – there are 300 different bird species on the island – and a picnic lunch of local honey and cheese. Afterwards, take the ferry back to Lauwersoog, then drive on to Pieterburen *(p294)* home of the fascinating Waddencentrum. Have dinner at De Oude Smidse *(www.deoudesmidse.eu)*, a bistro in a converted farmhouse where you can spend the night.

Day 6

Start the day with farm-fresh eggs and strong coffee. Follow a morning stroll through the botanical gardens with a stop at the Pieterburen Seal Sanctuary *(www.zeehondencentrum.nl)*. It's a short drive to the fairy-tale Menkemaborg castle *(www.menkemaborg.nl)* in Uithuizen *(p297)*. Arrive in good time in Groningen city *(p288)* to choose between the freshest fish and the excellent veggie options at local favourite De Kleine Heerlijkheid *(dekleineheerlijkheid.nl)*. Duck into craft brewer Baxbier Brouwerij *(p291)* for a nightcap, then fall into bed at the boutique Het Paleis hotel *(p288)*.

Day 7

Fill up on *wentelteefjes* (Dutch-style french toast) and overnight oats at Feel Good *(www.feelgoodgroningen.nl)*. Then wander over to Martinitoren, a sky-puncturing steeple with unparalleled views from the top. After, reward yourself at the square's buzzy food market. Finish in style at Prinsenhof *(www.prinsenhof.nl)*, a tribute to haute cuisine and a fitting end to the week.

←

1 Cycling through the morning mist along the IJssel, heading towards lovely Deventer.

2 A bright day for antiques hunting in Zutphen's the Brink.

3 Doesburg's famous mustard and vingegar museum.

4 The bucolic setting of the Openluchtmuseum in Arnhem.

4 DAYS

cycling along the River Ijssel

Day 1

Morning Slip into holiday mode in the delightful town of Kampen *(p331)*. Its cobbled streets inspire a slower pace of life. Explore the cigar-making rooms at De Eenhoorn *(www.eenhoorn.eu)*, then savour one of its single-origin coffees in the café.

Afternoon Cycle 14 km (9 miles) upriver to Zwolle *(p328)*, a handsome old trading centre. Take a picture with Rodin's *Adam* in Grote Kerkplein, then admire contemporary art at the Museum de Fundatie. Later, head to Hier en Daar *(www.hieren daar.nu)* to taste their organic wines.

Evening Feast on succulent seafood at De Librije *(p329)*, before checking into one of its rooms in the old prison.

Day 2

Morning *Hagelslag* (toast with chocolate sprinkles) is perfect fuel for the 37-km (23-mile) ride to pretty Deventer *(p330)*. Stroll along the cobbled Brink marketplace and buy *peperkoek* (gingerbread) at Jacob Bussink Koekwinkel *(www.deventer koekwinkel.nl)*, established in 1820.

Afternoon Cycle 17 km (10 miles) to Zutphen *(p352)*, and reward yourself with a glass of craft beer at Café Camelot *(p352)*. Then wander the town's fine medieval streets to take in the splendid *librije* (library) of St Walbrgiskerk.

Evening For dinner, enjoy Italian classics at Vaticano *(www.vaticano.nl)*. Then a blissful night awaits at Gravenhof *(www.hampshirehotelsgravenhofzutphen.com)*.

Day 3

Morning Rise early for a scenic 11 km (7-mile) ride down to tiny Bronkhorst *(p357)*, with a resident population of just 200 people. Pause for coffee at Het Kunstgemaal *(www.hetkunstgemaal.nl)*, overlooking bucolic scenes.

Afternoon Push on to Doesburg, 10 km (6 miles) away. Pause at La Fleur *(www. lunchroomlafleur.nl)* to have lunch in the leafy orangery, before learning how mustard-making has influenced the city at Doesburgsche Mosterd- en Azijnfabriek *(www.doesburgschemosterd.nl)*.

Evening Sample hearty Dutch classics, such as *mosterdsoep* (mustard soup), at De Liefde *(www.restaurantliefde.nl)*, but save room for the homemade ice cream.

Day 4

Morning Kickstart the day with a cycle to Arnhem *(p354)*, 70 km (43 miles) downriver. Arrive in time for brunch at Urban Chef *(www.urbanchef.nl)*, where organic and local is the name of the game.

Afternoon After a quick visit to Museum Arnhem *(www.museumarnhem.nl)*, cycle out to the Openluchtmuseum *(p355)* for insights into everyday Dutch culture.

Evening Tuck into breakfast for dinner at Den Strooper *(p356)* with Dutch *pannenkoeken* (pancakes) and an endless variety of toppings. End your trip rubbing shoulders with locals until the wee hours at the lively Cavern Café *(cafethecavern.nl)*, housed in an old city cellar.

Around the World

A raft of world cuisines is on offer across the Netherlands. Sample authentic Indonesian food at Den Haag's Tong Tong Fair *(tongtongfair.nl)* – the *nasi goreng* (fried rice) and gado-gado are legendary. For moreish Turkish food, Rotterdam is the place to be. Or taste it all at World of Food in Amsterdam *(worldoffood amsterdam.nl)*, where global flavours vie for attention.

←

Tucking into culinary feasts at the Tong Tong Fair in Den Haag

THE NETHERLANDS FOR
FOODIES

Buttery pies and pastries, moreish Edam and Gouda cheese, hearty meat dishes and fresh seafood – arguably the Netherlands' greatest gift to the world is its larder. Here we introduce the country's most enjoyable food experiences.

Market Life

Local markets are a staple across the country. There's nowhere better to sample regional specialities. Amsterdam's Noordermarkt *(p120)* delivers farm-fresh, organic fare to the city. Chat to cheesemakers and sample their wares at markets in Edam *(p196)* and Gouda *(p250)*. For the best in street food innovation, don't miss the Markthall *(markthal.klepierre.nl)* in Rotterdam.

EETCAFES

These neighbourhood bistros, which literally mean "eating café", developed out of early-19th-century living room cafés set up by landladies seeking to supplement their income. They are characterized by simple home-cooking, fuss-free service and beer, rather than wine, all for a low price.

Rotterdam's spectacular Markthal and *(inset)* Amsterdam's Noordermarkt ↑

TOP 5 ANNUAL MUST-EATS

Brabant Cherries
Enjoy juicy cherries from June to August.

Limburg Asparagus
This "white gold" is the star of Arcen in May.

Zeeland Samphire
Sample this salty grass from May to August.

Opperdoes Potatoes
Try this waxy potato from June to September.

Zeeland Oysters
Slurp down Pacific and Japanese varieties, both salty with a buttery bite, all winter long.

↑ Oysters and other seafood displayed outside Dries van den Berg's restaurant

Time-Honoured Traditions

Dutch home cooking has always had one foot in the past. To experience its roots, cycle Gelderland's orchard route, then hop over to Limburg to try your hand at baking *Limburgse vlaai* pie (fruit-filled pie) at Maastricht's De Bisschopsmolen (*www.bisschopsmolen.nl*), using age-old recipes. Over on the shores of IJsselmeer, visit Dries van den Berg (*www.driesvandenberg.nl*) a traditional smokehouse specializing in eel – discover the history in the museum, the flavours in the popular restaurant and how it's all done in their immersive smoker.

→ A creative plate, perfectly presented at Michelin-starred Inter Scaldes

Gourmet Stars

Join Dutch foodies feasting on deliciously daring plates at Michelin-starred sensations across the country. Try citrussy polder hare in a cream sauce at Inter Scaldes (*interscaldes.nl*) in Kruiningen and fermented langoustines at Overijssel's De Librije (*p329*). In the capital, book a seat at Vermeer (*p100*) for pared-down classics made using kitchen-garden produce.

Find Inspiration

For green inspiration look no further than the gorgeous gardens across the country. Start at spectacular Tuinen van Appeltern *(appeltern.nl)*. The Netherlands' largest show garden is an inspiring experience, with themed weekends, workshops and markets. Then drop in at the Keukenhof show gardens *(p252)*, Leiden's famed Hortus Botanicus *(p228)* and the intricately designed ornamental gardens at Paleis Het Loo *(p344)*. Finally, venture out to the German border to breathe in the fragrance of the roses at Arcen's Kasteeltuinen *(p384)*.

$\rightarrow$

Perfect symmetry in Kasteel Arcen's beautiful ornamental rose gardens

THE NETHERLANDS FOR
GARDENERS

Bursting with blooms, the Netherlands spells nirvana for green-fingered travellers. Marvel at beautifully landscaped gardens, visit fields of petal-perfect flowers and celebrate all things horticultural the Dutch way.

Delve into the Fields

The Netherlands' famous flower fields are as colourful as they are easy to explore. Hop on a boat or bike to experience a kaleidoscope of colour in the bulb fields *(p188)* around Haarlem and Leiden. Noordoostpolder in Flevoland also erupts into vibrant bloom each spring. Many farmers here offer guided tours of their fields and the chance to buy bulbs.

Celebrate Flower Power

Time your visit for Bloemen Corso (*p61*) to see glorious blooms paraded through towns and villages. Celebrate bulb-growing at the Aalsmeer Flower Festival, which takes place each June at the Bloemenlust. Can't get out of Amsterdam? Enjoy the heady fragrance of flowers at the famous floating Bloemenmarkt (*p125*).

←

Shopping at the floating flower market on the Singel canal in Amsterdam

↑ Wandering among box hedges at a Museum Van Loon Open Garden Day

Open the Garden Gate

Some private gardens open their gates to visitors at different times over the year, allowing green-fingered travellers to share secrets with some of the Netherlands best private gardeners. Visit De Stekkentuin (*www.destekkentuin.nl*), the cuttings garden, as part of Gardening in Flevoland to see 350 different plant species and collect a cutting to take home. In Amsterdam, Museum Van Loon (*p124*) orchestrates access to 30 rarely seen canal house gardens and quiet oases in the city.

↑ A stunning array of blooms at a tulip field at Hillegom

The Great Outdoors

With green spaces and parks galore, the country has plenty of space in which to get into the fresh air and let off steam. Leafy Vondelpark, Amsterdam's great green lung, has picnic tables and a prize of a playground in the centre. Or bring buckets and spades to Domburg's beaches *(p264)*; the waters are safe for swimming, and the sandy dunes are perfect for racing around. Connecting them is a network of canals. Most have canal boat tours, but the ones in Den Bosch travel underground to the delight of all who ride them.

$\rightarrow$

Leaping to new heights from wooden groynes that jut into the sea from one of Domburg's beaches

THE NETHERLANDS FOR
FAMILIES

Effortlessly easy to negotiate thanks to a completely child-friendly culture, the Netherlands is an ideal destination for families. Lakes and beaches are safe and clean, cycle paths are flat for everyone to enjoy, and its theme parks and fairy-tale forests will stimulate kids of all ages.

Magical Moments

The country is filled with sights to enthrall. In Kaatsheuvel, fall under the spell of Efteling *(www.efteling.com)*, a fairy-tale theme park where Dutch folktales weave their magic and little ones can hunt for giants, sprites and trolls. Let youngsters run around pint-sized Madurodam village *(p233)* by day and marvel as the streets glow with the magical light of 50,000 tiny lamps after dusk. In December, head to EYE *(p171)* for Magic Lantern shows and learn how to make your own.

$\leftarrow$

Costumed actors spinning tales at Efteling, before a rapt audience

---

💬 INSIDER TIP
When Nature Calls

The best places to find toilets – apart from inside museums – are train stations, cafés and department stores. Be prepared to buy a drink or pay a 50-cent fee.

On Two Wheels

Pick your route and saddle up. Cycling in the Netherlands offers myriad possibilities for kids: by tandem, on their own bike or even in a trailer. Pack a picnic to tour any part of the Linge cycle route, a pretty stretch of the EuroVelo 15, through orchard- and castle-rich De Betuwe. To the west, follow the Nieuwe Hollandse Waterlinie *(p218)* and cycle past 135 km (84 miles) of fortress-studded grassland. Alternatively, book with Dutch Bike Tours *(www. dutch-biketours.com)* to ride along well-maintained paths though the deer-inhabited forests of peaceful De Hoge Veluwe *(p346)*.

←

Cycling past towering trees in Nationaal Park De Hoge Veluwe

STAY

Camping Diever

All mod cons and long views of National Park Drents-Friese Wold from *boomhutten*, or Dutch treehouses.

🅰F2 🏠Haarweg 2, Diever 🌐camping diever.nl

€€€

Camping Reeënwissel

Comfy, sustainably made *boomhutten* 14 m (45 ft) up in the canopy.

🅰F2 🏠Bosweg 23, Hoogersmilde 🌐reeenwissel.nl

€€€

Landclub Ruinen

Enjoy the lap of luxury in *boomhutten*, each equipped with a hot tub, wood-burning stove and lofty terrace.

🅰F3 🏠Oude Benderseweg 11, Ruinen 🌐landclub ruinen.nl

€€€

Rainy Day Fun

Keep rainy days from being a washout with days out indoors. Embrace the world of Miffy at toddler-friendly Nijntje Museum *(p213)*, with its colourful rooms based on Dick Bruna's picture books. In Amsterdam, take young scientists to the hands-on labs of NEMO Science Museum *(p160)*, or let little chefs cook up a storm at the Kinderkook Kafe *(www.kinderkookkafe. nl)* in Vondelpark *(p148)*.

←

Hanging out with Miffy at the Nijntje Museum, where make-believe comes to life

Meet the Creatives

Once a Philips factory complex, Strijp-S in Eindhoven *(p370)* has been recast as an ideas lab for creative start-ups. Check out its array of Instagram-ready, achingly hip shops and trend-defining restaurants. NDSM *(p175)*, in an old industrial wharf on the River IJ in Amsterdam, was set up along the same principles. Come for the eye-catching murals by street art superstars and the innovative cafés housed in old shipping containers; stay to catch a movie at the outdoor summer cinema and to spend the night in an industrial crane.

→

The bright lights of Strijp-S's night scene reflected in the canal

THE NETHERLANDS FOR
BROEDPLAATSEN

An idea so good it could be bottled and sold, *broedplaatsen* is a local concept that transforms empty offices and derelict factories into creative hubs and affordable working spaces. The result? Run-down areas are revitalized and reclaimed by local people and the rewards are inspiring for everyone.

Reclaiming Public Spaces

We Are Public *(www.weare public.nl)* is a beyond-the-mainstream art calendar, with hand-picked daily events that take place in 12 cities. Take your pick from jazz in old factories and art exhibitions in repurposed office buildings to comedy in abandoned theatres and experimental dance in the street. City streets are reclaimed in other ways. In Delft and Amsterdam, find *speelstraaten* (play streets) closed off to traffic to provide a place for children to play.

←

We Are Public collaborators creating a fusion of art, advertising and protest

Tiny Houses, Big Ideas

The tiny house movement has gained a huge global following. Visit a zeitgeist-defining project in Almere *(p338)* to see how architects have created livable spaces in less than 50 sq m (540 sq ft) – a thought-provoking exercise in sustainability. Pick from a growing number listed on Airbnb.com to give tiny living a try.

← A bird's-eye view of the tiny house site in Almere

Urban Agriculture

Discover a big trend in the Netherlands: urban farm-to-table dining. At Rotterdam's *(p244)* Bistro Op het Dak *(www.ophetdak. com)* feast on dishes made from the organic veg, edible flowers and homemade honey produced in the rooftop farm of this repurposed office building. In Amsterdam, Restaurant de Kas *(www.restaurantdekas. com)* occupies the former municipal greenhouse – sample plant-to-plate dishes amid rows of growing fruit and veg.

↑ Picking from the menu in the leafy surroundings of Bistro Op Het Dak

TOP 5 RULES OF THE ROAD

Safety First
Always wear a helmet.

Stay Right
Always use the bicycle lane on the right-hand side of the road.

Stick to the Bike Path
Don't ride on footpaths or pavements.

Be Aware
Watch out for cars and pedestrians.

Lock It Up
Lock your bike up at an official city cycle rack.

THE NETHERLANDS FOR
CYCLISTS

Pancake-flat, the Netherlands is second to none for cyclists, with world-class infrastructure, a comprehensive bike lane network and countrywide two-wheeled options for all ages and abilities. Strap on your helmet, push the pedals and join the Dutch in their most natural state.

Kids on Wheels

Take a tip from Dutch parents and opt for a *bakfiets*, a sensible toddler transporter, when cycling with tots. Strap the kids into the box and pedal with ease on a child-friendly tour with We Bike Amsterdam *(www.webike amsterdam.com)*. The traffic-free bike paths and easy beach access along the Dutch Coastal Route are ideal for longer tours.

↑ Zipping over the canal bridges of Amsterdam in a sturdy *bakfiets*

Easy Does It

The Netherlands takes its cycling seriously and is geared up to cater for all abilities. Hire a tandem from Black Bikes (www.black-bikes.com) for easy rides along Amsterdam's canals. Similar to the tandem, side-by-side cycles are ideal for those with mobility, visual or hearing impairments. Accessible Travel Netherlands (www.accessible travelnl.com) can help with arranging hires. Want to try pedal power with a bit of a boost? Alley Cat (www.alleycatbikescoffee.nl) has charging points so you can leave your electric bike topping up while you recharge with a powerful caffeine hit.

→ An easy sunrise ride along a canal and (inset) hired bicycles from Black Bikes in Amsterdam

CYCLING SUPERHIGHWAYS

Some 35,000 km (21,750 miles) of cycle routes crisscross the Netherlands. The first, built in 2004, was between Breda and Etten-Leur. The country now has 26 fietssnelwegen – high-speed bicycle routes connecting major cities. Parallel to but segregated from railways and roads for motorized vehicles, these routes pass under main roads via tunnels where smart LEDs light up in response to cyclists' phones. When ready, the 60-km (37-mile) route from Eschende to Nijverdal will be the longest in the country.

↑ Competitors in the Fietselfstedentocht cycling event

Fiets of Endurance

Each December, hardcore cyclists from around the world flock to take part in the 8.5-km (5-mile) Dutch Headwind Cycling Championships, which crosses Zeeland's storm barrier, the Oosterscheldekering (p260). No sports bikes, gears or handle breaks are allowed – only pedal brakes. If you survive that, the Fietselfstedentocht (www.fietselfstedentocht.frl) is a two-wheel version of Friesland's famous 200-km (125-mile) ice-skating event - without the ice. Look out for it in June.

That's Saw Amazing!

Dutch woodworkers are well known for crafting *klompen*, the iconic wooden clog worn by farmers and gardeners for centuries. To see a traditional workshop, head to one of the country's open-air museums, such as the Zaanse Schans *(p198)*, to watch artisan woodworkers at the Kooijman Wooden Shoe Workshop *(www.wooden shoes.nl)*. Or give carpentry a go at Open Werkplaats Manu Forti *(www.manuforti. nl)* in Helmond *(p372)* and create your own version of a De Stijl-style chair.

←

Craftsman patiently finishing off a wooden piece at a traditional workshop

THE NETHERLANDS FOR
CRAFTERS

Crafting is firmly entrenched in the Dutch psyche, and crocheting, knitting, woodwork and textiles are all thriving. Pick up artisan goods, created using innovations alongside traditional techniques – or follow the DIY trend and unleash your creative side at workshops across the country.

💬 INSIDER TIP
Spinners' Paradise

Several sheep farms offer tours and the chance to see the sheep before they're sheared. At Purewol *(www. purewol.de)*, on the German border, you can buy raw sheep's wool in a rainbow of natural colours from more than 800 sheep of different breeds.

Spin a Long Yarn

Pack your needles and hooks and your latest work in progress and join one of the Netherlands' friendly knitting groups. Head to Wollyhood *(www.wollyhood. nl)* in Utrecht and meet local fellow stitchers at their weekly knitting and crochet café. Or stop by Rotterdam's popular Ja Wol *(www.ja-wol.com)* to perfect your Dutch cables and learn how to embroider delicate images over knitted and crocheted fabric. In Amsterdam, find a huge collection of gorgeous hand-dyed yarn at boutique Stephen & Penelope *(p91)*.

Of Warp and Weft

Textile production was once so integral to Dutch life that children were taught how to weave in schools, using paper yarn. At the fascinating Textielmuseum in Tilburg *(p368)* trace the history, then check out innovations in the manufacturing lab. Book a workshop to learn different techniques, from block-printing to weaving. See examples of hand-embroidered *kraplap* (a type of bib) at the Historisch Museum de Bevelanden *(www.hmdb.nl)* in Goes *(p264)*. In Volendam *(p197)*, traditional dress is still worn and can be admired by visitors.

→

Jacquard weaving on a demonstration loom at the Textielmuseum in Tilsburg

↑ Chatting at a Stephen & Penelope knitting group and *(inset)* colourful yarn for sale

Potter Away

Regional pottery styles flourish, but Delft's *(p238)* iconic blue-and-white glazed tiles, born during the 17th century, made Dutch ceramics famous. Pick up a paintpot and brush at De Delftse Pauw *(delftpottery.com)*, and create your own decorative tile, with help from a professional painter. The classes also take you through how the moulded-clay tiles are made.

↑ Decorating tiles using iconic Delft blue paint

Tulip fields on reclaimed land
in North Holland and *(inset)*
walking trails past windmills

THE NETHERLANDS FOR
THE GREAT
OUTDOORS

A shortcut to blending into this country of lakes, forest and canals is to escape the densely populated cities and join the Dutch in the wide open spaces where nature has been left to flourish – and, with so many options, it's never been easier to get out and explore.

Pick up a Paddle

In a country crisscrossed by canals, setting off to explore by boat is an obvious choice. Hire a canoe in North Brabant's Nationaal Park De Biesbosch *(np-debiesbosch. nl)* and paddle off for a night of *paalkamperen* (wild camping) and sleeping under the stars. A less rugged alternative are the rustic-but-cosy A-frame cabins and aquahomes accessible only by boat. For day trips buffeted by bracing North Sea breezes, head to Schiermonnikoog island *(p282)* to sail, canoe and kayak around its shores.

→

Canoeing through the peaceful, sun-dappled waters of Naational Park De Biesbosch

Hit the Trails

In a nation of land reclaimed from the sea, there are plenty of ways to dive in. Trails around Eilandspolder *(www.rondvaarteilandspolder.nl)* send you past reclaimed polders and colourful geometric fields. Hike or bike past dykes little changed since the 17th century, camera ready to capture their timeless quality. Alternatively, walk or cycle the trails that loop across the fens of the Nationaal Park Nieuw Land *(www.nationaalparknieuwland.nl)*, which sprawls across the bed of the reclaimed Zuiderzee bay. In the north, join Wadloopcentrum Fryslân *(www.wadlopen.net)* for a guided intertidal walk across the very bed of the Waddenzee – *wadlopen* (mud walking), also known as horizontal alpinism, is an exhilarating, unmissable and uniquely Dutch experience.

ISLANDS OF TOMORROW

In the middle of the Markermeer, one of Europe's largest lakes, five new man-made islands have been built. Created by the government as part of rewilding measures to reverse previous environmental damage in the area, the archipelago is intended to develop as a nature reserve and encourage wildlife to flourish. It is accessible by ferry from Lelystad.

Wildlife Watching

The vast tracts of woodland and marsh that make up Nationaal Park De Hoge Veluwe *(p346)* rustle, flutter and slither with wildlife. Pitch up at the car-free tent site and rise in time to see majestic stags and hoary boars stalking well-marked hiking trails. Don't forget to take your binoculars to Nationaal Park Utrechtse Heuvelrug *(www.np-utrechtseheuvelrug.nl)*, where the oak and beech forests and misty fens teem with crossbills, bluethroats and snipes.

→ Enjoying the well-marked trails that cut through Nationaal Park De Hoge Veluwe

THE NETHERLANDS FOR
ARCHITECTURE

Shaped by its long and storied past, the Netherlands is home to a trove of architectural splendours and a feast awaits design enthusiasts – from ancient brick churches and soaring Dutch Baroque canalside mansions to creaking windmills and striking contemporary structures.

Captivating Windmills

Ah, the picture-perfect windmill. The country's most Instagrammable symbol is also central to one of its most incredible feats of engineering (p200). Explore Zaanse Schans (p198), a 250-year-old windmill park that made Napoleon marvel. Then learn the history of polder-draining windmills at Kinderdijk (p251). In the capital, grab a beer and watch the sails of De Gooyer (p164) from the brewhouse next door.

Brightly coloured windmills, seemingly bobbing on the water, at Zaanse Schans ↓

Modern Marvels

In the 1950s, Rotterdam shook off the rubble of World War II, ushering in an era of Dutch architectural innovation. The city is full of mind-bending design – Blaak metro station (p249), the Markthal (www.markthal.klepierre.nl), the Kubuswoningen (p245) – see it all through expert eyes with Architecture Tours (www.architecturetours.nl). In Utrecht', admire Rietveld Schröderhuis (p214), a master reconception of residential design. The trompe d'oeil continues in the folding walls and sloping spires of EYE (p171) in Amsterdam, which is also home to the Amsterdam School's idealistic De Dageraad housing project (p170).

←—

Kubuswoningen in Rotterdam and (inset) Amsterdam's De Dageraad complex

Beautiful Baroque

The breathtaking Baroque core of Dutch cities dates from the 17th century. Put on comfy shoes for a self-guided Amsterdam walk (p126) and marvel at the magnificent merchant houses, all stepped gables and ornamented façades, lining the canals. A feast of Dutch Baroque treats awaits outside the capital. Den Haag (p230) brims with the legacy of master builder Pieter Post; explore the well-preserved Mauritshuis (p236), his best-known work.

> 💬 INSIDER TIP
> **Open Days**
>
> Each September, Open Monumentendag sees an A to Z of historic and contemporary buildings throw open their doors to the public for viewings (www.openmonumentendag.nl).

↑ Haarlem's Grote Kerk, a Baroque masterpiece, towering above the town

From Grape to Glass

Raise a glass to the sandy soil of Gelderland and the red loam of hilly Limburg – a new generation of vintners is making sure they bear fruit. In tiny Twijzel, sample wines made from Johanniter and Solaris grapes at Frysling (*www.frysling.nl*), named the country's best vineyard in 2018. The country's oldest winery, Wijngaard De Apostelhoeve (*www.apostelhoeve.nl*), will get you moving – chill out at its Rock O Vin festival, where bands are paired with wine. Slightly more sedate is a cycle tour through the country's largest winery, St Martinus (*www.wijngaardmartinus.nl*).

↑ Gathering to share a bottle of crisp white wine on a warm summer's day

THE NETHERLANDS
IN A GLASS

For tasty tipples, the Netherlands has you covered. Pop into a micro-pub, grab a seat at a classic brown bar or dive into a wine cellar – whether you opt for a refreshing craft beer, rejuvenating *jenever* or a crisp wine, the Dutch drinks cabinet has something to satisfy everyone.

Micro-brewery Jopen and ↑ (*inset*) having a drink at mega-brewer Heineken

Discover Jenever

Dutch for "juniper", *jenever* is not gin in disguise but a malted, grain-based spirit rich in botanicals. Savour it unadulterated, with a beer chaser, at Café De Eland *(p122)*, a classic Amsterdam brown café. Then train your nose for the liquor at Van Wees Distillery *(www.geneverschool.nl)*. The bar of the Jenever Museum in Schiedam *(p253)* is the perfect place to test your skills afterwards.

→

A tempting glass of clear, golden-tinged *jenever* surrounded by botanicals

INSIDER TIP
Jenever Festival

Visit Schiedam during the Jenever Festival *(www.jeneverfestival. nl)* in September and learn how to mix, shake and stir the potent liquor into cocktails in special workshops.

Cheers for the Beers

Full of buzzy brewhouses, the country reverberates with the craft beer boom. Tour Heineken *(www.theheinekencompany.com)* in Amsterdam to see production on a massive scale. Follow that up by learning the secrets of small-batch brewing at micro-brewery Jopen *(www.jopenkerk.nl)* in Haarlem. Alternatively, grab a seat in the 16th-century home of De Bekeerde Suster brewpub *(p89)* and rub shoulders with the locals as you sample local beer and homemade *bitterballen* (meatballs) with mustard.

TOP 5 UNMISSABLE CRAFT BEERS

Zatte
This golden brew from Brouwerij 't IJ *(www. brouwerijhetij.nl)* has light fruity flavours.

Mooie Nel IPA
Richly hoppy, Jopen's *(www.jopenbier.nl)* North Sea IPA is ideal after a day on the water.

Gold Ezelenbok
This robust double bock by SNAB *(www.snab.nl)* has mild hoppiness with caramel overtones.

Handlanger IPA
Kompaan's *(www. kompaanbier.nl)* award-winning brew has zingy citrus tones.

Gold Texels Springtij
This speciality brew with flowery aromas is made with pure dune water at Texelse Bierbrouwerij *(p279)*.

THE NETHERLANDS FOR
DUTCH MASTERS

Bursting with movement and dancing with colour, 17th-century Dutch canvases reveal a fierce cultural pride in the newly formed Dutch Republic. Dive into workshops, explore the artists' inspiration and admire the best of a movement that changed the art world.

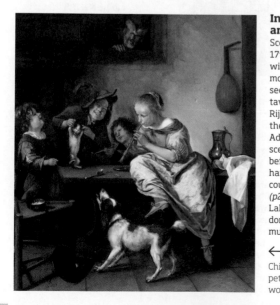

Interact with Domestic and Pastoral Scenes

Scenes of ordinary life leap from 17th-century canvases, alive with colour. Visit the country's most marvellous museums to see them. Study Jan Steen's tavern scenes in Amsterdam's Rijksmuseum *(p138)*, then see the real thing in a brown bar. Admire Carel Fabritius's pastoral scenes at the Mauritshuis *(p236)*, before experiencing them first hand on a cycle tour through the countryside around Den Haag *(p230)*. Leiden's Museum De Lakenhal *(p228)* is a cradle of domestic masterpieces – use the museum app to plan your visit.

←

Children with their household pets in Jan Steen's playful work, *The Dancing Lesson*

Get Creative

Workshops and classes get you closer than ever to the mind of the artist at studios and museums. At the lauded Vermeer Centrum *(p241)*, join a workshop to learn some of the master's techniques. The Young Rembrandt Studio *(Langebrug 89)* in Leiden is a great starting point to understand the young artist's craft through interactive displays. Then uncover the mature Rembrandt's unique paint-making methods and create your own technicolour palette at the Museum het Rembrandthuis *(p84)*. Alternatively, check out De Kat in Zaanse Schans *(p198)* – the only working windmill in the country that still makes oil paint.

← Vermeer's oil painting *View of Delft* and *(inset)* a paint-making demonstration at the Rembrandthuis

TOP 5 ART MUSEUMS

Rijksmuseum, Amsterdam
The best of 17th-century Dutch art *(p138)*.

Museum het Rembrandthuis, Amsterdam
The painter's house as it was in his time *(p84)*.

Mauritshuis, Den Haag
Home to a stellar array of 17th-century art *(p236)*.

Frans Hals Museum Hof, Haarlem
Focusing on works by the 17th-century master of portraiture *(p186)*.

Dordrechts Museum, Dordrecht
Workshops, tours and 400 years of Dutch art *(www.dordrechts museum.nl)*.

Face Painting

For a lesson in 17th-century portraiture, start at the Museum Het Rembrandthuis *(p84)*. Delve into Rembrandt's process via the stirring exhibits, then admire his exacting self-portraits in the galleries. Take a sketchbook and pens to the Frans Hals Museum Hof *(p186)* and try your hand at emulating Hals's wispy detail. In Amsterdam, join a Rijksmuseum *(p138)* drawing workshop to try out Judith Leyster's jaunty style.

Did You Know?

Judith Leyster, one of only two women in Haarlem's painters' guild, sued Frans Hals for poaching her assistant.

Judith Leyster's boisterous ↓ *The Jolly Drinker*, which hangs in the Rijksmuseum

Have a Punt

An oasis of calm away from the cities, the Maas river is a microcosm of Dutch boating life, with skiffs and day boats meandering past pastoral scenes. Join pleasure punters by hiring a sloop from Cafe-Maasterras 't Veerhuis *(www.sloephuren-limburg.nl)* in Wessem, a pretty Limburg backwater. In Amsterdam, take a Wetlands Safari *(www. wetlandssafari.nl)* to feel miles from the city. For something completely different, try your hand at *fierljeppen*, the age-old West Frisian sport of canal-vaulting.

← Paddling down green waterways on a Wetlands Safari canoe tour

THE NETHERLANDS
ON THE WATER

The Netherlands is bordered by the North Sea and the Waddenzee and contains the massive delta of the Rhine, Maas and Schelde rivers. Add to this a network of canals crisscrossing town and country, and the result is a vast aquatic playground ripe for water-based adventures.

Go With the Flow

The Netherlands' pristine lakes offer another side of the country. Catch the wind and waves with Leer Windsurfen *(www.leerwindsurfen.nl)* on Amstelmeer and soak up views of the tulip fields and farmlands from a distance. In picturesque Friesland, opt for a *skûtsje* (Frisian cargo barge) tour across a series of inter-connected lakes. Time it right over July–August to cheer skippers in the Sintrale Kommisje Skûtsjesilen *(www.skutsjesilen.nl)* races.

Did You Know?

The Netherlands has more than 6,000 km (3,730 miles) of canals and 17 per cent of its surface is water.

Water Lot of Seaside Fun

Delightfully golden arcs of sand are found all along the extravagantly indented coastline of the country. In Zeeland, the broad sandy beach at Domburg *(p264)*, peppered with groynes and beach huts, is perfect for families and offers an array of thrilling watersports. In the north, broad Egmond aan Zee *(p202)*, overlooked by the Jan van Speijk lighthouse, is bordered by undulating dunes, perfect for a walk. South Holland's white-sand Noordwijk beach is ideal for surfers, while the gnarly Wijk aan Zee in North Holland offers left and right walls and northwest swells. The harbour jetty throws up plenty of surprise rips too. Complete beginner? Sign up for lessons with Australian-run school and surf camp Ozlines *(www. ozlines.com)*.

$\longrightarrow$

Walking past the rows of groynes at Domburg and *(inset)* a surfer riding the North Sea swells

↑ Sailing a *skûtsje* past the 18th-century De Jager *paltrok* (smock mill) in Woudsend, Friesland

A YEAR IN
THE NETHERLANDS

JANUARY

△ **Nieuwjaarsduik** *(usually New Year's Day).* Hundreds of hearty Netherlanders plough into the freezing cold sea at Scheveningen.
International Film Festival Rotterdam *(late Jan).* Thousands descend on the city for 12 days of independent and experimental film and art screened during this prestigious film festival.

FEBRUARY

△ **Carnival** *(late Feb).* Drink, sing and dance among colourful crowds of costumed revellers at the pre-Lenten carnivals that take place across the southern and eastern Netherlands.

MAY

△ **National Mill Day** *(2nd Sat & Sun).* Over 950 windmills and watermills open their doors across the country. Mills are beautifully decorated with flags, flowers and angels.

JUNE

△ **Holland Festival** *(three weeks in Jun).* Explore Amsterdam through this huge performing arts festival, with free events across the city.
Oerol *(mid-Jun).* Ferry across to Terschelling for ten days of imaginative fine art and performing arts.

SEPTEMBER

Open Monumentendag *(2nd weekend).* All across the Netherlands hundreds of monuments, historical houses and lesser-known landmarks throw open their doors for free.
△ **Fruitcorso** *(late Sep).* Tiny Tiel gets taken over by the "Fruit Parade", featuring vintage cars decorated with fruit and vegetables – it's three days of extravagant good fun.

OCTOBER

△ **Amsterdam Marathon** *(mid-Oct).* Nearly 15,000 long-distance runners speed through the city centre in the Netherlands' biggest running event of the year.

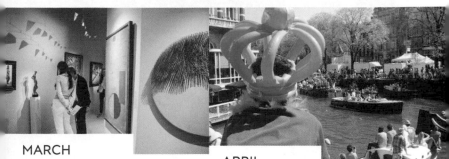

MARCH

△ **TEFAF Maastricht** *(early to mid-Mar)*. Drink in the world's best art, antiques and design at Maastricht's famous showcase.

Keukenhof *(late Mar–early May)*. Gardening enthusiasts throng to the world-famous floral displays in the bulb fields and hothouses near Leiden. Tulips galore.

APRIL

Bloemen Corso *(late Apr)*. Elaborate and fantastically colourful flower floats are paraded through a string of Dutch towns and villages.

△ **Koningsdag (King's Day)** *(27 Apr)*. Join the beer-swilling hordes clad in vibrant orange – the national colour – in a nationwide knees-up and drink a toast to the king's birthday.

JULY

Oud Limburgs Schuttersfeest *(1st Sun)*. Limburg hosts a colourful shooting competition in which teams dressed in traditional gear use vintage carabines to shoot lead bullets.

△ **North Sea Jazz Festival** *(mid-Jul)*. Rotterdam swings to the music of big-name Dutch and international jazz maestros performing at venues across the city.

AUGUST

△ **Amsterdam Gay Pride** *(1st or 2nd weekend)*. Performances and street parties celebrate the city's the LGBT+ community – don't miss the raucous "Canal Pride" flotilla.

De Parade *(mid-Aug)*. This travelling theatre festival wends its entertaining way from Rotterdam through Den Haag and Utrecht and ends with a bang in Amsterdam.

NOVEMBER

△ **Sint Maarten** *(11 Nov)*. Teeming crowds converge in Utrecht to fete the town's patron saint, St Maarten, with this glorious spectacle featuring elaborate light sculptures.

Sinterklaas Intocht *(2nd or 3rd Sun)*. Santa Claus and his helpers parade through the capital, dolling out sweets and little presents to hopelessly excited children.

DECEMBER

△ **Pakjesavond** *(5 Dec)*. Literally translated as "present evening", this is the day when Dutch children traditionally tear off the wrapping of their Christmas presents.

A BRIEF
HISTORY

Surrounded by great warring neighbours, the Netherlands has been shaped by a history that has seen high drama on land and at sea. Although it was only in the 19th century that it assumed its present shape, this small country is today an established and peaceful power in its own right.

Prehistoric and Roman Times

Flint tools discovered in Woerden suggest the Netherlands has been inhabited for at least 37,000 years. *Hunebedden* (megalithic tombs) can be seen near Emmen and earthen mounds in Friesland attest to Paleolithic efforts to keep the sea at bay. The Germanic Batavi and Frisii tribes and the Celtic La Tène and Belgae tribes farmed, foraged and fought tidal encroachment for agricultural gain for nearly a thousand years before the Romans arrived. In AD 69, the Batavi revolted but the Romans proved too strong and remained in power here until the 5th century AD, when new powers began to emerge.

> **Did You Know?**
>
> Pliny described the Dutch as "A wretched race... inhabiting... artificial mounds... like mariners on board a ship".

Timeline of events

800 BC

The Iron Age begins in the Netherlands as its peoples learn how to smelt the local ore.

486

Frankish king Clovis I wins a decisive battle against the Romans.

AD 69

The Batavi rise in rebellion against the Romans, as later famously recalled in several of Rembrandt's paintings.

732

Charles Martel, the first Carolingian king, defeats a Muslim army in one of Western Europe's most crucial engagements.

The Frisians, Franks and Carolingians

As the Roman empire started to collapse, legions stationed in this region were pulled back to Rome. The ensuing power vacuum was filled by two Germanic tribes, the Saxons, who would eventually become known as Frisians, and the Franks. After a series of conflicts, the Frisians were swept into the Frankish Merovingian empire at the 734 Battle of the Boarn. The Merovingians were supplanted by the Carolingians in 785, and relative stability followed under Holy Roman Emperor Charlemagne. He brought order out of chaos, but after his death in 814 power passed into the hands of the local barons.

The Emergence of Powerful Cities

Over the next few centuries, barons along the coast fended off Viking raids and encouraged the growth of towns, seeing them as potential sources of tax revenue. Towns with sea access, such as Deventer and Kampen, joined the Hanseatic League, a group of powerful trading cities. As their collective dominance grew, they secured an array of privileges, such as the right to pass laws, making some of them almost akin to city states.

[1] A map of lands occupied by the prehistoric Belgae tribespeople.

[2] Frost sparkling on a *hunebed* (megalithic stone tomb) in a wintry field outside Drenthe.

[3] Illustration of Romans and Bavatians at a marketplace, by Charles Rochussen (1889).

[4] Medieval portrait of King Charlemagne giving an audience to his courtiers.

754
Missionary St Boniface is murdered by Frisians, but the spread of Christianity continues.

800s–900s
Frankish and Frisian villages along the north coast are ravaged by Viking raids.

814
Charlemagne's empire, which includes the Netherlands, crumbles in the aftermath following his death.

c 1100
According to legend Amsterdam is founded by two Frisian fishermen on peaty marshland.

The Revolt of the Netherlands

In 1482, the Netherlands passed to the Habsburgs by dynastic happenstance. When Spain's fanatically Catholic Philip II, a Habsburg, took power in 1555, the scene was set for a confrontation. The Reformation had transformed the Netherlands, with people attracted to the beliefs of leading Protestant thinkers such as John Calvin and Martin Luther. Determined to subdue his heretical subjects, Philip sent in his army, triggering the savage Eighty Years' War. In 1578, Amsterdam's Catholic city government was deposed in favour of a Protestant one; known as the Alteration, this event had a significant impact on the city's churches and monasteries. A shaky peace was agreed in 1648, ending the war and making the Netherlands fully independent – the Verenigde Nederlanden (United Provinces).

The Dutch Golden Age

Free from the Habsburgs, the Dutch revelled in their new-found independence. Amsterdam flourished as a major trade hub for local goods as well as those from the Indies. Dutch banking and insurance corporations expanded the country's coffers, but

↑ Dutch ships at anchor in the Ij river at Amsterdam (1666)

Timeline of events

1482

After the death of Mary of Burgundy, the Netherlands is absorbed into the Habsburg empire.

1517

The Reformation begins when Martin Luther nails up his 95 theses against Catholicism.

1566

Dutch Protestants rampage through Catholic churches, enraging Philip II of Spain.

1584

A Catholic agent murders William the Silent, leader of the Dutch Protestants.

1598

Philip II of Spain, the most implacable foe of Dutch Protestantism, dies of cancer.

reckless speculation in the tulip trade led to the first stock market crash in 1637. Along the coast windmills proliferated, draining the water to create polder towns. On the seas, the navy developed a formidable reputation for fiercely protecting the country's expanding merchant fleet. The Protestant merchants, convinced their new wealth was a sign of God's pleasure, celebrated by commissioning handsome canal houses and vivid portraits of themselves and their families.

The Dutch Trading Empire

The Dutch merchant fleet initially concentrated on carrying Baltic grain to southern Europe, but in the early 17th century it extended its horizons, developing a network of trade routes that stretched around the globe. The powerful Dutch East India Company, founded in 1602, brought spices from Indonesia and India to Europe, and set up a trade monopoly with Japan in 1640. The Dutch West India Company, established in 1621, was given a monopoly over the Americas, including the slave trade. Both companies were ruthless in their exploitation of local peoples, and trade often anticipated colonial occupation.

⬆ Portrait of Martin Luther at the pulpit.

② A prominent Dutch merchant family, the Sams, committed to canvas with bold realism.

③ Bird's-eye view of a battle between the Dutch West India Company and the Spanish in 1636.

④ Illustration of the fortified Dutch East India Company's trading port in Hooghly, West Bengal, painted by Hendrik van Schuylenburgh (1665).

1606

Golden Age icon Rembrandt is born in Leiden, the ninth child of a middle-class miller.

1625

Dutch settlers in America found New Amsterdam, later renamed New York by the British.

1672

Rampjaar (Disaster Year) – the United Provinces is assailed on all sides, marking the end of the Dutch Golden Age.

1648

The Peace of Westphalia heralds the end of the Revolt of the Netherlands – and sparks the Dutch Golden Age.

1

2

3

From Republic to Kingdom

In the late 17th century, political and military power became ever-more concentrated in the hands of the House of Orange, aristocratic landowners who became monarchs in all but name. This state of affairs came to an abrupt end when the French Revolutionary army invaded the Netherlands in 1795. The French extinguished the privileges accumulated by the Dutch merchant elite and established the Batavian Republic. This was popular amongst many, but when Napoleon abolished this republic and installed his brother Louis as king, support for the French evaporated. At the end of the Napoleonic Wars, the victorious powers put William I, Prince of Orange, on the throne.

Colonialism

Driven initially by trade rather than territorial expansion, Dutch colonialism was orchestrated by chartered companies, mainly the Dutch West India and the Dutch East India companies. By the 1890s, most of the Netherlands' colonies and trade monopolies had been commandeered by the British. Nevertheless, a number of coastal countries remained under Dutch control,

↑ William I, king of the Netherlands, in a regal pose

Timeline of events

1806
Napoleon installs his brother Louis as the king of the Netherlands; Louis is deposed four years later.

1689
William III (1650-1702), the Prince of Orange, also becomes the king of England, Ireland and Scotland.

1890
Queen Wilhelmina becomes the first woman to occupy the Dutch throne - and rules for 58 years.

1917
The Act of Universal Suffrage gives the franchise to men over 25; two years later, women get the vote as well.

including what would become Indonesia. It was this region that the Dutch coveted most on account of its raw materials. Here, the Dutch installed a racist social order backed up by state-sponsored violence. During World War II, the Japanese occupied Indonesia, but after their defeat the Dutch ignored local nationalist feelings and attempted to reimpose colonial rule. The bloody war that followed, led by Indonesian nationalist leaders Sukarno and Hatta, ended in a unilateral declaration of Indonesian independence in 1949.

The Netherlands Today

The Netherlands managed to stay neutral in World War I, but was subject to a bitter and cruel occupation by the Nazis from 1940, which led to the virtual extermination of the Jewish population. Postwar reconstruction was rapid, and in 1957 the country became one of the six founding members of the European Economic Community (EEC). In the 1960s, Amsterdam was transformed from a somewhat conservative city into a hotbed of the hippy movement, spawning a radical eco-conscious movement that is a defining feature of the Netherlands today.

1 French army during the Napoleonic Wars. ↑

2 Wayang puppets depicting the Java War.

3 Heavily bombed Nijmegen in 1944.

4 Modern windmills.

Did You Know?

The Netherlands became the first country in the world to legalize same-sex marriage in 2001.

1953
Nearly 2,000 people drown when Zeeland sea defences are overwhelmed.

1966
Princess Beatrix marries a former German army officer, sparking riots.

2019
Dutch-based Ocean Cleanup pioneers technology to catch floating plastic waste on the ocean surface.

1944–5
Hundreds of Dutch citizens die of hunger and hypothermia before they are liberated by the Allies.

1972
The possession and use of cannabis is decriminalized in the Netherlands.

EXPERIENCE
AMSTERDAM

Amsterdam's colourful canal houses at sunset

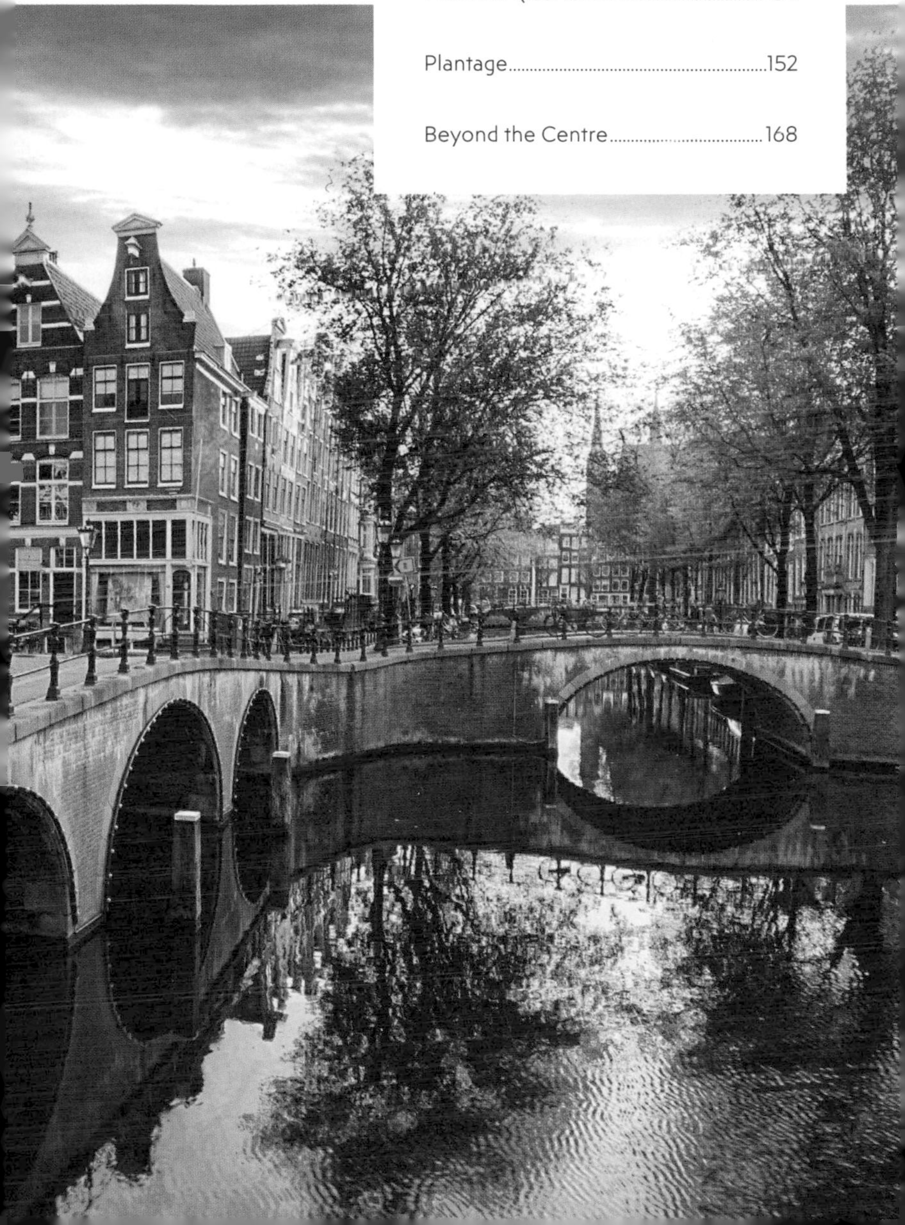

EXPLORE
AMSTERDAM

This guide divides Amsterdam into five sightseeing areas, as shown on this map, plus an area containing sights beyond the city centre. Find out more about each area on the following pages.

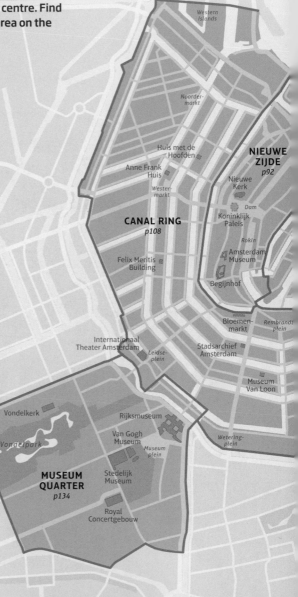

Western Islands

Noorder-markt

Huis met de Hoofden

Anne Frank Huis

Wester-markt

NIEUWE ZIJDE
p92

Nieuwe Kerk

Dam

Koninklijk Paleis

Rokin

CANAL RING
p108

Amsterdam Museum

Felix Meritis Building

Begijnhof

Bloemen-markt

Rembrandt plein

Internationaal Theater Amsterdam

Leidse-plein

Stadsarchief Amsterdam

Museum Van Loon

Vondelkerk

Rijksmuseum

Van Gogh Museum

Museum plein

Wetering-plein

Vondelpark

MUSEUM QUARTER
p134

Stedelijk Museum

Royal Concertgebouw

THE NETHERLANDS

AMSTERDAM

Centraal
Station

Stations-
plein

Museum Ons' Lieve
Heer op Solder

Oude Kerk

NEMO
Science Museum

Waag

Nieuw-
markt

Het
Scheepvaartmuseum

OUDE ZIJDE
p76

Stadhuis

Waterloo-
plein

Verzetsmuseum

Werfmuseum
't Kromhout

Museum
Willet-
olthuysen

Hermitage
Amsterdam

Hollandsche
Schouwburg

Artis

Magere
Brug

PLANTAGE
p152

Fredericks-
plein

Bonn
plein

Tropenmuseum

Dapper
plein

Oosterpark

0 metres   600
0 yards   600

N
↑

GETTING TO KNOW
AMSTERDAM

Amsterdam is divided by the many canals that give this city its unique character. The Grachtengordel – the ring of canals that defines the Oude Zijde and Nieuwe Zijde – encloses most of the city's top attractions, but there's much to discover beyond this watery perimeter.

PAGE 76

OUDE ZIJDE

The "Old Side" is the city's easternmost district and where Amsterdam has its roots. The area is an oddball: an intensely urban quarter where piety and porn sit side by side. While the glow of the Red Light District almost bathes the 14th-century Oude Kerk, the smell of incense does battle with the all-too familiar scent of marijuana wafting down the streets.

Best for
Heritage

Home to
Oude Kerk, Joods Historisch Museum, Museum Het Rembrandthuis

Experience
The Zeedijk – the main drag of Chinatown

PAGE 92

NIEUWE ZIJDE

Crammed with hotels, shops, bars and restaurants, this is Amsterdam's busiest tourist district. At its centre, the famous Dam Square bustles with visitors heading to the sights as street performers clamour to grab their attention. Enclaves like the serene Begijnhof provide a refuge from the "New Side's" relentless commercialism.

Best for
Sightseeing

Home to
Amsterdam Museum, Museum Ons' Lieve Heer op Solder

Experience
Jenever at a traditional brown bar

PAGE 108

CANAL RING

Curving between the IJ and the Amstel like concentric ripples in a pond, the Singel, Herengracht, Keizersgracht and Prinsengracht canals define Amsterdam's central canal ring. Compared with the cramped Nieuwe Zijde, this part of the city has a more spacious feel to it. Leidseplein square – the area's hub – is packed with open-air cafés, but it really comes into its own after dark, when music bars and dance clubs attract throngs of visitors and a sprinkling of locals. Its eastern section is defined by the Singel and the Amstel canals, while the Vijzelstraat and Vijzelgracht canals cut a straight line through its heart. At the north end of Vijzelstraat is the much-loved Bloemenmarkt and its floating flower vendors. To the west, once-raffish Jordaan now has a bohemian feel, with chic boutiques, galleries, cafés and bars satisfying every desire of a hip clientele.

Best for
Canal trips and scenic strolls, offbeat museums and multicultural street food

Home to
Anne Frank House, Museum Willet-Holthuysen

Experience
A ride along the area's picturesque canals aboard a pedal-driven "canal bike"

$\rightarrow$

MUSEUM QUARTER

For lovers of high culture, the Museumplein is what Amsterdam is all about. Three world-class museums and one of the world's great concert halls stand around a calm green space. Visitors flock to the square here to admire the Old Masters in the Rijksmuseum and the modernists in the Stedelijk Museum, but the Van Gogh Museum is the quarter's true star. Away from the Museumplein, you'll find elegant streets defined by wealth and taste.

Best for
World-class art and classical music

Home to
Rijksmuseum, Van Gogh Museum, Stedelijk Museum

Experience
The wealth of art on display in Musemplein, before having a picnic in Vondelpark

PLANTAGE

East of the Amstel, this immaculately planned peninsula of tree-lined avenues and gracious 19th-century buildings contrasts with the cramped streets of Oude Zijde, which is only a block or two away. At its centre are the green spaces of Artis – the city's zoo – and Hortus Botanicus Amsterdam, which kids will love exploring. On the gentrified Entrepotdok waterfront, centuries-old warehouses have been turned into upscale apartments. Where the waters of the Nieuwevaart and the Oosterdok meet, a flotilla of historic ships lies at anchor.

Best for
A family day out

Home to
Tropenmuseum, Het Scheepvaartmuseum, NEMO Science Museum

Experience
Music at the Muziekgebouw aan 't IJ concert hall

PAGE 168

BEYOND THE CENTRE

In this compact city, venturing outside the central core is quick and uncomplicated. A five-minute ferry ride north across the IJ lies the edgy neighbourhood of Noord. The 100-m- (328-ft-) high A'DAM Toren, with its trendy clubs and revolving restaurant, is the district's emblematic landmark of transformation. South of the centre, in the De Pijp area, the landscape changes. Striking Amsterdam School architecture contrasts with the older canal house façades. This is the city's most multicultural neighbourhood and Albert Cuypmarkt lies at its heart, fragrant with enticing scents and alive with the sounds of vendors' calls.

Best for
Edgy culture and nightlife

Home to
A'DAM Toren, EYE, NDSM

Experience
New horizons on the highest swing in Europe at A'DAM Toren and the variety of street food along Albert Cuypmarkt

OUDE ZIJDE

A scattering of archaeological finds suggests that this area was first settled around 2600 BC, but little is known of these Neolithic peoples. It is more certain that Amsterdam began life in the 12th century as a fishing village on the east bank of the Amstel, gaining in importance after the river was dammed about a century later. Over the course of the 14th century, new canals and walls – including the Oudezijds Voorburgwal and Oudezijds Achterburgwal – were built to protect what had become known as the Oude Zijde (Old Side). In the early 15th century, the district began an eastward expansion that continued into the 17th century. This growth was fuelled by an influx of Jewish refugees from Portugal fleeing the Inquisition. Many of these Sephardic Jews were craftsmen and merchants who brought wealth to their new, tolerant home, building schools and synagogues. The growing city also profited handsomely from the English wool trade, with ships sailing up the old Damrak canal right into the heart of the city. As the town developed, further canals were cut and, after a great fire in 1452 destroyed much of the area, timber buildings were banned in favour of brick and stone – both measures substantially transformed the appearance of this part of the city. Due to its large migrant population and proximity to the harbour, the area gradually became a centre for prostitution, but in the 20th century, concerns about human trafficking led to the curtailment of many "window brothel" licences. Now calmer and safer than before, the Oude Zijde is once again becoming a vibrant tourist hub.

OUDE ZIJDE

Must Sees

1. Oude Kerk
2. Joods Historisch Museum
3. Museum Het Rembrandthuis

Experience More

4. Nieuwmarkt
5. Portuguese Synagogue
6. Mozes en Aäronkerk
7. Waag
8. Zuiderkerk
9. Agnietenkapel
10. De Waalse Kerk
11. Stadhuis and the Dutch National Opera & Ballet Building
12. Hash Marihuana & Hemp Museum
13. Zeedijk
14. Montelbaanstoren
15. Waterlooplein
16. Schreierstoren

Eat

1. Eetcafé van Beeren
2. De Waag
3. Hemelse Modder
4. Oriental City

Drink

5. Café de Engelbewaarder
6. De Bekeerde Suster
7. Café de Sluyswacht

Shop

8. Stephen & Penelope
9. Knuffels Toyshop
10. Time Machine

1 OUDE KERK

♀F3 ♙Oudekerksplein 23 Ⓜ Centraal ⊞4, 14, 24
ⓒChurch: 10am–6pm Mon–Sat, 1–5:30pm Sun; tower:
Apr–Oct: 1–7pm Mon–Sat ⓔ27 Apr, 25 Dec Ⓦoudekerk.nl

Sitting incongruously in the heart of the Red Light District, the "Old Church" is Amsterdam's oldest and most stately monument.

Dedicated to St Nicholas, patron saint of the city, the Oude Kerk dates from the mid-13th century, when a wooden church was built in a burial ground on a sandbank. The present Gothic structure was built in the 14th century and has grown from a single-aisled church into a basilica. As it expanded, the building became a gathering place for traders and a refuge for the poor. Its paintings and statuary were destroyed after the Alteration *(p64)* in 1578, but the rare gilded ceiling and stained-glass windows remain. The world-famous organ was added in 1724. The church still holds services, but also hosts art exhibitions, performances and debates. Access to the tower is via guided tour only.

2,500
tombstones are found in the church floor.

The spire of the bell tower was built in 1565, but the 47-bell carillon was added in 1658.

Great Organ

Tomb of Admiral Abraham van der Hulst (1619–66), hero of the Second Anglo-Dutch War

Main entrance to church on Oudekerksplein

Illustration showing both the Oude Kerk's medieval exterior and its magnificent interior

← The medieval Oude Kerk, rising behind houses in the Red Light District

Brocaded
pillars

Tomb of the explorer
Admiral Jacob van
Heemskerk (1567–1607)

Lady
Chapel

1 Contemporary art exhibitions, such as Christian Boltanski's *NA*, contrast with the Oude Kerk's medieval interior.

2 The Lady Chapel (1552) has three restored stained-glass windows, including *The Death of the Virgin Mary* by Dirk Crabeth.

3 Delicate 15th-century gilded vault paintings decorate the ceiling of the nave. They were hidden under layers of blue paint in 1755 and not revealed until 1955.

17th- and 18th-century houses

Timeline

1250
The first wooden chapel is built.

1330
The church is dedicated to St Nicholas.

1578
The Calvinists triumph in the Alteration and iconoclasts destroy many of the statues in the church.

1724
▷ Christian Vater's oak-encased Great Organ, with its 4,000 pipes, is installed in the nave.

② 🖌️ Ⓜ️ 🖥️ 🏛️

JOODS HISTORISCH MUSEUM

📍G5 🏛️ Nieuwe Amstelstraat 1
Ⓜ️ Waterlooplein 🚋14 🚌 Muziektheater
🕐11am–5pm daily 🚫27 Apr, Jewish New
Year, Yom Kippur 🌐 jck.nl/en

From the first Jews to arrive in Amsterdam to the preservation of Jewish identity today, this museum tells the turbulent history of the Jewish community in the Netherlands.

This remarkable museum of Jewish heritage is housed in four monumental synagogues – the Grote Synagoge, Nieuwe Synagoge, Obbene Shul and Dritt Shul. Restored in the 1980s, they are connected by internal walkways. Three permanent multimedia exhibitions present the history and culture of the Jewish people in the Netherlands through paintings, drawings, artifacts, photographs, films and 3D displays. In addition, there are temporary exhibitions and a Children's Museum. This museum, the Portuguese Synagogue (p86) and the Hollandsche Schouwburg (p162) form the Jewish Cultural Quarter.

Nieuwe Synagoge (1752)

1 The main entrance to the museum is through the stately Grote Synagoge.

2 The Festival Prayer Book was presented to the city's Jewish community by printer Uri Phoebus ha-Levi in 1669.

3 The side galleries of the Nieuwe Synagoge house part of the permanent collection. Photographs and artifacts tell moving stories.

JEWS IN AMSTERDAM

The first Jew to gain Dutch citizenship, in 1597, was a member of the Portuguese Sephardi community. The Ashkenazi Jews from Eastern Europe came to Amsterdam later, in the 1630s. They were restricted to working in certain trades, but were granted full civil equality in 1796. With the rise of Zionism in the 19th century, Jewish identity re-emerged, but the Nazi occupation almost obliterated the community *(p67)*.

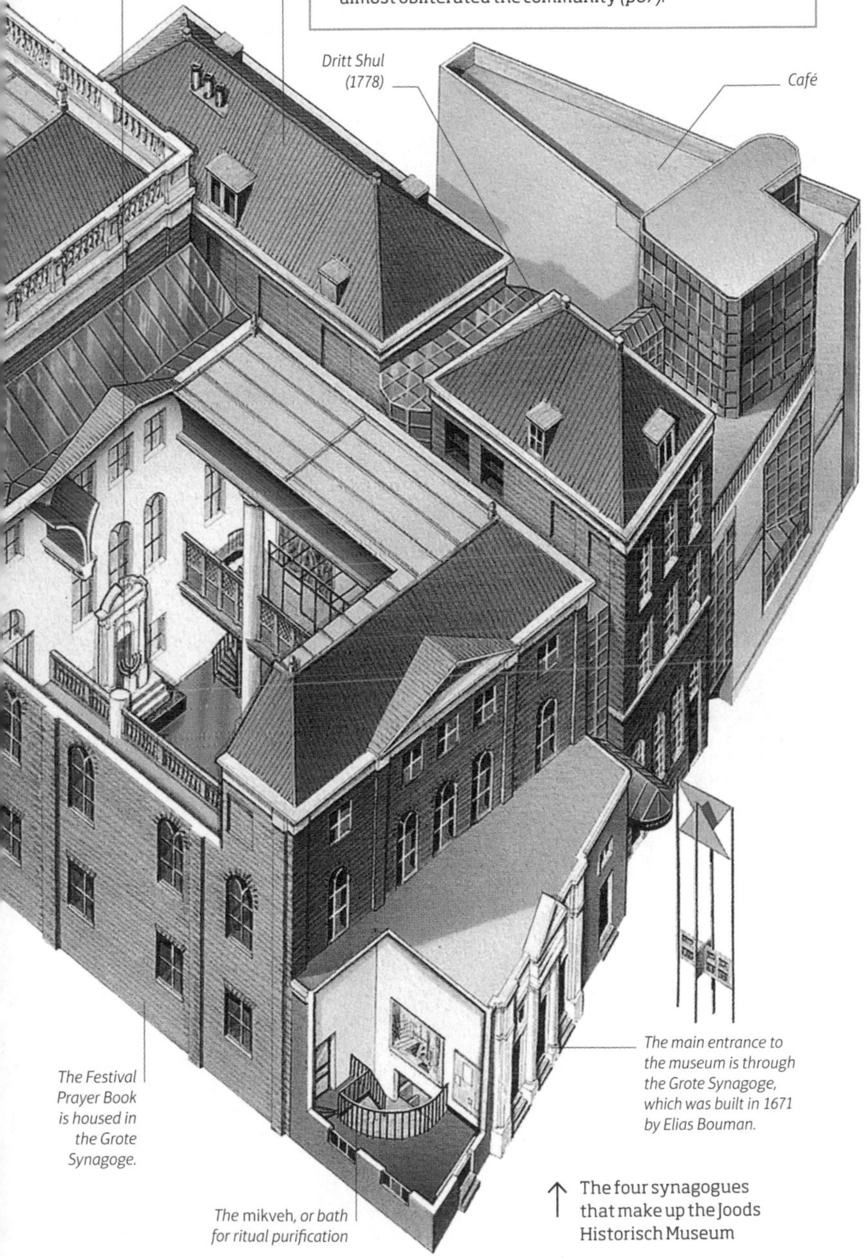

Hanukkah lamp

Obbene Shul (1685)
(Children's Museum)

Dritt Shul
(1778)

Café

The Festival
Prayer Book
is housed in
the Grote
Synagoge.

The mikveh, *or bath
for ritual purification*

The main entrance to
the museum is through
the Grote Synagoge,
which was built in 1671
by Elias Bouman.

↑ The four synagogues
that make up the Joods
Historisch Museum

A canvas set
up in the artist's
former studio ↑

INSIDER TIP
**Etching
Demonstration**

Don't miss the free,
daily etching and print-
mixing demonstrations
held in Rembrandt's
former graphic studio.
Learn about the etching
technique, the printing
process and graphic art.

MUSEUM HET REMBRANDTHUIS

⑨ G5 ⬛ Jodenbreestraat 4 Ⓜ Nieuwmarkt ⬛14 ⓞ10am–6pm daily
⬛27 Apr, 25 Dec ⬛ rembrandthuis.nl

The former home of Amsterdam's most famous artist – creator of
The Nightwatch, The Anatomy Lesson of Dr Nicolaes Tulp and over 300
other works – has been sensitively restored and converted into a
museum allowing an intimate glimpse into the life and times of
Rembrandt Harmenszoon van Rijn.

Rembrandt was an established portraitist,
married to the daughter of a wealthy
bourgeois family, when he bought this
red-shuttered house on the edge of the
Jewish district in 1639. By 1658, however,
his fortunes had changed. No longer an
artistic star, he was forced to sell his home.

Furnished according to the 1658
inventory, the house is now a museum
dedicated to the artist. On the first floor is
the studio where Rembrandt created many
of his most famous works. A room on the
mezzanine floor has some of his superb
etchings and paintings on display, and the
exhibition wing next door shows work by
his contemporaries. Younger visitors will
love the cabinet of curiosities on the
second floor, with its stuffed crocodiles,
narwhal tusks, skulls and fossils. Demonstrations of 17th-century etching and
paint-mixing are held daily.

The exterior of Rembrandt's home,
looking much as it did when he lived
here in the 17th century ↑

↑ A visitor admiring an exhibition
of Rembrandt's works alongside
paintings by artists he inspired

REMBRANDT'S SITTERS

Sephardi Jews fleeing the
Spanish Inquisition began to
arrive in Amsterdam in the
early 17th century. They
settled on the eastern
fringes of the Oude Zijde.
Many Sephardim were
already wealthy when they
arrived in Amsterdam, and in
Rembrandt's day this part of
town was an up-and-coming
neighbourhood. Its exotic,
striking young women
and craggy elders were
the perfect models for
Rembrandt's series of
paintings inspired by
Old Testament myths.

↑ Flea market at the Nieuwmarkt, with the Waag in the background

EXPERIENCE MORE

❹
Nieuwmarkt

📍G4 Ⓜ Nieuwmarkt
🚊4, 14, 24

An open, paved square, the Nieuwmarkt is flanked to its west by the Red Light District. With the top end of the Geldersekade, it forms Amsterdam's Chinatown. The Waag dominates the square, and construction of this gateway led to the site's development in the 15th century as a marketplace. When the city expanded in the 17th century, the square took on its present dimensions and was named the Nieuwmarkt. It retains an array of 17th- and 18th-century gabled houses. True to tradition, a flea market is held on Sundays during the summer.

The old Jewish Quarter leads off the square down St Antoniesbreestraat. In the 1970s, many houses here were demolished to make way for the metro, sparking clashes between protesters and police. The action of conservationists persuaded the council to adopt a policy of renovating rather than redeveloping old buildings. Photographs of their protests decorate the metro station.

---

❺ ◈ Ⓜ 🏛
Portuguese Synagogue

📍G5 🏠 Mr Visserplein 3
Ⓜ Waterlooplein 🚊14
🕐10am–4pm Sun–Fri
🚫27 Apr, Jewish hols
🌐esnoga.com

Elias Bouman's design for the Portuguese Synagogue is said to have been inspired by the Temple of Solomon in Jerusalem. Built for the wealthy Portuguese Sephardi community of Amsterdam and inaugurated in 1675, the huge brick building has a rectangular ground plan with the Holy Ark in the southeast corner, facing towards Jerusalem, and the *tebah* (the podium from which the service is led) at the opposite end.

The synagogue interior, with its pews made of mahogany, is illuminated by more than 1,000 candles and 72 windows. The wooden, barrel-vaulted ceiling is supported

---

> ## RED LIGHT DISTRICT
>
> Barely clad prostitutes bathed in a red neon glow and touting for business at their windows is one of the defining images of Amsterdam. The city's Red Light District, known locally as de Walletjes ("the little walls"), is concentrated around the Oude Kerk. Prostitution in Amsterdam dates back to the 13th century. By 1478, it had become so widespread that attempts were made to contain it. Today, hordes of visitors generate a buzz and, despite the sleaze, the council is trying to make this area more culturally attractive, promoting the bars, eateries and beautiful canal-side houses of this district.

by four Ionic columns. The main building holds the world's oldest functioning Jewish library, Ets Haim Livraria Montezinos, the contents of which are on UNESCO's World Heritage List.

6

Mozes en Aäronkerk

🌐 G5 🏠 Waterlooplein 205 Ⓜ Waterlooplein 🚋 14 🕐 For regular services & scheduled events (check website) 🌐 santegidio.nl

Designed by Flemish architect Tilman-François Suys in 1841, Mozes en Aäronkerk was built on the site of a hidden Catholic church. The later church took its name from the Old Testament figures depicted on the gable stones of the original building. These are now set into the rear wall. The church was restored in 1990 and services resumed in 2014 after an interruption of 34 years.

7 🍴

Waag

🌐 G4 🏠 Nieuwmarkt 4 Ⓜ Nieuwmarkt 🚋 4, 14, 24

The multiturreted Waag is the city's oldest surviving gatehouse. Built in 1488, it was then, and often still is, called St Antoniespoort. Public executions were held here, and condemned prisoners awaited their fate in the "little gallows room".

In 1617, the building became the Waaggebouw (public weigh house). Peasants had their produce weighed here and paid tax accordingly. Various guilds used the upper rooms of each tower.

From 1619, the Guild of Surgeons had a meeting room and anatomy theatre here. They added the central octagonal tower in 1691. Rembrandt's *Anatomy Lesson of Dr Nicholaes Tulp*, now in the Mauritshuis (p236), and *The Anatomy Lesson of Dr Jan Deijman*, in the Amsterdam Museum (p96), were commissioned by guild members to be hung here.

The weigh house closed in the early 19th century and the Waag has since served as a fire station and two city museums. It is now home to the restaurant In de Waag.

EAT

Eetcafé van Beeren
Friendly pub with modern Dutch fare and a cosy atmosphere.

🌐 G4 🏠 Koningsstraat 54 🕐 Dinner only 🌐 eetcafe vanbeeren.nl

€€€

In de Waag
Relaxed, candle-lit restaurant with terrace, serving hearty dishes.

🌐 G4 🏠 Nieuwmarkt 4 🌐 indewaag.nl

€€€

Hemelse Modder
Modern restaurant with refined dishes. Try the chocolate mousse.

🌐 G4 🏠 Oude Waal 11 🕐 Dinner only 🌐 hemelsemodder.nl

€€€

Oriental City
Busy Cantonese restaurant known for its dim sum.

🌐 F4 🏠 Oudezijds Voorburgwal 177-179 📞 020-626 8352

€€€

← The imposing 15th-century Waag lit up at dusk

8

Zuiderkerk

⊙ G5 ⌂ Zuiderkerkhof 72 Ⓜ Nieuwmarkt 🚋 14 ⒲ zuiderkerkamster dam.nl

Designed by Hendrick de Keyser in 1603 in the Renaissance style, the Zuiderkerk was the first Calvinist church to open in Amsterdam after the Alteration. The spire makes the building a prominent landmark, with its columns, decorative clocks and onion dome. The Zuiderkerk ceased to function as a church in 1929. It was restored in 1988 and now serves as an information centre and a commercial venue for events and private dinners. The surrounding community housing includes the "Pentagon" by Theo Bosch.

> The building boasts splendid acoustics and an impressive organ built by Christiaan Müller, one of the finest remaining in the world.

9

Agnietenkapel

⊙ F4 ⌂ Oudezijds Voorburgwal 231 Ⓜ Rokin 🚋 4, 14, 24 🚫 To the public ⒲ uva.nl

The Agnietenkapel was part of the convent of St Agnes until 1578, when it was closed after the Alteration. In 1632, the Athenaeum Illustre, the precursor of the University of Amsterdam, took over the building and by the mid-17th century it was a centre of scientific learning. It also housed the municipal library until the 1830s. The Agnietenkapel itself dates from 1470, and is one of the few Gothic chapels to have survived the Alteration. During restoration from 1919 to 1921, elements of Amsterdam School architecture were introduced (p172). Despite these changes and long periods of secular use, the building still has the feel of a Franciscan chapel. The large auditorium on the first floor is the oldest in the city. It has a lovely ceiling, painted with Renaissance motifs and a portrait of Minerva, the Roman goddess of wisdom and the arts. The Agnietenkapel once housed the University of Amsterdam Museum; now the museum's collection can be seen in Oude Turfmarkt 129 (next to the Allard Pierson Museum p102). A conference centre has taken its place.

10

De Waalse Kerk

⊙ F4 ⌂ Walenpleintje 157-159 Ⓜ Nieuwmarkt 🚋 4, 14, 24 🚫 For services and events only ⒲ dewaalsekerk.nl

The origin of this church dates back to 1409, when it started as a convent for laymen monks and was known as Paulusbroederkerk (Brother Paul Monastery). After 1550 it was handed over to the Huguenots – Protestant refugees from France – and was renamed Église Wallone. Services and regular lectures are still conducted here in French. The building boasts splendid acoustics and an

← The stunning spire of the Zuiderkerk reaches high above surrounding buildings

↑ The controversial Dutch National Opera & Ballet building beside the Amstel river

impressive organ built by Christiaan Müller, one of the finest remaining in the world.

Stadhuis and the Dutch National Opera & Ballet Building

🔲 G5 🏠 Waterlooplein 22
Ⓜ Waterlooplein 🚊 4, 14

Few buildings in Amsterdam caused as much controversy as the **Stadhuis** (city hall) and the **Dutch National Opera & Ballet**. Nicknamed the "Stopera" by protesters, the plan required the destruction of dozens of medieval houses, which were virtually all that remained of the original Jewish quarter, and the temporary relocation of a popular market. This led to running battles between squatters and the police.

The building, completed in 1988, is a huge confection of red brick, marble and glass. The complex has the largest auditorium in the country, and it is also home to the Netherlands' national opera and ballet companies.

Stadhuis
🏠 Waterlooplein 22
🕐 8am-6pm Mon-Fri; call 020-624 1111

Dutch National Opera & Ballet
🏠 Waterlooplein 22
🌐 operaballet.nl

Hash Marihuana & Hemp Museum

🔲 F4 🏠 Oudezijds Achterburgwal 148
Ⓜ Nieuwmarkt 🚊 4, 14, 24
🕐 10am-10pm daily 🔒 27 Apr 🌐 hashmuseum.com

This museum, which also has a branch in Barcelona, charts the history of hemp (marijuana). Exhibits refer back 8,000 years to early Asiatic civilizations, who used the plant for clothing and medicines. It was first used in the Netherlands, according to a herbal manual of 1554, as a cure

← Hash Marihuana & Hemp Museum sign

for earache. Until the late 19th century, hemp was also the main source of fibre for rope, and was therefore important in the Dutch shipping industry. Other exhibits relate to the psychoactive properties of this plant. They include an intriguing array of pipes and bongs (smoking devices), along with displays that explain smuggling methods. The museum also has a small cultivation area where plants are grown under artificial light.

⑬ Zeedijk

⑨ G3 Ⓜ Nieuwmarkt, Centraal Station 🚋 4, 14, 24, 26

Along with the Nieuwendijk and the Haarlemmerdijk, the Zeedijk (sea dyke) formed part of Amsterdam's original fortifications. Built in the early 1300s, some 30 years after Amsterdam had been granted its city charter, these defences took the form of a canal moat with piled-earth ramparts reinforced by wooden palisades. As the city grew in prosperity and its boundaries expanded, canals were filled in and the dykes became obsolete. The paths that ran alongside them became the streets and alleys which bear their names today.

One of the two remaining wooden-fronted houses in the city is at No 1. It was built in the mid-1500s as a hostel for sailors and is much restored. Opposite is St Olofskapel, built in 1445 and named after the first Christian king of Norway and Denmark. By the 1600s, the Zeedijk had become a slum. The area is on the edge of the city's Red Light District, and in the 1960s and 1970s it became notorious as a centre for drug-dealing and street crime. However, following an extensive clean-up campaign in the 1980s, the Zeedijk is much improved. Architect Fred Greves has built a Chinese Buddhist temple, Fo Kuang Shan.

> 💬 **INSIDER TIP**
> ### Shipping House
> Discover the marvellous Scheepvaarthuis, 450 m (492 yd) east of Zeedijk. Now the Grand Hotel Amrâth, it can be visited on guided tours organized by the Museum Het Schip (p171), which include lunch.

→
Decorated stalls awaiting opening time at Waterlooplein's flea market

⑭ Montelbaanstoren

⑨ G4 ⊓ Oude Waal/ Oudeschans 2 Ⓜ Nieuwmarkt 🚋 14 ⊙ To the public

The lower portion of the Montelbaanstoren was built in 1512 and formed part of Amsterdam's medieval fortifications. It lay just beyond the city wall, protecting the city's wharves on the newly built St Antoniesdijk (now the Oudeschans) from the neighbouring Gelderlanders.

The octagonal structure and open-work timber steeple were both added by Dutch sculptor and architect Hendrick de Keyser in 1606. In 1611, the tower began to list, prompting Amsterdammers to attach ropes to the top and pull it right again.

Sailors from the Dutch East India Company would gather at the Montelbaanstoren before being ferried in small boats down the IJ to the massive East Indies-bound sailing ships, anchored further out in deep water to the north. The building appears in a number of etchings by Rembrandt, and is still a popular subject for artists. It once housed the offices of the Amsterdam water authority but is currently unoccupied.

⑮ Waterlooplein

⑨ G5 Ⓜ Waterlooplein 🚋 14 ⊙ Market: 9:30am-6pm Mon-Sat 🖥 waterlooplein.amsterdam

The Waterlooplein is home to the oldest flea market in the country, dating from 1885 when two canals were filled in to create a market square. The area was originally known as Vlooyenburg, an artificial island built in the 17th century to house Jewish settlers. The original market disappeared during World War II, when most of the Jewish residents of Amsterdam were transported east by the Nazis. After the war, a popular flea market grew up in its place, and today the northern end of the square still hosts a lively mix of stalls.

SHOP

Stephen & Penelope

A knitter's paradise, with a huge selection of natural yarns, kits and accessories. Go along to the Craft Night (first Thursday of the month) or a weekly workshop.

⊙ G4 ⌂ Nieuwe Hoogstraat 29 ⓦ stephenand penelope.com

Knuffels Toyshop

A toyshop overflowing with soft toys, games and souvenirs, plus wooden shoes made in the on-site factory.

⊙ G4 ⌂ Sint Antoniesbreestraat 51 ⓦ knuffels.nl

Time Machine

A vintage clothing store with a funky selection of 70s and 80s attire and some unique designer pieces.

⊙ G4 ⌂ Nieuwe Hoogstraat 5 ☎ 020-625 3162

16

Schreierstoren

⊙ G3 ⌂ Prins Hendrikkade 94–95 Ⓜ Centraal Station 🚋 4, 14, 24, 26 ⊙ VOC Café Schreierstoren: 10am to late daily ⓠ Tower: to the public ⓦ schreierstoren.nl

The Schreierstoren (Weepers' Tower) was a defensive structure forming part of the medieval city walls, built in 1480. It was one of few fortifications not to be demolished as the city expanded beyond its medieval boundaries in the 17th century. The distinctive building now houses a basement café.

Popular legend states that the tower derived its name from the weeping (*schreien* in Dutch) of the women who came here to wave their men off to sea. It is more likely that the name comes from the tower's position on a sharp (*screye* or *scherpe*) bend in the old town walls. The earliest of four wall plaques, dated 1569, depicts a weeping woman with the inscription *scrayer hovck*, which means "sharp corner".

In 1609, Henry Hudson set sail from here in an attempt to discover a faster trading route to the East Indies. Instead, he unintentionally "discovered" the river in North America that still bears his name.

→

The Schreierstoren (Weepers' Tower) formed part of the original city fortifications

NIEUWE ZIJDE

The area to the west of the original course of the Amstel river was known as the Nieuwe Zijde (New Side), and, together with the Oude Zijde, formed the heart of the early maritime settlement. In 1345, the district was rejuvenated by the Miracle of Amsterdam: at a house on Kalverstraat, a dying man regurgitated the Eucharist, and even though this sacramental bread was thrown onto a fire, it would not burn. This event transformed the city into a place of pilgrimage and a chapel was built on the site, bringing commerce to the Nieuwe Zijde as worshippers passed through. Surprisingly, a great fire in 1452 also reinvigorated the Nieuwe Zijde. As part of the reconstruction, the broad Singel canal was cut, attracting the wealthy to the area. Fine quays, warehouses and merchants' homes sprang up where once there had been poverty. This medieval prosperity also manifested itself in the Begijnhof, almshouses built for the *begijns*, a lay sisterhood involved in good works. Over the next few centuries, the Amstel dam connecting the Oude and Nieuwe Zijdes gradually built up until it became wide enough to function as a town square, becoming not only a centre of commercial activity but also local government: in the 17th century, when Amsterdam was at the height of its powers, the Koninklijk Paleis was built on it to serve as the town hall. Today, Dam Square still plays an important role in public life, and its main artery, the Nieuwendijk, has become one of the city's principal shopping streets.

NIEUWE ZIJDE

Must Sees
① Amsterdam Museum
② Museum Ons' Lieve Heer Op Solder

Experience More
③ Nieuwe Kerk
④ Beurs van Berlage
⑤ Koninklijk Paleis
⑥ Allard Pierson Museum
⑦ Magna Plaza
⑧ Torensluis
⑨ Begijnhof
⑩ Nationaal Monument
⑪ Centraal Station
⑫ Ronde Lutherse Kerk
⑬ Sint-Nicolaasbasiliek

Eat
① Visrestaurant Lucius
② Vermeer
③ Café 't Gasthuys
④ Greenwoods Singel

Drink
⑤ In de Wildeman
⑥ Café Luxembourg
⑦ Café Van Zuylen

Stay
⑧ The Craftsmen Hotel
⑨ INK Hotel

1 🏛️ 🚶 🍴 🖼️ 🛍️

AMSTERDAM MUSEUM

📍E4 🏛️Kalverstraat 92, St Luciënsteeg 27 Ⓜ️Rokin
🚊2, 4, 11, 12, 14, 24 🕐10am–5pm daily 🔒27 Apr, 25 Dec
🌐amsterdammuseum.nl

The city's history museum explores Amsterdam's fascinating evolution from marshland to modern times, as well as the city's future. The setting tells a story just as varied as the one told by the main collection. The red-brick building began life as the Convent of St Lucien, before it was turned into a civic orphanage two years after the Alteration, in 1580.

↑ An interior courtyard of the red-brick Amsterdam Museum

The present building is largely as it was in the 18th century, with its 17th-century wings by Hendrick de Keyser and Jacob van Campen. At the heart of the collection within is Amsterdam DNA, a multimedia introduction to the development of Amsterdam, from its origins as a small fishing village in the Middle Ages to today's cosmopolitan city. Visitors can then explore the other rooms, where aspects of Amsterdam's history are dealt with in more detail, including the city's golden age in the 17th century. The Amsterdam Gallery covers both the past and the present, with exhibits ranging from 16th-century portraits to modern-day graffiti. Meanwhile, the Regents' Chamber and the Little Orphanage unlock the building's history.

Did You Know?

Boys and girls played in separate courtyards when the building was an orphanage.

A globe, crafted by Willem Blaeu (cartographer of the Dutch East India Company), on display in Amsterdam DNA to illustrate the city's history of overseas trade and colonial expansion ↓

Gallery Rooms

Amsterdam DNA

▼ This one-hour tour of the city's history explores Amsterdam's main cultural characteristics, including the spirit of enterprise, freedom of thought, civic virtue and creativity. Touch-sensitive screens and archival film footage are used to great effect.

Amsterdam Gallery

▶ Leading from Begijnensteeg into the museum, this covered "museum street" is free of charge. Don't miss Albert Jansz Vinckenbrinck's wooden statue of *David, Goliath and His Shield-Bearer* (1648–50).

Regents' Chamber

▼ Built in 1634, this room was the meeting place of the orphanage's directors (regents). Its fine ceiling, added in 1656, shows the orphans receiving charity. Portraits of the regents hang on the walls. The long table and cabinets are 17th century.

The Little Orphanage

▶ This exhibition gives children and parents the opportunity to experience life in a 17th-century orphanage. Along with authentically arranged classrooms, kitchens and animal sheds are talking exhibits and pop-up characters who tell visitors about their day-to-day lives.

← Exhibits from the 20th century on display in Amsterdam DNA

② ⌔ Ⓜ ▭ 🛍

MUSEUM ONS' LIEVE HEER OP SOLDER

📍 F3 🏠 Oudezijds Voorburgwal 38
🚋 4, 14, 24 🕐 10am-6pm Mon-Sat, 1-6pm
Sun & public hols 🗓 27 Apr 🌐 opsolder.nl

Tucked away on the edge of the Red Light District is a restored 17th-century canal house, with two smaller houses to the rear. The upper storeys conceal a secret Catholic church known as Our Lord in the Attic (Ons' Lieve Heer op Solder).

Our Lord in the Attic

After the Alteration of 1578, when Amsterdam officially became Protestant, many hidden Catholic churches were built throughout the city. Merchant Jan Hartman added this chapel to his house in 1663. It was extended in around 1735 to create more seating space. The building became a museum in 1888, and displays fine church silver, religious artifacts and paintings. Next door to the church is an exhibition space, café and shop.

Simple spout gable on the first house

Canal room

Main entrance

A chaplain's tiny box bedroom is hidden off a bend in the stairs. There was a resident chaplain in the church from 1663.

↑ Hartman's house on the canal, concealing the two smaller houses behind

↑ The three houses that make up the Museum Ons' Lieve Heer Op Solder

Wooden viewing gallery of the church

Sacristy, where vestments were kept

Did You Know?

The church is painted with a pigment known as *caput mortuum*, or "dead head" pink.

Our Lord in the Attic served the Catholic community until Sint Nicolaasbasiliek (p105) was finished in 1887.

The landing where the tiny wooden confessional stands was the living room of the rear house.

The 17th-century kitchen was originally part of the priest's living quarters.

Parlour

① Restored to its former opulence, the parlour is furnished in the Dutch Classical style of the 17th century.

② Unlike the rest of the house, Our Lord in the Attic has been restored to its 19th-century appearance, when it was last used by worshippers.

③ The canal room is where the 17th-century inhabitants would have spent the day.

EXPERIENCE MORE

3 🏛️💻🛍️

Nieuwe Kerk

📍E4 🚇Dam 🚊2, 4, 14,
17 🕐10am-5pm during
exhibitions only; check
website 🗓️27 Apr
🌐nieuwekerk.nl

Dating from the late 14th
century, Amsterdam's second
parish church was built as the
population outgrew the Oude
Kerk (p80). During its turbulent
history, the church has been
destroyed several times by
fire, rebuilt and then stripped
of its finery after the Alteration.
The structure reached its
present size in the 1650s.

The pulpit, not the altar, is
the focal point of the interior,
reflecting the Protestant belief
that the sermon is central to
worship. Unusually flamboyant for a Dutch Protestant
church, the pulpit was finished
in 1664 and took Albert
Vinckenbrink 15 years to carve.
Above the transept crossing,
grimacing gilded cherubs
struggle to support the corners of the wooden barrel

vault. Magnificent three-tiered
brass candelabra were hung
from the ceilings of the nave
and transepts during restoration work following the fire
of 1645. Other highlights of
the interior include Jacob van
Campen's great organ (1645),
which is adorned with marble
and wood cherubs, and a
colourful arched window in
the south transept, designed
by Otto Mengelberg in 1898.
In the apse is Rombout
Verhulst's memorial to
Admiral De Ruyter (1607–76),
who died at sea in battle
against the French.

4 🏛️🎨🍴💻🛍️

Beurs van Berlage

📍F3 🚇Damrak 243
🚊4, 14, 24 🕐10am-10pm
daily 🗓️1 Jan 🌐beursvan
berlage.nl

This striking Modernist
building, the city's former
stock exchange, was con-
structed in 1903 to a design
by the pioneering Dutch architect Hendrik Petrus Berlage
(1856–1934). The clean,
functional appearance of the
building marked a departure
from late 19th-century

BURGERZAAL, KONINLIJK PALEIS

Based on the assembly halls of ancient Rome, the 30-m-
(95-ft-) high Burgerzaal (Citizens' Hall) is an impressive
room at the heart of the Koninklijk Paleis. The hall's best
feature is its mid-18th-century marble floor, which is
inlaid with three large circular maps, each over 6 m
(19.5 ft) in diameter. These depict the night sky as seen
from the northern hemisphere, plus western and eastern
terrestrial hemispheres, all based on charts by the well-
known Dutch cartography Blaue family. Overlooking the
hall are great marble reliefs and sculptures, including
one of Atlas holding the world on his shoulders.

← Gothic Nieuwe Kerk, with its huge stained-glass windows

Revivalist architecture. Its curving lines, plain exterior and, above all, Berlage's imaginative use of red brick as a decorative construction material inspired the later architects of the Amsterdam School. It has an impressive frieze above the entrance showing the evolution of man from Adam to stockbroker. The building is entered through a 40-m (130-ft) clock tower that gives access to three massive halls once used as trading floors. Inside, the main hall is decorated with ceramic friezes depicting different labourers, including miners and coffee-pickers.

The Beurs is now used as a conference venue. It also hosts a variety of changing exhibitions and concerts, and there is a good

bistro. Guided tours of the building allow you to climb the bell tower for extensive views over Amsterdam.

 5

Koninklijk Paleis

📍E4 🏛Dam Square 🚋2, 4, 11, 12, 14, 24 ⏰Hours vary, check website 🌐paleis amsterdam.nl

The Koninklijk Paleis (Royal Palace), still used by the Dutch royal family for official events, was originally built as the city's Stadhuis (town hall). Construction of the sandstone building began in 1648, at the end of the Eighty Years' War, and it was completed in 1665. The Neo-Classical design of Jacob van Campen (1595–1657) reflected Amsterdam's new-found self confidence after the victory against the Spanish. In 1808, under Louis Napoleon, the town hall was converted into a palace.

The palace was thouroughly restored in the 20th century, which undid much of the work of Napoleon.

When not in use by the royal family, the palace is open to the public. Take time to admire the impressive façade, which is decorated with a large number of sculptures, mainly of allegorical figures. A flight of stairs takes visitors from street level up to the imposing bronze entrance gates of the grand Burgerzaal (Citizens' Hall). Inside the Vroedschapszaal (the Council Hall of the city fathers) are two fine fireplaces with mantelpieces by Govert Flinck and Han van Bronckhorst. The grisailles from 1738 are the work of Jacob de Wit.

DRINK

In de Wildeman
This tavern in a former distillery has at least 18 craft beers on tap and 200 more by the bottle.

📍F3 🏛Kolksteeg 3 ⏰Sun 🌐inde wildeman.nl

Café Luxembourg
An elegant café with Art Deco detailing and a large terrace perfect for people-watching, sipping Dutch gin, and indulging in a *kroket* (croquette) or two.

📍E5 🏛Spui 24 🌐cafeluxembourg. amsterdam

Café Van Zuylen
The pretty terrace of this classic brown café is located right on the 17th-century Torensluis bridge.

📍X9 🏛Torensteeg 4-8 📞020-639 1055

↑ The Neo-Classical façade of the Koninklijk Paleis, with fine sculptures intended to glorify the city

STAY

The Craftsmen Hotel

Formerly known as the Hotel Brouwer, this boutique hotel is set in an elegant 17th-century canal house. All the well-appointed, uniquely designed rooms feature canal views and traditional wooden floors.

📍E3 🏠Singel 83
🌐hotelthecraftsmen.nl

€€€

INK Hotel

Rain showers, a 24-hour fitness centre and romantic picnic packages are offered at this modern boutique hotel in the heart of the city.

📍F3 🏠Nieuwezijds Voorburgwal 67
🌐ink-hotel-amsterdam.com

€€€

6

Allard Pierson Museum

📍F5 🏠Oude Turfmarkt 127 🚊4, 14, 24 🕙10am–5pm Tue–Fri, 1–5pm Sat, Sun & public hols 🚫1 Jan, Easter Sun, 27 Apr, 25 Dec 🌐allardpiersonmuseum.nl

Amsterdam's only specialist archaeological collection is named after Allard Pierson (1831–96), a noted humanist and scholar. The collection was moved into this Neo-Classical building in 1976 and includes Cypriot, Greek, Egyptian, Roman, Etruscan and Coptic artifacts.

7

Magna Plaza

📍E4 🏠Nieuwezijds Voorburgwal 182 🚊1, 2, 5, 13, 14, 17 🕙10am–10pm daily 🚫27 Apr, 25 Dec, 1 Jan
🌐magnaplaza.nl

A post office building has been situated here since 1748. The present building was completed in 1899; the architect, C P Peters, was ridiculed for the extravagance of its Neo-Gothic design. In 1990 it opened as the city's first shopping mall.

8

Torensluis

📍E3 🏠Singel, between Torensteeg and Oude Leliestraat 🚊1, 2, 5, 13, 14, 17 🌐detorensluis.nl

The grand Torensluis is one of the oldest and widest bridges in the city. Built on the site of

← A statue of Thucydides at the Allard Pierson Museum

> 📷 PICTURE PERFECT
> **Canal View from Torensluis**
>
> The Torensluis is the ideal spot from which to snap a quintessential Amsterdam image. Capture canal boats chugging along against a backdrop of high-gabled canal houses.

↑ Retaining its former opulence, Magna Plaza's colonnaded interior

a 17th-century sluice gate, it took its name from a tower that stood here until demolished in 1829. The tower's outline is marked in the pavement. A lock-up jail built in the bridge's foundations in the 17th century has since been restored, and today hosts exhibitions. In summer, café tables on the bridge offer pleasant views down the Singel.

---

⑨
Begijnhof

⚐ E5 Ⓜ Spui (public entrance at Gedempte Begijnensloot) 🚊 2, 4, 11, 12, 14, 24 🕘 9am–5pm daily

The Begijnhof was originally built in 1346 as a sanctuary for the Begijntjes, a lay Catholic sisterhood who lived like nuns, although they took no monastic vows. In return for lodgings, these women undertook to educate the poor and look after the sick. Nothing survives of the earliest dwellings, but the Begijnhof, cut off from traffic noise, retains a sanctified atmosphere. Among the houses that overlook its well-kept green is the city's oldest surviving house at No 34. On the adjoining wall there is a collection of wall plaques taken from the houses. In keeping with the Begijntjes' religious outlook, the plaques have a biblical theme.

The southern fringe of the square is dominated by the Engelse Kerk (English Church), dating from the 15th century. Directly west stands the Begijnhof Chapel, a clandestine church in which the Begijntjes and other Catholics worshipped in secret until religious tolerance was restored in 1795. Stained-glass windows and paintings depict scenes of the Miracle of Amsterdam. Public tours are not allowed, and all visitors are requested to be quiet and not visit the Begijnhof in large groups.

↓ The Begijnhof, housing for the Catholic Begijntjes

No 19 has a plaque depicting the exodus of the Jews from Egypt.

The Begijnhof Chapel, a clandestine church (Nos 29–30), completed in 1680.

Houten House, No 34, is Amsterdam's oldest house, dating from around 1420.

Biblical plaques cover the wall behind No 34.

Engelse Kerk, a church built around 1419, was confiscated after the Alteration.

Main entrance from Gedempte Begijnensloot

Spui entrance

EAT

Visrestaurant Lucius
Lobster and crab dishes are specialities at this long-established seafood restaurant.

📍E4 🏠Spuistraat 247
🌐lucius.nl

€€€

Vermeer
This Michelin-starred restaurant sources much of its produce from nearby a rooftop garden and local farms to create an exquisite modern menu.

📍G3 🏠Prins
Hendrikkade 59-72
⏱Dinner only 🚫Sun
🌐restaurantvermeer.nl

€€€

Café 't Gasthuys
Take a seat on the canalside terrace of this brown café and watch the range of vessels passing by while sipping a glass of wine.

📍F5 🏠Grimburgwal 7
🌐gasthuys.nl

€€€

Greenwoods Singel
For a spot of tea or even a full breakfast, this English tearoom is worth the wait on weekends.

📍E3 🏠Singel 103
⏱Breakfast and lunch
only 🌐greenwoods.eu

€€€

10

Nationaal Monument

📍F4 🏠Dam 🚊4, 9, 14, 16

Sculpted by John Raedecker and designed by architect J J P Oud, the imposing 22-m (72-ft) obelisk in Dam Square commemorates the Dutch casualties of World War II. The monument was unveiled in 1956 and is fronted by two lions, heraldic symbols of the Netherlands. Embedded in the wall behind are urns containing earth from all the Dutch provinces as well as from the former Dutch colonies of Indonesia, the Antilles and Suriname.

11

Centraal Station

📍G2 🏠Stationsplein
Ⓜ Centraal Station 🚊2, 11,
12, 13, 17 ⏱Daily 🌐ns.nl

When the Centraal Station opened in 1889, it replaced the old harbour as the symbolic focal point of the city and curtained Amsterdam off from the sea. The Neo-Gothic red-brick railway terminus was designed by P J H Cuypers and A L van Gendt. Three artificial islands were created with 8,600 wooden piles supporting the structure. The twin towers and central section have architectural echoes of a triumphal arch. The façade's decorations show allegories of maritime trade, a tribute to the city's past. The station sees over 250,000 passengers pass through it every day.

12

Ronde Lutherse Kerk

📍F3 🏠Kattengat 2 🚊1, 2,
5, 13, 17 🚫To the public

This round church, also known as Nieuwe Lutherse Kerk or Koepelkerk, was designed by Adriaan Dortsman (1625–82) and opened in 1671. It is the first Dutch Reformed church

to feature a circular ground plan and two upper galleries, which give the whole congregation a clear view of the pulpit.

In 1882 a fire, started by careless plumbers, destroyed all but the church's exterior walls. When the interior and entrance were rebuilt in 1883, they were made more square and more ornate and a grand vaulted copper dome was added, replacing the earlier ribbed version.

Falling attendance led to the closure of the church in 1935. The building is now used by Renaissance Amsterdam Hotel as a business centre.

1,281

bridges span the 50 km (31 miles) of canals in Amsterdam.

Concerts are sometimes held here. Take time to admire the unique exterior, which stands out among the neighbouring canal houses.

---

13 🅜

Sint-Nicolaasbasiliek

📍 G3 🏠 Prins Hendrikkade 73 Ⓜ Centraal Station 🚊 4, 14, 24, 26 🕐 Noon–3pm Mon & Sat, 11am–4pm Tue–Fri 🌐 nicolaas-parochie.nl

Saint Nicholas is the patron saint of seafarers, and is an important icon in the history of the Netherlands. Many Dutch churches are named after him, and the Netherlands' principal day for the giving of presents, 5 December, is known as Sint Nicolaas Day.

Completed in 1887, Sint-Nicolaasbasiliek was designed by A C Bleys (1842–1912). It replaced some clandestine Catholic churches set up in the city when Amsterdam was officially Protestant. The

↑ Colourful stained-glass windows adorn Sint Nicolaasbasiliek's dome

splendid Neo-Renaissance exterior is forbidding, its twin towers dominating the city skyline. The church's monumental interior has squared pillars and coffered ceiling arches. Inside, look up to see the beautifully coloured stained-glass windows that decorate the dome.

← The circular Ronde Lutherse Kerk, with its copper dome, overlooking the canal

A SHORT WALK
NIEUWE ZIJDE

Distance 1.5 km (1 mile) **Nearest metro** Rokin
Time 15 minutes

Although much of the medieval Nieuwe Zijde has disappeared, the area is still rich in buildings that relate to the city's past. A walk up Kalverstraat to Dam Square, dominated by the Koninklijk Paleis and Nieuwe Kerk, and then down to Spui on Rokin takes you past examples of architecture from the 15th to the 20th centuries. You'll stroll past narrow streets and alleys that follow the course of some of the earliest dykes and footpaths. Along the way, pause at traditional gabled houses that have been turned into bustling shops and cafés. Financial institutions on Rokin and Nes have made way for chic department stores.

↑ The charming houses
of the Begijnhof

Kalverstraat, *a busy shopping area, took its name from the livestock market which was regularly held here during the 15th century.*

Wall plaques and maps showing the walled medieval city are on display in the **Amsterdam Museum** (p96), *a converted orphanage that dates from the 16th century.*

Two churches and one of the few remaining wooden houses in the city nestle in the **Begijnhof**'s *secluded, tree-filled courtyard (p103).*

START

ST LUCIENSTEEG

KALVERSTRAAT

FINISH

Caffè Esprit

SPUI

ROKIN

Built as the town hall, the **Koninklijk Paleis** (p101) has a Classical façade and fine sculptures that were intended to glorify the city and its government.

Much of the **Nieuwe Kerk** (p100) was destroyed in the great fire of 1645.

Locator Map
For more detail see p94

A **wall statue** depicting St Nicolaas – Amsterdam's patron saint – is thought to date from the 15th century.

Did You Know?

Dam Square derives its name from its original function – damming the Amstel river.

Two heraldic stone lions represent the Netherlands on the imposing **Nationaal Monument** (p104), a memorial to the Dutch who lost their lives in World War II.

As well as waxworks and animated scenes, there is a fine view of the city from **Madame Tussauds Amsterdam**.

Nes is one of Amsterdam's oldest streets and has been a centre for theatre for over 150 years.

0 metres 50
0 yards 50

→ People strolling past Madame Tussauds Amsterdam on Rokin

CANAL RING

In the early 17th century, the merchant classes, rich from booming maritime trade, sought to escape the overcrowding and industrial squalor of the old city. Construction of the Canal Ring, or Grachtengordel, began, and the city's three main canals – Herengracht, Keizersgracht and Prinsengracht – were dug as part of a comprehensive plan to extend the boundaries of a city bulging at the seams. The idea was both visionary and simple: the town bought the land, dug the canals and sold housing plots back to developers. Neither did the town's vision end there: buyers had to comply with exhaustive planning regulations stipulating plot sizes and even the colour of the front doors, which were painted in a shade known as "Amsterdam green". The wealthiest buyers built opulent mansions on a stretch of Herengracht known as the Golden Bend, the better-off lived on the main canals and the radial cross-streets had modest dwellings for the skilled artisans that were necessary for the whole plan to work. The end result was aesthetically sublime, with the architectural conformity animated by gable variations.

Around the same time, the marshy area west of Prinsengracht was laid out as an area for workers whose industries were banned from the city centre. Immigrants fleeing religious persecution also settled here. It is thought that Huguenot refugees called the district *jardin* (garden), later corrupted to Jordaan. This once poor area is now known for the *hofjes* (almshouses) that were built to serve residents in need. From the 1660s, the Canal Ring was extended east beyond the medieval city walls, and Reguliersgracht, now one of the city's prettiest canals, was cut. These new stretches of canal also soon became lined with merchants' mansions. Today, Amsterdam is at its most enchanting in the Grachtengordel, which has been designated a UNESCO World Heritage Site.

CANAL RING

Must Sees
① Anne Frank Huis
② Museum Willet-Holthuysen

Experience More
③ Haarlemmerpoort
④ Brouwersgracht
⑤ Felix Meritis Building
⑥ Westerkerk
⑦ Huis met de Hoofden
⑧ Rembrandtplein
⑨ Noorderkerk and Noordermarkt
⑩ Western Islands
⑪ Leidseplein
⑫ Foam Museum
⑬ De Krijtberg
⑭ Bijbels Museum
⑮ Looier Kunst en Antiekcentrum
⑯ Het Grachtenhuis
⑰ Stadsarchief Amsterdam
⑱ Magere Brug
⑲ Internationaal Theater Amsterdam
⑳ Museum Van Loon
㉑ Pathé Tuschinski
㉒ Munttoren
㉓ Bloemenmarkt

Eat
① Tujuh Maret
② Café Américain
③ Morlang

Drink
④ Café de Eland
⑤ Café Het Molenpad
⑥ Rose's Cantina

Stay
⑦ Ambassade Hotel
⑧ Hotel Dwars
⑨ Armada Hotel

ANNE FRANK HUIS

D3 **Prinsengracht 263-7** **13, 17** **Apr-Oct: 9am-10pm daily; Nov-Mar: 9am-7pm daily (to 9pm Sat)** **Yom Kippur** **annefrank.org**

Anne Frank's diary is a poignant portrait of a young girl growing up in times of oppression. Even those who have not read her diary will be moved by the annexe where she and her family hid.

On 6 July 1942, to avoid their Nazi persecutors, the Jewish Frank family moved from Merwedeplein to a secret annexe of Otto Frank's workplace on Prinsengracht. Anne; her mother, Edith; her father, Otto; and her older sister, Margot, lived hidden here for two years, along with the Van Pels family and dentist Fritz Pfeffer. It was here that Anne wrote her famous diary. On 4 August 1944, the annexe was raided by the Gestapo. All those hiding there were arrested and taken to Nazi concentration camps. Only Otto Frank survived.

The rear annexe is accessible via the reconstructed offices of Otto Frank. The building beside Anne Frank Huis holds various exhibitions. It also houses a café, shop and information desk. Tickets are only available online, for designated time slots; it's advisable to book well in advance.

Attic

The Van Pels family's room

Anne's bedroom

The Frank family's bedroom

Bathroom

Behind the hinged bookcase was a small suite of rooms where the Franks, Van Pels and Pfeffer lived.

↑ The plain façade, offering no clues to the secret annexe found inside

↑ Illustration showing the Anne Frank House's secret annexe

[1] Photographs of Anne - happy and carefree - before she went into hiding are displayed in the building beside the annexe.

[2] Anne and Fritz shared a room on the first floor of the annexe. On Anne's bedroom walls were photos of film stars, which she collected. Anne wrote most of her diary at the table here.

[3] Visitors to the Anne Frank House enter the annexe via the revolving bookcase that hid its entrance.

Main building housing the offices and warehouse of Otto Frank's pectin and spice business

THE DIARY OF ANNE FRANK

Otto Frank returned to Amsterdam in 1945 to discover that his entire family had perished: his wife, Edith, in Auschwitz and his daughters, Anne and Margot, in Bergen Belsen. Miep Gies, one of the family's helpers while they were in hiding, had kept Anne's diary. First published in 1947, it has since been translated into 70 languages, with some 20 million copies sold. For many, Anne symbolizes the six million Jews who were murdered by the Nazis in World War II.

2 🗡 Ⓜ 🏛

MUSEUM WILLET-HOLTHUYSEN

📍 F5 🏠 Herengracht 605 🚊 4, 14 🕐 10am–5pm daily 🚫 1 Jan, 27 Apr, 25 Dec
🌐 willetholthuysen.nl

A visit to Amsterdam wouldn't be complete without exploring one of the city's iconic canal houses. Named after its last residents, the Museum Willet-Holthuysen allows visitors a glimpse into the lives of the emerging merchant class who lived in luxury along the Grachtengordel (Canal Ring) in the 17th century.

The house, built in 1685, became the property of coal magnate Pieter Holthuysen (1788–1858) in 1855. It passed to his daughter Louisa and her art-connoisseur husband, Abraham Willet – both fervent collectors of paintings, glass, silver and ceramics. When Louisa died childless and a widow in 1895, the house and its many treasures were left to the city, on the condition that it became a museum bearing their names. Room by room, the house is gradually being restored, bringing it back to the time when Abraham and Louisa lived here.

Arguably, the most interesting part of the house is found below stairs. The 19th-century kitchen has been re-created using items salvaged from similar houses, including the sink and pump, and special exhibits illuminate the lives of the Willet-Holthuysens' servants.

> **When Louisa died childless and a widow in 1895, the house and its many treasures were left to the city, on the condition that it became a museum bearing their names.**

↑ The grand façade of the Museum Willet-Holthuysen

↑ The dining room, decorated with a copy of an 18th-century silk wallpaper

← The gentlemen's parlour, hung with opulent, heavy blue damask

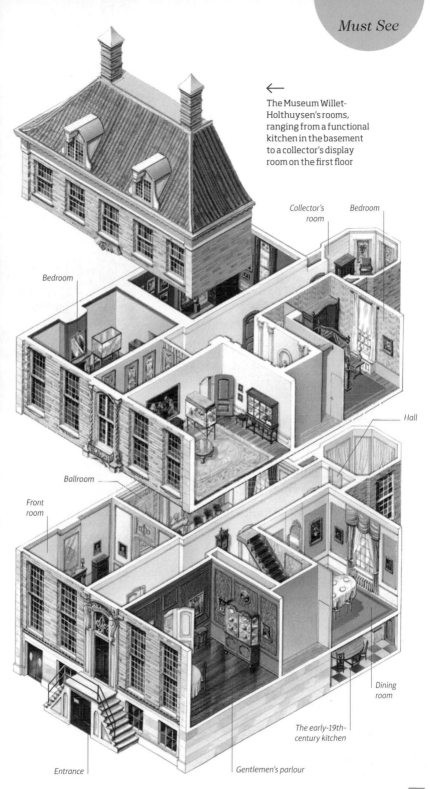

← The Museum Willet-Holthuysen's rooms, ranging from a functional kitchen in the basement to a collector's display room on the first floor

Collector's room

Bedroom

Bedroom

Hall

Ballroom

Front room

Dining room

The early-19th-century kitchen

Entrance

Gentlemen's parlour

EXPERIENCE MORE

③
Haarlemmerpoort

⚲ D1 **⌂ Haarlemmerplein 50** **🚊 3** **⊘ To the public**

Originally a defended gateway into Amsterdam, the Haarlemmerpoort marked the beginning of the busy route to Haarlem. The present gateway, dating from 1840, was built for King William II's triumphal entry into the city and named Willemspoort. However, as the third gateway to be built on or close to this site, it is still called the Haarlemmerpoort by Amsterdammers.

Designed by Cornelis Alewijn (1788–1839), the Neo-Classical gatehouse was used as tax offices in the 19th century and was made into flats in 1986. Traffic no longer goes through the gate, since a bridge has been built over the adjoining Westerkanaal.

Restorations are under-way for a restaurant and several housing units in the building, despite protests by local residents, and will be completed some time in 2020.

④
Brouwersgracht

⚲ E2 **🚊 3**

Brouwersgracht (Brewers' Canal) was named after the breweries established here in the 17th and 18th centuries. Leather, spices, coffee and sugar were also processed and stored here. Today, most of the warehouses, with their spout gables and shutters, are residences that look out onto moored houseboats.

⑤ ⊘
Felix Meritis Building

⚲ D5 **⌂ Keizersgracht 324** **🚊 2, 11, 12, 13, 17** **⊘ For renovation until early 2020** **🌐 felixmeritis.nl**

This Neo-Classical building is best viewed from the opposite side of the canal. Designed by Jacob Otten Husly, it opened in 1787 as a science and arts centre set up by the Felix Meritis society. The name means "happiness through merit". An association of wealthy citizens, the society was founded by the watch-maker Willem Writs in 1777, at the time of the Dutch Enlightenment (p77).

Five reliefs on the façade proclaim the society's interest in natural science and art. The building was fitted out with an observatory, library, labora-tories and a small concert hall. Mozart, Grieg, Brahms and Saint-Saëns are among the many distinguished musicians who have given performances in the society's hall.

In the 19th century, it became Amsterdam's main

←

Apartments overlooking houseboats on the Brouwersgracht canal

→

Grand Westerkerk, set alongside the Keizersgracht canal

> **🔍 HIDDEN GEM**
> ## Homo-monument
>
> The pink triangle used to "brand" homosexual men during World War II influenced Karin Daan's 1987 memorial to oppressed gay people. It is located in a quiet spot on busy Westermarkt.

cultural centre, and its concert hall inspired the design of the Concertgebouw (p146).

The Dutch Communist Party (CPN) occupied the premises from 1946, but cultural prominence was restored in the 1970s when the Shaffy Theatre Company used the building as a theatre and won acclaim for its avant-garde productions.

From 1988 the building housed the European Centre for Arts and Sciences. It is

25,000

bicycles end up in Amsterdam's canals every year.

DUTCH HOFJES

Before the Alteration, the Catholic Church often provided subsidised housing for the poor and elderly, particularly women. During the 17th and 18th centuries, hundreds of almshouse complexes, known as *hofjes,* were built - many are found in the Jordaan. Behind their façades lie pretty houses and serene gardens. Visitors are admitted to some but asked to respect the residents' privacy.

six burglars and cut off their heads. The sculptures are in fact portrayals of six classical deities (from left to right): Apollo, Ceres, Mars, Minerva, Bacchus and Diana. The design is sometimes attributed to Pieter de Keyser (1595–1676), son of Hendrick de Keyser.

The Huis met de Hoofden building has housed variously a business school, a conservatoire and the Bureau Monumenten en Archeologie. In 2006, it was purchased by the art collector and owner of the Bibliotheca Philosophica Hermetica, J R Ritman, and today the house features a cultural museum called the Embassy of the Free Mind.

undergoing extensive renovation and will reopen once more as a cultural centre in 2020.

Westerkerk

D3 **Prinsengracht 281** **13, 14, 17** **Hours vary, check website** **Dec-Mar** **westerkerk.nl**

Built as part of the development of the Canal Ring, this church has the tallest tower in the city at 85 m (279 ft), and the largest nave of any Dutch Protestant church. It was designed by Hendrick de Keyser, who died in 1621, a year after work began. Rembrandt was buried here but his grave has never been found. The organ shutters (1686) were painted by Gerard de Lairesse, with lively scenes showing King David and the Queen of Sheba. The tower,

which has stunning views, carries the crown bestowed on Amsterdam in 1489 by Maximilian, the Hapsburg emperor.

Huis met de Hoofden

E3 **Keizersgracht 123** **13, 14, 17** **10am-5pm Wed-Sat** **embassyofthe freemind.com**

Built in 1622, the Huis met de Hoofden (House with the Heads) is one of the largest double houses of the period. It takes its name from the six heads placed on pilasters along the façade. Legend has it that they commemorate a housemaid who surprised

→

A head from the façade of Huis met de Hoofden (House with the Heads)

Characterful houses along
one of Amsterdam's
boat-lined canals ↑

A GUIDE TO CANAL HOUSE ARCHITECTURE

Amsterdam's canalscape developed in the 15th century, when planning laws, plot sizes and the instability of the topsoil dictated that façades were uniform in size and built of lightweight materials. Canal house owners stamped their own individuality on the buildings by adding decorative gables, ornate doorcases and varying window shapes.

WORKING WITHIN RISTRICTIONS

Taxes were levied according to width of façade, so canal houses were often long and narrow, with an *achterhuis* (back annexe) used for offices and storage. With space at a premium, few canal houses allowed side access, so goods had to be unloaded from canal boats to the *achterhuis* using more creative means. Pulleys were added to the gables so that items could be winched up to the height of the attic and then transferred through the windows. Façades were also angled towards the canals to allow easier access. A law dating from 1565 restricted this lean to 1:25, to limit the risk of buildings collapsing into the streets.

GABLES

The term "gable" refers to the front apex of a roof. Amsterdam's canal houses were first topped with gables to disguise the steepness of their roofs, under which goods were stored. As the city's merchants grew richer and more individualistic, they decorated the gables on their properties with scrolls, crests, and even with coats of arms.

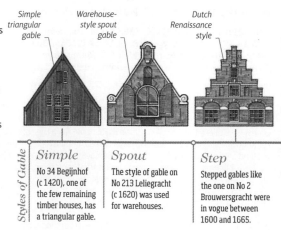

Simple triangular gable

Warehouse-style spout gable

Dutch Renaissance style

Styles of Gable

Simple

No 34 Begijnhof (c 1420), one of the few remaining timber houses, has a triangular gable.

Spout

The style of gable on No 213 Leliegracht (c 1620) was used for warehouses.

Step

Stepped gables like the one on No 2 Brouwersgracht were in vogue between 1600 and 1665.

Did You Know?

Canal houses tilt to allow goods to be winched to the attic without crashing into the windows.

↑ View of the Golden Bend on the Herengracht Canal, Amsterdam (c 1694), an etching by Jan van Call

WALL PLAQUES

Carved and painted stones were used to identify houses before street numbering was introduced in the 19th century. Many reflect the owner's occupation. Examples include an anchor on a building that was once a sailors' hostel, or a scene from Noah's Ark, designating that the building was a refuge for the poor.

CORNICES

Decorative top mouldings, called cornices, became popular from 1690 onwards when the fashion for gables declined. In the 18th century, the fashion was for ornate Rococo balustrades, but by the 19th century, cornices had become unadorned.

GOLDEN BEND

The stretch of the Herengracht between Leidenstraat and Vijzelstraat was first called the "Golden Bend" in the 17th century, because of the great wealth of the ship-builders, merchants and politicians who lived here. With its glowing standstone façades – a far more expensive material than brick – this collection of buildings still merits this name today.

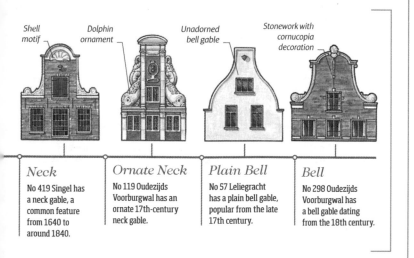

Shell motif *Dolphin ornament* *Unadorned bell gable* *Stonework with cornucopia decoration*

Neck
No 419 Singel has a neck gable, a common feature from 1640 to around 1840.

Ornate Neck
No 119 Oudezijds Voorburgwal has an ornate 17th-century neck gable.

Plain Bell
No 57 Leliegracht has a plain bell gable, popular from the late 17th century.

Bell
No 298 Oudezijds Voorburgwal has a bell gable dating from the 18th century.

Catching up with friends under cherry blossom on Rembrandtplein

8

Rembrandtplein

F5 4, 9, 14

Formerly called the Botermarkt, after the butter market held here until the mid-19th century, this square acquired its present name when the statue of Rembrandt was erected in 1876.

Soon afterwards, Rembrandtplein developed into a centre for nightlife with the opening of various hotels and cafés. The N H Schiller Hotel and Café Schiller both opened in 1892. De Kroon, which epitomizes a typical grand café, dates from 1898. The popularity of Rembrandtplein has endured, and the café terraces are packed during summer with people enjoying a pleasant drink and watching the world go by.

A 3D bronze-cast representation of Rembrandt's *The Night Watch* sits in the square as well.

9

Noorderkerk and Noordermarkt

E2 Noordermarkt 44-48 3, 10, 13, 14, 17 Church: 10:30am-12:30pm Mon, 11am-1pm Sat; general market: 9am-1pm Mon; Boerenmarkt: 9am-5pm Sat noorderkerk.org

Built for poor settlers in the Jordaan, the North Church was the first in Amsterdam to be constructed in the shape of a Greek cross. Its layout around a central pulpit allowed the congregation in the encircling pews to see and hear well.

The church, designed by Hendrick de Keyser, was completed in 1623. By the entrance is a sculpture of three bound figures, inscribed: "Unity is Strength". It commemorates the Jordaan Riot of 1934. On the south façade, a plaque recalls the 1941 February Strike, protesting the Nazis' deportation of Jews.

Since 1627, the square that surrounds the Noorderkerk has been a market site. At that time, it sold pots and pans and *vodden* (old clothes), a tradition that continues today with a flea market. Since the 18th century, the area has been a centre for bed shops. Bedding, curtains and fabrics are

TOP 3 CITY MARKETS

Lindengracht market
9am-4pm Sat
Over 200 stalls are filled with local produce and knick knacks.

Noordermarkt
9am-1pm Mon, 9am-3pm Sat
Traditional market with a focus on organic goods.

Westerstraat market
9am-1pm Mon
Over 150 stalls sell new and vintage clothing, shoes and accessories.

still sold on Monday morning along Westerstraat, as well as vinyl records, vintage clothing and other second-hand items. At 9am on Saturdays, the hugely popular Boerenmarkt sells health foods, crafts and candles.

⑩ Western Islands

⚲ E1 🚊 3

This district comprises three islands built on the IJ in the early 1600s to quarter warehouses and shipyards.

Merchant and developer Jan Bicker bought Bickerseiland in 1631. Today, the island is a mix of colourful apartment blocks and a jumble of houseboats. Realeneiland has the pretty waterside street of Zandhoek, and a row of attractive 17th-century houses built by the island's founder, Jacobsz Reaal. Prinseneiland is dominated by characterful warehouses, many now apartments.

⑪ Leidseplein

⚲ D6 🚊 1, 2, 5, 7, 10

Amsterdam's liveliest square, Leidseplein developed in the 17th century as a wagon park. It takes its name from the Leidsepoort, the massive city gate demolished in 1862, which marked the beginning of the route out to Leiden.

During the day, the square is buzzing with fire-eaters, buskers and other street performers playing to café audiences. It is also popular with pickpockets. At night, it is the focal point for the city's youth, who hang out in the many bars, cafés, restaurants, nightclubs and cinemas here.

→

Outdoor exhibition organized by the Foam Museum

⑫ 🖼 💻 🏛

Foam Museum

⚲ F6 🏛 Keizersgracht 609 Ⓜ Vijzelgracht 🚊 24 🕐 10am-6pm Sat-Wed, 10am-9pm Thu & Fri 🕐 27 Apr 🌐 foam.org

Three elegant 17th-century canal houses on the Keizersgracht have been joined together and beautifully renovated to create this labyrinth of modern rooms filled with photographs.

Foam (Fotografiemuseum Amsterdam) is dedicated to exhibiting and celebrating every form of photography, from historical to journalistic, cutting-edge to artistic. The museum has an international outlook – photographs exhibited here are taken all over the world by photographers from a variety of cultures and backgrounds.

The museum holds four major exhibitions a year and 15 smaller ones, showcasing both established figures and emerging local talent.

Foam prides itself on being an interactive centre for photography where amateurs can learn more about the art by meeting professionals, attending lectures and taking part in discussion evenings. Foam also hosts pop-up exhibitions in different neighbourhoods to make photography accessible to all.

EAT

Tujuh Maret
Indonesian cuisine is a Dutch favourite and this cosy restaurant offers just that, including *rijsttafel* (a large assortment of small dishes).

⚲ F6 🏛 Utrechtsestraat 73 🌐 tujuhmaret.nl

€€€

Café Américain
Enjoy brunch at this lovely historical Art Deco bar in the American Hotel, with excellent cakes, coffee and cocktails.

⚲ D6 🏛 Leidsekade 97 🌐 cafeamericain.nl

€€€

Morlang
Dine inside this classy candle-lit lunch and dinner spot. The vegetarian-friendly menu features a delicious green curry.

⚲ E5 🏛 Keizersgracht 451 🌐 morlang.nl

€€€

13

De Krijtberg

Q E5 **⌂** Singel 448
▦ 1, 2, 5 **◷** Noon-1:15pm &
5-6:15pm Mon & Fri, noon-
6:15pm Tue-Sat, 9am-
6:30pm Sun **Ⓦ** krijtberg.nl

An impressive Neo-Gothic church, the Krijtberg (or "chalk hill") replaced a clandestine Jesuit chapel in 1884. It is officially known as Franciscus Xaveriuskerk, after St Francis Xavier, one of the founding Jesuit monks.

Designed by architect Alfred Tepe (1840–1920), the church was built on the site of three houses; the presbytery beside the church is on the site of two other houses, one of which had belonged to a chalk merchant – hence the church's nickname of "chalk hill".

The back of the church is wider than the front, extending into the space once occupied by the original gardens. The narrowness of the façade is redeemed by its two magnificent, soaring, steepled towers.

The ornate interior of the building contains some good examples of Neo-Gothic design. The colourful stained-glass windows, walls painted in stunningly bright colours and liberal use of gold are in striking contrast to the city's austere Protestant churches. A statue of St Francis Xavier stands in front and to the left of the high altar; one of St Ignatius, co-founder of the Jesuits, stands to the right.

Near the pulpit is an 18th-century wooden statue of the Immaculate Conception, which shows Mary trampling the serpent while surrounded by angels. The statue used to be housed in the original hidden chapel.

DRINK

Café De Eland
Gezelligheid (a kind of social cosiness) is experienced at its best here at this typical Dutch bar with excellent *bitterballen* (fried meatballs) and beer.

Q D4 **⌂** Prinsengracht 296 **☏** 020-623 7654

Café Het Molenpad
A classic Amsterdam brown café that's had a modern facelift and is the perfect spot for *borrel* - having drinks and snacks with friends.

Q D5 **⌂** Prinsengracht 653 **Ⓦ** cafehet molenpad.nl

Rose's Cantina
Established South American restaurant with cocktails, a "tequila library" and delicious Mexican fare, plus a DJ on weekends.

Q E6 **⌂** Reguliers-dwarsstraat 38-40 **Ⓦ** roses-amsterdam.nl

← The colourful interior of the De Krijtberg, with its brightly painted walls and stained-glass windows

A visitor at Het Grachtenhuis (Museum of the Canals) admires maps of the city

HIDDEN GEM
Houseboat Museum

The Houseboat Museum (houseboatmuseum.nl), moored on the Prinsengracht, offers an interesting glimpse of what it would be like to live in one of Amsterdam's floating homes.

14
Bijbels Museum

9 D5 **A** Herengracht 366–368 **5** 1, 2, 5 **4** Herengracht/ Leidsegracht **0** 10am–5pm daily **4** 1 Jan, 27 Apr **W** bijbelsmuseum.nl

Reverend Leendert Schouten founded the Bible Museum in 1860, when he put his private artifact collection on public display. In 1975, the museum moved to its present site, two 17th-century houses designed by Dutch architect Philips Vingboons. The museum's highlights include a copy of the Book of Isaiah from the Dead Sea Scrolls and the Delft Bible (1477).

15
Looier Kunst en Antiekcentrum

9 C5 **A** Elandsgracht 109 **5** 7, 10, 17 **0** 11am–6pm Mon & Wed–Fri, 11am–5pm Sat & Sun **4** Tue & public hols **W** antiekcentrum amsterdam.nl

The Looier antiques centre is a vast network of rooms in a block of houses near the canal. Its 55 stalls sell everything from glassware to dolls and paintings to jewellery.

16
Het Grachtenhuis

9 D5 **A** Herengracht 386 **5** 2, 11, 12 **0** 10am–5pm Tue–Sun (daily Jun–Aug) **4** 27 Apr, 25 Dec **W** grachtenhuis.nl

Het Grachtenhuis was designed in 1663–5 by Philips Vingboons (1607–78), the architect of the Cromhouthuis – Bijbels Museum.
Once the home of merchants and bankers, this ornate canal house is now the Museum of the Canals. Using interactive displays, it tells the story of town planning and engineering for the creation of Amsterdam's triple canal ring. The ground floor has been restored to its 18th-century splendour, complete with original wall paintings. The upper rooms showcase detailed models, films and 3D animation on the construction of the canals, along with the stately mansions that line the route.

17
Stadsarchief Amsterdam

9 E6 **A** Vijzelstraat 32 **5** 16, 24 **0** 10am–5pm Tue–Fri, noon–5pm Sat & Sun **4** Mon & public hols **W** amsterdam.nl

The Stadsarchief, the city's municipal archives, moved from their former location in Amsteldijk to this vast building in 2007. Designed by K P C de Bazel, one of the principal representatives of the Amsterdam School of Architecture, the edifice was completed in 1926 for the Netherlands Trading Company. In spite of much renovation work at the end of World War II and in the 1970s, the building retains many original features, such as colourful floor mosaics (designed by De Bazel himself). There is a permanent display of treasures from the archives in the monumental vaults.

→ Statue of workers outside the Stadsarchief, the city's municipal archives

STAY

Ambassade Hotel

Ten canal houses have been merged to create this stunning and spacious boutique hotel.

📍 E5 🏠 Herengracht 341 🌐 ambassade-hotel.nl

€€€

Hotel Dwars

Nine characterful, cosy rooms decorated with modern and vintage furniture. It's great value for money.

📍 F6 🏠 Utrechtsedwarsstraat 79 🌐 hoteldwars.com

€€€

Armada Hotel

Antique-filled, uniquely decorated 300-year-old canal house turned hotel with modern amenities and in-room breakfast on request.

📍 F6 🏠 Reguliersgracht 31 🌐 hotelseven bridges.nl

€€€

18

Magere Brug

📍 G6 🏠 Amstel 🚊 4

Of Amsterdam's 1,281 bridges, Magere Brug (Skinny Bridge) is the best known. The original drawbridge was built in about 1670. According to legend, it was named after two sisters called Mager, who lived either side of the Amstel. It is more likely that the bridge's name comes from its narrow (*mager*) design.

The present drawbridge was put up in 1969 and, though wider than the original, it still conforms to the traditional double-leaf style. Constructed from African azobe wood, it was intended to last 50 years. The bridge is opened a few times every day. It has been featured in many films, including the James Bond film *Diamonds are Forever*.

19

Internationaal Theater Amsterdam

📍 D6 🏠 Leidseplein 26 🚊 1, 2, 5 🕐 Box office: noon-6pm Mon-Sat 🌐 ita.nl

This Neo-Renaissance building is the most recent of the city's three successive municipal theatres, its predecessors having burned down. The Internationaal Theater Amsterdam (ITA, and previously know as Stadsschouwburg) was designed by Jan Springer and A L van Gendt, who was responsible for the Royal Concertgebouw (*p146*) and for part of the Centraal Station (*p104*).

The former home of the Dutch national ballet and opera companies, the theatre today stages plays by local drama groups such as the resident Toneelgroep, as well as international companies, including many English-language productions. The foyer houses a popular restaurant.

20

Museum Van Loon

📍 F6 🏠 Keizersgracht 672 🚊 24 🕐 10am-5pm daily 🚫 Public hols 🌐 museum vanloon.nl

The Van Loons were one of Amsterdam's most prestigious families in the 17th century. They did not move into this house on the Keizersgracht, however, until 1884. Designed by Adriaan Dortsman, No 672 is one of a pair of symmetrical houses built in 1672 for Flemish merchant Jeremias van Raey. In 1752, Dr Abraham van Hagen

↑ Magere Brug is illuminated at night by strings of lights

and his wife, Catharina Elisabeth Trip, moved in, followed by the Van Loons.

In 1973, after many years of restoration, it opened as a museum. Its collection of Van Loon family portraits stretches back to the early 1600s. To the rear of the house, the old coach house holds an intriguing display on how the slave plantations of Suriname provided the basis for the van Loon fortune.

Pathé Tuschinski

📍F5 🏛Reguliers-breestraat 26-34 🚊4, 9, 16 🕐Box office: 9:30am-10pm daily 🌐pathe.nl

Abraham Tuschinski's cinema and variety theatre caused a sensation when it opened in 1921. Until then, Amsterdam's cinemas had been sombre places; this was an exotic blend of Art Deco and Amsterdam School architecture (p172). Built in a slum area known as Devil's Corner, it was designed by Heyman Louis de Jong and decorated by Chris Bartels, Jaap Gidding and Pieter de Besten. In its

→ Bloemenmarkt's floating flower stalls lining the Singel canal

heyday, Marlene Dietrich and Judy Garland performed here. Now a six-screen cinema, the building has been meticulously restored. The best way to appreciate its opulence is to see a film.

㉒ Munttoren

📍E5 🏛Muntplein 🚊4, 9, 14, 16 🕐Munttoren: to public 🛍Gift shop: 10am-6pm Mon-Sat

The polygonal base of the Munttoren (Mint Tower) formed part of a gate in Amsterdam's medieval wall. Fire destroyed the gate in 1618, but the base survived. In 1619, Hendrick de Keyser added the clock tower; François Hemony, the set of bells in 1699. During the 1673 French occupation, the city mint was housed here.

㉓ Bloemenmarkt

📍E5 🏛Singel Ⓜ️Rokin 🚊4, 14, 24 🕐9:30am-5pm daily

On the Singel, west of Muntplein, is the last of the

TULIP MANIA

Tulip mania seized Amsterdam in the 1630s. The exotic, Asian bulbs tempted investors and their value soared. At the height of the craze, a single rare bulb could cost more than 10,000 guilders – as much as a grand canal-side town house. Tempted by the chance to get rich quick, even ordinary folk invested their savings in the flowers, only to lose them when the bubble inevitably burst and prices collapsed in 1637.

city's floating markets. In the past, nurserymen sailed up the Amstel from their small-holdings and moored here to sell cut flowers and plants directly from their boats.

Today, the stalls are still floating but are now a permanent fixture on the canal. Despite the sellers' tendency to cater purely for tourists, with prices reflecting this, the displays of fragrant seasonal flowers and bright spring bedding plants are always beautiful to look at.

A CANAL WALK

DAM SQUARE TO KEIZERSGRACHT

Did You Know?

The Yab Yum brothel once made €40,000 in one night.

Distance 850 m (880 yd) **Nearest tram** Dam **Time** 10 minutes

The walk along Amsterdam's finest canals begins in Dam Square. Leave the square by walking down Paleisstraatpast, passing the Koninklijk Paleis (p101). Cross Nieuwezijds Voorburgwal and Spuistraat, and turn left to stroll along the left bank of Singel.

This canal served as a moat around the city until 1585, when Amsterdam expanded. The Singel is the nexus of the city's second-largest Red Light District. As you walk along, you'll pass both opulent mansions and former brothels, including the infamous Yab Yum.

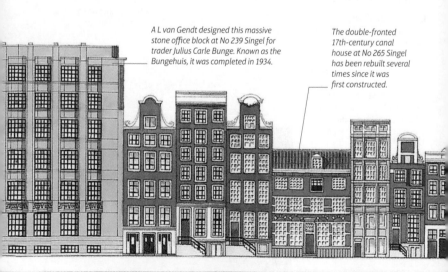

A L van Gendt designed this massive stone office block at No 239 Singel for trader Julius Carle Bunge. Known as the Bungehuis, it was completed in 1934.

The double-fronted 17th-century canal house at No 265 Singel has been rebuilt several times since it was first constructed.

3

① The imposing Bungehuis office block is located at No 239 Singel.

② A vibrant orange boat floats down the Singel, passing the diverse façades that line this canal.

③ The Singel is home to the Bloemenmarkt *(p125)* which floats on the water.

After passing the contrasting 18th-century façades of Nos 317 and 319 Singel, turn right onto Oude Spiegelstraat to cross Herengracht. Walk along Wolvenstraat until you reach Keizersgracht. Turn the page to continue your stroll along the waterways.

Locator Map

The stepped gable at No 279 Singel dates from the 19th century. Most of the houses along this canal were built between 1600 and 1665.

These houses, Nos 289–293, stand on an alley once called Schoorsteenvegersteeg (chimney sweeps' lane), which was home to many immigrant chimney sweeps in the 19th century.

The opulent former brothel of Yab Yum occupied the 17th-century canal house at No 295 Singel. The interior has been preserved as a museum.

1

2

A CANAL WALK
KEIZERSGRACHT TO HERENGRACHT

Distance 700 m (765 yd) **Nearest tram** Spui **Time** 10 minutes

Keizersgracht is known as "the emperor's canal", and with good reason. A stroll along this canal takes in highly decorated façades, including No 319, which is covered with scrolls, vases and garlands.

After marvelling at the tiny 345a Keizersgracht, cross Huidenstraat to reach the magnificent section of the canal illustrated below.

Cross the Leidsegracht, which marks the end of Daniel Stalpaert's city expansion plan of

Jacob de Wit – the artist – bought Nos 383 and 385 Keizersgracht, living in No 385 until his death in 1754.

De Vergulde Ster (Gilded Star), at No 387 Keizersgracht, was built in 1668 by the municipal stonemasons' yard. It has an elongated neck gable and narrow windows.

No 399 Keizersgracht dates from 1665, but the façade was rebuilt in the 18th century. Its achterhuis (back annexe) has been perfectly preserved.

1 No 401 Keizersgracht has a highly decorated gable, with friezes of cherubs.

2 Boats are moored alongside Nos 401 and 403 Keizersgracht.

3 A *rondvaartboot* passes under the bridge on Keizersgracht that crosses over the Leidsegracht canal.

1664. It has a mixture of fine 17th- and 18th-century canal houses. Turn left onto Leisestraat and walk to Koningsplein, then take the left bank of the Herengracht. On the next page, the stroll will continue on Herengracht.

Locator Map

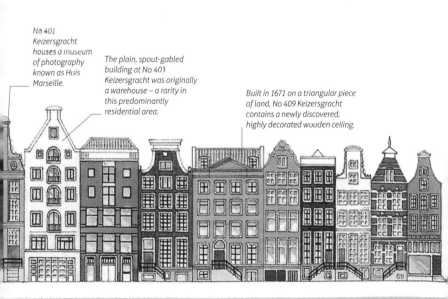

No 401 Keizersgracht houses a museum of photography known as Huis Marseille.

The plain, spout-gabled building at No 403 Keizersgracht was originally a warehouse – a rarity in this predominantly residential area.

Built in 1671 on a triangular piece of land, No 409 Keizersgracht contains a newly discovered, highly decorated wooden ceiling.

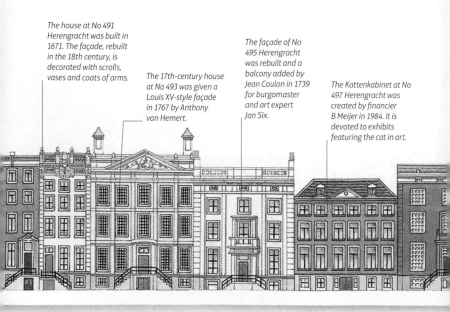

3

① Verdant trees line the canal in front of No 493 Herengracht.

② The Kattenkabinet represents itself with a simple black-and-white sign showing a cat walking away from the viewer.

③ The grand exteriors of No 497 - the Kattenkabinet - and No 499 Herengracht.

Locator Map

at the corner of Herengracht and Thorbeckeplein which contrast with the grand neighbouring buildings.

At Thorbeckeplein, take the bridge to the right, which marks the beginning of Reguliersgracht. Follow the left bank.

No 499 Herengracht, like many of the other houses on the canal, has been converted into offices.

No 507 Herengracht was home of mayor Jacob Boreel. His house was looted during riots in 1696 in retaliation for the burial tax he introduced to the city.

No 509 Herengracht looks very different to its neighbours because of its Art Deco balconies and bold three-dimensional design.

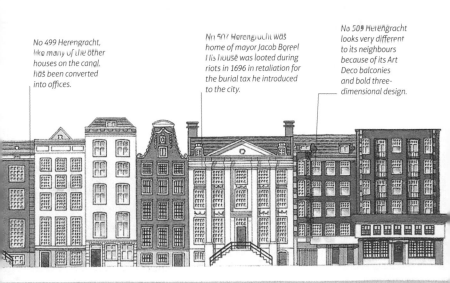

1

2

A CANAL WALK

REGULIERSGRACHT TO THE AMSTEL

Distance 750 m (820 yd) **Nearest tram** Rembrandtplein **Time** 10 minutes

The final part of the walk takes you along Reguliersgracht – one of the city's most famous canals. Before you begin, pause where the canal crosses Herengracht to see 15 bridges in total, including the one that you're standing on.

Continue past the buildings shown below and then cross Keizersgracht. You'll pass Nos 57, 59 and 63 Reguliersgracht, which have ornate stone, brick and woodwork façades.

Turn left by the church and take the left bank of Prinsengracht. You should be ready

19
—
arched stone bridges cross the Reguliersgracht.

The spout-gabled 16th-century warehouses at Nos 11 and 13 Reguliersgracht are called the Sun and the Moon.

Three houses boasting typical neck gables, at Nos 17, 19 and 21 Reguliersgracht, are now much sought-after addresses.

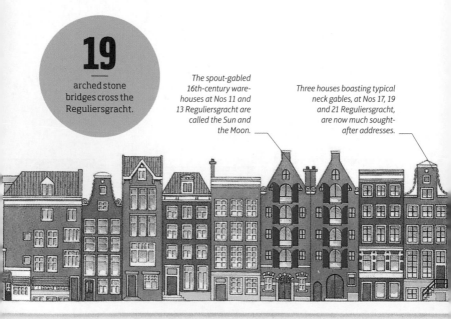

3

① With their distinctive red shutters, Nos 11 and 13 Reguliersgracht are identical, hence their nicknames, the Sun and Moon.

② The seven bridges that cross Reguliersgracht make a great picture.

③ Nos 37 and 39 can be found at the intersection with Keizersgracht.

Locator Map

for a break. Stop for lunch at Brasserie NeL at No 10 Amstelveld or a refreshing beverage at Café Marcella, at No 1047ª Prinsengracht, which is a typical local bar with outside seating in the summer. Refreshed, follow the Prinsengracht to the Amstel river.

The Nieuwe Amsterdammer, *a weekly magazine aimed at Amsterdam's Bolshevik intelligentsia, was published at No 19 Reguliersgracht from 1914 to 1920.*

The façades of Nos 37 and 39 Reguliersgracht lean towards the water, showing the danger caused by subsidence when building on marshland.

MUSEUM QUARTER

This area of Amsterdam was little more than farms and smallholdings until the late 19th century, when the city burst out from its restraining canals, swallowing up the farmland with a slew of housing developments. The city council was, however, very alert to charges of profit-making and philistinism, not least because the famed German composer Johannes Brahms had been scathing about Amsterdam's lack of culture when he visited in the city in the 1870s. With this in mind, the councillors designated this district an area of art and culture and set into motion plans for the creation of three great cultural centres. The first two were built in the 1880s: the Concertgebouw (concert hall), constructed to make a musical point to anyone who agreed with Brahms, and the Rijksmuseum, planned as a repository of art from the so-called "golden age" of the 17th century. The next decade saw the building of Stedelijk Museum; initially home to an eclectic collection of artifacts, it became a museum of modern art in 1905. A fourth centre, the Van Gogh Museum, followed in 1973, with a striking extension added in 1999. The area around the museums rapidly became a central space in the city, used for national celebrations, commemorations and political demonstrations, and is still seen as the spiritual home of the city's freethinkers. In the early 2010s, all four of these great museums were revamped and refurbished to form what is now Amsterdam's Museum Quarter, one of the city's biggest attractions.

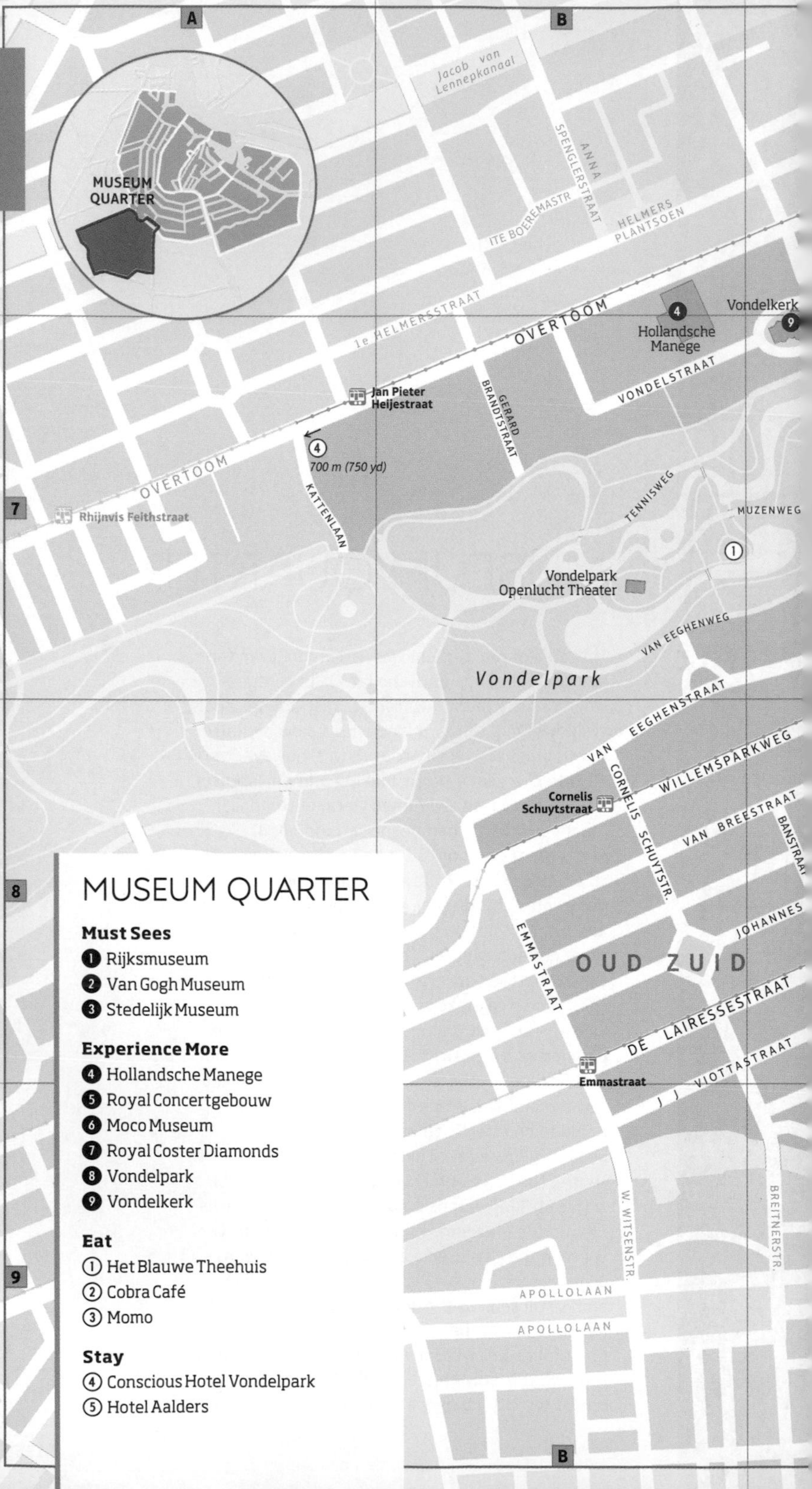

Jacob van Lennepkanaal

SPENGLERSTRAAT

ANNA

ITE BOEREMASTR

HELMERS
PLANTSOEN

MUSEUM
QUARTER

1e HELMERSSTRAAT

OVERTOOM

VONDELSTRAAT

4 Hollandsche
Manège

Vondelkerk

9

Jan Pieter
Heijestraat

GERARD BRANDTSTRAAT

OVERTOOM

4
700 m (750 yd)

KATTENLAAN

TENNISWEG

MUZENWEG

Rhijnvis Feithstraat

Vondelpark
Openlucht Theater

1

VAN EEGHENWEG

Vondelpark

VAN EEGHENSTRAAT

CORNELIS SCHUYTSTR.

WILLEMSPARKWEG

Cornelis
Schuytstraat

VAN BREESTRAAT

BANSTRAAT

EMMASTRAAT

JOHANNES

OUD ZUID

DE LAIRESSESTRAAT

Emmastraat

J J VIOTTASTRAAT

W. WITSENSTR.

BREITNERSTR.

APOLLOLAAN

APOLLOLAAN

MUSEUM QUARTER

Must Sees
1 Rijksmuseum
2 Van Gogh Museum
3 Stedelijk Museum

Experience More
4 Hollandsche Manege
5 Royal Concertgebouw
6 Moco Museum
7 Royal Coster Diamonds
8 Vondelpark
9 Vondelkerk

Eat
① Het Blauwe Theehuis
② Cobra Café
③ Momo

Stay
④ Conscious Hotel Vondelpark
⑤ Hotel Aalders

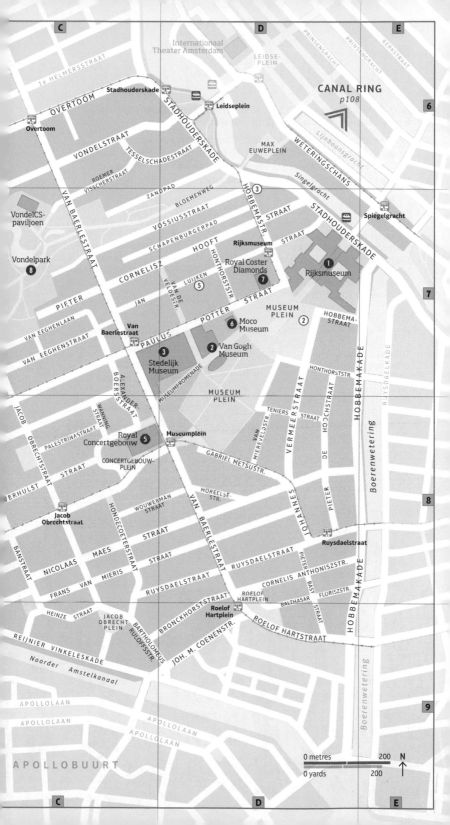

1 🗺️ Ⓜ️ 🍴 🛍️ 🛍️

RIJKSMUSEUM

📍 D7 🏛️ Museumstraat 1 🚊 2, 5, 12 🚋 Stadhouderskade ⏰ 9am–5pm daily (garden, shop and café to 6pm) 🌐 rijksmuseum.nl

The Rijksmuseum is a familiar Amsterdam landmark and possesses an unrivalled collection of Dutch art, begun in the early 19th century. The vast museum can seem overwhelming, but with such a wealth of things to see, it's no wonder that it's the city's most-visited museum.

The Rijksmuseum began life as the Nationale Kunstgaleriij in Den Haag. In 1808, King Louis Napoleon ordered the collection to be moved to Amsterdam and it briefly occupied the Koninklijk Paleis before it moved to its present location in 1885.

A competition to design the collection's new home was won by the architect P J H Cuypers. His red-brick building was initially criticized, most vehemently by Amsterdam's Protestant community, for its Catholic Neo-Renaissance style. King William III famously refused to set foot inside.

Nowadays, the building is fondly regarded and it forms the background of many of the images taken by novice photographers in the city due to its iconic exterior and beautifully tended gardens, which make for the perfect shot in every season.

> 💬 INSIDER TIP
> **Beat the Queue**
>
> The only way to walk straight inside the museum is to book a guided tour. Otherwise, get there at 9am or 3:30pm, and avoid Fridays and weekends.

The building is fondly regarded and it forms the background of many of the images taken by novice photographers in the city.

↑ Rembrandt's *The Night Watch* is the museum's most-prized possession and its most-visited piece

→

A huge 17th-century model of the *William Rex*, housed in the Rijksmuseum

TOP 5 UNMISSABLE EXHIBITS

The Night Watch (1642)
This vast canvas was commissioned by an Amsterdam militia.

The Milkmaid (1658)
The stillness and light are typical of Vermeer.

St Elizabeth's Day Flood (1500)
Painting of a 1421 flood by an unknown artist.

The Square Man (1951)
This painting is typical of Appel's CoBrA work.

Shiva Nataraja (c 1100-1200)
Bronze statue of the Hindu god dancing.

↑ The red-brick, Neo-Renaissance façade of the Rijksmuseum

Exploring the Rijksmuseum

The Rijksmuseum is almost too vast to be seen in a single visit. If time is short, visit the Gallery of Honour, taking in Frans Hals, Vermeer and scores of other Old Masters, to finally arrive at Rembrandt's *The Night Watch* at the centre of the building. Visitors with more time shouldn't miss the museum's other collections, spanning from the 11th century to the present day. Paintings, sculpture, historical objects and applied arts are shown side by side, emphasizing contrasts and connections. A pavilion houses the Asiatic Collection.

↑ Visitors admiring the art, and taking a break, in one of the galleries

8,000
───
pieces are displayed in the Rijksmuseum's 100 rooms.

The Gallery of Honour is lined with 17th-century masterpieces ↓

GENRE PAINTING

For the contemporaries of Jan Steen (1625–79), this cosy everyday scene was full of symbols that are obscure to the modern viewer. The dog on the pillow may represent fidelity, and the red stockings the woman's sexuality; she is probably a prostitute.

Gallery Guide

Medieval and Renaissance Art

The first specifically "Dutch" paintings, these works are mostly religious, such as *The Seven Works of Charity* (1504) by the Master of Alkmaar. As the 16th century progressed, religious themes were superseded by pastoral subjects; by 1552, paintings like Pieter Aertsen's *The Egg Dance* were full of realism.

17th-Century Art

▶ By the Alteration in 1578 (p64), Dutch art had moved away completely from religious to secular themes. Artists turned to realistic portraiture, land-scapes, still lifes, seascapes, domestic interiors (including genre work) and animal portraits. Don't miss Rembrandt's paintings and Vermeer's *The Milkmaid (right)*.

18th-Century Art

The still lifes of the 17th century turned into satirical "conversation pieces". *The Art Gallery of Jan Gildemeester Jansz* (1794), by Adriaan de Lelie (1755–1820), shows an 18th-century salon crowded with 17th-century works.

19th-Century Art

The early 19th century is represented by the Dutch romantics, who all reinterpreted the art of landscape painting but in contrasting styles. Artists such as Johannes Tavenraat and Wijnand Nuijen excelled in painting stormy and dramatic scenes, while Andreas Schelfhout preferred to paint more temperate and serene landscapes.

20th-Century Art

A small collection of 20th-century works are found under the museum's roof. Along with clothing, photography and sculpture, works by artists Le Corbusier and Karel Appel are on display. The FK 23 Bantam biplane, designed by Koolhoven for the British Aerial Transport Company, is a highlight of this section.

Asiatic Art

The pavilion between the main building and the Philips Wing is testament to the skill of artists and artisans in early Eastern cultures. Some of the earliest artifacts are the most unusual, such as tiny bronze Tang dynasty figurines from 7th-century China. Later exhibits include a 10th century Hindu statue entitled *Heavenly Beauty*.

Special Collections and Philips Wing

◀ The Special Collections gallery in the basement is a treasure trove of delftware, porcelain and much more. Temporary exhibitions are held in the Philips Wing *(left)*.

VAN GOGH MUSEUM

📍D7 🏠Museumplein 6 🚊2, 5, 12 🕐May-Jun & Oct: 9am-6pm daily (to 9pm Fri); Jul-Sep: 9am-7pm Sun-Thu, 9am-9pm Fri & Sat; Nov-Apr: 9am-5pm daily (to 9pm Fri) 🌐vangoghmuseum.com

When the troubled painter Vincent van Gogh died of a gunshot wound in 1890, he was on the verge of stardom. His brother Theo, an art dealer, amassed a collection of 200 of his paintings and 500 drawings. These, with around 700 letters by the artist, form the core of the world's largest Van Gogh collection.

The Van Gogh Museum is based on a design by De Stijl architect Gerrit Rietveld (1888–1964) and opened in 1973. A freestanding wing, designed by Kisho Kurokawa, was added in 1999.

The ground floor displays Van Gogh's numerous self-portraits chronologically. Paintings from his Dutch period and from his time in Paris and Provence are on the first floor, along with works by other 19th-century artists. The second floor focuses on Van Gogh's personal life, with a selection of letters. Works from his final year are shown on the third floor, as well as works by later artists who were influenced by him.

The main entrance is through the Exhibition Wing, which houses temporary exhibitions. Every Friday night, the central hall is turned into a bar, with lounge chairs and DJs.

→ The curvaceous Van Gogh Museum sitting on the manicured Museumplein

Did You Know?

Van Gogh claimed that all his work was "based to some extent on Japanese art".

← One of Van Gogh's most famous works, *Vincent's Bedroom in Arles* (1888), painted to celebrate his domestic stability at the Yellow House in the south of France

AN ARTIST'S LIFE

Vincent van Gogh (1853–90), born in Zundert, began painting in 1880. He worked in the Netherlands for five years before moving to Paris, later settling in Arles. After a fierce argument with Gauguin, he cut off part of his own ear; his mental instability forced him into a psychiatric hospital in Saint-Rémy. He sought help in Auvers, where he shot himself, dying two days later.

↑ Visitors milling around the entrance hall of the Van Gogh Museum

③ 🖼 🍴 🛍

STEDELIJK MUSEUM

📍D7 🏛Museumplein 10 🚊2, 5, 12 🕐10am–6pm daily (to 10pm Fri) 🌐stedelijk.nl

Built to house a collection bequeathed to the city by art connoisseur Sophia de Bruyn in 1890, the Stedelijk Museum became the national museum of modern art and design in 1938, displaying works by artists such as Picasso, Matisse, de Kooning, Chagall, Malevich and Appel, and designers including Rietveld.

The museum is housed in two contrasting spaces. The Neo-Renaissance main building was designed by A W Weissman (1858–1923) in 1895. The façade is adorned with turrets and gables and with niches containing statues of artists and architects, including Hendrick de Keyser and Jacob van Campen, architect of the

Koninklijk Paleis (*p101*). The Stedelijk's modern addition – the Benthem Crouwel Wing – opened in 2012. The giant "bathtub" appears to float, due to its continuous glass walls at ground level; it remains a love-it-or-loathe-it addition to the city's architecture.

Inside, both spaces are ultramodern, making a perfect backdrop for the museum's 90,000 modern and contemporary artworks. The collection represents virtually every artistic movement of the 20th and 21st centuries, including examples of the De Stijl, Pop Art

←

The futuristic Benthem Crouwel Wing - known as the "bathtub" - illuminated in the evening

1988

Three paintings by Van Gogh, Jongkind and Cézanne were stolen from the museum.

EXPERIENCE Museum Quarter

↑ *The Fiddler* (1912–13), by Marc Chagall (1887–1985), was inpired by the artist's memories of St Petersburg and his new surroundings in Paris

and CoBrA groups. It also houses a small group of works by Post-Impressionists, including Van Gogh and Cézanne, to highlight the late 19th century. The museum holds collections from present-day artists in a larger exhibition space, with a restaurant and a terrace overlooking Museumplein. Performances and film screenings are also staged here.

TOP 5 PERMANENT ARTISTS ON DISPLAY

Willem de Kooning (1904–97)
This Dutch Abstract Expressionist often focused on the female figure.

Kazimir Malevich (1878–1935)
Russian founder of Suprematism, an abstract movement which experimented with colour.

Jean Tinguely (1925–91)
The Swiss sculptor crafted humorous moving sculptures.

Karel Appel (1921–2006)
A Dutch member of the short-lived, experimental CoBrA movement.

Ernst Ludwig Kirchner (1880–1938)
The German Expressionist was inspired by the art of early African and Asian cultures.

↑ The light and airy space that houses the museum's shop

EXPERIENCE MORE

4

Hollandsche Manege

B6 **Vondelstraat 140**
1 **10am-11pm Mon-
Fri, 10am-6pm Sat & Sun**
**dehollandsche
manege.nl**

The Dutch Riding School was
originally situated on the
Leidsegracht, but in 1882 a
new building was opened,
designed by A L van Gendt
(1835–1901) and based on
the Spanish Riding School
in Vienna.

The riding school was
threatened with demolition in
the 1980s, but was saved after
a public outcry. Reopened in
1986 by Prince Bernhard, it
has since been restored to
its former glory.

The Neo-Classical indoor
arena features gilded mirrors
and moulded reliefs of horses'
heads on its elaborate plaster-
work walls. Some of the
original wrought-iron stalls
remain and sound is muffled
by sawdust. At the top of the
staircase, one door leads to a
balcony overlooking the
arena, another to the café.

5

Royal Concertgebouw

C8 **Concertgebouw-
plein 10** **2, 3, 5, 12, 16**
**Box office: 1-7pm Mon-
Fri, 10am-7pm Sat & Sun**
concertgebouw.nl

Following an architectural
competition held in 1881,
the Dutch architect A L van
Gendt was chosen to design
a vast new concert hall for
Amsterdam. The resulting
Neo-Renaissance building has
an elaborate pediment and
colonnaded façade, and houses
two concert halls. Despite
Van Gendt's lack of musical
knowledge, he managed to
produce near-perfect acoustics in the Grote Zaal (main
concert hall), which is
renowned the world over.

The concert hall has been
renovated several times,
most recently in 1983, when
serious subsidence threatened the building's entire
foundation. To remedy this,
the whole superstructure had
to be raised up off the ground
while the original supporting
piles, which rested on sand
13 m (43 ft) underground,
were removed and replaced
by concrete piles sunk into
the ground to a depth of 18 m
(59 ft). A glass extension and
new entrance were added by
Dutch architect Pi de Bruijn in
1988. The original entrance
was relocated round to the
side of the building.

Though primarily designed
to hold concerts, the Royal
Concertgebouw also hosts
business meetings, exhibitions, conferences, political
meetings and occasional
boxing matches.
Every Wednesday
(except during

The collonaded façade of
the Royal Concertgebouw
lit up after dark ↑

July and August) a free concert takes place, starting at 11:30am.

Moco Museum

📍D7 🚊Honthorststraat 20 🚋1, 2, 5, 7, 12, 19 🚊Stadhouderskade ⏰10am-6pm daily; check website for later openings 🌐mocomuseum.com

The exterior of this beautiful 20th-century mansion, designed by Eduard Cuypers, the nephew of the prominent 20th century architect Petrus J H Cuypers, belies the groundbreaking collection housed inside.

Carefully curated by private collectors, the exhibits at the Modern Contemporary (Moco) Museum include pieces by artists who expose the irony at work in modern society.

The collection includes Roy Lichtenstein's Pop Art and more than 90 original works by the street artist Banksy. The British activist's indoor pieces are far less exposed than his usual murals and make for an interesting contrast when compared to the few works rescued from buildings that are also on display here.

↑ Café tables lining the Museumplein in front of Royal Coster Diamonds

Royal Coster Diamonds

📍D7 🚊Paulus Potterstraat 2-6 🚋2, 5 ⏰9am-5pm daily 🚫1 Jan, 25 Dec 🌐coster diamonds.com

One of Amsterdam's oldest diamond factories, Coster was founded in 1840. Twelve years later, Queen Victoria's consort, Prince Albert, honoured the company by giving them the task of repolishing the great Koh-i-Noor (mountain of light) diamond. This blue-white stone is one of the treasures of the British crown jewels and weighs in at 105.6 carats. A replica of the coronation crown, which incorporates a copy of the fabulous stone, is found in Coster's spacious entrance hall.

More than 1,000 people visit the factory each day to witness the processes of grading, cutting and polishing the stones. The goldsmiths and diamond-cutters work together in the factory to produce customized items of jewellery. In the Diamond Museum, the history of the diamond is traced, from its creation deep in the earth to the dazzling stones that are a girl's best friend.

EAT

Het Blauwe Theehuis
Find calm respite at the iconic Blue Teahouse with a beer and a sandwich.

📍B7 🚊Vondelpark 5 📞020-662 0254

€€€

Cobra Café
Famous for its tasty apple pie, Cobra also serves other snacks such as pancakes and *krokets* (croquettes).

📍D7 🚊Hobbemastraat 18 🌐cobracafe.nl

€€€

Momo
This Asian fusion bar and restaurant serves delectable sushi, bento boxes and seafood tapas.

📍D6 🚊Hobbemastraat 1 🌐momo-amsterdam.com

€€€

Cyclists taking a break beside the lake in Vondelpark ↑

⑧ 🍴 🥤

Vondelpark

📍 C7 🏠 Stadhouderskade 🚊 1, 2, 3, 5, 12 🕐 24hrs daily

In 1864, a group of prominent Amsterdammers formed a committee with the aim of founding a public park, and raised enough money to buy 8 ha (20 acres) of land. J D and L P Zocher, a father-and-son team of landscape architects, were commissioned to design the park in typical English landscape style. They used vistas, pathways and ponds to create the illusion of a large natural area, which was opened to the public on 15 June 1865, as the Nieuwe Park. The park's present name was adopted in 1867, when a statue of Dutch poet Joost van den Vondel was erected in the grounds. After raising more money, by June 1877 the park reached its current size of 47 ha (116 acres).

The park now supports around 100 plant species and 127 types of tree. Squirrels, hedgehogs and ducks mix with a huge colony of bright green parakeets. Cows, sheep, goats and even a lone llama graze in the park's pastures. Vondelpark welcomes about 10 million visitors a year, and is popular for dog-walking and jogging. Free concerts are given at the **Openlucht Theater** (open-air theatre) or at the bandstand in summer. Set in the northeasternmost corner of the park is the lovely **VondelCS-paviljoen**. This flamboyant Neo-Renaissance-style building first opened in 1881 as a café and restaurant. After World War II, it reopened as a cultural centre. In 1991, the pavilion was renovated once more, and the complete Art Deco interior of the 1910 Cinema Parisien, Amsterdam's first cinema, was moved into one of the rooms.

The pavilion underwent extensive renovations in recent years and now functions as a TV and radio media centre, complete with a café and restaurant. The surrounding garden has been beautifully re-landscaped.

Openlucht Theater

🏷️ 📍 X9 🕐 Jun–last week Aug: Wed–Sun 🌐 openluchttheater.nl

💬 INSIDER TIP
Rollerblading in Vondelpark

Don rollerblades for a different way of exploring Vondelpark's network of cycle paths. Rent wheels or book a training session with Skate Dokter (www. skatedokter.nl).

JOOST VAN DEN VONDEL

Joost van den Vondel (1587-1679) was to Dutch poetry and drama what Rembrandt was to painting. Many of his history plays, like *Gijsbrecht van Amstel,* first performed in 1638, and *Joannes de Boetgezant* (1662), were hailed as masterpieces. After converting to his wife's Catholic faith, he became an advocate of religious tolerance. That made him unpopular with hard-line Calvinists and, despite his fame, he died an impoverished man.

VondelCS-paviljoen

ⓉⓈ 🅟 4 D2 🏠 Vondelpark 3 🚋 2, 12, 17 🕐 10am–6pm daily (during events hours vary) 🆆 vondelcs.nl

---

9

Vondelkerk

🅟 C7 🏠 Vondelstraat 120 🚋 1, 3, 12 🕐 To the public

The Vondelkerk was the largest church designed by P J H Cuypers, architect of Centraal Station. Work began in 1872, but funds ran out by the following year. Money gathered from public donations and lotteries allowed the building to be completed by 1880.

When fire broke out in November 1904, firefighters saved the nave by forcing the burning tower to fall away into Vondelpark. A new tower was added later by the architect's son, J T Cuypers. The church was deconsecrated in 1979 and converted into offices in 1985.

STAY

Conscious Hotel Vondelpark

Just a short walk from Vondelpark, this hotel has stylish modern rooms and a pleasant organic café.

🅟 A7 🏠 Overtoom 519 🆆 conscioushotels.com

€€€

Hotel Aalders

A good value, family-run hotel with clean, functional ensuite rooms.

🅟 D7 🏠 Jan Luijkenstraat 13-15 🆆 hotelaalders.nl

€€€

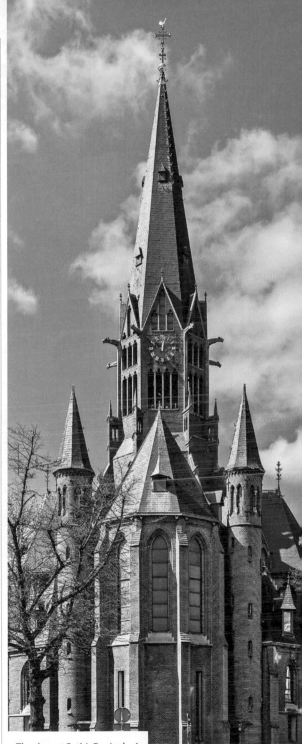

The elegant Gothic Revival Vondelkerk, set at the edge of Vondelpark ↑

A SHORT WALK
MUSEUM QUARTER

Distance 1.5 km (1 mile) **Nearest tram**
Rijksmuseum **Time** 15 minutes

The green expanse of Museumplein was once bisected by a busy main road known locally as the "shortest motorway in Europe". Dramatic renovation in the 1990s transformed it into a stately park, fringed by Amsterdam's major cultural centres. This is one of the wealthiest districts in the city, with wide streets lined with grand houses. After the heady delights of the museums, why not window-shop at the upmarket boutiques along the exclusive P C Hooftstraat and Van Baerlestraat, or watch the diamond polishers at work in Royal Coster Diamonds?

↑ The modern exterior of the Van Gogh Museum

VAN DER VELDESTR

PAULUS POTTERSTRAAT

Van Baerlestraat, lined with designer clothing shops

START

The **Stedelijk Museum** (p144) houses the civic collection of modern art, and also stages controversial contemporary art exhibitions.

VAN BAERLESTRAAT

The **Royal Concertgebouw** (p146), designed by AL van Gendt, has a Classical façade and a concert hall with near-perfect acoustics.

The modern wing of the **Van Gogh Museum** (p142), an elegant oval shape, is dedicated to temporary exhibitions of 19th-century art.

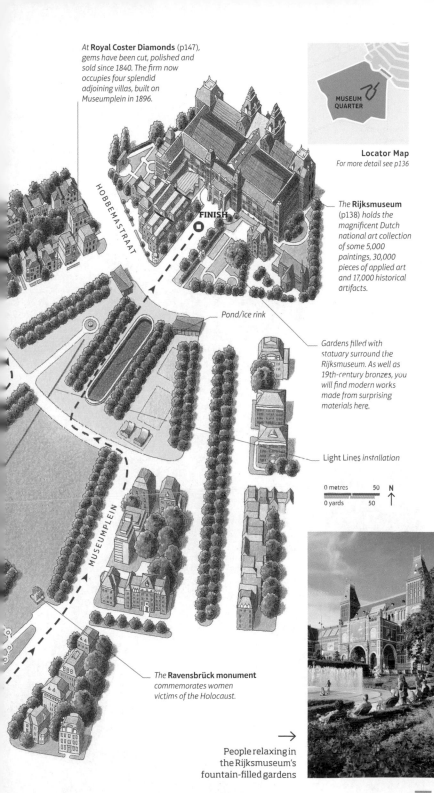

At **Royal Coster Diamonds** (p147), gems have been cut, polished and sold since 1840. The firm now occupies four splendid adjoining villas, built on Museumplein in 1896.

Locator Map
For more detail see p136

MUSEUM QUARTER

HOBBEMASTRAAT

FINISH

The **Rijksmuseum** (p138) holds the magnificent Dutch national art collection of some 5,000 paintings, 30,000 pieces of applied art and 17,000 historical artifacts.

Pond/ice rink

Gardens filled with statuary surround the Rijksmuseum. As well as 19th-century bronzes, you will find modern works made from surprising materials here.

Light Lines *installation*

| 0 metres | 50 |
| 0 yards | 50 |

N

MUSEUMPLEIN

The **Ravensbrück monument** commemorates women victims of the Holocaust.

→ People relaxing in the Rijksmuseum's fountain-filled gardens

PLANTAGE

Known as the "plantation", this area was once green parkland beyond the city walls. Its leafy streets today look and feel very different from the city centre, which – as it turns out – is entirely accidental. When the canals of the Grachtengordel were dug in the 17th century, the original plan was to extend them to include the Plantage district. However, in 1672, the country suffered the Rampjaar (Disaster Year), when the Dutch were assailed on all sides – by the German principalities, the English and the French. The economy nose-dived and there were no buyers for housing plots in the Plantage, which was, as a result, turned over for use as allotments and orchards. Indeed, in 1682 a prime lot went to Hortus Botanicus, one of Europe's oldest botanical gardens and still a popular attraction, and later, in the 1830s, the Artis zoo was allocated a large portion of the Plantage. By the 1880s, with its green spaces intact, the district had become popular for its cafés, dance halls and theatres. One of these theatres, the Hollandsche Schouwburg, once at the heart of the city's Jewish community, was turned into a deportation centre for arrested Jews during the German occupation in World War II. The area also has a long maritime association. In 1655, following their defeat in the First Anglo-Dutch War, the government decided to build a naval wharf on Kattenburg island, adding an arsenal a few years later. Since 1972, this building has housed the national maritime collection at the Scheepvaart Museum. Today, the Plantage remains one of the greenest and loveliest parts of Amsterdam, well worth a leisurely exploration.

PLANTAGE

Must Sees

1. Tropenmuseum
2. Het Scheepvaartmuseum
3. NEMO Science Museum

Experience More

4. Hortus Botanicus
5. Hollandsche Schouwburg
6. National Holocaust Museum
7. Amstelsluizen
8. Koninklijk Theater Carré
9. Entrepotdok
10. Hermitage Amsterdam
11. Werfmuseum 't Kromhout
12. De Gooyer Windmill
13. Verzetsmuseum

Eat

1. Café Restaurant De Plantage
2. Bloem Eten en Drinken
3. Brouwerij Het Ij

Stay

4. Hotel Arena
5. Hotel Rembrandt

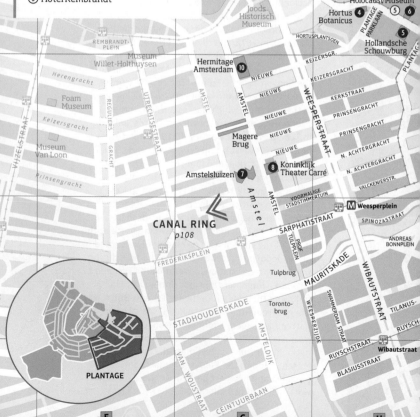

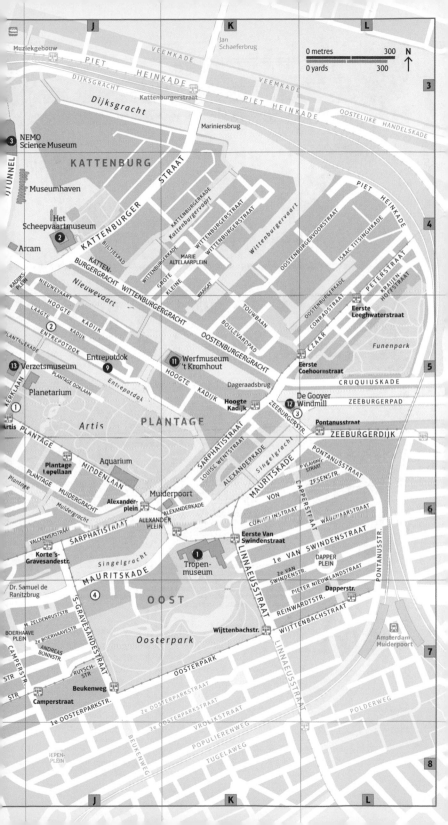

> **INSIDER TIP**
> **Take a Tour**
>
> Free tours often run on Sundays, or you can book a group tour for an insight into either the history of the building and the meaning behind its decor, or the way different cultures experience love.

The cavernous central hall ↑
reflecting the building's
grand beginnings

❶ 🗺️ Ⓜ️ 🍴 🖥️ 🛍️

TROPENMUSEUM

📍K6 🏛️Linnaeusstraat 2 🚊3, 7, 14, 19 🕐10am–5pm Tue–Sun (daily during school hols) 🚫1 Jan, 27 Apr, 25 Dec 🌐tropenmuseum.nl

This fascinating museum reflects the Netherlands' colonial history, as well as the diversity of the country today. The displays of art objects, photographs and film focus on widely different cultures in the tropics and subtropics. Children will love the interactive Tropenmuseum Junior.

Built to house the Dutch Colonial Institute, this vast complex was finished in 1926 by architects M A and J Nieuwkerken. The exterior of what is one of the city's finest historic buildings is decorated with symbols of imperialism, such as stone friezes of peasants planting rice. In 1978, the Royal Tropical Institute opened this fascinating ethnographic museum here, across three levels of galleries leading from the huge central hall. One floor holds treasures from Indonesia, Papua New Guinea and Southeast Asia. The collection aims to show the things that unite all cultures,

↑ The museum's exterior, made from red brick

from love to death. On the upper floors, static and interactive displays explore diverse topics, including body art and Afrofuturism. Temporary exhibitions are held in the North Wing on the ground floor and the Park Hall on the second floor.

Tropenmuseum Junior promotes the importance of children learning about different cultures. This immersive experience allows kids to see, hear, smell and taste what it's like to live in a different country. Youngsters board a simulated plane and on reaching their destination, meet "guides" who introduce them to local everyday life. The destination (most recently Morocco) changes every two and a half years.

Intricate carving with animal and canoe-prow motifs

Human figures on each others' shoulders

←

A Bisj pole from New Guinea: a South Pacific ritual totem carved from the root and trunk of a massive wild nutmeg tree to satisfy the spirits of cannibalized men

↑ The wood-and-tree-bark *Pustaha* (Book of Divinations), containing prescriptions applied by a Toba Batak village healer-priest in North Sumatra

② 🏛️ 🍴 🛍️

HET SCHEEPVAART MUSEUM

📍 J4 🏠 Kattenburgerplein 1 🚌 22 🚢 Oosterdok, Kattenburgergracht 🕐 9am–5pm daily
🌐 hetscheepvaartmuseum.com

Once the arsenal of the Dutch Navy, this vast Classical sandstone building was constructed by Daniël Stalpaert in 1655 around a massive courtyard. The admiralty stayed in residence until 1973, when the building was converted into the Maritime Museum. A renovation project has returned the building to its former glory, and the former artillery courtyard now has a stunning glass roof.

↑ The modern glass roof, inspired by navigational lines

Visitors of all ages enjoy the museum's interactive exhibitions and displays of 400,000 maritime objects. Don't miss the free audio tour. The open courtyard gives access to the three wings of the building, each with its own theme. Oost (East) has displays of maritime objects, maps, paintings, globes and model yachts. In Noord (North), visitors can take a journey back to the 17th century using the latest virtual reality technology. Climb aboard the East Indiaman *Amsterdam* moored outside at the dock: haul up cargo, crawl through the hold and even fire a cannon. The museum's West wing has interactive exhibits geared towards children, such as a lifesize board game and "Tale of the Whale".

1. "Tale of the Whale" starts with the first whaling expeditions in the 16th century, when whales were thought to be fearsome sea monsters, and finishes with today's efforts to preserve them from extinction.

2. Antique nautical maps and modern globes are on display.

3. The museum has a fine collection of beautifully decorated model boats. It features examples of pleasure craft through the ages, from the 17th century to the present day. Each one is a work of art, with exquisitely painted details.

1

2,300

piles driven into the bed of the Oosterdok support the building.

2

3

The museum sitting majestically in its watery surroundings, with the *Amsterdam* moored outside

3 ⊗ 🍴 💻

NEMO SCIENCE MUSEUM

📍 H3 🏠 Oosterdok 2 Ⓜ Centraal Station 🚊 1, 2, 4, 5, 9, 13, 14, 16, 17, 26 🚌 22 🕐 10am–5:30pm Tue–Sun; during school holidays: 10am– 5:30pm daily; rooftop open until 9pm in summer 🚫 27 Apr 🌐 nemosciencemuseum.nl

Amsterdam's dazzling science and technology museum, NEMO, is an unmissable family destination, with five floors of interactive exhibitions, theatre shows, films, workshops and demonstrations.

NEMO Science Museum occupies a striking curved building designed by Italian architect Renzo Piano, famous for the Centre Georges Pompidou in Paris and the London's Shard. Clad in verdigris-green copper, it juts out over the water by 30 m (99 ft) to form a counterpoint to the mouth of the IJ tunnel under the river. Inside it's a wonderland for inquiring minds of all ages, with five levels of entertaining demonstrations of the principles that govern the world around us and plenty of hands-on kit to interact and experiment with. Changing exhibits from the museum's extraordinary collection of scientific and technological artifacts celebrate humankind's ingenuity, from 19th-century galvanometers to the iconic Walkman.

The motorway approach to the tunnel under the IJ is beneath the building.

MUSEUM GUIDE

Level 1 (first floor) of the NEMO Science Museum will give visitors a glimpse into how science works. On levels 2 and 3 you can unravel everyday technology and learn about the cosmos. On level 4, discover NEMO's brand new "Humania" exhibition and learn how your own head, heart and body work. Don't forget to visit the museum's rooftop, which is home to "Energetica", an open-air exhibition where visitors can explore various forms of energy generation and capture.

Visitors can experience the energy generated from wind, water and the sun at "Energetica" on the rooftop.

Discover mathematics all around you in the "World of Shapes".

Become a logistics expert at "The Machine"

See how natural phenomena like light, sound and static electricity work in the interactive exhibition, "Sensational Science".

The entertaining "Chain Reaction" show demonstrates cause and effect and action and reaction, with plenty of audience participation.

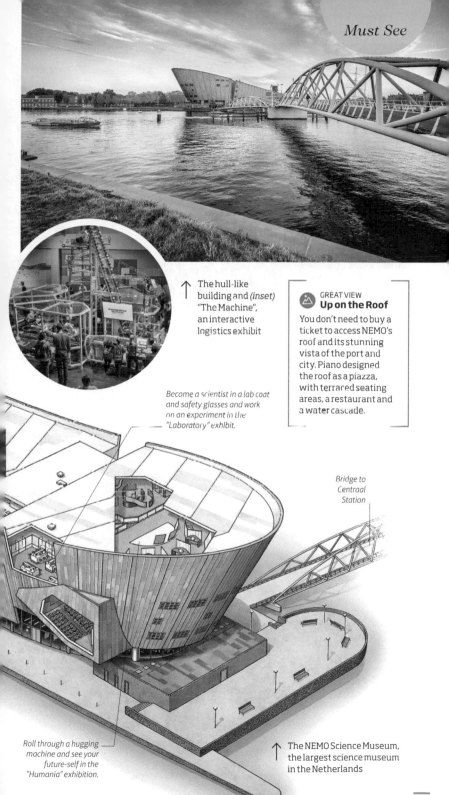

↑ The hull-like building and *(inset)* "The Machine", an interactive logistics exhibit

GREAT VIEW
Up on the Roof

You don't need to buy a ticket to access NEMO's roof and its stunning vista of the port and city. Piano designed the roof as a piazza, with terraced seating areas, a restaurant and a water cascade.

Become a scientist in a lab coat and safety glasses and work on an experiment in the "Laboratory" exhibit.

Bridge to Centraal Station

Roll through a hugging machine and see your future-self in the "Humania" exhibition.

↑ The NEMO Science Museum, the largest science museum in the Netherlands

→

The lovely glass-domed Palm Greenhouse of Hortus Botanicus

EXPERIENCE MORE

④ 🔋 Ⓜ 🖥 🗂

Hortus Botanicus

📍H5 🏛Plantage Middenlaan 2 Ⓜ Waterlooplein 🚋9, 14 ⏰10am–5pm daily 🚫1 Jan, 25 Dec 🌐dehortus.nl

Beginning life as a small apothecary herb garden in 1682, this green oasis in the centre of Amsterdam now holds one of the world's largest botanical collections. Its range of flora expanded when tropical plants were brought back by the Dutch East India Company. In 1706, it became the first place outside Arabia to succeed in cultivating the coffee plant.

The medicinal herb garden has several species of plants that were available in the 17th century and are of great importance to medicine. The glass-domed Palm Greenhouse, built in 1912, contains a collection of palms, conservatory plants and cycads, including one that is more than 400 years old. The

modern glass-and-aluminium Three Climate Greenhouse, designed by Moshé Zwarts and Rein Jansma, was opened in 1993 for tropical, subtropical and desert plants. There is also a Butterfly Greenhouse, with many species flying around, and a shop where you can purchase plants and gardening tools. The restored orangery has a café and terrace, where art shows with a botanical theme are held.

---

⑤

Hollandsche Schouwburg

📍H5 🏛Plantage Middenlaan 24 🚋14 ⏰11am–5pm daily 🚫27 Apr, Rosh Hashanah (Jewish New Year), Yom Kippur 🌐jck.nl/en

Part of the Jewish Cultural Quarter (*p82*), this former theatre is now a memorial to the 104,000 Dutch Jewish victims of World War II. Thousands of Jewish people were

detained here before being deported to concentration camps. After the war, the building was abandoned until 1962.

A basalt column with a base in the shape of the Star of David now stands on the site of the stage. Written behind it is: "To the memory of those taken from here". Following its restoration in 1993, the building became an education centre. On the ground floor, a candle illuminates the names of the war victims. Upstairs, there is a poignant permanent exhibition on the persecution of the Jews in the Netherlands from 1940 to 1945.

> 💬 INSIDER TIP
> **Oosterpark**
>
> Every morning, Tai Chi enthusiasts can join others in the peaceful, uncrowded Oosterpark. Open-air lessons take place next to the vintage bandstand and are free of charge – just turn up to take part.

6

National Holocaust Museum

📍H5 🚊Plantage Middenlaan 27 🚋14 🕐11am–5pm daily 🚫27 Apr, Rosh Hashanah, Yom Kippur 🌐jck.nl/en

The National Holocaust Museum features a wide range of semipermanent and temporary exhibitions that delve deep into the personal histories of the victims of the Holocaust. The displays focus mainly on the situation in the Netherlands, but there are also exhibits on the international context. The museum will close for renovation in 2020 and reopen in 2022.

7

Amstelsluizen

📍G6 🚇Weesperplein 🚋4, 7, 9, 10, 14

The Amstelsluizen, a row of sturdy wooden sluice gates spanning the Amstel river, form part of a complex system of sluices and pumps that ensure Amsterdam's canals do not stagnate. Four times a week in summer and twice a week in winter, the sluices are closed while fresh water from lakes north of the city is allowed to flow into the canals. Sluices to the west of the city are left open, allowing the old water to flow into the sea. The Amstelsluizen date from 1673, and were operated manually until 1994.

8

Koninklijk Theater Carré

📍G8 🚊Amstel 115–125 🚇Weesperplein 🚋4, 7, 9, 10 🕐Box office: 4–6pm daily 🌐carre.nl

During the 19th century, the annual visit of the Carré Circus was a popular city event. In 1868, Oscar Carré built temporary wooden premises for the circus on the banks of the Amstel. The city council considered these a fire hazard, so Carré persuaded them to accept a permanent building. Built in 1887, the new structure included a circus ring and a stage., and a Classical façade decorated with sculpted heads of dancers, jesters and clowns.

The Christmas circus is still one of the annual highlights at the theatre, but for much of the year the stage is taken over by concerts and blockbuster musicals.

9

Entrepotdok

📍J5 🚋9, 14, 32 🚌22, 43

The redevelopment of the old warehouses at Entrepotdok has revitalized this dockland complex. During the mid-19th century, it was the greatest warehouse area in Europe. The quayside buildings are now a lively complex of homes, offices, cafés and restaurants. Some of the original façades of the warehouses have been preserved, and the interiors have been opened up to provide an attractive inner courtyard. Café tables are often set out by the canal, next to rows of brightly coloured houseboats and barges that are moored along the waterway.

Former warehouses bordering the pleasant Entrepotdok canal ↑

10

Hermitage Amsterdam

📍 G6 🏛 Amstel 51
Ⓜ Waterlooplein 🚋 4, 9, 14
🚏 Muziektheater 🕐 10am–5pm daily 🚫 27 Apr, 25 Dec
🌐 hermitage.nl

In the early 1990s the State Hermitage Museum in St Petersburg, Russia, chose Amsterdam as the ideal city in which to open a satellite museum. Housed in the former Amstelhof – a shelter for poor elderly women (p117) – the museum displays temporary exhibitions drawn from the Hermitage's rich collection, including Russian artifacts, ancient Greek and Roman treasures, and works by Dutch masters. The museum has an auditorium and a children's wing, as well as a fine restaurant, Neva, which is open to all.

11

Werfmuseum 't Kromhout

📍 K5 🏛 Hoogte Kadijk 147 🚋 9, 10, 14 🚌 22, 43
🚏 Oosterdok or Artis
🕐 9:30am–3:30pm Tue, noon–4pm every third Sun
🌐 kromhoutmuseum.nl

The Werfmuseum 't Kromhout is one of the oldest working shipyards in Amsterdam, and is also the site of a ship engine museum. Ships were being built here as early as 1757. In the second half of the 19th century, production changed from sailing ships to steamships. As ocean-going ships got bigger, the yard, due to its relatively small size, turned to building lighter craft for inland waterways. Today the yard is used only for restoration and repair work.

In 1967, the Prince Bernhard Fund bought the site, saving it from demolition. The Amsterdam Monuments Fund later became involved to safeguard the shipyard's future as a historical site and helped turn it into a museum.

The museum is largely dedicated to the history of marine engineering, concentrating on work carried out at the shipyard, with steam engines, maritime photographs and ephemera. Another point of interest is the shipyard's forge featuring interesting tools and equipment. Some impressive historical ships are moored at the quayside. The museum's eastern hall is sometimes used for receptions and dinners.

12

De Gooyer Windmill

📍 K5 🏛 Funenkade 5 🚋 10, 14 🚫 To the public

Of the six remaining windmills within Amsterdam's boundaries, De Gooyer, also known as the Funenmolen, is the

10,000

windmills once dotted the Dutch landscape.

The De Gooyer Windmill, a Dutch icon in the centre of Amsterdam

STAY

Hotel Arena
With 139 rooms and suites, decorated in tones of grey and white, this hotel has views over Oosterpark and a pretty courtyard.

J7
's-Gravesandestraat 55 **hotelarena.nl**

€€€

Hotel Rembrandt
This small hotel in a 19th-century merchant's house offers single, double and family sized en-suite rooms. One has a copy of Rembrandt's *The Night Watch*.

H5 **Plantage Middenlaan 17** **hotelrembrandt.nl**

€€€

most central. Dominating the view down the Nieuwevaart, the windmill, built around 1725, was the first corn mill in the Netherlands to use streamlined sails. It first stood to the west of its present site, but the Oranje Nassau barracks, built in 1814, acted as a windbreak, and, as a result, the mill was moved piece by piece to the Funenkade. The octagonal wooden structure was rebuilt on the stone foot of an earlier water-pumping mill, demolished in 1812.

By 1925, De Gooyer was in a very poor state of repair and was bought by the city council, which fully restored it. Since then, the lower part of the mill, with its neat thatched roof and tiny windows, has been a private home, though its massive sails still creak into action sometimes. Next to the mill is the IJ brewery, with its own tasting room *(p163)*.

13

Verzetsmuseum

H5 **Plantage Kerklaan 61** **9, 14**
10am–5pm Mon–Fri, 11am–5pm Sat & Sun
1 Jan, 27 Apr, 25 Dec
verzetsmuseum.org

Located in a building that used to be the home of a Jewish choral society, the Resistance Museum holds a fascinating collection of memorabilia recording the activities of Dutch Resistance workers in World War II. It focuses on the courage of the 25,000 people who were actively involved in the movement. On display are false documents, weaponry, film clips, photographs and equipment and personal items belonging to the workers.

By 1945, there were 300,000 people in hiding in the Netherlands, including Jews and anti-Nazi Dutch. Events organized by the Resistance, like the February Strike against the deportation of the Jews, are brought to life by exhibits showing where the refugees hid and how food for them was smuggled in.

The museum includes a special children's wing, Verzetsmuseum Junior, in which the real-life wartime experiences of children are told. The story begins via a time machine that transports visitors back to the 1940s.

The Portrait Gallery of the 17th century, at Hermitage Amsterdam

A SHORT WALK
PLANTAGE

Distance 2.5 km (1.5 miles) **Nearest tram** Artis
Time 25 minutes

With its wide, tree-lined streets and painted sandstone buildings, the Plantage is a graceful and often overlooked part of the city. Though it seems like a quiet part of town, there is a lot to see and do, with a diverse range of popular attractions that can get very busy on sunny days. The area, which is dominated by the Artis complex, has a strong Jewish tradition, and several monuments commemorate Jewish history in Amsterdam, including a basalt memorial in the Hollandsche Schouwburg. The cafés of the Entrepotdok offer a pleasant setting for a relaxing coffee, within earshot of the zoo.

Entrepotdok was the largest warehouse development in Europe during the 19th century. It has been redeveloped and transformed into a quayside housing, office and leisure complex (p163).

Inspired by an Italian palazzo, **De Burcht** was the headquarters of the Dutch Diamond Workers' Union.

PLANTAGE PARKLAAN

START

PLANTAGE KERKLAAN

FINISH

The old glasshouses at **Hortus Botanicus** Amsterdam have been restored, and a new one erected to hold tropical and desert plants (p162).

Moederhuis – Aldo van Eyck's refuge for pregnant women – has a colourful, modern façade intended to draw people inside.

Little remains of the **Hollandsche Schouwburg**, a former theatre which is now a sombre monument to the deported Jews of World War II (p162).

Part of the Artis zoo complex, **Micropia** is the world's first museum dedicated to microbes and micro-organisms, with cutting-edge displays.

The domed **Planetarium** explores humankind's relationship with the stars. Interactive displays show the positions of the planets.

← Greenhouse at Hortus Botanicus Amsterdam

The Entrepotdok warehouses,
redeveloped in the 1980s

Locator Map
For more detail see p154

More than 900 species,
including a pride of
lions, live in the **Artis
zoo complex**, which
occupies a beautifully
laid-out garden site.

Did You Know?
——
Artis is short for
Natura Artis Magistra,
a Latin phrase
meaning "Nature is the
teacher of art".

Artis restaurant

PLANTAGE MIDDENLAAN

The building that once
stood here has been
demolished and a new one
is under construction.

| 0 metres | 100 |
| 0 yards | 100 |

N

→
Exploring exhibits at
the Micropia museum in
the Artis zoo complex

BEYOND THE CENTRE

In the late 19th century, an overcrowded Amsterdam burst out from its restraining canals in a frenzy of development. The first major push south of the Singel canal was De Pijp, a working-class district built in the 1870s to relieve the overcrowded Jordaan. De Pijp was constructed quickly and cheaply, and its affordability attracted students, immigrants and artists who gave it a lively, bohemian vibe. In 1901, a reforming Housing Act led to the clearance of Amsterdam's slums and, in the 1910s, innovative housing schemes such as De Dageraad and Het Schip were built by Amsterdam School architects. In 1946, the world's biggest shipbuilding yard, NDSM, was set up on the north shore of the IJ. It closed down in 1984, and, by the 1990s, artists were squatting in its abandoned buildings; the site is now the anchor of one of the most exciting cultural hubs in the city.

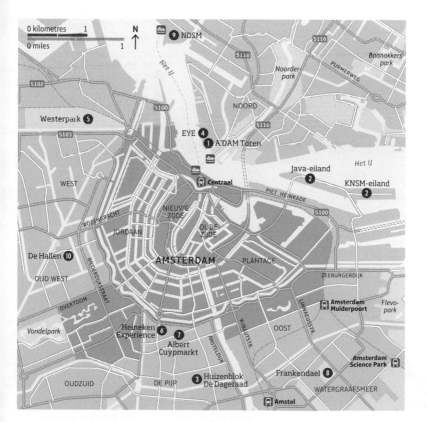

EXPERIENCE

❶
A'DAM Toren

🏠 Overhoeksplein 1
Ⓜ Centraal Station
🚌 38 🚇 Buiksloterweg
🕐 Hours vary, check
website 🌐 adamtoren.nl

Amsterdam's skyline is free
of skyscrapers, so locals look
across the IJ river at the great
tower, A'DAM Toren, with some
affection. An icon of the post-
industrial Noord, the 100-m-
(328-ft-) high multi-storey
colossus has become the city's
most exciting cultural complex.
The 22-storey tower was built
for oil giant Royal Dutch Shell
in 1971 and acted as the company's headquarters until 2009.
Many locals still call it the
"Shelltoren" (Shell Tower). It is
now packed with places to eat,
drink, dance and shop, and one
of the city's classiest hotels –
Sir Adam. A high-speed
elevator whisks visitors to
A'DAM Lookout on the 21st
floor for an unbeatable

360-degree view of the city.
Thrill-seekers, unsatisfied by
the observation deck alone,
can soar 100 m (328 ft) above
the city on "Over the Edge",
a two-seater swing.

---

❷
Java-eiland and KNSM-eiland

🏠 Java-eiland and KNSM-
eiland 🚊 10 🚌 41, 42

Situated side by side in the
eastern docklands of the city
are the islands of Java-eiland,
which is long and narrow, and
the broader KNSM-eiland.
Java-eiland, designed by
Sjoerd Soeters during the
1990s, demonstrates a wide
variety of architectural styles.
By combining these styles
with a number of canals
across the island, the architect
created an authentic
Amsterdam canal
atmosphere. This is
enhanced by the many

> **A high-speed
> elevator whisks
> visitors to A'DAM
> Lookout on the 21st
> floor for an unbeat-
> able 360-degree
> view of the city.**

shops and small cafés.
KNSM-eiland is slightly
broader, giving architect Jo
Coenen the space to create a
central avenue flanked on
either side by tower blocks.

---

❸
Huizenblok De Dageraad

🏠 Burgemeester
Tellegenstraat 128
🚊 4, 12 🕐 1–5pm Thu–Sun

One of the best examples of
Amsterdam School architec-
ture (p172), De Dageraad (the
Dawn) housing project was

→
Relaxing beneath
cherry trees in
Westerpark in spring

developed for poorer families following the Housing Act of 1901, by which the city council condemned slums and rethought housing policy. Architect H P Berlage drew up plans for the suburbs, aiming to integrate rich and poor by juxtaposing their housing. After Berlage's death, Piet Kramer and Michel de Klerk adopted his ideas. From 1918–23, they designed this complex for the De Dageraad housing association.

---

4 ⊗ 🍴 🖵 🏛

EYE

🏛 IJpromenade 1
🚊 Buiksloterweg ⏰ 11am–5pm daily 🌐 eyefilm.nl/en

The EYE is a merger between the Filmmuseum, which was previously housed for almost 40 years in what is now VondelCS (p148), and several other Dutch cinematic organizations. The museum's huge collection tells the story of the Netherlands film industry, from silent films at the end of the 19th century to advances in digital technology and 3D cinema today. There is a wide-ranging display of movie memorabilia, including photographs, soundtracks, equipment and posters.

The EYE occupies a sleek white building that resembles a giant eye. Inside are four cinemas, an exhibition space and a café-restaurant, with a waterside terrace that offers stunning views across the harbour on sunny days. In the basement, visitors can watch silent films from the museum's

←
A'DAM Toren beside the Ij river, dominating the skyline of Noord

vast collection in specially designed viewing capsules with three-seater sofas. A room also plays a 360-degree projection of film clips. Entrance to the basement is included in the cost of a cinema or exhibition ticket.

5

Westerpark

🏛 Polonceaukade
🚌 5 🚊 21, 22, 48, 248
🌐 westergasfabriek.com

The wasteland that surrounds Amsterdam's former gasworks (Westergasfabriek) was transformed into a green, 14-ha (35-acre) park in the early 2000s. Today, facilities include playgrounds, bars, restaurants, performance spaces and the Ketelhuis cinema.

The gasworks itself has been redeveloped and is rented out to various associations that organize music and food festivals, a variety of performances and exhibitions. Nearby is Het Schip (The Ship). Designed by Michel de Klerk in 1919, this block contains 102 homes and the **Museum Het Schip**, which displays a restored 1920s "working-class" apartment.

Museum Het Schip
⊗ 🕐 🏛 Oostzaanstraat 45
⏰ 11am–5pm Tue–Sun
🌐 hetschip.nl

EAT

Restaurant Pllek
A cool veggie hotspot housed in shipping containers.

🏛 TT Neveritaweg 59
🌐 pllek.nl

€€€

Moon
This upmarket revolving restaurant is perfect for special occasions.

🏛 Overhoeksplein 3
🌐 restaurantmoon.nl

€€€

Café-Restaurant THT
This lively café-cum-bar is set in the old Shell factory canteen.

🏛 Tolhuistuin,
Tlhuisweg 3
🌐 tolhuistuin.nl

€€€

Café Noorderlicht
This greenhouse café is cosy in winter and hosts live music in summer.

🏛 NDSM Plein 102
🌐 noorderlichtcafe.nl

€€€

THE AMSTERDAM SCHOOL

The industrial revolution at the end of the 19th century led to a boom in the growth of the Netherlands' towns. New districts grew around Amsterdam to accommodate the growing number of factory workers required in the city. The architects of these districts, who sought new elements for decorating building façades, became known collectively as the Amsterdam School. Their designs were characterized by unique rooflines, ornamental brickwork, cornices, window frames and corner formations which gave the façades "movement".

THE ARCHITECTURE OF THE AMSTERDAM SCHOOL

From 1911 to 1923, the members of the Amsterdam School built a large number of office and residential complexes. One of the greatest examples of these is the Scheepvaarthuis (1913-16 and 1926-8), today the Grand Hotel Amrâth Amsterdam, which also organizes tours for non-residents. Designed by the Van Gendt brothers and J M van der Meij, it was the first building to be completed entirely in the Amsterdam School style. Michel de Klerk, who later designed Het Schip (p171), was also involved in the project. A former post office, Het Schip was transformed into an apartment complex by De Klerk.

The vision of the Amsterdam School isn't just writ large on the city's buildings. Street furniture created by the group can be found all over the city. In the Spaarndammerbuurt neighbourhood in particular, many examples can still be seen, including fire alarms, cable boxes and post boxes.

Curves and serpentines on façades are typical features of the Amsterdam School.

An astonishing variety of decoration was achieved with this kind of brickwork.

↑ The Scheepvaarthuis (Shipping House), today a hotel, set on the Waalseilandgracht

> **The vision of the Amsterdam School isn't just writ large on the city's buildings. Street furniture created by the group can be found all over the city.**

Interiors and exteriors are characterized by an excess of Expressionist glass ornamentation and detail.

↑ The striking exterior of Het Schip, designed by Michel de Klerk

H P BERLAGE (1856-1934)

Berlage studied at the technical college of Zürich from 1875 to 1878, where he came into contact with architects such as Gottfried Semper and Viollet-le-Duc. Inspired by their ideas, he developed his own style, which incorporated traditional Dutch materials. It later evolved into the Amsterdam School style of architecture. Berlage designed not only buildings but also interiors, furniture and graphics. In 1896, he was appointed to design the Beurs, the new stock exchange in Amsterdam *(p100)*. Completed in 1903, it is an austere building whose structure is clearly visible. Berlage was also active as a town planner. His design of the Amsterdam-Zuid district consists of monumental residential blocks.

SCULPTURE OF H P BERLAGE BY HILDO KROP

→ Visitors to the Heineken Experience learning about the brewing process

STAY

Clink NOORD
For the budget-conscious traveller, Clink offers both friendly dorms and en-suite private room options.

🏠 Badhuiskade 3
🌐 clinkhostels.com

€€€

Volkshotel
The rooftop of this arty and modern hotel features hot tubs with city views and a lively cocktail bar.

🏠 Wibautstraat 150
🌐 volkshotel.nl

€€€

Tire Station
A modern, eco-friendly hotel with excellent dining options, a complimentary wine hour, and bike rentals.

🏠 Amstelveenseweg 5
🌐 conscioushotels.com

€€€

Lloyd Hotel
This hotel offers individually decorated rooms by Dutch designers, in a variety of prices to suit most budgets.

🏠 Oostelijke Handelskade 34
🌐 lloyd.nl

€€€

6

Heineken Experience

🏠 Stadhouderskade 78
🚋 7, 10, 16 🕐 Hours vary, check website; under 18s with parents only 🕐 1 Jan, 25 Dec 🌐 heineken experience.com

This historic 1867 building once housed the Heineken brewery. Now it offers an exhibition of how beer is made, culminating in a visit to the tasting room, where you can sample the beer.

7

Albert Cuypmarkt

🏠 Albert Cuypstraat 🚋 4, 16 🕐 9am–5pm Mon-Sat 🌐 albertcuyp-markt. amsterdam

The market running along Albert Cuypmarkt began trading in 1904 shortly after the expansion of the city. The wide street, once a canal, is named after the Dutch landscape painter Albert Cuyp (1620–91). Today, the market thoroughfare is lined with colourful stalls. Described by the stallholders as "the best-known market in Europe", it attracts some 20,000 visitors on weekdays and often twice

as many on Saturdays. Vendors sell everything you would expect from a Dutch market – fresh fish, poultry, cheese, fruit and clothes – but the real highlight here is the mouthwatering street food. All through the bazaar, the sound of frying and the scents of dishes from around the globe fill the air.

8 🍴 🖼️

Frankendael

🏠 Middenweg 72 🚋 9 🚌 41, 65, 101, 136, 152, 157 🏠 Gardens: dawn to dusk 🌐 huizefrankendael.nl

During the early part of the 18th century, many of Amsterdam's wealthier citizens built country retreats south of Plantage Middenlaan on reclaimed land called the Watergraafsmeer. The elegant Louis XIV-style Frankendael is the last survivor. The house is closed to the public, except during special events; the best views of the ornamented façade are from Middenweg. This is also the best place to view

→ Eduardo Kobra's *Let Me Be Myself* on the outside of the street art museum in NDSM

the fountain made in 1714 by Ignatius van Logteren (1685–1732), a sculptor who, along with his son, played a central role in the development of Amsterdam's Louis XIV style.

Behind the house is a small formal garden, and beyond lies a landscaped, English-style garden both of which are open to the public. There are also allotment gardens. The coach house is now home to café-restaurant Merkelbach and the conservatory is home to De Kas restaurant.

NDSM

🏠 Neveritaweg 61
🆆 ndsm.nl

The giant factory building at the heart of the former NDSM shipyard (on the banks of the IJ river) has become the core of Amsterdam's most vibrant cultural quarter. Some of the city's hottest young creative talents live and work here in spaces created from vintage shipping containers. Those wanting to find out about

NDSM's history and future can take a guided tour of the complex and meet some of the "city nomads" who make this area buzz.

Crammed with quirky shops and craft studios, bars, cafés, restaurants and nightspots, the complex also attracts visitors with its festivals, dance events and exhibitions. It even has its own artificial beach – Pllek – where city slickers sunbathe, practise yoga and listen to live music. In the summer months, Sunscreenings takes over the beach for its packed open-air cinema season. It seems appropriate that this colourful area became the home of the

world's largest street art museum in late 2019. Lasloods, NDSM's cavernous former welding hangar, has been transformed by specially commissioned works created by street art superstars from around the world. Don't miss Brazilian Eduardo Kobra's huge, 240-sq-m (2,583-sq-ft) mural of Anne Frank, *Let Me Be Myself*, on the exterior of the building.

De Hallen

🏠 Hannie Dankbaar Passage 33 🚊 7, 17
🕐 7am-1pm Sun-Thu, 7am-3pm Fri & Sat 🆆 dehallen-amsterdam.nl

A huge, unused tram depot has been transformed into an upscale cultural and commercial centre consisting of a range of designer shops, restaurants, bars and an international food market, as well as a cinema complex and a hotel. Visitors can also take guided tours of De Hallen and its neighbourhood that offer a glimpse into the architecture of the area.

![Let Me Be Myself mural of Anne Frank on the exterior of NDSM's Lasloods building]

EXPERIENCE
THE NETHERLANDS

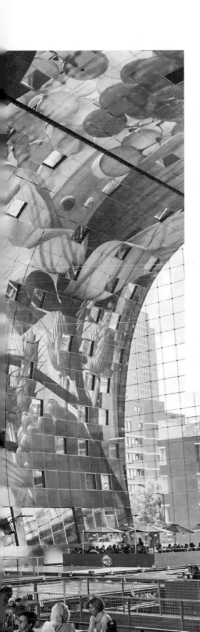

NORTH HOLLAND

North Holland, a chubby finger of land extending up from Amsterdam as far as the island of Texel, is mainly rural, its flat polder landscapes framed in the west by sea-facing sand dunes and in the east by two vast artificial lakes, the Markermeer and the IJsselmeer. These twin freshwater lakes were created from the old Zuiderzee, which was separated from the ocean in 1932 by the building of the remarkable 30-km- (19-mile-) long Afsluitdijk dam. Before the dam was constructed, the turbulent waters of the Zuiderzee were a constant danger to the region's seaports, which played a major part in the voyages of the Dutch East India Company and whose merchants became wealthy from the trade in exotic imports. Cities such as Hoorn and Enkhuizen boomed in the 17th century, benefiting from an integrated trading system: Dutch ships imported Baltic grain in exchange for spices, sugar, tea, coffee and tobacco, all of it merchandise that had been procured by brutal colonial exploitation and, in the case of the West Indies, slavery – the Dutch were heavily involved in the Atlantic slave trade.

Less historically tainted, perhaps, are towns such as Edam and Alkmaar, both of which became famous for their cheese in the 16th century and still make a tidy living from their popular cheese markets. The beautiful bulb fields in the south have also played an important role in the region's economy since the 16th century. Today, tourism is a major economic driver of North Holland, with traditional villages, picturesque seaports and coastal resorts attracting visitors in their millions.

NORTH HOLLAND

Must Sees

1 Haarlem
2 The Bulb Fields
3 Zuiderzeemuseum
4 Alkmaar

Experience More

5 Edam
6 Monnickendam
7 Voldendam
8 Marken
9 Jisp
10 De Beemster
11 Broek in Waterland
12 Zaanse Schans
13 Naardermeer
14 Hoorn
15 Egmond
16 Velsen/Ijmuiden
17 Den Helder
18 Medemblik
19 Heemskerk
20 Amstelveen
21 Ouderkerk aan de Amstel
22 Stoomgemaal De Cruquius
23 Zandvoort
24 's-Graveland
25 Aalsmeer
26 Muiden
27 Naarden
28 Hilversum
29 Laren

Julianadorp

Callantsoog

Noordhollands

Petten

Groet **N9**

Schoorl

Bergen

Bergen aan Zee

ALKMAAR 4

EGMOND 15

Heiloo

N203

Limmen

A9

Newcastle

Castricum

Uitgeest

N8

HEEMSKERK 19

IJMUIDEN 16 **16**

VELSEN

Santpoort

A9

Bloemendaal

HAARLEM 1 Zwanenburg

ZANDVOORT 23

North
Sea

THE BULB FIELDS 2 **22 STOOMGEMAAL DE CRUQUIUS**

A5

Hoofddorp **N201**

N208

Noordwijkerhout

Lisse

N207 **A4** *Westeinder-plassen*

Noordwijk

A44

N207

Katwijk aan Zee

SOUTH HOLLAND
p222

Ter Aar

0 kilometres   10
0 miles   10

N
↑

Noordzee

❶ HAARLEM

🗺 C3 **🚗 20 km (12 miles) W of Amsterdam**
🚉 Haarlem **ℹ Grote Markt 2** **🌐 haarlemmarketing.nl**

A prosperous city in the 17th century, Haarlem retains much of its historic character, with its brick-paved lanes around the Grote Markt.

Haarlem had grown into a thriving cloth-making centre by the 15th century. Today, the city is the commercial capital of Noord Holland province. It is the centre of the Dutch printing, pharmaceutical and bulb-growing industries, but there is little sign of this in the delightful pedestrianized streets of the historic heart of the city. Most of the sights of interest are within easy walking distance of the Grote Markt, a lively square packed with ancient buildings, cafés and restaurants. Old bookshops, antiques dealers and traditional food shops are all to be discovered in nearby streets.

The Hoofdwacht is a 17th-century former guard house.

The Grote Markt is the bustling centre of the city.

BARTELJORISSTAAT

KONING STRAAT

⑥

GROTE MARKT

GR. HOUTSTR.

⑦ *Museum Haarlem (550m)*
↓
⑧ *Frans Hals Museum Hof (600m)*
↓

1 The Teylers Museum's two-storey Oval Hall was added in 1779, and contains glass cabinets full of bizarre minerals and cases of intimidating medical instruments.

2 Grote Markt square is bordered with busy pavement restaurants and cafés. It has been the meeting point for the towns-people for centuries.

3 An iconic Haarlem landmark, Molen De Adriaan - a windmill on the Spaarne river - makes for a beautiful photograph at sunset.

Statue of Laurens Jansz Coster (1370–1440), who is believed to have invented printing in 1423, 16 years before Gutenberg.

④ Haarlem Station (600m)

↓ Illustration of the historic centre of Haarlem

Did You Know?

The Hero of Haarlem was a little boy who plugged a leaking dyke with his finger.

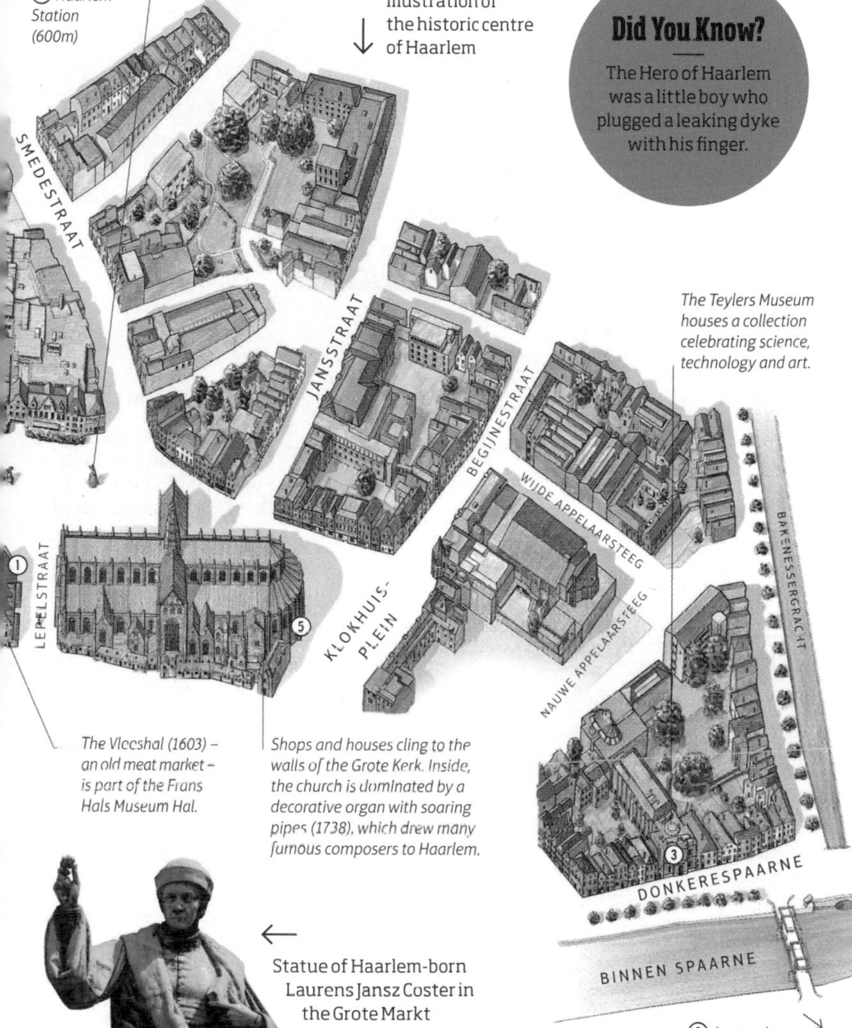

SMEDESTRAAT

JANSTRAAT

BEGIJNESTRAAT

The Teylers Museum houses a collection celebrating science, technology and art.

WIJDE APPELAARSTEEG

BAKENESSERGRACHT

LEPELSTRAAT

①

KLOKHUIS-PLEIN

⑤

NAUWE APPELAARSTEEG

The Vleeshal (1603) – an old meat market – is part of the Frans Hals Museum Hal.

Shops and houses cling to the walls of the Grote Kerk. Inside, the church is dominated by a decorative organ with soaring pipes (1738), which drew many famous composers to Haarlem.

③

DONKERESPAARNE

BINNEN SPAARNE

← Statue of Haarlem-born Laurens Jansz Coster in the Grote Markt

② Amsterdamse Poort (450m) ↘

THE MAN WHO BUILT HAARLEM

Haarlem's historic centre bears the stamp of Lieven de Key (1560–1627). Originally from Ghent, he was commissioned as city architect in 1592. Much of Haarlem had been destroyed by fire in 1576, so he had a free hand to rebuild the city in Dutch Renaissance style, with features such as richly patterned red, black and white brickwork, miniature spires and crow-stepped gables.

EAT

Brick
A stylish, industrial-chic restaurant with a choice of tasting menus. The focus is on seafood and refined Dutch specialities.

🏠 Breestraat 24-26
🌐 restaurantbrick.nl

€€€

Table 24
Indulge in Dutch-style tapas and good wine at this trendy spot, right in the heart of Haarlem.

🏠 Oude Groenmarkt 24
🕐 Dinner only
🌐 table24.nl

€€€

↑ The turreted medieval Amsterdamse Poort gateway

① De Hallen

🏠 Grote Markt 16 🕐 11am-5pm Tue-Sat, noon-5pm Sun & public hols 🗓 1 Jan, 25 Dec 🌐 franshals museum.nl

The Verweyhal (museum of modern art) and the Vleeshal (exhibition space), both in the Grote Markt, are part of the Frans Hals Museum (p186). The Verweyhal houses exhibitions of Dutch Expressionism, Impressionism, the CoBrA School (p204) and contemporary works. It is named after the painter Kees Verwey, whose Impressionist still lifes are an important feature of the collection.

The heavily ornamented Vleeshal (meat market), just to the west of the church, houses temporary exhibitions of modern art. It was built in 1602 by the city surveyor, Lieven de Key, and has a steep stepped gable that disguises the roof line. The extravagantly over-decorated miniature gables above each dormer window bristle with pinnacles. A giant painted ox's head on the façade signifies an earlier function of the building.

---

② Amsterdamse Poort

🏠 Amsterdamsevaart
🕐 To public

The imposing medieval gateway that once helped protect Haarlem lies close to the west bank of the Spaarne river. The Amsterdamse Poort was one of 12 gates guarding strategic transport routes in and out of Haarlem. Built in 1355, much of the gate's elaborate brickwork and tiled gables date from the late 15th century.

The city defences were severely tested in 1573, when the Spanish, led by Frederick of Toledo, besieged Haarlem for seven months during the Dutch Revolt. The city fathers agreed to surrender the town on terms that included a general amnesty for all of its citizens. The Spanish appeared to accept the fathers' terms, but once the city gates were opened, they marched in and treacherously slaughtered nearly 2,000 people – almost the entire population of the city.

---

③ 🖊 🖨 🛍

Teylers Museum

🏠 Spaarne 16 🕐 10am-5pm Tue-Fri, 11am-5pm Sat & Sun 🗓 Closed 1 Jan, 5 & 25 Dec 🌐 teylersmuseum.nl

This museum was established in 1778 by the silk merchant Pieter Teyler van der Hulst to encourage the study of science and art. Its collection of scientific paraphernalia, fossils and drawings is displayed in Neo-Classical splendour in a series of 18th-century rooms. The two-storey Oval Room was added in 1779 and contains glass cabinets of minerals and cases of medical instruments.

---

④ Haarlem Station

🏠 Stationsplein

The first Dutch railway line opened in 1839 and ran between Haarlem and Amsterdam. The original station, built in 1842, was refurbished in Art Nouveau style between 1905–1908. The grandiose brick building has an arched façade and rectangular towers. Its interior is decorated with coloured tiles depicting modes of transport. Also notable is the woodwork of the ticket offices and highly decorative wrought ironwork.

⑤ ✎ Grote Kerk

🏛 Grote Markt 22 🕐 10am–5pm Mon–Sat (Jul & Aug: also noon–4pm Sun) 🚫 Public hols 🌐 bavo.nl

The enormous Gothic edifice of Sint Bavo's Great Church, often referred to simply as Grote Kerk, was a favourite subject of the 17th-century Haarlem School artists Pieter Saenredam (1597–1665) and Gerrit Berckheijde (1639–98). Built between 1400 and 1550, the church and its ornate bell tower dominate the market square. The construction of a stone tower commenced in 1502, but the pillars started to subside. A new wooden tower, covered in lead, was erected in 1520.

The church has a high, delicately patterned, vaulted cedarwood ceiling, white upper walls and 28 supporting columns. The intricate choir screen, like the magnificent brass lectern in the shape of a preening eagle, was made by master metalworker Jan Fyerens in about 1510. The choirstalls (1575) are painted with coats of arms, and the armrests and misericords are carved with caricatures of animals and human heads. Not far away is the simple stone slab covering the grave of Haarlem's most famous artist, Frans Hals.

→ Grote Kerk, boasting an elaborately decorated bell tower

The Grote Kerk has one of Europe's finest and most flamboyant organs, built in 1735 by Christiaan Müller. In 1738 Handel tried the organ and pronounced it excellent. It also found favour with Mozart, who shouted for joy when he gave a recital on it in 1766. The organ is still often used for concerts.

---

⑥ Stadhuis

🏛 Grote Markt 2 ☎ 14 023 🕐 11am–4pm Tue–Sat

Haarlem's Stadhuis (town hall) has grown rather haphazardly over the centuries and is an odd mixture of architectural styles dating from 1250. The oldest part of the building is the beamed medieval banqueting hall, originally known as the Gravenzaal. Much of this was destroyed in two great fires in 1347 and 1351, but the 15th-century panel portraits of the counts of Holland can still be seen

The wing of the town hall bordering the Grote Markt was designed by Lieven de Key in 1622. It is typical of Dutch Renaissance architecture, combining elaborate gables, ornate painted detail and Classical features. In a niche above the main entrance is a plump allegorical figure of Justice, bearing a sword in one hand and scales in the other as she smiles benignly upon the cafés in the market below.

A free exhibition on the history of the city is on display in the vaulted cellars.

---

⑦ ✎ Museum Haarlem

🏛 Groot Heiligland 47 🕐 Noon–5pm Mon & Sun, 11am–5pm Tue–Sat 🚫 Public hols 🌐 museumhaarlem.nl

Located in one of Haarlem's prettiest streets, St Elisabeth's Gasthuis was built in 1610, around a pretty courtyard. A stone plaque carved above the former main doorway in 1612 depicts an invalid being carried off to hospital. After extensive restoration in the 1980s, this almshouse became Haarlem's principal history museum.

The museum features an interesting display of artifacts that focus on the city's history and its environs. A programme of changing exhibitions connect the past with the present day.

⑧ 🗡 🎨 🍴 🛍

FRANS HALS MUSEUM HOF

🏛 Groot Heiligland 62 🕐 10am–6pm Tue–Sat, noon–5pm Sun (to 4pm public hols) 🚫 1 Jan & 24, 25, 31 Dec 🌐 franshalsmuseum.nl

This fascinating museum focuses on works by Dutch artist Frans Hals (c 1582–1666), who introduced a new realism into painting, capturing the essence of his subjects through impressionistic techniques.

In his 80s, Hals still painted passionate portraits, such as *Governesses of the Old Men's Home* (1664). The Old Men's Home depicted in his painting became the Frans Hals Museum Hof in 1913. There is also a selection of paintings from the 16th and 17th centuries by other Haarlem artists. The best direction to take through the museum is counterclockwise, as exhibitions of the works of Frans Hals, other portraits, still lifes and pieces of genre painting are displayed in roughly chronological order. Each room displays works by contemporary artists alongside the Old Masters to show interesting points of contrast. The museum will be renovated at the end of 2020; check the website for details.

↑ *Satire on Tulip Mania* (c 1640) by Jan Brueghel the Younger (1601–78)

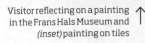

Visitor reflecting on a painting in the Frans Hals Museum and *(inset)* painting on tiles ↑

↑ The Renaissance courtyard garden,
perfect for a quiet moment when
visiting the Frans Hals Museum Hof

Cycling through the
endless tulip fields between
Haarlem and Leiden ↑

❷

THE BULB FIELDS

🗺C3 **🚉Haarlem**

Occupying a 30-km (19-mile) strip between Haarlem and Leiden, the Bloembollenstreek is the main bulb-growing area in the Netherlands. The most cultivated bulbs in the Netherlands include gladioli, lilies, daffodils, hyacinths, irises, crocuses and dahlias, but tulips are still by far and away the country's most popular flower.

When to Go

From late January, the polders (land reclaimed from the sea) bloom with a series of vividly coloured bulbs, beginning with early crocuses and building to a climax around mid-April, when the tulips flower. Late-blooming flowers, such as lilies, extend the season into late May.

Aalsmeer

This town is home to the world's largest flower auction – the Bloemenveiling Royal FloraHolland *(p206)*. As the 12.5 billion cut flowers and pot plants sold here annually all have a short shelf life, speed is of the essence. A reverse auction is held. The price decreases as the big-screen auction clock counts down and buyers stop the clock at any price point. Visitors can watch the proceedings from a viewing gallery above the trading floor.

Keukenhof

Situated on the outskirts of Lisse, this garden was set up in 1949 as a showcase for Dutch bulb growers and is now planted with some 7 million bulbs *(p252)*. Keukenhof is at its most spectacular from late March to late May, when drifts of daffodils, hyacinths and tulips form Japanese cherry trees shed snowy blossom early in the season, and there are splashes of azaleas and rhododendrons later in the year.

TOP 5 **TOP FIVE DUTCH BULBS**

Aladdin Tulip
A lily-shaped flower, which has red petals with yellow tips.

China Pink Tulip
Delicate stems are crowned with vibrant pink flowers.

Tahiti Daffodil
Double-formed, golden-yellow petals nestle in a small orange centre.

Minnow Daffodil
A fragrant, miniature daffodil with cream-coloured blooms.

Blue Jacket Hyacinth
Striped petals form a cone of blue flowers, with a heady scent.

↑ Carpets of tulips and grape hyacinths snaking through the Keukenhof gardens

→ A field carpeted with stripes of different coloured tulips in Lisse

Rows of beautiful pink
tulips blooming in
the fields in Groningen ↑

THE NETHERLANDS IN BLOOM

The Dutch love affair with flowers began rather unromantically in homes during the 17th century, when flowers were used to keep bad smells at bay. The aesthetic aspect soon developed, and today the Netherlands is one of the world's most important flower-growing countries, with an unrivalled distribution system.

PERFECT CONDITIONS

The Netherlands is indeed the land of flowers *par excellence*. The sandy soil in the high areas behind the dunes of Holland is known as *"geest soil"* and is very well suited for cultivating bulbs. The annual flower competition *(bloemen corso)* in the bulb-growing region is a grand event. Meanwhile, rose fields abound north of the southern province of Limburg, where every year a special rose competition is held.

TULIPS

The Netherlands is synonymous with one flower above all others. Tulips were introduced to Holland from Turkey in the 17th century. Pretty much as soon as the flowers were introduced, they became the subject of an unparalleled speculative bubble known as "tulip mania" *(p125)*. Today the tulip is considered a quintessentially Dutch product, with innumerable varieties.

Types of Bulb

Daffodil	*Crocus*	*Hyacinth*	*Tulip*
Not all daffodil bulbs can survive the winter. Plant your bulbs before the first frost for the best chance of success.	This flower is vibrant. Crocus bulbs should be planted in September and positioned 8-10 cm (3-4 inches) apart.	These bulbs range in colour from violet red to white. Plant the bulbs in early autumn in sun or partial shade.	Tulip bulbs are highly resistant to disease and pests. Late summer is the best time to get the bulbs in the ground.

CUT FLOWERS FROM DUTCH NURSERIES

As consumers have become increasingly demanding, the number of flower species and varieties is constantly on the rise. Consumer tastes vary from place to place: in France, gladioli are very popular, whereas in Great Britain, it is lilies and carnations. In Asia, tulips are in great demand. All of these flowers, and more, are grown in the Netherlands.

The iris flowers and bulbs are perennial favourites.

The chrysanthemum originated in China, where it was first cultivated as a flowering herb.

Dahlias come in 20,000 varieties, and yield gorgeous blooms.

The lilac is often bought for its sweet fragrance.

The carnation is loved as a spray.

The rose is known as "the queen of flowers", first cultivated in China over 5,000 years ago.

> Pretty much as soon as the flowers were introduced, they became the subject of an unparalleled speculative bubble known as "tulip mania".

FLOWER-SELLERS

Flower-sellers are part and parcel of the Netherlands' street scene. Perhaps the most famous example is Amsterdam's floating Bloemenmarkt *(p125)*, but flower markets can also be found indoors, in places such as stations or shopping centres. Whereas in most countries, cut flowers are considered expensive and a luxury, in the Netherlands, they are practically a daily shopping item and quite cheap.

Iris

The tall, beautiful iris, comes in many colours. Blooming in June, it is rugged, reliable, and easy to grow.

↑ Stalls at Amsterdam's Bloemenmarkt, selling seed packets and bulbs

3 ⚐ 🍴 🛍

ZUIDERZEEMUSEUM

🅰D3 🏠Wierdijk 12-22, Enkhuizen 🚆Enkhuizen 🚌From the station 🕐Apr-Oct: 10am-5pm daily; Nov-Mar: 10am-5pm Sat, Sun & holidays (indoor museum only) 🚫25 Dec 🌐zuiderzeemuseum.nl

Step back in time at this fascinating open-air museum which recreates daily life in a traditional fishing village on the Zuiderzee – a bay of the North Sea – in the early 20th century.

Enkhuizen was one of several villages around the Zuiderzee whose fishing-based economy was devastated when access to the North Sea was blocked by the construction of the Afsluitdijk dam in 1932. The village's fortunes were revived with the opening of this museum complex. The *binnenmuseum* (indoor museum) focuses on the Zuiderzee's history, including an impressive display of historic boats. The *buitenmuseum* (open-air museum) consists of rescued buildings, reconstructed to create a typical Zuiderzee village, with demonstrations of local crafts.

Marine Hall

→ The open-air museum, with its recreated houses and harbour

← Traditional houses, lime kilns and modern boats at the museum

Bottle-shaped lime kilns were used to burn shells to make quicklime.

Barges carry visitors to the open-air museum.

Did You Know?

Herring is preserved by being smoked over smouldering woodchips.

Must See

1 Modern Dutch culture is presented on Delft blue tiles at the Contemporary Delft installation by Hugo Kaagman.

2 At the houses from Urk, daily life on the island in 1905, including washing clothes, is recreated by actors.

3 Housed in an old warehouse of the Dutch East India Company, the Marine Hall contains sailing and fishing boats.

Contemporary Delft installation

The builders of this late-19th-century church disguised the organ in a cupboard to avoid a tax.

Houses in this area are from Zoutkamp.

A working windmill

Visitors can sample delicious preserved herring here.

Houses from Urk

In "Keeping House" a 1930s "housewife" describes her daily life over a cup of tea.

SAILING TRIPS

Enjoy the calm inland waters of the IJsselmeer aboard a traditional vessel, such as *Aaltje Angelina*, a 22-m (72-ft) *stevenaak* (sailing boat), which offers accommodation for 12. If time is short, take a day trip or sunset cruise on the Markermeer aboard *Zuiderzee*, a traditional *tjalk*, or sailing barge (*www.zuiderzeezeiltochten.nl*).

4

ALKMAAR

A C3 **A** 41 km (25 miles) north of Amsterdam ☒ ☒
i Waagplein 2; www.vvvhartvannoordholland.nl

This old town has over 400 historic monuments, and the street layout has barely changed over the centuries. Along the canals, old merchants' houses and small courtyards can still be seen.

①

Stedelijk Museum

A Canadaplein 1 **O** 11am–5pm Tue–Sun **☒** 1 Jan, 27 Apr, 25 Dec **W** stedelijk museumalkmaar.nl

The Stedelijk Museum is one of the oldest museums in the country, dating back to 1875, though its current location and modern building dates from 2000. The museum retells the history of the city and surrounding area mostly via paintings, with masterpieces ranging from the 17th century to the present day works. The museum is also known for its large collection of Bergen School art from the 1920s and 1930s. Opt for a light lunch on the sunny terrace of the museum café in the summer, with views of the Grote Sint-Laurenskerk.

②

Hollands Kaasmuseum

A Waagplein 2 **O** Hours vary; check website **W** kaasmuseum.nl

Inside the monumental Waaggebouw (weigh house) from the 16th century, this museum is dedicated to two of the most famous cheeses in the Netherlands – Edam and Gouda. Artifacts, interactive exhibits and games explore the history of cheesemaking.

③

Kaasmark

A Waagplein **O** Apr–Oct: 10am–1pm Fri (Jul & Aug: also 7–9pm Tue) **W** kaasmarkt.nl

Alkmaar is famous for its traditional *kaasmarkt* (cheese market), which dates back to 1365. The large yellow wheels of cheese arrive by barge. They are tossed from the barges by four groups of porters from the 400-year-old cheese porters' guild. The porters are dressed in white and divided into groups by the colour of their hats. The cheese is loaded onto sledges, which the porters run with to the Waaggebouw, where the cheese is weighed. Once tasting has taken place, the

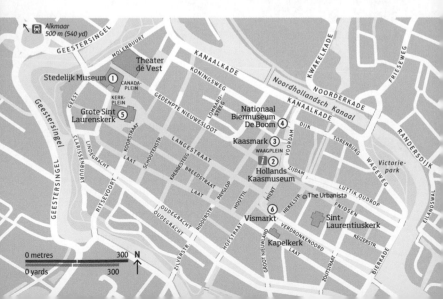

A Alkmaar
500 m (540 yd)

Stedelijk Museum ①

Theater de Vest

Grote Sint Laurenskerk ⑤

Nationaal Biermuseum De Boom ④

Kaasmark ③

i ②

Hollands Kaasmuseum

The Urbanista

Vismarkt ⑥

Sint-Laurentiuskerk

Kapelkerk

Victorie-park

0 metres   300
0 yards   300
N

↑ The great Gothic Waaggebouwe presiding over Alkmaar's canal

cheese is auctioned off by a system called *handjeklap*, with sellers clapping each other on the hands.

④

Nationaal Biermuseum De Boom

🏠 Houttil 1 🕐 1–4pm Mon-Sat (Apr-Oct: Fri from 11am) 🚫 public hols 🌐 biermuseum.nl

Housed in an impressive 17th-century building, formerly the biggest brewery in town, this museum explores a millennium of beer drinking in the Netherlands. It illustrates, for example, how in the Middle Ages Alkmaar lacked a supply of safe drinking water, so brewers would ship barrels of clean water from the surrounding dunes and streams, and then make it into beer.

The collection of equipment demonstrates the beer-making process over the last 100 years, ranging from copper vats, kettles, barrels and bottles to examples of the modern laboratory technology that breweries now use. There is also a reconstruction of an old café interior. Under the same roof is a lovely waterside café and a "tasting house" where over 80 different beers, many of them Dutch, can be sampled.

⑤

Grote Sint-Laurenskerk

🏠 Koorstraat 2 🕐 May-Oct: 11am-5pm Tue-Sun; Nov-Apr: times vary, check website 🌐 grotekerk-alkmaar.nl

This 15th-century church has one of the most important organs in Europe, built in 1639–46, and is noteworthy for its painting on the ceiling depicting the Last Judgment by Jacob Cornelisz van Oostsanen. The scene was painted on nine wooden panels in 1518–19. In 1885, due to water damage, the panels were taken to the Rijksmuseum, only to return here during the German occupation. In the summer, organ concerts are held at the church; details of times and dates are available from the local tourist (VVV) office located in the Waaggebouw.

⑥

Vismarkt

🏠 Verdronkenoord 114 🕐 daily 🌐 alkmaar.nl

On the corner where Mient meets Verdronkenoord is the old Vismarkt (fish market), dating back to the 1500s and still in use until 1998. The low, colonnaded stalls are covered to protect the traders and their wares from the elements, and contain brick and stone benches where catches of fish were displayed to customers. The current buildings date back to the mid-18th century.

EXPERIENCE MORE

5

Edam

△ D3 ● 𝑖 Damplein 1;
**www.vvv-edam
volendam.nl**

Edam is known worldwide for its eponymous semi-hard cows-milk cheese. The town's cheese market was established in the Middle Ages, and thrived as a busy hub where local farmers sold their wares. The market is still held on Wednesday mornings in July and August, with traders dressed in traditional costume.

Founded in the 12th century, the town has many historical buildings, including the brightly painted Waag (weigh house). Nearby, the 17th-century stained-glass windows in the Grote Kerk are considered some of the finest in Holland.

The **Edams Museum** is located in a 16th-century merchant's house. Here you can see 17th-century portraits of famous Edammers, such as Trijntje Keever, who was supposedly a staggering 2.5 m (8.2 ft) tall.

Edams Museum
⊗ 🏠 Damplein 1 & 8 ⏰ Apr-Oct: 10am–4:30pm Tue–Sun 🌐 edamsmuseum.nl

←

A sculpture of cheese carriers in Edam's cheese market

Did You Know?

In the 1600s, Dutch merchant ships sailed with stocks of long-lasting Edam cheese on board.

6

Monnickendam

△ D3 ● 𝑖 Zuideinde 2;
www.laagholland.com

This old fishing town on the Gouwzee was originally founded by monks. Today, medieval buildings still line its streets, including the pretty 17th century Waag (weigh house) and the Stadhuis (town hall), with its 15th-century mechanical carillon tower: every hour, clockwork horsemen parade outside. The **Waterlandsmuseum de Speeltoren** is located within the Stadhuis clock tower, with

↑ The village of Volendam with its colourful wooden houses beside the canal

EAT

E' Barrage

Classics like escargot and steak tartare are staples at this stylish French restaurant.

🅰D3 🏠Damplein 7, Edam 🌐 ebarrage.nl

€€€

De Waegh

This brasserie offers hearty Dutch dishes including smoked eel and tomato soup.

🅰D3 🏠Middendam 5-7, Monnickendam 🌐dewaegh.com

€€€

Lotje Wine & Dine

Marina-side dining with excellent seafood and local dishes with an Asian twist.

🅰D3 🏠Haven 148, Volendam 🌐lotjewinedine.nl

€€€

exhibits exploring the history of Monnickendam and the surrounding countryside.

Waterlandsmuseum de Speeltoren

🏠Noordeinde 2 ⏰Apr-Oct: 11am-5pm Tue-Sat (Jul & Aug: also 1-5pm Mon); Nov-Mar: 11am-5pm Sat & Sun 🌐despeeltoren.nl

---

7

Volendam

🅰D3 🚌 ℹZeestraat 37; www.vvv-volendam.nl

Perched along a dyke on the edge of the Markermeer, this picturesque old fishing village is famous for its colourful wooden houses and quaint fishing boats, and attracts a huge number of visitors each year. Traditional costume is also one of this town's biggest attractions: for folk festivals, the women dress in bodices, lace caps and brightly striped skirts; the men don loose trousers and jackets. In the town centre there are various spots where visitors can dress up and have their photo taken.

On the other side of the dyke is a different Volendam: an ancient, atmospheric maze of narrow streets, wooden houses and little canals.

8

Marken

🅰D3 🚌🚲From Volendam 🌐vvv-waterland.nl

For almost eight centuries, Marken was a fishing community that saw little change. The construction of a causeway linking Marken to the mainland in 1957 put an end to its isolation. The island, however, has kept its original atmosphere, retaining its wooden houses built on mounds and piles to guard against flooding. Het Paard Lighthouse is a famous landmark. **Marker Museum**, located in six historic houses, gives a flavour of past and present life in Marken. There is also a cheese factory and clog-making workshop.

Marker Museum

🏠Kerkbuurt 44-47 ⏰10am-5pm daily 🌐markermuseum.nl

9

Jisp

🅰C3 🚌 🌐onsdorpjisp.nl

The old whaling village of Jisp, on one of the many former Zuiderzee islands, retains a 17th-century feel. The Stadhuis and *dorpskerk* (village church) are worth a visit. The village lies in the middle of the Jisperveld, a nature reserve that is home to many different birds, such as lapwings, black-tailed godwits, redshanks, ruffs and spoonbills. The reserve makes a lovely spot for cycling, rowing or fishing trips. The tourist office, VVV, has information about the various excursions offered.

← A typical farm surrounded by flowering bulb fields in Middenbeemster

10

De Beemster

🅐 C3 🚌 🛈 VVV Middenbeemster; www.beemsterinfo.nl

The polder of Beemster was once a lake that was drained by hydraulic engineer Jan Adriaansz Leeghwater in 1612. Laid out in a neat grid of fields cut through by canals and roads, this unusual region has hardly changed since the 17th century, and in 1999 it was named a World Heritage Site by UNESCO. You can see historic objects and period rooms in the **Museum Betje Wolff**.

Museum Betje Wolff

🏛🏛🏛 🏠 Middenweg 178, Middenbeemster 📞 0299-681968 🕐 May-Oct: 11am-5pm Tue-Fri, 2-5pm Sat &Sun; Nov-Apr: 2-5pm Sun 🚫 1 Jan, 27 Apr, 25 Dec

---

CZAAR PETERHUISJE (TSAR PETER'S HOUSE)

In 1697, Tsar Peter I of Russia visited the shipyards of Zaandam during his Grand Embassy of Europe, a diplomatic mission to strengthen Russian ties with Western Europe. In Zaandam, the tsar lodged with Gerrit Kist, a local tradesman, to learn about local Dutch ship-building techniques. The tradesman's tiny wooden house was supplied with a stone casing and foundations for the Tsar's protection. Peter paid many more visits to the town; his last was in 1717. Today this humble house, one of the oldest wooden dwellings in Holland, attracts a great number of visitors and forms part of the Zaans Museum.

11

Broek in Waterland

🅐 D3 🚌 🌐 laag holland.com

In the 17th century, this charming little village was used as a retreat for sea captains of the East India Company. Ornate, colour-coded clapboard villas still line the cobbled streets of Broek in Waterland: the captains lived in the pastel-tinted houses and non-seafarers in the ones painted grey. Along the Havenrak, the road winding along the lake, fine examples of *kralentuinen*, mosaics made from blue glass beads brought back by merchants from the East Indies, can be seen in several of the gardens.

To explore the village from a different perspective, take a boat trip on the serene surrounding waterways; canoes and small motorboats can be rented from **Broeker Bootverhuur**, 3.5 km (2 miles) from the village centre.

Broeker Bootverhuur
⊗ 🏠 Belmermeer 5 🌐 fluisterbootvaren.nl)

12

Zaanse Schans

🅐 C3 🏠 Schansend 7, Zaandam 🚌 🕐 Apr-Oct: 9am-5pm daily; Nov-Mar: 10am-5pm daily 🌐 dezaanseschans.nl

The Zaanse Schans is the tourist heart of the Zaan region. This open-air museum, created in 1960, has typical Zaan houses, windmills and buildings. When it's windy, you will be able to see the windmills working. The products (oil, paint, mustard) are for sale. All the houses are built from timber, as stone houses would sink at once into the soft peat earth, and wood was readily available from local sawmills when they were built. Zaanse Schans is also home to the first 1887 shop of Albert Heijn (whose legacy includes

→ Iconic windmills lining the banks of the Zaan at Zaanse Schans

the upmarket supermarket chain of the same name), which is today a baking museum and cheese factory. The **Zaans Museum** showcases the history of the region. Pleasure boats offer trips on the Zaan.

At the **Molenmuseum** (Windmill Museum) at Koog on the Zaan, you will learn everything you need to know about the windmills of the Zaan region.

Zaans Museum

⊛⊜🅟 🅐Schansend 7, Zaandam 🅞Apr–Oct: 9am–5pm daily; Nov–Mar: 10am–5pm daily 🅒1 Jan, 25 Dec 🅦zaansmuseum.nl

Molenmuseum

⊛ 🅐Museumlaan 18, Koog a/d Zaan 🅞Tue–Sun 🅒1 Jan, Easter Sun, Whitsun 🅦zaanschemolen.nl

---

13

Naardermeer

🅐D4 🅘Meerkade 2, Naarden; www.natuur monumenten.nl

The Naardermeer is the oldest protected nature reserve in the Netherlands, comprising a large area of lakes and marshland renowned for its thriving bird and plant life. As well as

---

> **The Naardermeer is the oldest protected nature reserve in the Netherlands, comprising a large area of lakes and marshland renowned for its thriving bird and plant life.**

breeding colonies of cormorants and purple herons, several other bird species such as the marsh harrier, the bittern, the reed warbler and the spoonbill can also be observed in the reserve. Discerning botanists will spot an array of unusual orchids, rare mosses and fungi that grow here.

The Vereniging Natuurmonumenten (Nature Reserve Association) has set out several walking tours around the area, which are accessible to everyone. From April to November there are guided boat tours on the lakes.

14

Hoorn

🅐D3 🚌 🚉 🅘Schuitjeskade 1; www.hoorn.nl

Hoorn's rich past, as the capital of the ancient province of West Friesland and one of the great seafaring towns of the 16th century, has produced many

beautiful buildings. In the town centre seek out the Late Gothic Oosterkerk, a national heritage site, for its marvellous Renaissance façade.

Hoorn's historic past is set out in the **Westfries Museum** in a collection of art and artifacts from around the globe. A glimpse of the more recent past and a nostalgic trip down memory lane can be experienced at the **Museum van de Twintigste Eeuw** (Museum of the 20th Century).

Westfries Museum

⊛ 🅐Rode Steen 1 🅞Hours vary, check website 🅦westfriesmuseum.info

Museum van de Twintigste Eeuw

⊛⊜ 🅐Krententuin 24 🅞10am–5pm Mon–Fri, from noon Sat–Sun & holidays 🅒1 Jan, 27 Apr, 25 Dec 🅦museumhoorn.nl

WINDMILLS

Since the 13th century, windmills have been an inseparable part of the landscape of Holland. They have been used for a variety of purposes, including milling corn, extracting oil, sawing wood and pumping excess water from the polders. Windmills consist of a fixed tower and a cap, which carries the sails. The sails can be very dangerous when they are turning – hence the Dutch saying, "Een klap van de molenwiek hebben" ("To be struck by a windmill"), that is, to have a screw loose. The Netherlands had thousands of windmills in earlier times, but since the arrival of modern machines, particularly wind turbines, their number has dropped to just over 1,000. Many are still working and are open for visits.

TYPES OF WINDMILL

Windmills were adapted to perform certain roles and became specialized, each with its own particular function. For example, flour mills were used to mill grain, polder mills drained wet lands and *paltrok* mills could saw huge trees.

FLOUR MILLS

One of the most distictive types of windmill found in Holland is the flour mill. They are ubiquitous throughout the country, and many are still in operation. Flour mills tend to be the same shape as gigantic pepper grinders and were once covered with reeds. The millstones were linked to the sails by the spindle and gearwheels and milled wheat, barley and oats.

↑ A flour mill in the old town of Laren *(p207)*

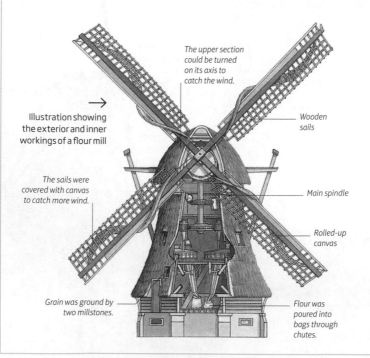

→ Illustration showing the exterior and inner workings of a flour mill

The upper section could be turned on its axis to catch the wind.

Wooden sails

The sails were covered with canvas to catch more wind.

Main spindle

Rolled-up canvas

Grain was ground by two millstones.

Flour was poured into bags through chutes.

PALTROK MILLS

Paltrok, or smock, mills were developed for use as sawmills around 1600. They were so called because of their resemblance to the smocks that were commonly worn at the time. These windmills were mounted on a circular track, allowing them to rotate in their entirety. Generally, smock mills were used to saw *wagenschot* - entire oak trunks that had been split in two.

BELT, BERG OR TOREN MILLS

Belt or *berg* mills have an extra-high body because of surrounding buildings or trees. A mound *(berg)* built at the base of the mill provides access to the sails. *Toren* mills (tower mills) have a cylindrical brick body and a cap that can be rotated from inside. Only four survive in Holland today.

Sail

Ridge post

Saw floor

Underneath the porch is a crane for lifting the tree trunks from the water.

The mill house is divided into two wings.

Did You Know?

If someone is acting strangely, the Dutch say that they have been "struck by a windmill".

Under the cap the wind shaft propels the heavy brake wheel.

↑ Illustration showing a typical *paltrok* mill used in the 15th century

Other Types of Mill

Polder

Polder mills for draining became common during the 17th century. Standing in groups, they were each responsible for part of the pumping.

Stander (Post)

The oldest type of mill in Holland, *post* mills were used to grind corn. They differ from other flour mills because the entire wooden body rotates on a central wooden post.

Wipmolen

A later version of the *stander* mills, *wipmolen* were designed to pump water. Unlike polder mills, the smaller body rotates on a fixed, pyramidal base.

15

Egmond

C3 Voorstraat 141, Egmond aan Zee; www.vvvegmond.nl

Egmond is divided into three parts: Egmond aan de Hoef, Egmond-Binnen and the seaside resort of Egmond aan Zee, where there is a sandy beach, a lighthouse and walking trails to explore. The Counts of Egmond, a rich and powerful Dutch family, once lived in Egmond aan de Hoef. Only the foundations remain of the *kasteel* (castle), which is open to visitors. In Egmond-Binnen, the beautiful **Egmond Abbey**, is the site of the oldest abbey in Holland and Zeeland. However, in 1573, this 10th-century structure was destroyed by Sonoy, chief of the Beggars of the Sea pirate fleet *(p255)*. It was not until 1934 that a new abbey was built. Benedictine monks still live here today. Within the abbey is the Abdijmuseum (Abbey Museum) and a candle factory. There is a small shop here too, where candles, oils and condiments made by the monks can be purchased.

Egmond Abbey
Vennewatersweg 27, Egmond Sun & Mon
abdijvanegmond.nl

16

Velsen/IJmuiden

C3 Marktplein 33; 020-702 6000

Holland's largest fishing port is IJmuiden – as visitors can guess from the penetrating smell of fish and the wonderful restaurants in the port. The Noordersluis (north lock), which forms part of the North Sea canal lock system, is one of the biggest locks in the world. While coming across you will pass by the Hoogovens (blast-furnaces), where you can take a round trip on a steam train.

The area around Velsen was inhabited in Roman times; archaeological finds are exhibited in the **Ruïne van Brederode**, a 13th-century fortress. You will also feel you are going back in time with a visit to the Romanesque Engelmunduskerk. **Buitenplaats Beeckestijn** is one of the many houses built on the coast in the 17th and 18th centuries by rich Amsterdammers. Its gardens, as well as the period rooms on the ground floor, are open to the public.

Ruïne van Brederode
Velserenderlaan 2, Santpoort Mar-Oct: noon-5pm Wed & Fri, 11am-5pm Sat & Sun ruinevan brederode.nl

Buitenplaats Beeckestijn
Rijksweg 134 House: 11am-4pm Thu-Sun; garden: daily buitenplaats beeckestein.n l

17

Den Helder

C2 Willemsoord 52A; www.topvan holland.nl

Perched on the northernmost tip of the North Holland peninsula, Den Helder has been a base for the Dutch Royal Navy since the 18th century. The **Marinemuseum** has displays of Dutch marine history from 1488. Another highlight of the town is the the North Sea Aquarium, housed within Fort Kijkduin, where a glass tunnel weaves among the fish.

Marinemuseum
Hoofdgracht 3
10am-5pm daily
marinemuseum.nl

→ The 12th-century tympanum above the entrance to Egmond Abbey

←
Slot Assumburg and its manicured gardens, Heemskerk

STAY

Hoeve Meerzicht
A converted barn turned B&B on a working farm, complete with cows and sheep that little ones will adore.

🅰D3 🏠Monnickenmeer 4, Monnickendam ⓦhoevemeerzicht.nl

€€€

Inntel Hotel Zaandam
An unusual and colourful modern hotel made up of various traditional houses stacked together.

🅰C3 🏠Provincialeweg 102, Zaandam ⓦinntel hotelsamsterdam zaandam.nl

€€€

Graaf van Hoorn
A beautiful boutique guesthouse located in a historic home from 1592.

🅰D3 🏠Grote Noord 3, Hoorn ⓦgraafvan hoorn.nl

€€€

Hotel Merlet
At the edge of huge dunes and green pastures, this resort-like family-friendly hotel is ideal for nature lovers.

🅰C3 🏠Duinweg 15, Schoorl ⓦmerlet.nl

€€€

---

18 Medemblik

🅰D2 🚆 ⓦmedemblik.nl

Many pretty 17th-century houses can still be found in Medemblik, which today is well known for its sailing competitions. On the harbourfront is the **Kasteel Radboud**, built in 1288, worth visiting for its little museum. On the town's outskirts, an old pumping station is home to **Het Nederlands Stoommachine-museum**, a collection of steam-driven industrial machinery.

Kasteel Radboud
🅰🅰 🏠Oudevaartsgat 8 🕐Hours vary, check website ⓦkasteelradboud.nl

Het Nederlands Stoommachinemuseum
🅰🅰 🏠Oosterdijk 4 🕐10am–5pm Tue–Sun ⓦstoommachinemuseum.nl

19 Heemskerk

🅰C3 🚆 ⓦheemskerk zeevantijd.nl

An obelisk honouring Dutch artist Maarten van Heemskerck stands in the cemetery of the 17th-century Hervormde Kerk (Reformed Church). Slot Assumburg (Assumburg Castle), dating from the 15th century, was built on the site of a 13th-century fortified house. Slot Marquette is just as old but acquired its present form only two centuries ago. **Fort Veldhuis** is part of the Stelling van Amsterdam, a 135-km (84-mile) defensive line that encircles Amsterdam. It is now a museum, dedicated to the sacrifices made by pilots during World War II.

Fort Veldhuis
🅰🅰 🏠Genieweg 1 📞0251-230670 🕐May–Oct: Sun

⑳ Amstelveen

🅐C4 🚍 🆆amstelveen.nl

Amstelveen is home to many interesting modern art museums, such as **Museum Jan van der Togt**, with its unique collection of glass objects. The **Cobra Museum voor Moderne Kunst** (Cobra Museum of Modern Art) looks at the work of the CoBrA group, established in 1948 by Danish, Belgian and Dutch artists. During its existence, CoBrA abandoned dreary postwar art and introduced modern art to the Netherlands. The Electrische Museumtramlijn is a quirky museum with a collection of electric trams which used to run along the Haarlemmermeer railway. On Sundays from April to October you can take a return trip to Amsterdam from Amstelveen on a historic tram.

To the west of Amstelveen, the Amsterdamse Bos (Amsterdam Forest) unfolds towards Amsterdam, and makes for lovely rambling and picnicking.

Museum Jan van der Togt

🔖🔖 🅐Dorpsstraat 50 🕐11am–5pm Tue–Sun 🚫1 Jan, 27 Apr, 25 Dec 🆆jvdtogt.nl

Cobra Museum voor Moderne Kunst

🔖🔖 🅐Sandbergplein 1–3 🕐11am–5pm Tue–Sun 🚫1 Jan, 27 Apr, 25 Dec 🆆cobra-museum.nl

---

㉑ Ouderkerk aan de Amstel

🅐C4 🚍Amstelveen

This pretty village at the junction of the Amstel and

DRINK

Grand Café de Bosbaan
With views of the lake and surrounded by forest, visit this peaceful spot for a coffee.

🅐C4 🅐Bosbaan 4, Amstelveen 🆆debosbaan.nl

De Voetangel
Relax with a beer on this restaurant's terrace, where three rivers converge in the heart of Ouderkerk.

🅐C4 🅐Rondehoep Oost 3, Ouderkerk 🚫Sun & Mon 🆆voetangel.nl

Cherry blossom in bloom in Amsterdamse Bos (Amsterdam Forest) ↑

the Bullewijk rivers has been a favourite with Amsterdammers since the Middle Ages. They had no church of their own until 1330, and worshippers had to travel to the 11th-century Ouderkerk that gave the village its name. The Old Church was destroyed in a tremendous storm in 1674, and a fine 18th-century church now stands on its site. Today, Ouderkerk aan de Amstel is popular with cyclists who come to enjoy its water-front cafés and restaurants.

Stoomgemaal De Cruquius

🅐 C3 🄰 Cruquiusdijk 27 🚌 🄾 Apr-Oct: 10am-5pm Mon-Fri, 11am-5pm Sat & Sun; Nov-Mar: 1-5pm Mon-Fri, 11am-5pm Sat & Sun 🆆 haarlemmermeer museum.nl

The Stoomgemaal (steam-driven pumping station) at De Cruquius is one of the three steam-driven pumping stations used to drain the great lake Haarlemmermeer. It has not been in use since 1933 and is now a museum.

The original steam engine is in the machine hall, which has eight pumps moved by beams. An exhibition gives a comprehensive overview of water management in the Netherlands.

㉓ Zandvoort

🅐 C3 🄰🚌 🄳 Bakkerstraat 2b; www.vvvzandvoort.nl

Once a fishing village, Zandvoort is now a modern seaside resort where in the summer, half the population of Amsterdam relaxes on the beach or wanders the busy main street known as Kerkstraat. The pretty village

↑ Visitors to Zandvoort stroll along the busy main street, Kerkstraat

centre still retains its old fishermen's houses. Zandvoort is famous for its motor racing circuit, **Circuit Zandvoort**, which has a history going back over 70 years. The track has been restored and is now attempting to achieve its former status. To escape the crowds, ramble through the dunes and parklands at Amsterdamse Waterleidingduinen.

Circuit Zandvoort
🄾 🄰 Burg van Alphenstraat 108 🄾 Daily during meets 🆆 circuitzandvoort.nl

---

RECLAIMED LAND

The Netherlands is continually increasing in size. Various methods of reclaiming low-lying land, such as building dykes around marshy areas, have been employed as far back as the 11th century. In the 17th and 18th centuries, deep lakes like the Haarlemmermeer were drained with the help of windmills. The far-reaching IJsselmeer polders - fertile farmlands - were created after the Zuiderzee was closed off using ingenious reclamation methods. Even now, huge efforts are being made to extend areas of reclaimed land - hence the new Amsterdam residential area of IJburg, which has sprung up from the IJmeer.

24
's-Graveland

🅰D4

The village of 's-Graveland is set amid wooded countryside to the east of Amsterdam. In the 17th century, nine country estates were built here for rich Amsterdammers. Today, there are five parks in the surrounding area: the **Bezoekers-centrum Gooi-en Vecht-streek** (visitors' centre) has information on walking trails.

Bezoekerscentrum Gooi-en Vechtstreek
🅐Noordereinde 54b
🅒10am–5pm Tue–Sun
🆆natuurmonumenten.nl

25
Aalsmeer

🅰C4 🚌

Aalsmeer is a famous centre for floriculture, holding the biggest flower auction in the world, the **Bloemenveiling Royal FloraHolland**. There are also many nurseries around Aalsmeer, where new plant varieties are developed.

Bloemenveiling Royal FloraHolland
🅐Legmeerdijk 313
🅒7–11am Mon–Wed & Fri, 7–9am Thu 🆆royalflora holland.com

26
Muiden

🅰D4 🚌

In the Middle Ages, the pretty town of Muiden was an out-port for Utrecht, but later became part of the defence system of the Stelling van Amsterdam *(p203)*, together with fort island **Pampus**. The town is mainly known for its castle, the **Muiderslot**, which is more than 700 years old and was built by Floris V. After his death it was demolished and rebuilt. The most famous inhabitant, 17th-century poet PC Hooft, formed the Muiderkring (Muiden Circle), a circle of friends occupied with literature and music.

Pampus
🚢From Herengracht 33
🅒Hours vary according to ferry, check website
🆆pampus.nl

Muiderslot

🅐Herengracht 1
🅒Hours vary, check website
🆆muiderslot.nl

27
Naarden

🅰D4 🚌

The fortified town of Naarden lies behind a double ring of canals and walls. The original town is thought to have been founded in the 10th century, then later destroyed and rebuilt around 1350. In the 15th and 16th centuries, it was occupied in turn by the Spanish and the French. The Spaanse Huis (Spanish House), which was converted into the Waag (weigh house), is home to the **Comeniusmuseum**, which explores the life and ideas of the Czech scholar Jan Amos Comenius (1592–1670), who is buried in Naarden. The **Nederlands Vestingmuseum** (Fortress Museum) is in one of the six bastions of the fortress and has an exhibition on the Hollandse Waterlinie, a strip of land flooded as a defence line in Holland, and of Naarden's eventful past.

↑ The Muiderslot in Muiden, protected by its wide moat and towering walls

Inside the Nederlands Instituut voor Beeld en Geluid, Hilversum

Comeniusmuseum

🏛 ♿ 🅰 Kloosterstraat 33
🕐 Noon–5pm Tue–Sun
🌐 comeniusmuseum.nl

Nederlands Vestingmuseum

🏛 ♿ ⬆ 🅰 Westwalstraat 6
🕐 10:30am–5pm Tue–Sun
🌐 vestingmuseum.nl

28

Hilversum

🅰D4 🚌🚆 ℹ Stationsplein 27; www.vvvhilversum.nl

Known as the media centre of the Netherlands, this leafy town is home to a large number of broadcasting companies. It also claims the **Nederlands Instituut voor Beeld en Geluid**, an archive and museum of audio-visual culture with fascinating temporary exhibits housed in a striking modern building.

The town is peppered with historic buildings designed by architect Willem Dudok (1884–1974), a representative of the

Nieuwe Bouwen, such as the 1931 Raadhuis (town hall), with its towers and beautiful interior. The **Museum Hilversum**, which combines the Goois Museum and the Dudok Centrum, illuminates the past of Het Gooi and features an archaeological collection. The Neo-Gothic Sint-Vituskerk, designed by P J H Cuypers (*p386*), with its 98-m (322-ft) tower is worth a visit.

Nederlands Instituut voor Beeld en Geluid

🅰 Media Parkboulevard 1
🕐 10am–5pm Tue–Sun
🌐 beeldengeluid.nl

Museum Hilversum

🅰 Kerkbrink 6 🕐 11am–5pm daily 🗓 27 Apr 🌐 museum hilversum.nl

---

29

Laren

🅰D4 🚌

Alongside pretty villas and country houses, Laren has

many converted farmhouses. In the 19th and early 20th centuries, Laren and its surroundings were the inspiration for many landscape and interior painters, such as Mauve, Israëls and the American W Singer. The **Singer Museum** has been set up in his old house. Here you can see his work and that of other 19th- and 20th-century artists. There is also a sculpture garden. Sint-Jansbasiliek (1925) towers above the Brink and its charming restaurants.

Singer Museum

🏛 ♿ 🏠 🅰 Oude Drift 1
🕐 11am–5pm Tue–Sun
🌐 singerlaren.nl

EAT

Spandershoeve

At this award-winning authentic Indonesian restaurant, try tasty lunch specials in a tropical outdoor setting.

🅰D4 🅰 Bussumer grintweg 46, Hilversum 🌐 spandershoeve.nl

€€€

DRINK

Joseph aan de Poel

A stylish bar and restaurant with gorgeous sunset views.

🅰C4 🅰 Stommeerweg 72, Aalsmeer 🌐 joseph aalsmeer.nl

De Vitrine van Demmers

Beer is the speciality at this old-school brown café, with seasonal local brews on tap.

🅰D4 🅰 Marktstraat 52, Naarden 🌐 vestinggilde.nl

UTRECHT

The region of Utrecht has had a long and bumpy history. At its heart lies the lively city of Utrecht, home to one of the country's most prestigious universities. The city has its origins in the mid-1st century AD, when the Romans built a camp by a ford *(trecht)* in the Rhine, but it only came to prominence after the consecration of its first bishop seven centuries later. Thereafter, a series of powerful bishops created an independent mini-state that paid fealty to the Holy Roman Emperor. In 1528, Henry of the Palatinate, Prince-Bishop of Utrecht, transferred his secular authority to Emperor Charles V, a shrewd move given that the people of Utrecht were restless, objecting to both the autocratic powers of the bishop and his Catholicism – the city was among those at the forefront of the Protestant Reformation. In 1579, in the early stages of what became known as the Dutch Revolt, rebels signed the Union of Utrecht in opposition to the Habsburgs, an event seen as the beginning of the Verenigde Nederlanden (United Provinces), the nascent Dutch republic. It was also in Utrecht city, by accident rather than design, that the Treaty of Utrecht was signed in 1713, ending a long series of bitter wars between Europe's ruling dynasties. In 1853, when the bishopric of Utrecht was reinstated, the city once again became the centre of Dutch Catholicism. In the early 20th century, the region developed strong connections with the De Stijl modernist art movement with the building of Piet Mondriaan's house in Amersfoort and the Rietveld Schröderhuis in Utrecht city. Today, the region is a major economic force – Utrecht university is a great source of economic and artistic development, and the region is at the forefront of the Dutch IT industry and home to major Dutch corporations and a modern manufacturing industry.

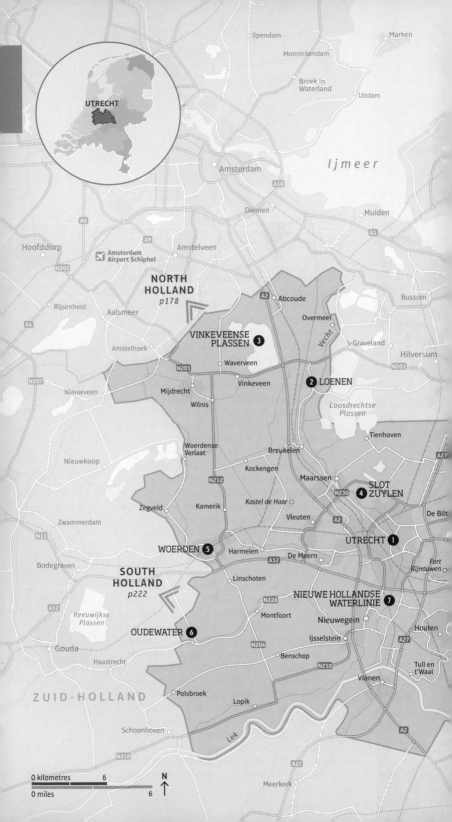

FLEVOLAND

Almere-buiten

Almere

Almere-haven

N305

Huizen

FLEVOLAND
p332

Eemdijk

Eemnes

⓭ BUNSCHOTEN-
SPAKENBURG

Kasteel
Groeneveld

⓼ BAARN

⓬ SOESTDIJK

⓽
LAGE
VUURSCHE

⓼ SOEST

Bilthoven

⓯ AMERSFOORT

Soesterberg

Leusden

GELDERLAND
p340

Hoevelaken

Voorthuizen

Zeist

UTRECHT

Utrecht
Heuvelrug

Scherpenzeel

Lunteren

Woudenberg

Driesprong

Driebergen

Ede

Werkhoven

Von Gimborn
Arboretum

⓮ DOORN

Veenendaal

't Goy

Langbroek

Leersum

⓰ AMERONGEN

Bennekom

Cothen

Elst

Wageningen

WIJK BIJ
DUURSTEDE ⓾

Neder Rijn

Lek

Culemborg

Maurik

RHENEN ⓫

Neder Rijn

Kesteren

Zoelen

Buren

A boat passes a café on one of Utrecht's many canal-side wharfs →

❶
UTRECHT

🅐D4 🚗57 km (35 miles) SE of Amsterdam 🚉Hoog Catherijne
ℹ️Domplein 9; www.visit-utrecht.com

Utrecht, founded by the Romans in AD 47, has been a bishopric and university town for centuries. It has grown into a lively city, thanks to its central position. The Oudegracht (Old Canal), lined with broad quays, cellar bars and cafés, threads its way through the city.

①
Domkerk

🅐Achter de Dom 🕐Daily
🌐domkerk.nl

Construction of a cathedral began in 1254. Today, only the north and south transepts, two chapels and the choir remain, along with the 15th-century cloisters and a chapterhouse (1495), which is now part of Utrecht University.

Outside the church is a giant boulder, dated 980 and covered with runic symbols. It was presented to Utrecht by the Danish people in 1936, to commemorate Denmark's early conversion to Christianity by missionaries from Utrecht. The soaring 112-m- (367-ft-) high Domtoren has always stood apart from the cathedral.

②
Museum Catharijneconvent

🅐Lange Nieuwstraat 38
🕐10am–5pm Tue–Fri,
11am–5pm Sat, Sun &
public hols 🚫1 Jan, 27 Apr
🌐catharijneconvent.nl

The beautiful former convent of St Catherine (1562) is now home to a fascinating museum dealing with the often troubled history of religion in the Netherlands. On the upper floors, a series of model church interiors highlight the changes in religious philosophies through the ages. They range from the lavish statues and paintings in a Catholic church to the more austere, unadorned interiors typical of Protestant churches.

③
Museum Speelklok

🅐Buurkerk on Steenweg 6
🕐10am–5pm Tue–Sun
(daily during school hols)
🚫1 Jan, 27 Apr, 25 Dec
🌐museumspeelklok.nl

This magical place displays a collection of mechanical musical instruments, from the 18th century to the present day. Fairground organs compete with music boxes, clocks, carillons, pianolas and automated birds. These instruments are demonstrated on guided tours, during which visitors are encouraged to sing and dance along. The restoration of instruments can be observed in the workshop.

EAT

Meneer Smakers
Bright and friendly canal-side restaurant serving artisan burgers.

🅐Nobelstraat 143
🌐smakers.nl

€€€

→
Making friends with
Miffy the little rabbit at
the Nijntje Museum

④ 🏃 🖼 🖵 🛍
Nederlands Spoorwegmuseum

🏠 Maliebaanstation
🕙 10am–5pm Tue–Sun
(daily during school hols)
🚫 1 Jan, 27 Apr 🌐 spoorweg
museum.nl

The headquarters of the Dutch railways is based in Utrecht, so it is fitting that the town has a superb railway museum. Inside, there are modern rail accessories. Outside, visitors can explore steam engines, carriages, trams and signal boxes in five railway "worlds", each with its own theme. Using costumed actors, the museum's "Dream Journeys" experience recreates a journey on the legendary Orient Express from Paris to Constantinople. It summons up the glamour and romance of the golden age of steam.

_____

⑤ 🏃 🖵 🛍
Nijntje Museum

🏠 Agnietenstraat 2
🕙 10am–5pm Tue–Sun
🚫 1 Jan, 27 Apr, 25 Dec
🌐 nijntjemuseum.nl

Reserve your ticket online for the always popular Nijntje Museum. It is dedicated to the most famous *nijntje* (little rabbit) in the Netherlands – Miffy – and her creator, Dick Bruna (1927–2017). Inside, younger kids can explore ten themed rooms inspired by characters from Bruna's many picture books, listen to story readings, or get stuck in at a creative workshop. It's a playful, lighthearted learning experience that avoids being too commercialized.

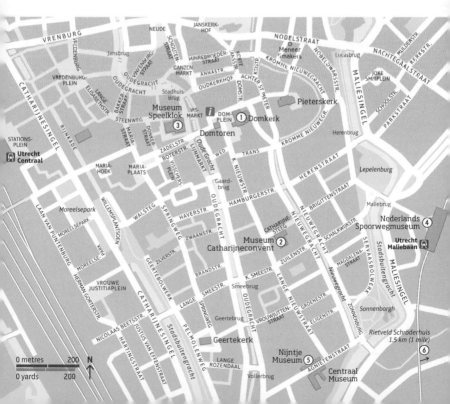

0 metres 200
0 yards 200
N

⑥ ⊘ ⊗ 🖐

RIETVELD SCHRÖDERHUIS

🏠 Prins Hendriklaan 50 🚌 8 🕐 Tue–Sun, for guided tours only (book ahead online) 🚫 1 Jan, 27 Apr, 25 Dec 🌐 rietveldschroderhuis.nl

One of the key figures of the Dutch art movement known as De Stijl, Gerrit Rietveld is perhaps best known for his furniture designs, but he was also an influential architect, as evidenced by this stunning house.

The bold use of modular components, intersecting planes and colour that characterizes furniture pieces such as Rietfeld's iconic *Red and Blue Chair* are given full expression in this revolutionary domestic dwelling. When designing the house, Rietveld worked in close collaboration with his client, Truus Schröder-Schräder, a devotee of the avant-garde who lived here from 1924 until her death in 1985. The house was to epitomize all that was "modern" and broke with many of the architectural standards of the time. This can be seen in the design of the top floor, which may be divided in several ways by sliding partitions, according to the requirements of the inhabitants. The house was declared a World Heritage Site by UNESCO in 2000.

> When designing the house, Rietveld worked in close collaboration with his client, Truus Schröder-Schräder, a devotee of the avant-garde who lived here from 1924 until her death in 1985.

💬 INSIDER TIP
Rietveld Route

Gerrit Rietveld's influence is visible in many spots in Utrecht, his home town. To see more of his extraordinary work, cycle or walk the 5-km (3-mile) Rietveld Route. Along the way see his old furniture workshop on Adriaen van Ostadelaan, other buildings he designed and more. Download a free map from www.rietveld schroderhuis.nl.

DE STIJL

This Dutch artistic movement, founded in 1917, aimed to integrate art further into everyday life. Proponents wanted to bring painting and architecture closer together in a new way. The geometrical design and use of colour in the Rietveld Schröderhuis are both expressions of this idea. Rietveld was a member of De Stijl from 1919, as was the artist Piet Mondrian, famous for his blocky primary colours.

←
The striking exterior; after his wife's death, Rietveld moved in here with Mrs Schröder

Sliding partitions enabled the top floor to be divided into separate rooms for the Schröder children.

The skylight in the roof above the stairs allows additional light to reach the top floor.

Rietveld designed the unusual "Hanging Lamp" in around 1922.

To reflect modern times, functional items like the drainpipe and fuse box were given prominent locations.

The dining corner has a spectacular feature: when the windows are opened, the corner disappears.

The Rietveld ↑
Schröderhuis with interior cutaway

The up-to-date intercom sign instructed visitors to "First ring. If no answer use mouthpiece".

EXPERIENCE MORE

② Loenen

Ⓐ D4 🚍

In the 10th century, this place was called Lona, meaning "water" or "mud". Loenen fell under two jurisdictions and has two courts dating from the beginning of the 18th century. Loenen aan de Vecht, now a protected village, is famous for its rural atmosphere, castles and country estates complete with coach houses and boathouses. **Kasteel Loenersloot**, on the bank of the Angstel, dates back to the 13th century, though only the round defence tower remains.

Kasteel Loenersloot
🚲 Ⓐ Rijksstraatweg 211 🕐 By appt only 🌐 utrechts-landschap.nl/loenersloot

③ Vinkeveense Plassen

Ⓐ C4 🚍 🌐 recreatiemidden nederland.nl

The site of De Vinkeveense Plassen (Vinkeveense Lakes) was once marsh. The thick peat was dug up to be used as

---

KASTEEL DE HAAR

Just outside Utrecht stands one of the most impressive castles in the country - Kasteel De Haar *(kasteeldehaar. nl)*. Originally the site of a castle built in 1391, the current Neo-Gothic structure dates from 1892 and is largely the work of P J H Cuypers. It is surrounded by an estate of over 55 ha (135 acres), complete with ponds, canals, rose gardens and bridges.

---

fuel for nearby towns, earning the people here a good living. The peat was therefore dug up more and more, leading to a large area of lakes.

Today, the lakes attract many watersports enthusiasts, cyclists and walkers who come to enjoy this tranquil area. When it's not the breeding season, you can take a rowing boat through the nature reserve of Botshol, which is home to marsh and grassland birds.

---

④

Slot Zuylen

Ⓐ D4 🚍 Castle: Tournooi-veld 1, Oud-Zuilen 🕐 Apr-Oct: 11am–5pm Tue-Sun; Nov-Mar: 11am–5pm Sat & Sun 🗓 1 Jan, 27 Apr & 25, 26 & 31 Dec 🌐 slot zuylen.nl

The original U-shaped Slot Zuylen castle was built around 1520 on the remains of a medieval residential tower. In the 18th century, extensive rebuilding brought the castle into line with contemporary architectural style.

The author Belle van Zuylen (1740–1805) was one of the castle's famous inhabitants, renowned for her correspondence at home and abroad, which she cleverly used to show her modern attitude. Several rooms are furnished as they were when she resided here.

The serpentine wall that runs alongside the castle provides so much protection that even in this cool sea climate, subtropical fruits such as peaches and grapes can flourish here.

---

⑤ Woerden

Ⓐ C4 🚃 🚍

Woerden came into being on the dykes along the Rhine and Lange Linschoten. It has been besieged many times but always managed to hold out. Between 1575 and 1576, during the Thirty Years' War, the Spaniards tried to conquer Woerden, as did the French in 1672, but neither succeeded.

Impenetrable Kasteel van Woerden (Woerden Castle), built between 1405 and 1415, offers a lovely weekend high tea (kasteelwoerden.nl).

---

⑥

Oudewater

⚠C4 🚌 ℹLeeuwer ingerstraat 10; www. oudewater.net

The counts of Holland and the bishops of Utrecht fought fiercely for the little town of Oudewater, which was converted into a border stronghold by Floris V. In 1349, Oudewater was captured by Jan van Arkel, the Bishop of Utrecht. In 1572, Oudewater sided with the Prince of Orange and, as a result, the town was seized in 1575 by the Spanish. They exacted a bloody revenge by burning it to the ground.

The town's most famous attraction is the scales, dating from the 16th century, known

↑ The 16th-century Heksenwaag in Oudewater, used to weigh "witches"

as the **heksenwaag** (witches' scales). Women who were suspected of witchcraft came here to be weighed. If their weight and their outward appearance tallied, they were given a certificate as proof of their innocence. Oudewater was the only place where "witches" could be legally weighed in public.

Heksenwaag

⊘ 🏠Leeuweringerstraat 2 🕐Apr–Oct: 11am–5pm Tue–Sun 🌐heksenwaag.nl

← The pretty village of Loenen aan de Vecht lies on the Vecht river

DRINK

Badhu

This popular Arabian restaurant is set in a 1920s bathhouse and serves afternoon chai (high tea Arabian style) and evening cocktails.

🅐D4 🅠Willem van Noortplein 19, Utrecht 🆆badhu.nl

Theehuis Fort WKU

Visit this cosy teahouse inside the old fort waiting room, with both a fireplace and a sunny terrace.

🅐D4 🅠Lange Uitweg 42, Tull en 't Waal 📞030-634 2199 🅠Nov-Mar: Sat & Sun

---

Café De Engel

High tea and wine options are available at this modern bar, along with plenty of good beer and snacks.

🅐D4 🅠Markt 26, Wijk bij Duurstede 🆆engelrestaurant.nl

7

Nieuwe Hollandse Waterlinie

🅐D4 🆆nieuwe hollandsewaterlinie.nl

The Nieuwe Hollandse Waterlinie (New Dutch Waterline), laid out from 1815 to 1940, comprises 45 forts, 6 fortresses and 2 castles, from Muiden and Naarden in North Holland to Werkendam in North Brabant. The Waterline was intended as a defence against invading armies; a wide strip of land would simply be flooded. Utrecht's installations are now being protected, and have been put forward for UNESCO's World Heritage Site register. The original reconnaissance positions and unimpeded lines of fire will hopefully be preserved. The best are at Rijnauwen, Groenekan and Tull en 't Waal.

8

Baarn/Soest

🅐D4 🅟🚌 🅘Lt Gen van Heutszlaan 7, Baarn; 035-544 9649

During the 17th century, regents and wealthy

INSIDER TIP
Fortress Cycling Route

You can bike, canoe or walk along the scenic Nieuwe Hollandse Waterlinie route of about 135 km (84 miles), passing by dozens of fortresses, lakes, grasslands and picturesque villages.

merchants had splendid summer residences built in Baarn and its environs. This place has retained its leafy, elegant appearance.

The Rococo-style **Kasteel Groeneveld**, built in 1710, lies in the middle of a 1.3 sq km (0.5 sq mile) park with a café in its former stables.

Soest's past is pre-9th century, and the old centre remains largely in its original state. The church dates from 1400. The surrounding area is beautiful and offers a wealth of leisure activities.

Kasteel Groeneveld

♿ 🅠Groeneveld 2 🕐Castle: 11am-5pm Tue-Sun; park: sunrise-sunset Tue-Sun 🅠Castle: 1 Jan, 27 Apr, 25 & 31 Dec 🆆kasteelgroeneveld.nl

People cycling through the park towards Kasteel Groeneveld in Baarn

↑ The 13th-century castle, Kasteel Duurstede, in Wijk bij Duurstede

the Iron Age. The Late Gothic Cuneratoren (Cunera Tower), built between 1492 and 1531, escaped the bombs of World War II. The Raadhuis (town hall) dates from the Middle Ages.

East of the town is the **Ouwehands**, a zoo with tigers, pandas, monkeys and elephants. In the large "bear wood", the *berenbos*, brown bears and wolves wander free. Other attractions include a tropical aquarium and plenty of children's activities.

Ouwehands Dierenpark
⊛⊕⊜⊚ ⌂ Grebbeweg 111
⊙ 10am-5pm daily (till 6pm some days, check website)
ⓦ ouwehand.nl

---

⑫

Soestdijk

Ⓐ D4 ⌂ Amsterdamse-straatweg 1, Baarn
⊙ 11am-5pm Fri-Sun (also Tue-Thu in summer)
ⓦ paleissoestdijk.nl

Just outside the town of Baarn lies Paleis Soestdijk, built in 1674 as a place for Viceroy William III to hunt. In 1815, it came into the hands of the crown prince, who later became King William II. Paleis Soestdijk will be redeveloped into housing, a hotel, shops and other public spaces beginning in 2022.

⑨

Lage Vuursche

Ⓐ D4 🚌

The name "Furs" for Lage Vuursche has been around since 1200, though the village itself has existed only since the 17th century. The village, surrounded by woodland, is popular with ramblers. The small octagonal castle Drakenstein (1640–43), is the home of Princess Beatrix, former Queen of the Netherlands.

---

⑩

Wijk bij Duurstede

Ⓐ D4 🚌 🛈 Markt 24; 0343-575995

Dorestad was an important trade centre in Carolingian times. Plundering Vikings and a shift in the river basin of the Rhine led to its decline, until Wijk (near Dorestad) emerged and became the home of the Utrecht bishops. The **Kasteel**

Duurstede dates from the 13th century, when it was originally built as a donjon, the castle's fortified inner tower, surrounded by a moat.

Kasteelpark Duurstede
⊜ ⌂ Langs de Wal 6
⊙ Castle: Apr-Oct: 10am-5pm Tue-Sun (hours vary during events, check website); park: open daily ⓦ kasteel duurstede.nl

---

⑪

Rhenen

Ⓐ D4 🚌🚌 🛈 Markt 20; 0317-612333

Rhenen lies on the north bank of the Rhine, at the border between Betuwe and the Utrecht Heuvelrug. This area was inhabited as far back as

→
Sculpture of a Danube Mermaid in the gardens of Soestdijk Palace

13

Bunschoten-Spakenburg

🅰D4 🚌🅒 Oude Schans 90;
www.spakenburg.nl

Over the years, Bunschoten and Spakenburg have merged into one another. Farming was Bunschoten's traditional livelihood, and there are pretty farms to see here. Spakenburg was once a fishing town; its smoke-houses, fishermen's houses and shipbuilding yard are reminders of this time. **Museum Spakenburg** brings this era back to life.

Museum Spakenburg

🅰🅒🅒🅒 🅰 Oude Schans 47–63 🅒 Apr–Oct: 1:30–5pm Mon, 10am–5pm Tue-Sat; Nov–Mar: noon–4pm Wed–Sat 🅦museum spakenburg.nl

14

Doorn

🅰D4 🚌
🅒 Langbroekerweg 10;
www.opdeheuvelrug.nl

Doorn, originally called Thorheim (home of Thor, god of thunder), is a pretty village in wooded surroundings. Its greatest attraction is **Huis Doorn**, where the German Kaiser, Wilhelm II, lived with his retinue after World War I. There is now a pavilion commemorating World War I and its impact on the Netherlands.

The village's **Von Gimborn Arboretum** is a botanical garden founded in 1924. One of the country's largest gardens, it has ten huge sequoia trees. Although best visited in spring and summer, the gardens contain plants for all seasons.

> One of the country's largest gardens, Von Gimborn Arboretum has ten huge sequoias. Although best visited in spring and summer, the gardens contain plants for all seasons.

Huis Doorn

🅰🅒🅒🅒
🅰 Langbroekerweg 10
🅒 1–5pm Tue-Sun
🅦 huisdoorn.nl

Von Gimborn Arboretum

🅰 🅰 Velperengh 13
🅒 Daily 🅦 botanis chetuinen.nl

15

Amersfoort

🅰D4 🅰🚌 🅒Breestraat 1;
www.vvvamersfoort.nl

The town centre of quaint Amersfoort is defined by small streets with old houses and gardens. The **Museum Flehite** explores the history of Amersfoort. The town was the birthplace of Piet Mondriaan, the leading light of the De Stijl and Neo-Plasticist movements. The house where he was born is home to the **Mondriaanhuis voor Constructieve en Concrete Kunst**, a study centre and archive of his life and work. On the edge of

town, **Kunsthal KAdE** curates exhibitions on contemporary art and culture, architecture and design. The library, the Amersfoort Archives, is a must visit.

Some 4 km (2 miles) from Amersfoort, in the village of Leusden, **Kamp Amersfoort** is a grim reminder of the area's history. A Dutch army barracks was transformed in 1941 into a work camp for more than 35,000 prisoners.

Museum Flehite
⊗ 🅰 Westsingel 50
🅾 11am–5pm Tue–Sun
🅲 Public hols
🅦 museumflehite.nl

Mondriaanhuis voor Constructieve en Concrete Kunst
⊗ 🅐 🅰 Kortegracht 11
🅾 11am–5pm Tue–Sun
🅲 1 Jan, 27 Apr, 25 Dec
🅦 mondriaanhuis.nl

Kunsthal KAdE
🅐🅣 🅰 Eemplein 77
🅾 11am–5pm Tue–Sun
🅲 1 Jan, 27 Apr, 25 Dec
🅦 kunsthalkade.nl

Kamp Amersfoort
⊗ 🅰 Loes van Overeemlaan 19, Leusden 🅾 Mar–Oct: 9am–5pm Tue–Fri, noon–4pm Sun & public hols; Nov–Feb: 10am–4pm Tue–Fri, noon–4pm Sun & public hols
🅦 kampamersfoort.nl

16

Amerongen

🅰 D4 🚍 🅸 0343-412015

Situated on the bank of the lower Rhine, which can be crossed by ferry, Amerongen lies in the ridge of hills known as the Utrechtse Heuvelrug, a national park. The highest point in the ridge is marked by Amerongense Berg, which has earned the name "mountain", despite being just 69 m (225 ft) high. The town originally lay on the Via Regia, the "royal route" that ran from Utrecht to Cologne. From the 17th to 19th centuries, tobacco was grown in this area, evident by the drying sheds that are still standing. Be sure to have a proper look at an old drying

shed in the **Tabaksteelt Museum**. In 1672, the town's castle, **Kasteel Amerongen**, was destroyed by the French; it was later rebuilt in the Dutch Classical style.

Tabaksteelt Museum
⊗ 🅰 Burg Jhr van den Boschstraat 46 🅾 Apr–Oct: 1–5pm Tue–Sun 🅦 tabak steeltmuseum.nl

Kasteel Amerongen
⊗⊗🅣 🅰 Drostestraat 20 🅾 Apr–Oct: 11am–4pm Tue–Sat, noon–4pm Sun; Nov–Mar: 11am–3pm Thu–Sat, noon–3pm Sun 🅦 kasteelamerongen.nl

---

EAT

Moeke Rhenen
A local favourite, this riverside restaurant has a lovely terrace and excellent pub fare.

🅰 D4 🅰 Veerplein 1, Rhenen 🅦 moeke rhenen.nl

€€€

Nul33
Bright and modern eatery in the heart of town, with a fresh Dutch menu that will suit most tastes.

🅰 D4 🅰 Langestraat 76, Amersfoort 🅦 nul33.nl

€€€

Restaurant Robberse Eiland
Enjoy a glass of wine and the catch of the day at the water's edge.

🅰 D4 🅰 Oud-Loosdrechtsedijk 234, Loosdrecht 🅦 restaurant-robberse-eiland.nl

€€€

← Traditional fishing boats moored in the fishing village of Bunschoten-Spakenburg

1 VOOR €4
EN
3 VOOR €10,-
tijd nodig
VOOR HOUDEN
Seasons
Tasteful
Gezellig

SOUTH HOLLAND

South Holland was part of the Roman province of Germania Inferior, but after the departure of the Romans, the region became part of the Frisian kingdom, and then the Frankish empire. In 690, the Frankish king gave Anglo-Saxon monks permission to spread Roman Catholicism, and they gradually converted the region to Christianity. Between the 9th and the 13th centuries, the influence of the counts of Holland, who took up residence in The Hague, attracted trade with Flanders, Germany and England, and settlements in the region slowly grew into rich towns, from Leiden and The Hague to Rotterdam, Delft and Dordrecht. As they grew and prospered, each these cities maintained a fierce independence while still cooperating with ech other. As a result, they came to dominate the Netherlands politically, socially and culturally. In the 16th century, it was South Holland that led the Dutch Revolt against the Catholic Habsburgs, and after the war, it was South Holland that benefited most in economic terms from the imperialism of the West and East India companies in what has traditionally been called the "Golden Age" of the Netherlands. Although there were differences between these cities – Rotterdam focused on its shipping industry from the 14th century onwards; Leiden was famous for its university, founded in 1575; The Hague became the country's political centre; Delft was home to William the Silent, the greatest Protestant rebel of them all – their histories and fortunes have largely mirrored each other. As a result, South Holland is today the country's financial powerhouse, with its bulb fields and tourism, shipping and petrochemical industries driving its economy and its continued success crucial to the Netherlands as a whole.

SOUTH HOLLAND

Must Sees
1. Leiden
2. Den Haag
3. Delft
4. Rotterdam
5. Gouda

Experience More
6. Kinderdijk
7. Middelharnis
8. Geodereede
9. Hellevoetsluis
10. Keukenhof
11. Lisse
12. Scheveningen
13. Schiedam
14. Maassluis
15. Reeuwijkse Plassen
16. Gorinchem
17. Nieuwpoort
18. Leerdam
19. Brielle
20. Dordrecht

Noordwijk aan Zee

Katwijk aan Zee

Wassenaar

N44

SCHEVENINGEN 12

DEN HAAG 2

Rijswijk

Nootdorp

Monster

Wateringen

DELFT 3

Hull, Harwich

Hoek van Holland

Naaldwijk

A4

A13

Europoort

Oostvoorne

MAASSLUIS 14

A20

SCHIEDAM 13

North Sea

BRIELLE 19

Vlaardingen

Strype

N57

A15

Spijkenisse

Hoogvliet

Goeree

HELLEVOETSLUIS 9

Oude Maas

GOEDEREEDE 8

Stellendam

Zuidland

Oud-Beijerland

Piershil

Klaaswaal

Melissant

N215

MIDDELHARNIS 7

Zuid-Beijerland

A29

Renesse

N57

Brouwershaven

Overflakkee

Den Bommel

Herkingen

Serooskerke

N59

ZEELAND
p256

Oude-Tonge

Willemstad

N57

N59

Bruinisse

Zierikzee

Dinteloord

ZEELAND

A4

0 kilometres   10

0 miles   10

N

❶
LEIDEN

🗺 C4 🚉 Leiden Centraal 🛈 Stationsweg 41; www.visitleiden.nl

Leiden is famous for its university, the oldest and most prestigious in the Netherlands. During termtime, the streets are crowded with students cycling between lectures or packing the cafés and bookshops.

Lieden university was founded in 1575 by William of Orange (*p68*), a year after he relieved the town from a year-long siege by the Spanish. As a reward for their endurance, William offered the citizens of Leiden a choice: the building of a university or the abolition of tax. They chose wisely, and the city's reputation as a centre of intellectual and religious tolerance was firmly established. English Puritan dissidents, victims of persecution in their homeland, were able to settle here in the 17th century before undertaking their epic voyage to the New World.

A number of excellent museums document Leiden's eventful history, which included the Eighty Years' War and the 17th century, when the town was a centre for worldwide trade. This age also saw the birth of the city's most famous son – Rembrandt – in June 1606. Look for the wall plaque on the façade of his birthplace on Weddesteeg.

1

↑
⑥ *Museum Volkenkunde* (900m/984yd)

Langebrug is lined with student accommodation.

LANGEBRUG

PAPENGRACHT

RAPENBURG

⑤

HOUTSTRAAT

③

NONNENSTRAAT

↑ A café on one of Leiden's picturesque canals, which are lined with modern and 17th-century buildings

Illustration showing ↑ the area around Pieterskerk in Leiden

1 The verdant Hortus Botanicus Leiden contains many beautiful features, such as this waterfall.

2 Artifacts from Ancient Greece are exhibited in the Rijksmuseum van Oudheden.

3 Pieterskerk has a dramatic interior, with beautiful vaulting.

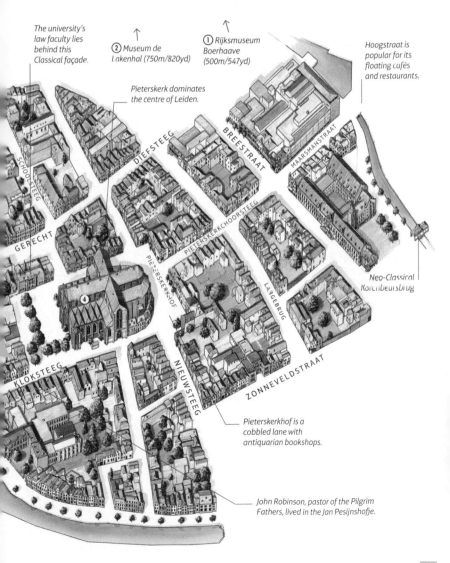

The university's law faculty lies behind this Classical façade.

2 Museum de Lakenhal (750m/820yd)

1 Rijksmuseum Boerhaave (500m/547yd)

Hoogstraat is popular for its floating cafés and restaurants.

Pieterskerk dominates the centre of Leiden.

SCHOOLSTEEG

GERECHT

KLOKSTEEG

DIEFSTEEG

BREESTRAAT

MAARSMANSTRAAT

PIETERSKERKCHOORSTEEG

PIETERSKERKHOF

LANGEBRUG

NIEUWSTEEG

ZONNEVELDSTRAAT

Neo-Classical Korenbeursbrug

Pieterskerkhof is a cobbled lane with antiquarian bookshops.

John Robinson, pastor of the Pilgrim Fathers, lived in the Jan Pesijnshofje.

EAT

Grand Café van Buuren

Soups, salads and mighty sandwiches, with fillings such as pulled chicken and avocado, feature on the lunch menu here.

⌂ Stationsweg 7
ⓦ grandcafevan buuren.nl

€€€

Crabbetje

This upmarket seafood restaurant serves platters piled high with sole, lobster and oysters.

⌂ St Agatenstraat 5
ⓦ visrestaurant crabbetje.nl

€€€

---

① ⊗ ⊡

Rijksmuseum Boerhaave

⌂ Lange St Agnietenstraat 10 ⊙ 10am-5pm Tue-Sun & public hols (daily during school hols) 🔒 1 Jan, 27 Apr, 3 Oct & 25 Dec ⓦ rijks museumboerhaave.nl

The museum is named after the great Dutch professor of medicine, botany and chemistry Herman Boerhaave (1668–1738). The collection reflects the development of mathematics, astronomy, physics, chemistry and medicine. Exhibits range in time from a 15th-century astrolabe and surgical equipment of yesteryear to early electron microscopes.

→

Children looking down microscopes at the Rijksmuseum Boerhaave

---

② ⊗ Ⓜ ⊡ 🏛

Museum de Lakenhal

⌂ Oude Singel 32
⊙ 10am-5pm Tue-Fri, noon-5pm Sat & Sun
ⓦ lakenhal.nl

The Lakenhal (cloth hall) was the 17th-century headquarters of Leiden's cloth trade. Built in 1640 in Dutch Classical style by Arent van 's-Gravesande, it now houses the municipal museum.

One of the most famous works of art is Lucas van Leyden's Renaissance triptych of *The Last Judgment* (1526–7), which was rescued from the city's Pieterskerk during the religious struggles of 1566. A wing of the museum, built in the 1920s, offers an expansive silver collection, and exhibits covering the local weaving industry. Not to be missed is a big bronze *hutspot*, or cauldron, allegedly left behind by the Spanish when William of Orange broke the siege in 1574. At that time, the cauldron would have contained a wholesome spicy stew that the starving people ate. Traditionally this meal is cooked every year on 3 October, to commemorate Dutch victory over the Spanish *(p66)*.

---

③ ⊗ Ⓜ 🏛

Hortus Botanicus Leiden

⌂ Rapenburg 73 ⊙ Apr-Oct: 10am-6pm daily; Nov-Mar: 10am-4pm Tue-Sun
🔒 3 Oct, 24 Dec-1 Jan
ⓦ hortusleiden.nl

Leiden's botanical garden was founded in 1590 as part of the university. Some of the varied trees and shrubs, including a 350-year-old laburnum, reflect the garden's history.

Today, the Hortus Botanicus features a modern reconstruction of an earlier walled garden, called the Clusiustuin. Other visual delights include hothouses full of exotic orchids, rose gardens and an exquisite Japanese garden.

---

④ ⊗ ⊡

Pieterskerk

⌂ Kloksteeg 16
⊙ 11am-6pm daily, unless special events are taking place (check website for details) 🔒 3 Oct & 31 Dec
ⓦ pieterskerk.com

This impressive Gothic church dedicated to St Peter was built in the 15th century in rose-pink brick, and stands in a leafy

→

Museum Volkenkunde, sitting on the river

GREAT VIEW

De Burcht

Sitting between two channels of the Rijn atop a grassy man-made mound, which is thought to be of Saxon origin, this citadel overlooks the town below. Climb to the top of this odd 12th-century fortress and peer over the crenellated battlements.

square surrounded by elegant houses. Pieterskerk was deconsecrated in 1971 and is now used as a community centre. The church is worth a visit for its austere interior and its magnificent organ, built by the Hagenbeer brothers in 1642 and enclosed in gilded woodwork. The floor of the nave is covered with worn slabs, marking the burial places of 17th-century intellectuals such as Puritan leader John Robinson and 17th-century artist Jan Steen. A long-term restoration project started in 2001 and discoveries made during this are displayed in the church.

⑤ Rijksmuseum van Oudheden

🏛 Rapenburg 28 🕐 10am–5pm Tue–Sun 🚫 1 Jan, 27 Apr, 3 Oct, 25 Dec 🌐 rmo.nl

The Dutch museum of antiquities, established in 1818, is Leiden's main attraction. The centrepiece of the collection is the Egyptian Temple of Taffeh, reassembled in the main exhibition hall in 1978. It dates from the 1st century AD, and from the 4th century AD was dedicated to Isis, Egyptian goddess of fertility.

The museum's rich collection of Egyptian artifacts, which includes wonderful painted sarcophagi, occupies the first two floors. There are also impressive displays of musical instruments, textiles and shoes, expressive Etruscan bronze work and fragments of Roman mosaics and frescoes.

The presentation has been designed with children in mind, with interactive exhibits and multimedia reconstructions of daily life in ancient Egypt, Greece and Rome.

⑥ Museum Volkenkunde

🏛 Steenstraat 1 🕐 10am–5pm Tue–Sun (daily during school hols) 🚫 1 Jan, 27 Apr, 3 Oct, 25 Dec 🌐 volkenkunde.nl

This excellent ethnological museum, founded in 1837, houses collections from non-Western cultures. Individual displays are linked together to create a worldwide cultural journey that shows both the differences and connections between cultures. Temporary exhibitions include deep dives into different living conditions across the world, from the Arctic wastes to the hills of China, adding to this eclectic museum's wide appeal.

19

windmills once stood on Leiden's high walls.

②

DEN HAAG

🅰B4 🚗56 km (35 miles) SW of Amsterdam 🚉Centraal Station, Koningin Julianplein; Station Hollands Spoor (HS), Stationsplein 🅸Spui 68; noon–6pm Mon, 10am–6pm Tue–Fri, 10am–5pm Sat, noon–5pm Sun; www.denhaag.com

Den Haag ('s-Gravenhage or The Hague) became the political capital of the Netherlands in 1586 and is home to prestigious institutions such as the Dutch Parliament and International Court of Justice.

① 🔄 🅼

Binnenhof

🅰Binnenhof 8a 🕐For guided tours only; book via website 🕐Sun, public hols 🆆prodemos.nl

The former castle of the Counts of Holland is now home to the Dutch Parliament and the office of the Prime Minister of the Netherlands. Known as the Binnenhof, this complex of buildings sits beside the castle's former moat – the Hofvijver. In the centre of the courtyard stands the fairy-tale, double-turreted Gothic Ridderzaal (Hall of the Knights). This was the 13th-century dining hall of Floris V, Count of Holland (1254–96). Since 1904, the hall's function has been mostly ceremonial; it is used for the opening of the Dutch Parliament by the monarch (Prinsjesdag, the third Tuesday in September), and for other state occasions. It is open to visitors when parliament is not in session. Tours take in the Ridderzaal and the debating chambers.

② 🔄 🅼

Museum Bredius

🅰Lange Vijverberg 14 🕐11am–5pm Tue–Sun 🕐1 Jan, 27 Apr, Easter & 25 Dec 🆆museumbredius.nl

Dr Abraham Bredius was an art historian and collector as well

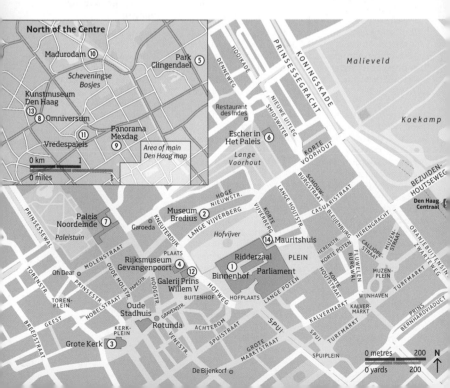

North of the Centre

Madurodam ⑩
Park Clingendael ⑤
Scheveningse Bosjes
Kunstmuseum Den Haag ⑬
⑧ Omniversum
Vredespaleis ⑪
Panorama Mesdag ⑨
Area of main Den Haag map
0 km   1
0 miles   1

Restaurant des Indes
Escher in Het Paleis ⑥
Lange Voorhout

Paleis Noordeinde ⑦
Paleistuin
Garoeda
Museum Bredius ②
Hofvijver
Mauritshuis ⑭
Rijksmuseum Gevangenpoort ④
Oh Dear
Galerij Prins Willem V ⑫
Ridderzaal
PLEIN
Binnenhof ① Parliament
Oude Stadhuis
Rotunda
Grote Kerk ③
De Bijenkorf

Den Haag Centraal

0 metres   200
0 yards   200

↑ The grand Binnenhof, sitting on the tranquil waters of the Hofvijver lake

as director of the Mauritshuis (*p236*) from 1895 to 1922. On his death in 1946, he bequeathed his collection of 17th- and 18th-century art to the city of Den Haag. This bequest is displayed in a distinguished 18th-century merchant's house on the north side of the Hofvijver lake, and features around 200 17th-century paintings, including famous works by Dutch Masters such as Rembrandt and Jan Steen, as well as others by lesser-known artists.

The building itself has undergone considerable renovation and boasts a fine collection of antique furniture, delicate porcelain and beautifully engraved silverware.

③

Grote Kerk

🏠 Rond de Grote Kerk 12
🕐 During summer months; check website for details
🌐 grotekerkdenhaag.nl

In its present form, the Grote Kerk dates mainly from 1539, but major rebuilding between 1985 and 1987 has restored it to its former glory. Its most impressive feature is a stained-glass window that depicts Charles V, the Holy Roman Emperor, kneeling at the feet of the Virgin Mary.

④

Rijksmuseum Gevangenpoort

🏠 Buitenhof 33 🕐 For guided tours only 🚫 Mon, 1 Jan, 24, 25 & 26 Dec
🌐 gevangenpoort.nl

The Gevangenpoort (Prison Gate) was originally the main gateway to the 14th-century castle of the Counts of Holland. Later, it was turned into a jail,

← A delicately carved marble statue in the Grote Kerk

becoming infamous during a period of violent social unrest in the late 17th century when burgomaster Cornelis de Witt was confined and tortured here. Both he and his brother Jan were subsequently tried for heresy, and torn limb from limb outside the prison gate by a rioting mob.

The gate is now a prison museum. The guided tour explores a unique collection of torture instruments, accompanied by a stereo soundtrack of bloodcurdling screams.

↑ The picturesque Japanese Garden, a highlight of Park Clingendael

---

(5) 🖼️

Park Clingendael

🏠 Entrance from Alkemadelaan or the Ruychrocklaan 📞 070-3533000 🚌 18 🕐 Park Clingendael: sunrise-sunset daily; Japanese Garden: end Apr-mid-Jun & Oct: sunrise-sunset daily

This country estate already existed in the 16th century, when it had a large, formal French-style garden. In 1830 it was converted into a pretty landscaped park. It contains a Dutch garden, a rose garden, grazing land for animals, rhododendron woods and an ancient beech tree.

Overgrown bunkers in the woods are a sombre reminder of World War II, when the Netherlands was occupied and the most senior German authorities took up quarters in Huis Clingendael.

At the centre of the park lies the famous Japanese Garden, which was laid out in 1903 on the instructions of Baroness Marguérite Mary after a trip to Japan. The tea house and all the stones and ornaments in the garden were brought over from Japan by boat at the time.

---

(6) 🖼️🖼️🖼️

Escher in Het Paleis

🏠 Lange Voorhout 74 🚊🚌 🕐 11am-5pm Tue-Sun 🕐 1 Jan, 3rd Tue in Sep, 25 Dec 🌐 escherinhetpaleis.nl

A large proportion of the graphic artist Maurits Cornelis Escher's (1898–1972) work is displayed in the Paleis Lange Voorhout, where Queen Emma and Queen Wilhelmina once lived. The permanent exhibition includes well-known works such as *Day and Night, Rising and Falling* and *Belvédère*. In addition to graphic works, there are sketches, personal documents and photographs. The museum also features the Escher Experience, a virtual journey through his world.

Did You Know?

Den Haag was once a hunting spot for the Count of Holland; "s-Gravenhage", means "the Count's woods".

---

(7)

Paleis Noordeinde

🏠 Noordeinde 68 🕐 Only the Paleistuin (garden) is open, sunrise-sunset daily 🌐 koninklijkhuis.nl

In 1640, Stadholder Frederik Hendrik had his mother's house converted into a palace built in the Dutch Classical style. The property of the Princes of Orange since William V (1748–1806), this is the building where the present King of the Netherlands, Willem-Alexander, has his offices, and also where he leaves from for the state opening of parliament.

---

(8) 🖼️🖼️

Omniversum

🏠 President Kennedylaan 5 🚊 17 🚌 24 🕐 Daily, from 10:30am (9:30am school and public hols) 🌐 omniversum.nl

The Omniversum (next to the Kunstmuseum Den Haag) is a cross between a planetarium and a high-tech cinema. It puts on a programme of films of space flights, volcanic eruptions and ocean life.

⑨

Panorama Mesdag

🏠 Zeestraat 65 🕐 10am–5pm Mon–Sat, 11am–5pm Sun 🚫 1 Jan, 25 Dec Ⓦ panorama-mesdag.com

This painted cyclorama is important both as a work of Dutch Impressionism and as a rare surviving example of 19th-century entertainment. The vast painting, the largest circular canvas in Europe, is 120 m (400 ft) in circumference and lines the inside wall of a circular, canopied pavilion. The optical illusion makes visitors feel that they are standing in the old fishing village of Scheveningen.

The astonishingly realistic effect of the painting is achieved through the brilliant use of perspective, enhanced by natural daylight from above. It was painted in 1881 by members of the Dutch Impressionist School, led by H W Mesdag (1831–1915) and his wife,

Sientje (1834–1909). George Hendrik Breitner (1857–1923) later added a group of cavalry officers charging along the beach on horseback. Constructed specially for the painting, the building itself has been renovated and extended, creating more space for temporary exhibitions.

---

⑩

Madurodam

🏠 George Maduroplein 1 🕐 Hours vary daily, check website Ⓦ madurodam.nl

This 1:25 scale model of a Dutch city consists of replicas of the Binnenhof in Den Haag, Amsterdam canal houses, Rotterdams' Europoort, Schiphol airport, windmills and bulb fields. At night it is lit up.

Madurodam was opened in 1952, designed by J M L Maduro in memory of his son George, who died at Dachau concentration camp in 1945.

Miniature buildings in the re-created city of Madurodam

EAT

Restaurant des Indes

The opulent restaurant of Den Haag's grandest hotel serves French-inspired, classically presented steak and seafood such as Dover sole.

🏠 Lange Voorhout 54-56
🕐 Sun & Mon
🌐 desindes.nl

€€€

Garoeda

This long-established restaurant, which opened in 1949, serves Indonesian meat, fish and vegetable dishes, including satay skewers and *rijsttafels* (small dishes served with rice).

🏠 Kneuterdijk 18A
🌐 garoeda.com

€€€

Vredespaleis

🏠 Carnegieplein 2
🕐 Visitors' centre: Tue-Sun 🕐 Public hols & when court is in session
🌐 vredespaleis.nl

In 1899, Den Haag played host to the first international peace conference. This led to the subsequent formation of the Permanent Court of Arbitration, which had the aim of maintaining world peace. To provide a suitably august home for the court, the Scottish-born philanthropist Andrew Carnegie (1835–1919) donated $1.5 million towards the building of the mock-Gothic Vredespaleis (Peace Palace), which was designed by French architect Louis Marie Cordonnier.

The enormous palace was completed in 1913, and many of the member nations of the Court of Arbitration contributed to the interior's rich decoration. Today, the Vredespaleis is the seat of the United Nations' International Court of Justice, which was formed in 1946 as successor to the Permanent Court of Arbitration. There is a visitors' centre but the building itself is open to the public only on a guided tour (check dates and book tickets via the website).

Galerij Prins Willem V

🏠 Buitenhof 33 🕐 Noon-5pm Tue-Sun 🕐 1 Jan, 25 Dec 🌐 mauritshuis.nl

In his youth, Prince William V was a collector of 17th-century paintings. His collection was opened to the public in 1774, inside this former inn, which the prince had converted for use as his *kabinet* – the 18th-century Dutch word for an art gallery. The Galerij is the oldest art gallery in the Netherlands. The 18th-century fashion for covering every available inch

↑ Visitors viewing art at Galerij Prins Willem V

Vredespaleis, home to the International Court of Justice ↓

↑ Mother and child admiring artworks in the Kunstmuseum Den Haag

of wall space with paintings has been retained, and so pictures are hung high and close together. Many of Prince William's original purchases are still to be seen. Old Master paintings by Rembrandt, Jan Steen and Paulus Potter (1625–54) are included in a collection that consists principally of typically Dutch 17th century landscapes, genre paintings, "conversation pieces" and recreations of important historical events.

⑬ 🎨 🖼 🖥 🛍

Kunstmuseum Den Haag

🏛 Stadhouderslaan 41
🕐 10am-5pm Tue-Sun
🚫 25 Dec 🌐 kunstmuseum. nl

This is one of the city's finest museums. The delightful building was the last work of H P Berlage, the father of the architectural movement known as the Amsterdam School *(p172)*. The museum was completed in 1935, a year after Berlage's death, and is built in sandy-coloured brick on two storeys around a central courtyard, with every room open to daylight.

The museum houses 160,000 pieces of art and the

world's largest collection of paintings by Piet Mondriaan. Its many exhibits are displayed in three sections. Highlights of the superb applied arts section include antique delftware, Islamic and Oriental porcelain.

Costumes and musical instruments dating from the 15th to the 19th centuries are too fragile to be put on permanent display, but selected items are regularly exhibited.

The "Wonder kamers" or "Wonder Rooms" are housed in the museum's basement,

which is a labyrinth of 13 thematic rooms featuring quirky displays, aimed especially at teenage visitors.

With as many as 35 temporary exhibitions each year and an extensive exhibition programme, the Kunstmuseum offers something for everyone – topics ranging from the role of the colour black in the history of fashion to Picasso's Cubist sculptures have all had their place in the museum's programme.

Be sure to get a ticket online before you go.

THE INTERNATIONAL COURT OF JUSTICE

Den Haag is known the world over for being home to the International Court of Justice - the highest court of the United Nations. The court's 15 judges are elected for nine-year terms by the UN General Assembly and Security Council, and are tasked with settling legal disputes between states, submitted by UN members. It's often confused with both the Court of Justice of the European Union, based in Luxembourg, and the European Court of Human Rights, in Strasbourg.

↑ The magnificent Mauritshuis building, reflected in the Hofvijver

⑭ ⬙ ⑯ ⑰ ⬚ ⬛

MAURITSHUIS

🏠 Plein 29, Den Haag 🚆 From Den Haag CS: 2, 3, 4, 6, 15; from Den Haag HS: 1 🚌 From Den Haag CS: 22; from Den Haag HS: 18 🕐 1-6pm Mon, 10am-6pm Tue-Sun (to 8pm Thu) 🚫 1 Jan, 25 Dec 🌐 mauritshuis.nl

One of the finest galleries in the Netherlands, the Mauritshuis justifies this claim with its Old Masters, exquisitely presented in period rooms with sparkling chandeliers and immense painted ceilings.

After he was recalled as captain general of Brazil, Johan Maurits of Nassau commissioned this graceful house. It was completed in 1644 by Pieter Post in the North Dutch Classical style with influences from the Italian Renaissance, and has a marvellous view of the Hofvijver. After the death of Maurits in 1679, the house passed to the State and, in 1822, became the home of the royal painting collection. Though the collection is not large, it is almost exclusively composed of superior works by Old Masters. An additional exhibition wing has been added to the museum, connected to the historic building by an underground foyer, which also houses a brasserie and shop.

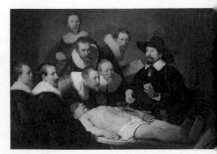

↑ Rembrandt's painting *The Anatomy Lesson of Dr Nicolaes Tulp* (1632)

TOP 5 PAINTINGS IN THE MAURITSHUIS

Girl with a Pearl Earring (1665-7)
At the mid-point of his career, Johannes Vermeer painted this haunting portrait.

The Anatomy Lesson of Dr Nicolaes Tulp (1632)
Rembrandt's painting of surgeons examining a corpse reflects the growing interest of the time in anatomy and science.

The Goldfinch (1654)
Tiny, delicate work of a European goldfinch by Carel Fabritius.

Hunting for Lice (c 1652-3)
Gerard ter Borch's scene of a mother grooming her child's hair.

Roses in a Glass Vase (c 1640-45)
Delicate still life by Jacob van Hulsdonck.

Girl with a Pearl Earring (1665), painted by Johannes Vermeer ↑

GALLERY GUIDE

Set over three floors, the arrangement of the paintings changes frequently in order to cover all aspects of the collection, so check the current display on the museum's website. All of the paintings are label-led with the artist, title and year.

↑ One of the beautiful galleries in the Mauritshuis, which is hung with fine paintings from top to bottom

SCHOOLSTRAAT

ST AGATHA PLEIN

OUDE DELFT

① ⑤

③

DELFT

🅰B4 🚗50 km (31 miles) SW of Amsterdam
🚉 ℹ️Kerkstraat 3; www.delft.com

The charming town of Delft is known the world over for its blue-and-white pottery, but it is equally celebrated as the resting place of William of Orange (1533–84) and as the birthplace of artist Jan Vermeer (1632–75).

Delft dates back to 1075, its prosperity based on the weaving and brewing industries. The town is renowned in Holland as being the resting place of William of Orange (1533–84), the "father of the Netherlands". William led the resistance against Spanish rule in the Eighty Years' War (p64) from his Delft headquarters; his victory meant religious freedom and independence for the Dutch.

Delft became the Republic's main arsenal, the site, in October 1654, of an enormous gunpowder explosion that destroyed much of the medieval town. The centre was rebuilt at the end of the 17th century and has remained relatively unchanged – houses in Gothic and Renaissance styles still stand along the tree-shaded canals. Town life is concentrated on the Markt, with the town hall at one end and the Nieuwe Kerk at the other.

Delft is world-famous for its blue-and-white pottery (p242). Visitors can dip into the scores of shops selling antique and modern hand-painted delftware or take a tour of local factories.

The Oude Delft is lined with canal-side houses in Renaissance style.

Chapel of St Hippolytus (1396)

Did You Know?

Vermeer's nickname is "The Sphinx of Delft" because so little is known of his life.

↑ Delft's pretty canal banks, perfect for people-watching with an alfresco coffee

THE ASSASSINATION OF WILLIAM OF ORANGE

In 1581, Philip II declared William of Orange *(p64)* an outlaw and offered a huge reward for his assassination. Balthasar Gérard, a fervent Catholic, masqueraded as a French nobleman and gained William's trust. On 10 July 1584, Gérard shot William at his headquarters in Delft, now the Museum Prinsenhof Delft. Projected silhouettes here re-enact the assassination, and the bullet holes can still be seen in the staircase wall.

← The centre of Delft, dominated by two iconic churches

CHOORSTRAAT

VROUWJUTTENLAND

HIPOLYT JSBUURT

PAPENSTRAAT

UEVLOUW

④

VOLDERSGRACHT

STR

③

KERK

CAMARETTEN

JWSTRAAT

MARKT

BOTER BRUG

OUDE LANGENDIJK

WIJNHAVEN

Stadhuis (1618)

Vleeshal (1650)

② *Royal Delft (1.6 km/1 mile)* ↓

PEPER STRAAT

💬 INSIDER TIP
Delftware

Instead of buying the famed hand-painted porcelain in the expensive boutiques in the centre of the town, head to a local factory. Their shops are often reasonably priced and you can take a tour.

The Oude Kerk's bell tower, seen from one of Delft's many canal bridges

①

Oude Kerk

🏠 Heilige Geestkerkhof 25 🕐 Apr-Oct: 9am-6pm Mon-Sat; Nov-Jan: 11am-4pm Mon-Fri, 10am-5pm Sat; Feb & Mar: 10am-5pm Mon-Sat 🌐 onkd.nl

Although a church has existed on this site since the 11th century, the original building has been added to many times. The ornate, but leaning, clock tower was built in the 14th century, and the Flamboyant Gothic north transept was added in the early 16th century. The interior is dominated by a carved wooden pulpit with an overhanging canopy. The floor is studded with 17th-century gravestones, many beautifully decorated. A simple stone tablet at the east end of the north aisle marks the burial place of Johannes Vermeer. In the north transept lies Admiral Maarten Tromp (1598–1653), who defeated the English fleet in 1652.

②

Royal Delft

🏠 Koninklijke Porceleyne Fles, Rotterdamseweg 196 🕐 Apr-Oct: 9am-5pm daily; Nov-Mar: 9am-5pm Mon-Sat, noon-5pm Sun 🔒 25 & 26 Dec, 1 Jan 🌐 royaldelft.com

There were once more than 30 delftware factories in this area. De Porceleyne Fles (established in 1653) is the only factory still producing the typical white pottery with delicate blue hand-painted decorations known as delftware. A visit includes a tour of the factory and the opportunity to watch the artists at work.

There is a small museum displaying pieces produced by the factory. Vermeer's dining room has been recreated, and the Royal Treasury shows the delftware especially designed for the Dutch royal family.

If you fancy trying your hand at creating your own decorative masterpiece, you can sign up for a workshop of earthenware painting with Delft blue paint. The lunchroom serves afternoon tea (advance booking required), allowing you the chance to sip tea and nibble petits fours from fine Delft blue crockery.

③

Nieuwe Kerk

🏠 Markt 🕐 Apr-Oct: 9am-6pm Mon-Sat; Nov-Jan: 11am-4pm Mon-Fri, 10am-5pm Sat; Feb & Mar: 10am-5pm Mon-Sat 🌐 onkd.nl

Standing in the market square opposite the city hall, the

DELFTWARE

Delftware stems from majolica, introduced to the Netherlands by 16th-century Italian immigrants who began producing tiles with Dutch designs, such as birds and flowers. By the next century, however, traders had started to deal in delicate Chinese porcelain, leading to the eventual collapse of the market for the less-refined Dutch earthenware. Towards 1650, though, the Chinese example was adopted and craftsmen designed plates, vases and bowls depicting landscapes, biblical tableaux and scenes of everyday life. De Koninklijke Porceleyne Fles (Royal Delft) – the last remaining earthenware factory from the 17th century – is open for tours *(www.royaldelft.com)*.

↑ A pair of souvenir Delftware porcelain clogs

→ Model of a galleon in the Museum Prinsenhof Delft

Nieuwe Kerk was built between 1383 and 1510, but much of the original structure was restored following a fire in 1536 and the explosion at the national arsenal in 1654. Work on the church continued for many years, and it was not until 1872 that P J H Cuypers *(p386)* added the statuesque 100-m (320-ft) tower to the Gothic façade. To climb the tower's 376 steps, buy a token from the church. The climb is quite strenuous but worth it for a great view across Delft and its surroundings. The tower also has a fine set of bells.

The burial vaults of the Oranje Nassau Dutch royal family are in the crypt of this empty, cavernous church, but the most prominent feature is the mausoleum of William of Orange *(p64)*. Originally a modest monument, it was replaced in 1623 by this richly decorated tomb, designed by Hendrick de Keyser. It is carved from striking black and white marble, with heavy gilded detailing. At its heart is a sculpture of William, seated and impressive in his battle dress, and at each corner stand bronze figures representing the Virtues. Close to William is his dog, who died a few days after his master, and at the foot of the tomb is a trumpeting angel – symbol of Fame.

④ ⑯ Ⓜ 💻 🎒

Vermeer Centrum Delft

🏛 Voldersgracht 21
🕐 10am–5pm daily
🖥 vermeerdelft.nl

Little is known about the life of Delft's most famous and enigmatic artist, Johannes Vermeer (1632–75). In a series of beautiful displays, the Vermeer Centrum uncovers some of the mysteries surrounding this man. Visitors are introduced to the artist and the city where he lived all his life. Life-size copies of all his paintings are on display, including *Girl with a Pearl Earring* (1665-7). On the upper floors, some of his painting techniques are explained, particularly his use of perspective, colour and light. Changing exhibitions focus on the symbolic messages in his paintings. Tours are conducted in English on Sundays.

⑤ ⑯ 💻 🎒

Museum Prinsenhof Delft

🏛 St Agathaplein 1
🕐 11am–5pm daily
🚫 1 Jan, 27 Apr, 25 Dec
🖥 prinsenhof-delft.nl

This tranquil Gothic building, formerly a convent, now houses Delft's history museum, but is better known as the place where William of Orange was assassinated. He requisitioned the convent in 1572 for his headquarters during the Dutch Revolt. In 1584, by order of Philip II of Spain, William was shot by Balthasar Gérard. The bullet holes in the main staircase wall can still be seen. The museum houses a rare collection of antique Delftware, displayed alongside fine tapestries, silverware, medieval sculpture and a series of portraits of the Dutch royal family. The museum café has a terrace in the lovely garden.

POTTERY AND TILES

When in 1620 exports of porcelain from China to Europe fell because of domestic troubles in China, Dutch potters seized the opportunity and started to produce their own wares, imitating the Chinese style on a large scale. The city of Delft became one of the prime centres for the production of this china, which reached the peak of its popularity between 1660 and 1725. The style later experienced a revival during the Art Nouveau and Art Deco periods, when Dutch potters such as Theo Colenbrander achieved international renown.

DELFTWARE

Although tin-glazed earthenware was also made in other parts of the Netherlands, "Delft" came to describe almost all earthenware made in the Netherlands during this period. Any piece made after 1650 will always have a workshop mark, and later works will include the glazer's initials, as well as a code denoting the year it was made and a serial number. The popularity of delftware has fluctuated throughout the centuries, but one shop that has managed to survive is De Koninklijke Porceleyne Fles, or Royal Delft, founded in 1653. The business was bought in 1876 and revived by Joost Thooft, whose initials can still be seen on the workshop's mark. The exquisite painting on the porcelain continues to be done by hand, although the rest of the manufacturing process no longer involves the craft's traditional methods.

Stylized flowers *reflect the Italian majolica tradition.*

The lily *often features as a corner motif on Dutch tiles.*

↑ An antique blue-and-white tile from the 17th century

← A display of Delft blue plates, featuring a mix of traditional and modern designs

↑ A skilled artist painting a vase at De Koninklijke Porceleyne Fles

Theo Colenbrander (1841–1930) was one of the biggest names in Art Nouveau pottery. Originally an architect, he became known for his fanciful floral-based designs for the Rozenburg earthenware and porcelain factory in The Hague, where he was chief designer from 1884 to 1889. As celebrated as his designs were, the ceramics had limited commercial success. One reason for this was their expense – a reflection of the labour-intensive production. In addition to pottery, he designed wallpaper and carpets, and also worked as a graphic and interior designer.

**EARTHENWARE BOWL
BY THEO COLENBRANDER**

TILES

Majolica wall tiles – decorated earthenware on a tin-glazed background – were made for the first time in the Netherlands during the 16th century, with production reaching its peak in the 17th century. Until 1625, polychrome decoration predominated, after which the majority of tiles were painted in blue on white. Major centres were Makkum – where in the 17th century the Tichelaar family firm, which operates to this day, was established – as well as Harlingen, Delft, Gouda, Amsterdam, Utrecht and Haarlem.

4

ROTTERDAM

🄰 C5 🄰 65 km (40 miles) SW of Amsterdam ✈ 6 km
(4 miles) NW 🚇 Stationsplein 🚌 🄵 Rotterdam Centraal
station and Coolsingel 114; www.rotterdam.info

Rotterdam's ancient heart was ravaged during World
War II, due to its large port. Much of the city has been
rebuilt in experimental styles, resulting in some of
Europe's most original and innovative architecture.

① 🤿 🎠 🖥 🏛

Maritiem Museum Rotterdam

🄰 Leuvehaven 1 🕙 10am–
5pm Tue–Sat (Jul–Aug: also
11am–5pm Sun & Mon)
🚫 Public hols 🖥 maritiem
museum.nl

Rotterdam occupies a
strategic maritime position.

The city sits where the Rijn
(Rhine), Europe's most
important river, meets the
North Sea and, as a result,
has always been a centre for
trade. Today, barges from
Rotterdam transport goods
deep into the continent, and
ocean-going ships carry
European exports around the
world. Rotterdam is therefore
a fitting city for a museum

dedicated to the historic
seafaring prowess of
the Netherlands.

Prince Hendrik, brother of
King William III, founded this
museum in 1873. Highlights
include the oldest model ship
in Europe, a miniature version
of one of Columbus's cargo
ships. Also worth a visit is the
museum harbour, where you
can explore artfully restored
barges and steamships.

Children will love the interactive Professor Splash area
where they can play games
while learning about ships and
what it's like to work in a port.

←

Historic boats in the
Maritiem Museum
Rotterdam harbour

← The striking tilting yellow cubes of the Kubuswoningen

③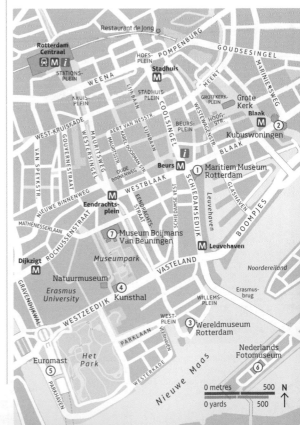

Wereldmuseum Rotterdam

🏠 Willemskade 25 🕙 10am–5pm Tue–Sun 🚫 Public hols 🌐 wereldmuseum.nl

During the 17th century, the city fathers amassed a superb ethnological collection. The Wereldmuseum displays 1,800 artifacts from Indonesia, the Americas and Asia, and presents audiovisual displays of theatre, film, dance and music. The museum reflects 127 of the 170 different nationalities represented in Rotterdam. After exploring the collection, you can take a break in the café, which offers river views.

②

Kubuswoningen

🏠 Overblaak 70 🕙 10am–6pm daily 🌐 kubuswoning.nl

Much of Oudehaven, the old harbour area of Rotterdam, was bombed in World War II and it has largely been rebuilt in daring and avant garde styles. The pencil-shaped apartment block, Blaaktoren, and the adjacent "cube houses", Kubuswoningen, were designed by architect Piet Blom (1934–99), and built in 1982–4. The Structuralist buildings were designed to integrate with their surroundings, but also to encourage social interaction among its occupants.

The Kubuswoningen are extraordinary apartments, set on concrete stilts and tilted at a crazy angle. Each cube contains three floors. The lowest floor creates a triangular living space, with its windows looking down on the street, while the second floor houses the bedrooms and has sky-facing windows. The top floor forms a three-sided pyramid, with 18 windows and 3 hatches, offering amazing views. Residents have specially designed furniture to fit the sloping rooms.

EUROPOORT HARBOUR CRUISES

The Europoort, which is the area on the south side of Rotterdam's harbour, stretches along the Rijn between the city and the North Sea. A cruise around this bustling part of the harbour is a rare opportunity to see some of the world's largest ships up close. Visitors who prefer to stay on dry land can see some of these steel behemoths loading and unloading right in the city centre at Spido (*www.spido.nl*), where wharves and quays service around 32,000 container ships yearly.

④ 🏛 🍴 🛍

Kunsthal

📍 Westzeedijk 341, Museumpark 🕐 10am-5pm Tue-Sat, 11am-5pm Sun 🚫 Mon, 1 Jan, 27 Apr, 25 Dec 🌐 kunsthal.nl

From costume and art to inventions and photography, the Kunsthal delivers exciting exhibitions that alternate between traditional "high art" and pop culture. There is no permanent collection. The eye-catching building was designed in 1998 by Rotterdam's Rem Koolhaas, whose other works include the Beijing headquarters for China Central Television. His innovative use of materials such as corrugated plastic and an orange steel girder that sticks out over the edge of the roof draw attention.

EUROMAST ABSEILING

From May to September, adventurous visitors to Rotterdam can abseil down the Euromast. The 100-m (328-ft) descent from the viewing platform takes around 15 minutes. Adrenaline junkies are accompanied by an instructor and must be over 16. The €55 ticket includes admission to the Euromast. See www.abseilen.nl for details.

⑤ 🏛 🍴 🛍

Euromast

📍 Parkhaven 20 🕐 Apr-Sep: 9:30am-10pm daily; Oct-Mar: 10am-10pm daily 🌐 euromast.nl

This futuristic structure, one of the most famous in Rotterdam, enjoys sweeping views of the city. At a height of 100 m (328 ft), the lower section, which was built in 1960, has a viewing platform with a restaurant. A high-speed lift zooms up to the top in minutes. In 1970, the Space Tower added another 85 m (279 ft) to the structure to make this the tallest structure in the Netherlands. An exterior "space cabin" ascends a further dizzying 58 m (190 ft) from the viewing platform.

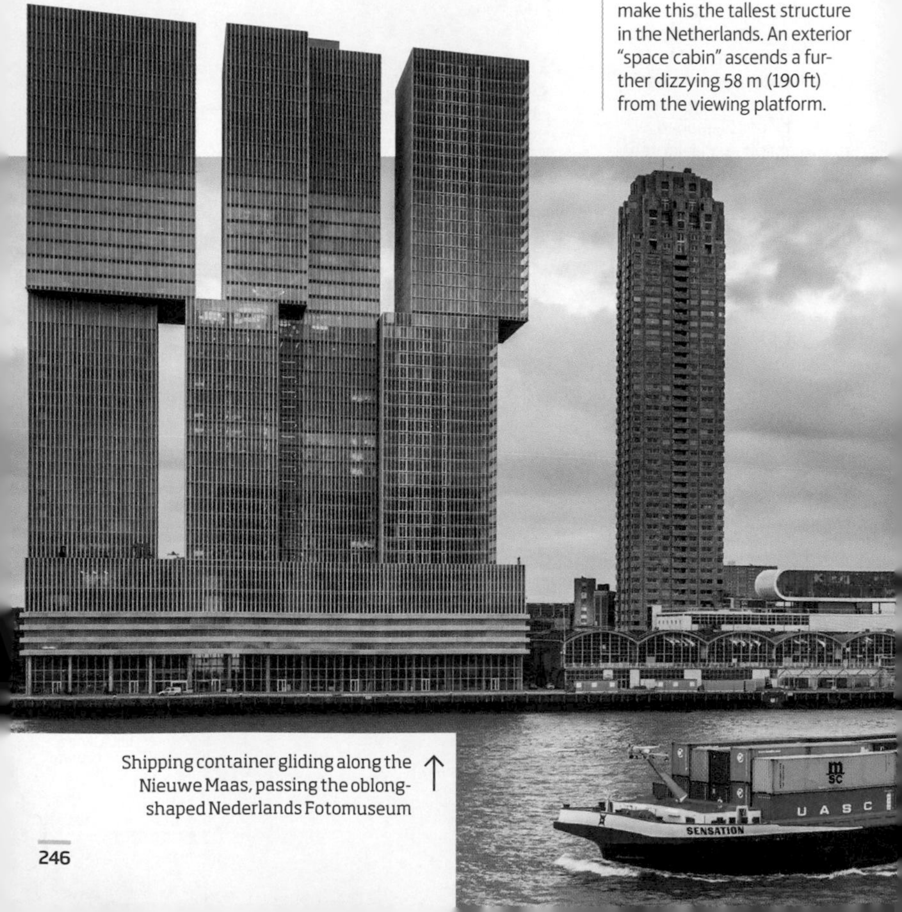

Shipping container gliding along the ↑ Nieuwe Maas, passing the oblong-shaped Nederlands Fotomuseum

⑥ Nederlands Fotomuseum

🏛 Gebouw Las Palmas, Wilhelminakade 332
🕐 11am–5pm Tue–Sun
🚫 1 Jan, 27 Apr, 25 Dec
🌐 nederlandsfoto museum.nl

In the heart of Rotterdam's former industrial area, the restored warehouse Las Palmas, once the workshop of the Holland America transatlantic shipping line, now houses the Dutch Photography Museum. This is an impressive archive dedicated to amassing and conserving the heritage of images created by Dutch photographers. Fascinating and ever-changing exhibitions showcase treasures from the archives alongside works by foreign photographers, comparing and contrasting the examples. The large gallery space is very open. Prints and a good selection of books are available at the museum shop.

⑦ Museum Boijmans Van Beuningen

🏛 Museumpark 18–20
🕐 Currently closed for renovation 🌐 boijmans.nl

The museum is named after two art connoisseurs – F J O Boijmans, who bequeathed his paintings to Rotterdam in 1847, and D G van Beuningen, whose heirs donated his collection to the State in 1958. The resulting collection is one of the Netherlands' finest, known for its Old Masters but covering the whole spectrum of art, including the medieval works of Jan van Eyck, rare glassware, Surrealist paintings and contemporary art. While the museum is closed for renovation, parts of the collection will be shown around the city (check the website for details), and from 2021 onwards they will appear in the new open-access art storage facility, the Boijmans Van Beuningen Depot, also in the Museumpark.

TOP 5 EXHIBITS IN BOIJMANS VAN BEUNINGEN

Tower of Babel (c 1556)
Pieter Bruegel depicts the building of the Old Testament skyscraper.

The Pedlar (c 1502)
Bosch's painting is an allegory of human temptation.

Titus at his Desk (1655)
Rembrandt's portrayal of his frail son.

Three Marys at the Tomb (c 1425–35)
Biblical scene by Jan and Hubertus van Eyck.

Projet pour la toile "Premier Amour" (1952)
Man Ray's jagged geometric abstract painting.

Did You Know?
Covering 105 sq km (41 sq miles), Rotterdam is the biggest port in Europe.

A SHORT WALK
ROTTERDAM

Distance 1.5 km (1 mile) **Nearest metro**
Churchillplein **Time** 25 minutes

This route takes you through the area to
the south of the town centre, which was
devastated by heavy bombing in May 1940.
On your way you will see the Witte Huis
(White House), one of the few buildings spared
by the bombs. Further on you will pass
unusual modern architecture, such as the
cube-shaped apartments Het Potlood ("the
pencil"), and the maritime museum, devoted
to the history of shipping. In front of this
museum is a monument by Ossip Zadkine,
which is one of the symbols of Rotterdam.
The undeveloped area around Blaak station
was completely built up before the bombing.

The Schielandhuis, *built
between 1662 and 1665, is one
of the few surviving buildings
from the 17th century.*

De Verwoeste Stad (The
Devastated City) *is a statue by Ossip
Zadkine in front of the maritime
museum (p244). It commemorates
the bombing of May 1940.*

START

The old armoured vessel
De Buffel, *now open to
visitors, was for many
years a training ship.*

B L A A K

G L A S H A V E N

B O O M P J E S

FINISH

↑ *The Devastated City,* one of
Rotterdam's finest sculptures

← Commuters outside the striking Blaak metro and railway station

The **Blaak metro and railway station** *has a futuristic canopy designed by architect H C H Reijnders.*

Het Potlood *("the pencil"), an unusually shaped apartment block near Blaak station, was designed by Piet Blom.*

Kubuswoningen, *a bizarre creation (1978–84) by architect Piet Blom, are cube-shaped apartments, among the city's most striking modern buildings (p245).*

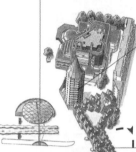

The **Witte Huis** *(White House) is one of the few buildings to have survived the World War II raids. For a long time, it was one of the tallest office blocks in Europe.*

Willemswerf *is one of Rotterdam's highest and most impressive office blocks. The 1989 building, which is completely white, is a design by architect W G Quist.*

VERLENGDE WILLEMSBRUG

0 metres 100
0 yards 100

N

5

GOUDA

📍 C4 **🏛 South Holland** **🚻** **ℹ Markt 35; www.welcometogouda.com**

Granted its city charter by Floris V in 1272, pretty, canal-crossed Gouda is most famous for its cheese market, where the eponymous cheeses, made in the surrounding area, are still traded in the traditional way.

Thanks to its strategic position on the Hollandse IJssel and the Gouwe river, by the 15th century Gouda had developed into a flourishing centre for beer brewing and the textile industry. However, Gouda became economically and politically isolated during the Thirty Years' War. The town recovered in the 17th and beginning of the 18th century due to its trade in cheese, candles and pipes.

From April to August, its Thursday morning cheese market is held on an enormous three-sided square around the Stadhuis, which dates from 1450 and is one of the oldest in the Netherlands. The Museum Gouda (municipal museum) is in the former Catharina Gasthuis (St Catherine's hospital), which dates from the 14th century and later. The museum features Hague School paintings and unusual 16th-century altarpieces. If you're not visiting in market season, the former cheese weighhouse, the Waag, is now a Gouda cheese museum, where you can taste and buy year round.

↑ City canals linked to the Gouwe, enabling the trade in cheese and other goods

Did You Know?

Gouda's Gothic St Janskerk church, famed for its stained glass, is the longest in the Netherlands.

THE WINDOWS OF ST JANSKERK

This church is noted for its magnificent stained-glass windows, the gift, originally, of its rich Catholic benefactors and then, after the Reformation (*p64*), of wealthy Protestant patrons. They are unusual in that their subject matter - and even their treatment of Biblical themes - reveals much about the politics and events of the time, in particular the Thirty Years' War. A tour is recommended.

↓ Cheese wheels for sale in front of the turreted, Flemish-Gothic Stadhuis

↑ A family enjoy a bike ride along Kinderdijk's windmill-lined canal

EXPERIENCE MORE

6 (P)

Kinderdijk

🅰 C5 🚌 90 from Rotterdam Lombardijen station; 18 from Dordrecht Centraal Station 🛈 Nederwaard 1; www.kinderdijk.nl

The famous 19 windmills which were used to drain the Alblasserwaard in the past are situated where the Noord and the Lek converge. New *boezems* (drainage pools) and windmills were needed time and time again as the land settled. The group of windmills is a UNESCO World Heritage Site.

7

Middelharnis

🅰 B5 🚌 436 from Rotterdam Zuidplein

During the 16th century, Middelharnis became the regional port, and until the end of the 19th century, fishing remained the most important source of income.

The Late Gothic cruciform church (15th century) stands at the heart of the village. Outside the town hall (1639) hang wooden blocks that women branded as gossips had to carry through the town as punishment.

8

Goedereede

🅰 B5 🚇 Metro R'dam CS to Spijkenisse, then 111 to Hellevoetsluis, then 104

Goedereede was an important port in the 14th and 15th centuries until it began to silt up. The early harbour houses are reminiscent of the livelier days of old.

9

Hellevoetsluis

🅰 B5 🚇 Metro Rotterdam CS to Spijkenisse, then 101 🛈 Industriehaven 8; 0181-314479

At the end of the 16th century, this was a naval port for the States of Holland. Within the old fortifications are the Prinsehuis, the 17th-century lodgings of the Admiralty of the Maze, the dry dock and Fort Haerlem. The **National Brandweermuseum** (Fire Service Museum) also houses the tourist information office.

Nationaal Brandweermuseum
🔄 🅐 Industriehaven 8 🕐 Apr-Oct: 10am-4pm Wed-Sun 🔲 nationaal brandweermuseum.nl

7 million

The number of flower bulbs currently planted in the gardens at Keukenhof.

⑩ Keukenhof

🅐C4 🚌854 (from Leiden Centraal Station), 858 (from Schiphol airport) 🕐Late Mar-mid-May: 8am-7:30pm daily 🌐keukenhof.nl

A wooded park spanning 32 ha (79 acres) and located close to Lisse, the Keukenhof is one of the most spectacular public gardens in the world. It was set up in 1949 as a show-case for bulb growers and currently has around 7 million bulbs planted in it. Dazzling narcissi, tulips and hyacinths bloom from the end of March to the end of May.

⑪ Lisse

🅐C4 🚌50 (from Leiden and Haarlem) 🛈Heereweg 219; www.vvvlisse.nl

Visit the town of Lisse at the end of April for the **Bloemen Corso** (flower parade, p60), a vibrant procession of floats that travels from Noordwijk to Haarlem, where they are illuminated at night.

The **Museum De Zwarte Tulp** (Black Tulip Museum) covers the history of bulb growing, illustrates the life cycle of bulbs and touches upon "tulipmania" in 1620–37 (p125), when rare tulip bulbs became worth their weight in gold.

Just outside Lisse is **Huys Dever**, a fortified residential tower which dates from the second half of the 14th century. It now houses a a small archeological museum.

Bloemen Corso

🌐bloemencorso bollenstreek.nl

Museum De Zwarte Tulp

⊛⊜ 🏠Heereweg 219 🕐10am-5pm Tue-Sun 🚫Public hols 🌐museumdezwartetulp.nl

Huys Dever

⊛ 🏠Heereweg 349a 🕐2-5pm Wed-Sun 🚫Public hols 🌐kasteeldever.nl

⑫ Scheveningen

🅐B4 🚋1 🚌22 🛈Spui 68, Den Haag; 070-361 8860

Previously a spa town, this pleasant seaside resort is just 15 minutes by tram from the centre of Den Haag. It had its heyday in the 19th century and is now a curious mixture

Colourful carpets of tulips adorn the Keukenhof gardens ↑

of faded charm and modern garishness, though it remains a popular holiday resort.

At **Sea Life Scheveningen** you can look through transparent tunnels at stingrays, sharks and other sea creatures. **Muzee Scheveningen** is devoted to the history of the village and the spa. Tours of Scheveningen lighthouse can also be booked. Designed by Wim Quist, **Museum Beelden aan Zee** (Seaside Sculpture Museum) displays an array of contemporary sculptures on the theme of the human figure.

Although the seaside resort has all but swallowed up the original fishing village, there is still a harbour and a large fish market. Fishing boat trips can be booked on the southern side of the harbour.

Sea Life Scheveningen
♻🚌 🚪 Strandweg 13 🕐 Apr–Jun & Sep–Oct: 10am–7pm daily; Jul & Aug: 10am–8pm daily; Nov–Mar: 10am–6pm daily 🗓 25 Dec 🌐 visitsealife.com

Muzee Scheveningen
♻🚌🚶 🚪 Neptunusstraat 90–92 🕐 10am–5pm Tue–Sat, noon–5pm Sun 🗓 1 Jan, 27 Apr, 25 Dec 🌐 muzee scheveningen.nl

Museum Beelden aan Zee
♻🚌🚶 🚪 Harteveltstraat 1

↑ Aerial view of the pleasure pier in the seaside town of Scheveningen, Den Haag

🕐 10am–5pm Tue–Sun 🗓 1 Jan, 27 Apr, 25 Dec 🌐 beeldenaanzee.nl

---

13
Schiedam
🅰C5 🚪 ℹ Lange Kerkstraat 39; www.sdam.nl

Schiedam was granted its city charter in 1275 and soon afterwards expanded into a centre for trade and fishing. It became the centre of the *jenever* (Dutch gin) industry. Its production is still important to the town, as evidenced by the five tallest windmills in the world and the old warehouses and distilleries. In the bar of the **Jenever Museum**, you can familiarize yourself with the enormous range of Dutch *jenevers* and liqueurs.

The **Stedelijk Museum** (Municipal Museum), with exhibits of contemporary art and on modern history, is in the former St-Jacobs Gasthuis. Its main attraction is the collection of artwork by the group known as CoBrA (consisting of painters from Copenhagen, Brussels and Amsterdam).

Stedelijk Museum
♻🚶 🚪 Hoogstraat 112 ☎ 010-246 3666 🕐 11am–5pm Tue–Sun 🗓 1 Jan, 25 Dec

Jenever Museum
🚪 Lange Haven 74 🕐 11am–5pm Tue–Sun & public hols 🗓 1 Jan, 27 Apr, 25 & 26 Dec 🌐 jenevermuseum.nl

---

14
Maassluis
🅰B4 🚪 ℹ Heldringstraat 101; www.ervaar maassluis.nl

The settlement of Maassluis grew up around the locks, which date from 1367; the herring trade brought prosperity to the town. The historic town centre is adorned with 17th-century buildings, such as the Grote Kerk, with its famous organ, and the Stadhuis.

15
Reeuwijkse Plassen
🅰C4 ℹ 0182-589110

The picturesque Reeuwijk lake district was formed through peat excavation. Narrow roads pass through the rectangular lakes, which owe their shape to former parcels of land. The best way to explore this area is by bicycle, on foot or, in the summer, on a boat trip through this typically Dutch lakeland scenery.

⑯ Gorinchem

🅰C5 🚊 ℹ️ Groenmarkt 8;
www.mooigorinchem.nl

Gorinchem, situated on the Linge and the Waal, was the property of the Lords van Arkel in the 13th century. They were driven out by Count William VI and the town was then absorbed into Holland. Fortifications built at the end of the 16th century are still partially intact and offer marvellous views over the water meadows and the Waal. Of the four town gateways, only the Dalempoort remains. The Linge harbour, in the heart of the town, is still mostly authentic, especially the narrow part.

On the other side of the Waal is the 14th-century **Slot Loevestein**. It has a very eventful history as a toll castle, a defence point along the Hollandse Waterlinie (a strip of land flooded as a defence line, (*p218*) and a state prison in the 17th century. Today it houses a medieval and archaeological museum. From Gorinchem, the castle can be reached by ferry, changing at Woudrichem.

Slot Loevestein

🦿🦿🦿🦿🦿 🚗 Poederoijen
🚌 May, Jun & Sep: Tue–Sun; Jul & Aug: daily; Oct–Apr: weekends ⏰ May, Jun & Sep: 11am–5pm Tue–Sun; Jul & Aug: 11am–5pm daily; Oct–Apr: 11am–5pm Sat & Sun 🔒1 Jan, Good Friday, 27 Apr, 25 Dec 🌐 slotloevestein.nl

---

→

The pretty streets of the port town of Brielle in the summer

EAT

De Vitamine Kantine
Freshly squeezed fruit and vegetable juices, smoothies, salads and sandwiches are eaten guilt-free here.

🅰C5 🏠 Langendijk 38, Gorinchem 🔒 Sun
🌐 devitaminekantine.nl

€€€

Restaurant 't Veerhuys
Choose from more than 140 different sweet and savoury *pannekoeken* (Dutch pancakes).

🅰D5 🏠 Kerkstraat 93, Leerdam 🔒 Mon
🌐 veerhuys.com

€€€

Villa Augustus
This large, airy restaurant inside a former pump house is surrounded by gardens that supply ingredients for the menu.

🅰C5 🏠 Oranjelaan 7, Dordrecht 🌐 villa-augustus.nl

€€€

---

⑰ Nieuwpoort

🅰C4 🚌 90 from Utrecht

The whole of this magnificent fortified town, which obtained its city charter in 1283, has been declared a listed area. The 17th-century street layout is practically intact. The Nieuwpoort city walls, which are also intact, were originally built to ward off attacks from the French but served mainly to protect the town against flooding. The stunning monument that is the former town hall, built over the inundation lock, dates from 1696, while the arsenal dates from 1781.

⑱ Leerdam

🅰D5 🚊 ℹ️ Kerkstraat 55;
www.leerdamglasstad.nl

Leerdam is renowned for its glass industry. Royal Dutch Glass Factory designs by Berlage, Copier and other artists can be admired in the **Nationaal Glasmuseum** (National Glass Museum), and traditional crystal production can be observed at Royal Leerdam Kristal. Fort Asperen, on the Linge, is one of the best-preserved defence points remaining along the Nieuwe Hollandse Waterlinie (*p218*).

Nationaal Glasmuseum

🦿🏠 🏠 Lingedijk 28-30
⏰ 10am–5pm Tue–Sat, noon–5pm Sun 🌐 nationaal-glasmuseum.nl

---

⑲ Brielle

🅰B5 🚇 Metro Rotterdam CS to Spijkenisse, then 103
ℹ️ Markt 1; 0181-475475

The magnificent port of Brielle is a protected town. The 18th-century fortifications

THE BEGGARS OF THE SEA

The Beggars of the Sea were a pirate fleet of minor Dutch and Flemish nobles who had fled at the beginning of the Inquisition. They plundered other ships and caused trouble in English and German ports. They were forced to leave England in 1572. With no clear plan, they entered the town of Brielle, which they held "for the Prince". Other towns joined the Beggars of the Sea or were forcibly occupied by them. Their pursuits represented the first steps towards Dutch independence from Spain and the creation of Dutch sea power.

are still mostly intact. The town, birthplace of Admiral van Tromp, held a strategic position until the 1872 opening of the Nieuwe Waterweg (new waterway). The **Historisch Museum Den Briel** (Brielle History Museum) depicts this and the famous Beggars of the Sea invasion in 1572. The tourist information office is inside the museum. The 15th-century St-Catharijnekerk, in Brabant Gothic style, rises from the surrounding buildings.

Historisch Museum Den Briel

⊛ ⓐ ⬛ Markt 1 ⏰ 10am–5pm Tue–Sat, 1–5pm Sun 🔒 Public hols 🌐 historischmuseum denbriel.nl

---

⑳ Dordrecht

🄰 C5 🚉 ℹ️ Spuiboulevard 99; www.vvvdordrecht.nl

The oldest town in Holland, Dordrecht received its city charter in 1220 and was the most important harbour and commercial town of the region until the 1500s. Even after being outstripped

by Rotterdam, Dordrecht remained an important inland port. In the city's old port area, mansions, warehouses and almshouses are reminders of its long and rich history.

The **Grote Kerk** (13th to 17th century), in the Brabant Gothic style, has an ornate interior and is located in the central market square. Huis Simon van Gijn, in an 18th-century house with period rooms, has a collection of old prints, clothes and toys. The shady **Hof** (Court of Justice), built in 1512, contains the **Statenzaal** (State Room). This is where the States of Holland met for the first time in 1572,

thus laying the foundation of the independent Republic of the Netherlands.

Grote Kerk

⊛ ⓐ ⬛ Lange Geldersekade 2 ⏰ Apr–Oct: 10:30am–4:30pm Tue–Sat, 10–4pm Sun; Nov & Dec: 2–4pm Tue, Thu & Sat 🌐 grotekerk-dordrecht.nl

Hof and Statenzaal

⊛ ⓐ ⬛ Hof 6 ⏰ 11am–5pm Tue–Sun 🔒 25 Dec, 1 Jan 🌐 hethofvannederland.nl

↑ Huis Simon van Gijn, the 18th-century house-turned-museum of a wealthy trader

ZEELAND

Tucked away in the southwest corner of the country, watery Zeeland comprises a lattice of islands and peninsulas within the massive delta of the Rhine, Maas and Schelde rivers. Relatively remote, the region was always a bit player in the history of the Netherlands, passed between rival Dutch and German counts in the medieval period before joining the revolt against the Habsburgs in the 16th century and eventually becoming part of the Verenigde Nederlanden (United Provinces).

Given that the land is low and flat – and often below sea level – it is no surprise that from the earliest recorded times, storms and floods have taken their toll on the region. Although Zeeland has a number of fine churches and public buildings dating as far back as the 14th century, there are very few houses more than 50 years old in coastal areas. As a result, the region has always had a great determination to keep the waters at bay, with land reclamation schemes, canals and dams gradually changing the landscape forever. During World War II, Zeeland's vulnerability was cruelly demonstrated when both the Allies and the Germans deliberately flooded parts of the region for tactical reasons. However, this was almost insignificant compared to the catastrophic North Sea flood of 1953, when 1,836 people died, 47,000 houses were destroyed and agricultural land was ruined by salt water and tonnes of sand. The government's response was immediate: the launch of the Delta Project, an extraordinarily complex scheme of dams, sluices, locks, dykes and storm surge barriers that was only completed in the 1990s. With climate change concerns growing, the Zeeland government adopted an action plan in 2019 for the formulation of adaptation strategies to mitigate the negative impact of rising sea levels on the region, its economy and its people.

ZEELAND

Must Sees
1. Oosterscheldekering
2. Middelburg

Experience More
3. Domburg
4. Goes
5. Yerseke
6. Veere
7. Vlissingen
8. Westkapelle
9. Zierikzee
10. Haamstede
11. Cadzand
12. Terneuzen
13. Brouwershaven
14. Hulst
15. Tholen
16. Sluis
17. Bruinisse
18. St Annaland
19. St Maartensdijk
20. Nisse

Strype

N57

Goeree

Goedereede

N57

ZEELAND

N215

Middelharnis

Renesse

BROUWERSHAVEN

N57

13

SOUTH
HOLLAND
p222

N59

Serooskerke

10

HAAMSTEDE

*Schouwen-
Duiveland*

Dreischor

Oude-Tonge

N59

N59

ZIERIKZEE **9**

Nieuwekerk

BRUINISSE **17**

N257

Ouwerkerk

St Philipsland

Dinteloord

Colijnsplaat

N256

ST ANNALAND **18**

Stavenisse

Steenbergen

*Noord-
Beveland*

Oosterschelde

Tholen

Oud-Vossemeer

N286

N656

Kortgene

19 ST MAARTENSDIJK

Wolphaartsdijk

Wemeldinge

THOLEN **15**

NORTH
BRABANT
p358

N256

4 GOES

5 YERSEKE

Lewedorp

Kapelle

Bergen
op Zoom

A4

Zuid-Beveland

20 NISSE

Kruiningen

N659

N62

Z E E L A N D

Krabbendijke

Hoogerheide

Hoedekenskerke

A58

Ellewoutsdijk

Westerschelde

Ossendrecht

Kloosterzande

E34

N689

12 TERNEUZEN

Vlaanderen

Hoek

N62

Zaamslag

N290

Nieuw-Namen

R2

Philippine

Sluiskil

N290

Axel

14 HULST

Boekhoute

N258

Verrebroek

B E L G I U M

N62

Zelzate

E34

Stekene

Kemzeke

Vrasene

Zwijndrecht

N70

OOSTERSCHELDE-KERING

A5 ⬛ Deltapark Neeltje Jans, Faelweg 5, Vrouwenpolder 🚌133 ⏰Apr-Oct: 10am-5:30pm daily; Nov-Mar: 10am-5pm Wed, Sat & Sun 🌐neeltjejans.nl

The mighty storm surge barrier that protects the estuary environment of Oosterschelde National Park and its agricultural hinterland is a remarkable feat of engineering, testament to the ingenuity of the Dutch in protecting their land.

After the disastrous floods of 1953, which hit Zeeland heavily, the battle to remove the danger of the sea once and for all was on. It took 13 years and €3.6 billion (two-thirds of the cost of the entire Delta Works plan for this stretch of coast) to build the Oosterscheldekering storm surge barrier. After much deliberation, the decision was made to keep open the estuary and to preserve the salty estuary habitat. A half-open multiple buttress dam was built, with 62 sliding gates, which are closed on average once a year during heavy storms. This keeps the water salty and has preserved the unique salt marshes and mud flats of the Oosterschelde. An artificial island, Neeltje Jans, was created, on which the piers for the barrier were assembled before being taken by special barges to their positions. Now the task is finished, the Deltapark educational and recreational centre occupies the island; from here you can visit the barrier from the inside, take a boat trip to view it from the outside, and join a guided tour of the surrounding dune landscape.

> **INSIDER TIP**
> **Family Fun**
>
> Don't leave the kids behind on a trip to the storm surge barrier. The Deltapark Neeltje Jans has lots of family attractions, including a water splash park, an aquarium, feeding time for the seals and sea lions and, thrillingly, a hurricane machine in which you can experience nature's raw power.

The Oosterscheldekering storm surge barrier, its operation powered by wind turbines ↑

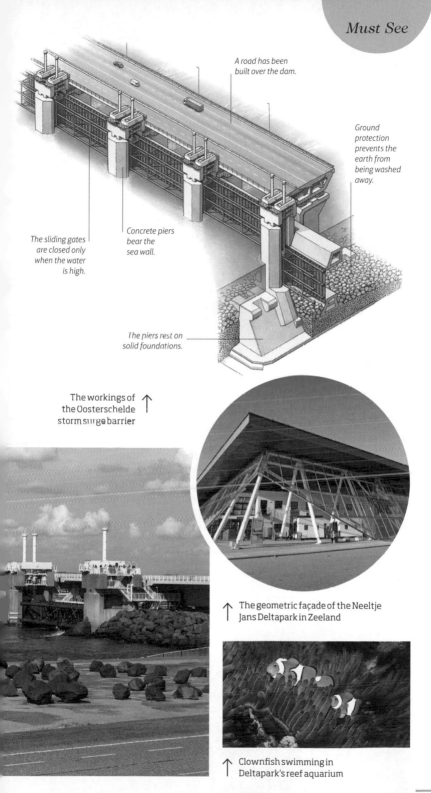

A road has been built over the dam.

Ground protection prevents the earth from being washed away.

The sliding gates are closed only when the water is high.

Concrete piers bear the sea wall.

The piers rest on solid foundations.

The workings of ↑ the Oosterschelde storm surge barrier

↑ The geometric façade of the Neeltje Jans Deltapark in Zeeland

↑ Clownfish swimming in Deltapark's reef aquarium

The Lange Jan tower, capped with a golden "crown", presiding over Middelburg ↑

Zeeuws Archief, the archives of the province, are housed in the historic Van de Perre House on the Hofplein.

②

MIDDELBURG

⚠ A5 🏠 200 km (124 miles) SW of Amsterdam 🚆🚌
ℹ Markt 51; www.uitinmiddelburg.nl

Even with the reconstruction necessitated by bombing in 1940, Middelburg remains a beautiful old-world town redolent of the 17th century, when the Dutch East India Company flourished in the port area along the quay.

Nowhere are the rewards of years of careful rebuilding more evident than at Middelburg Abbey, a magnificent complex that dominates the historic centre. At Nos 3–4 Abdij, the old monks' quarters house the Zeeuws Museum, where eclectic displays such as the Chamber of Wonders and a costume collection are imaginatively presented. The entire old town area is perfect for strolling, with lots to discover. Outside the centre, families – especially with younger children – should head for Minimundi, a fun little amusement park with a model village and plenty of gentle rides.

HOFPLEIN WAGENAARSTRAAT

LANGE NOORDSTRAAT

The 15th-century Stadhuis (town hall) has been restored.

← Narrow cobbled street winding through Middelburg's historic centre

Cafés in the lively market square, overlooked by the Late Gothic Stadhuis ↓

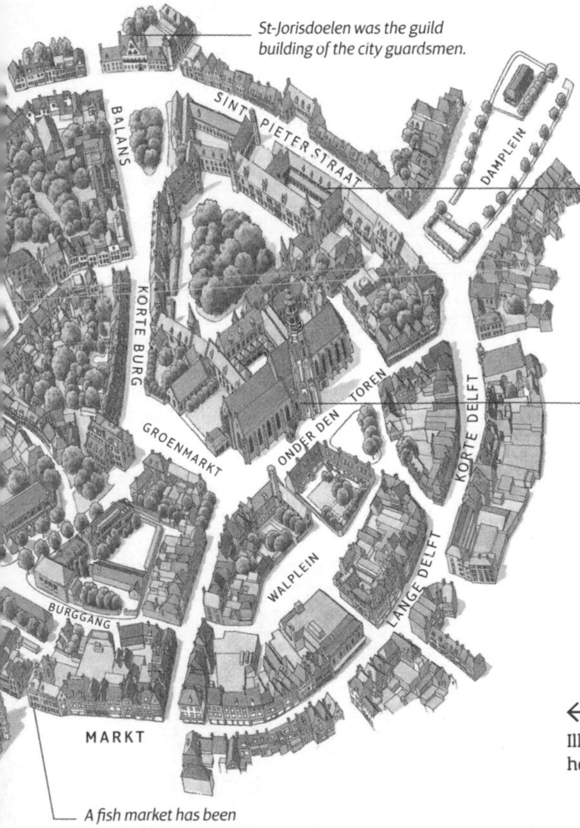

St-Jorisdoelen was the guild building of the city guardsmen.

BALANS

SINT-PIETER-STRAAT

DAMPLEIN

The Abbey dates from 1100, when it was inhabited by Norbertine monks from Antwerp.

KORTE BURG

ONDER DEN TOREN

KORTE DELFT

Lange Jan – "Long John" – is the 91-m (300-ft) tower of the Nieuwe Kerk in the abbey complex. Climb the 200 steps to the top for stunning views.

GROENMARKT

WALPLEIN

LANGE DELFT

BURGGANG

← Illustration of the historic heart of Middelburg

MARKT

A fish market has been recorded here since 1559.

EXPERIENCE MORE

❸ Domburg

🏔A5 🚌 ℹ️ **Schuitvlotstraat 32; www.vvvzeeland.nl**

Domburg was one of the first seaside resorts in the Netherlands. In the 19th century, this little town on the northwest coast of Walcheren was popular among prominent Europeans, who came here to relax and recuperate in the chic seaside hotels on the dunes. Today it is a popular holiday destination, receiving thousands of visitors each year.

To the west of the town are the pretty nature reserve of De Manteling, popular with hikers and cyclists, and the site of Westhove castle, which was the Abbot of Middelburg's country house until the 16th century. The castle now houses a youth hostel, and within its former orangery is **Terra Maris**, Zeeland's natural landscape museum.

Terra Maris

♿🚻🛍 🏠 Duinvlietweg 6
🕐 May-Oct: 10am-5pm daily; Nov-Apr: noon-4pm Wed-Sat, 11am-5pm Sun 🌐 terra maris.nl

❹ Goes

🏔B5 🚌 🚉 ℹ️ **Singelstraat 13; 0113-235990**

Some of the historical towns of Zeeland are charming yet sleepy, but Goes is wide awake. Every Tuesday there is an old-fashioned market featuring fabrics and groceries which takes place on the Grote Markt, a square full of Zeeland atmosphere. There is a Saturday market in the square too, with the emphasis on fish, cheese and other fresh produce. The Raadhuis (town hall), dating from 1463 (but rebuilt between 1771 and 1775), stands at the front of the square, representing the magistrates' power with all its bulk and loftiness. The Rococo interior, with its grisailles and stucco ceiling, is particularly attractive. The majestic St-Maria-Magdalenakerk (Church of Mary Magdalen), built during the course of the 15th and 16th centuries, rises up behind the town hall. The church's impressive cruciform basilica has been restored and its fine organ is often put through its paces in regular music recitals.

OOSTERSCHELDE AQUACULTURE

Aquaculture has flourished along the Oosterschelde since 1870, when parts of the estuary bed were cleared to farm nutrient-rich molluscs. Yerserke is particularly well known for its delicious shellfish, and its oyster and mussel farms can be visited on a guided tour through the Zeeland tourist board (*www.vvv zeeland.nl*).

❺ Yerseke

🏔B6 🚌 🚉 ℹ️ **Kerkplein 1; 0113-571864**

Yerseke is situated along the southern edge of the Oosterschelde estuary. The nature reserve Yerseke Moer, to the west of the village, shows how the island used to look: a desolate patchwork of inlets, hamlets, rough pasture lands, coves, peat moors and water holes. To the east of Yerseke lies the submerged land of Zuid-Beveland, lost in the St-Felixstormvloed (St Felix storm flood) of 1530.

↑ The Westkapelle sea wall, part of the Dutch coastal flood defence system

6
Veere

🅰 A5 🚌 𝒊 Grote Markt 5; www.vvvzeeland.nl

Past and present merge in the town of Veere. Modern pleasure boats moor along the quay opposite the Gothic façades of Het Lammetje (The Lamb, 1539) and De Struijs (The Ostrich, 1561). These Schotse Huizen (Scottish Houses) serve as a reminder of the time that the port was important for its trade in precious Scottish wool. Other monuments to Veere's past are the Stadhuis (1474), the Campveerse Toren, a tower dating to around 1500, and the OL-Vrouwekerk (Church of Our Lady), dating from the 15th–16th centuries.

7
Vlissingen

🅰 A6 🚌 🚉 𝒊 Spuistraat 46; www.vvvzeeland.nl

The main thrust behind the economy of Vlissingen, the largest town in Zeeland, is its busy ports. Vlissingen,

←

St-Maria-Magdalenakerk, soaring over the main square in Goes

with its large harbour and shipyards, has always been of great military significance. In the early 19th century, the town was badly damaged during the the Napoleonic Wars. One of the few remaining historic buildings to have withstood the ravages of the years is the Arsenaal, dating from 1649. A second arsenal from 1823 is now the **Amusement Park Het Arsenaal**, an adventure park with water rides and activites such as paintball and mini golf.

Amusement Park Het Arsenaal

⊛ 🏠 Arsenaalplein 7 📅 Apr–Nov 10am–6pm 🔗 arsenaal.com

8
Westkapelle

🅰 A5 🚌 𝒊 Zuidstraat 154; www.vvvzeeland.nl

The most impressive sight In Westkapelle is its impressive sea wall. In former times, this seaside village lay securely behind the dunes, but these were washed away by storms in the 15th century. A dyke was built to protect the village from the sea, and was completed in 1458. Westkappelle's lighthouse, once a church, also dates

from this period. During World War II, the dyke was bombed by the Allies in order to flood Walcheren so it could be liberated. Exhibits at the **Polderhuis Westkapelle** museum explore the town's history, including the wartime years.

Polderhuis Westkapelle

⊛ ☺ 🏠 Zuidstraat 154 📅 Apr–Oct: daily; Nov–Mar: Wed–Sun 🔗 polderhuis westkapelle.nl

← A café overlooking the old harbour in the charming town of Zierikzee

SHOP

Klompenmakerij Traas

Watch how wooden clogs are made at this century-old factory and sales shop.

🅰B6 🅰Westdijk 3, Heinkenszand 🕒Sun
🆆klompen.com

De Man die Bakt

Artisan bakery that produces high-quality breads and pastries, including the very Dutch *krentenbollen* (raisin buns).

🅰B5 🅰Meelstraat 31, Zierikzee 🕒Sun-Tue
🆆demandiebakt.nl

Streekshop De Paardenstal

Delightful souvenir shop in an old converted horse stable, with goods that include locally produced preserves, wine, cheese, chocolates and other goodies.

🅰B5 🅰Markt 4, Aardenburg
🆆streekproductjes.nl

9

Zierikzee

🅰B5 🚍 ℹ Nieuwe Haven 7; www.vvvzeeland

With 568 listed houses, Zierikzee ranks eighth in the list of historic Dutch towns. The impressive city gateways can be seen from afar. The many café terraces on the Havenplein offer a marvellous view of the two harbour entrances and ornate mansion houses on Oude Haven (Old Harbour), and the trickle of the Gouwe, the creek that brought trading prosperity to the town. Strolling through the narrow streets along the new and old harbours, you will chance upon passageways that offer glimpses of old façades, such as that of the 14th-century De Haene house, the former Stadhuis, which is now the **Stadhuismuseum**. Nearby, the Gothic Gravensteen (1524–6), once the home of the Count of Holland, can

be visited on a guided tour organized via the museum.

The Zierikzee skyline shows the still unfinished Dikke Toren (Great Tower), construction of which began in 1454. At 130 m (425 ft), it must have been the highest point of the colossal 12th-century St-Lievenskerk, which burnt to the ground in 1832.

One of the most famous historic events in Holland, the revolt of Zierikzee in 1472 against Charles the Bold, is re-enacted each summer.

Some 7 km (4 miles) west of Zierikzee is Ouwerkerk, where you'll find the fascinating **Museum Watersnood 1953** devoted to the floods of 1953.

Stadhuismuseum

⊘ 🅰Meelstraat 6 🕒11am-5pm Tue-Sat, 1-5pm Sun
🆆stadhuismuseum.nl

Museum Watersnood 1953

⊘⊘⊘ 🅰Weg van de Buitenlandse Pers 5
🕒Hours vary, check website
🆆watersnoodmuseum.nl

10

Haamstede

🅰A5 🚍 ℹ 0111-450524

Haamstede is a peaceful town built around a church. The nearby **Slot Haamstede**,

→ The solitary Plompetoren, all that is left of a now-submerged church

a castle dating from the 13th century, is surrounded by a park with pleasant walks.

Westerschouwen, 5 km (3 miles) southwest of Haamstede, has an impressive landscape and illustrious past. The barren dunes lie on the western edge, with a scattering of gorse in places, in others covered with coniferous forest. You can climb to the top of **Plompetoren**, the tower of the now-submerged Koudekerke, which rises from the salt marshes. On the edge of the dunes is the pretty Slot Moermond, a castle which dates back to the 13th century.

Slot Haamstede

🏠 Haamstede 🔵 Grounds only; castle closed to public
🌐 natuurmonumenten.nl

Plompetoren

🏠 Koude Kerkseweg 12
🕐 10am–6pm daily

11

Cadzand

🅰 A6 🔵 Boulevard de Wielingen 44d; 0117-391298

The modern seaside resort of Cadzand is particularly popular for its wide stretch of sand. A common pursuit here is to search for fossilized sharks' teeth. Along the

dunes are dignified seaside hotels reminiscent of those of Domburg. A little way past Cadzand is the Zwin nature reserve, which extends as far as Knokke in Belgium. The resort of Nieuwvliet lies to the east of Cadzand.

12

Terneuzen

🅰 B6 🚉 🔵 Noordstraat 62; 0115-760122

Terneuzen is a major port. The sea locks in the Kanaal van Gent naar Terneuzen (Gent–Terneuzen canal), built between 1825 and 1827, are also impressive. The town has industrial areas to the north and nature reserves to the west (De Braakman) and the east (Otheense Kreek).

13

Brouwershaven

🅰 B5 🚉

Quiet Brouwershaven combines a historic centre with a modern port. The Havenkanaal that flows to the marina and the Stadhuis date from 1599. The 14th-century St-Nicolaaskerk (Church of St Nicholas) is a monument to past glory. The town experienced another period of prosperity in the 18th century as an outport to Rotterdam, until the Nieuwe Waterweg (new waterway) was built in 1870. For more information

on the town's history visit the **Brouws Museum**.

Brouws Museum

♿🕐 🏠 Haven Zuidzijde 15 🕐 1–5pm Mon–Fri
🌐 brouwsmuseum.nl

14

Hulst

🅰 B6 🚉 🔵 Steenstraat 37; 0114-315221

Cross over the Westerschelde and you are simultaneously in Flanders and in the Netherlands. Towering over Hulst is St-Willibrordus-basiliek (St Willibrordus Basilica). Generations of Keldermans, a Mechelen building family, have worked on this church. One unusual feature in Hulst is the trio of hostels, once safe houses for the monks from the Flemish abbeys of Ten Duinen, Baudelo and Cambron.

Nearby is the former village of Hulsterloo, famous from the medieval epic *Reynard the Fox*.

> 💬 INSIDER TIP
> ### Verdronken Land van Saeftinghe
>
> Some 10 km (6 miles) from Hulst, this nature reserve, the "Drowned land of Saeftinghe" makes for an exciting day trip, with its fast-moving tides and great bird-watching (*www.saeftinghe.eu*).

DUNES

The Dutch coast is famous for its dunes, which can reach heights of up to 10 m (33 ft). These natural sea walls, with a vegetation of their own, were used in earlier times as common ground for cattle grazing in the absence of sufficient grassland. They now play an important role in the purification of water. The dunes are also a particularly popular recreational area - many of the protected dune areas are open to ramblers and cyclists.

NATURE RESERVES

The dunes provide a habitat for a wide range of wildlife, supporting over 50 per cent of the Netherlands' biodiversity. Protected against such environmentally damaging influences as industry and land development, they are becoming important nature reserves. Vegetation includes gorse, spindle trees, creeping willow and hawthorn, while resident and migratory birds found here include curlews, tawny pipits and sometimes ospreys. During World War II, anti-tank trenches with steep banks were built in the Midden-Heeren dunes (in Nationaal Park Zuid-Kennemerland), which now provide a home for the rare kingfisher. Mammals roaming the dunes include deer, rabbits, Highland cattle and bison.

> The dunes also provide a habitat for a wide range of wildlife, supporting over 50 per cent of the Netherlands' biodiversity.

↑ A common kingfisher, one of many bird species that inhabit the dunes

The sea supplies the sand from which the dunes are built.

On the beach, the dry, white sand drifts and piles up.

The first row of dunes, golden in colour because of the overgrowth, has higher summits.

↑ Looking out over the dunes in Nationaal Park Zuid-Kennemerland

WATER COLLECTION

Drinking water has been collected from underground reservoirs beneath the dunes of North and South Holland since the 19th century. The process was developed as a means of supplying safe drinking water to the country's densely populated cities, in order to combat the rise of diseases such as chloera. Initially the water was piped directly from the dunes – which collect fresh water in the form of precipitation – but this led to a build up of salt in the supply. To remedy the problem, an innovative new system was set up whereby river water from inland was piped to the dunes to undergo a natural filtration process. This method is still in use today.

ORIGINS OF THE DUNES

Dunes are created by a process that occurs time and time again during storms on the country's long, flat beaches. The sand carried by the sea dries on the surface of the beach and is then dragged by the wind like a white shroud over the beach. Held back by any obstacles in its way, the sand starts to accumulate. If the obstacle is a plant, a dune begins to form. Plants involved in forming dunes, such as sand couch grass *(Elymus farctus)*, are called pioneer plants. They must be able to tolerate being buried by the sand and also be able to grow back through the sand. After the initial dune formation, marram grass often begins to stabilize the new dune with its enormous root system. When the sea breaks through dunes that have collapsed or have been cut through, it creates a sea inlet, or channel, around which an entire vegetation system develops, attracting many different species of birds.

Marram grass is a sturdy plant whose root system holds new dunes together. It plays an important role in the formation and protection of Holland's dunes.

The dune overgrowth becomes richer as it moves inland, as limestone is replaced by humus.

↑ Vegetation-covered dunes along the windswept Zeeland coast

$\rightarrow$ The historic town of Sluis, much restored after bomb damage in World War II

⑮ Tholen

🅰 B5 📧 ℹ️ Markt 1, St Maartensdijk; 0166-663771

Tholen is a Zeeland town with a Brabant flavour. Two buildings dominate the town – the marvellous Stadhuis (1452), with its robust battlements, and the **OL-Vrouwekerk** (Church of Our Lady), dating from the 14th to 16th centuries. The **Kapel van het St-Laurensgasthuis** (St Laurensgasthuis Chapel), now a residential home, stands opposite the church. Even though Tholen became a fortified town in the 16th century, it has retained its old character. Gothic façades everywhere are a reminder of its former prosperity.

Did You Know?

The ancestors of US presidents Theodore and F D Roosevelt came from Tholen.

⑯ Sluis

🅰 A6 📧 ℹ️ Groote Markt 1; 0117-461700

The Zeeland-Flanders landscape is scarred by the effects of floods and the dykes built to deal with them. Both polders and inner dykes bear witness to the constant struggle with the sea. The liberation of Zeeland-Flanders in 1944 was also hard fought, devastating towns and villages such as Sluis. The 14th-century Stadhuis, with its belfry, the only one existing in the Netherlands, was restored after 1945; a colourful statue, the "Jantje van Sluis", stands in one of the belfry's windows.

St-Anna-ter-Muiden, 2 km (1.5 miles) to the west of Sluis, is a village beloved by artists. Once prosperous, the town now has just a few houses around the square, with a village pump and the stump of a tower. To the south is the oldest town in Zeeland, Aardenburg. The Romans built a fort here in the 2nd century to ward off Saxon pirates. Aardenburg later became one of the most powerful towns in Flanders, a status reflected in its church, **St-Baafskerk**, a flawless 13th-century example of the Scheldt Gothic style famous for its painted sarcophagi. The **Gemeentelijk Archeologisch Museum Aardenburg** deals solely with the Romans.

Gemeentelijk Archeologisch Museum Aardenburg

⊛⊛ 🏛 Marktstraat 18 🕐 May-Oct: 10am-5pm Tue-Fri, 1-5pm Sat & Sun 🆆 museumaardenburg.nl

⑰ Bruinisse

🅰 B5 📧 ℹ️ VVV Zierikzee; 0111-410940

Bruinisse is now mainly a centre for watersports. The modern bungalow park Aqua Delta is situated outside the old village next to the marina.

To get an idea of what this countryside looked like in earlier times, visit the *ringdorp* (circle-shaped village) Dreischor, 10 km (6 miles) west of Bruinisse. It has a typical village church and town hall. On the edge of the

village is **Goemanszorg**, an agricultural museum devoted to farming past and present.

Goemanszorg

⊗ ☺ 🏠 Molenweg 3, Dreischor ⏰ 11am–5pm Tue–Sun & public hols ⓦ goemanszorg.nl

⑱

St Annaland

🅰 B5 🚌 ℹ Markt 1, St Maartensdijk; 0166-663771

Tholen is Zeeland's least well-known island: a landscape of poplars and pollard willows, fields and quiet towns, such as St Annaland, with its picturesque harbour. An interesting reminder of Zeeland's past is the **Streekmuseum De Meestoof** (Madder Museum). The cultivation of the madder plant and the processing of its root into a red dye was, until the 19th century, one of the main livelihoods of the region.

Streekmuseum De Meestoof

⊗ 🏠 Bierensstraat 6 ⏰ Apr–Oct: 2–5pm Tue–Sat ⓦ demeestoof.nl

⑲

St Maartensdijk

🅰 B5 🚌 ℹ Markt 1; 0166-663771

St Maartensdijk was once the seat of the powerful Lords van Borssele. The remains of the tomb of Floris van Borssele (who died in 1422) and his wife are still to be seen in a burial chapel of the slender 14th- to 15th-century church. The most impressive part of the town itself is the Markt, with its 16th-century houses and elegant Stadhuis.

⑳

Nisse

🅰 B6 🚌 ⓦ nisse-info.nl

Nisse is a typical Beveland village with square, ford and church. The church, the **Mariakerk**, is worth a visit; though it does not look like much from the outside, inside you will be surprised by unique, 15th-century frescoes and wood carvings depicting the saints, scenes from the life of Mary and the coats of arms of the Lords van Borssele. The surrounding landscape of Zak van Zuid-Beveland is characteristic of this region – a succession of polders, divided by dykes covered with flowers and grazed by sheep.

Mariakerk

⊗ 🏠 Dorpsplein 49 ⏰ Jul–Aug: 1:30–5pm Sat ⓦ mariakerk-nisse.nl

---

EAT

Restaurant Smaek
Family-friendly eatery near St Maartensdijk.

🅰 B5 🏠 Gorishoeksedijk 25, Scherpenisse ⓦ restaurant-smaek.nl

€€€

Het Badpaviljoen
High above the dunes, this gorgeous seaside restaurant is known for its amazing seafood.

🅰 A5 🏠 Badhuisweg 21, Domburg ⓦ hetbadpaviljoen.nl

€€€

WEST FRISIAN ISLANDS

Trailing across the northern edge of the Netherlands are the West Frisian Islands, a scattered archipelago of low-lying islands and islets, only five of which are inhabited, the last remaining fragments of an ancient sandbank that once stretched from Cap Gris Nez in France to Esbjerg in Denmark. At the end of the last Ice Age, about 12,000 years ago, sea levels rose as the ice melted, and tidal action created a long barrier of sand dunes over 500 km (310 miles) long. This was then breached by the sea to form the islands and the mud flats behind them. The sea has constantly been eroding this sandbank, creating the shallow Waddenzee behind and washing away much of the peat soil that lay beyond the dunes. Given the precariousness of the islands, it seems surprising that they seem to have been populated in Roman times by a few hardy settlers, presumed to be Frisians, who built artificial mounds (terpen) to keep themselves safe from the sea and eked out a living by farming, fishing and collecting shellfish. On some of the islands, notably Schiermonnikoog, the Frisians were reinforced by a few monks, who added a degree of order, constructing dykes and dams from the 13th century until the Reformation in the 16th century. The islands prospered in the 17th century due to their links with the Dutch East India Company and in the 19th century due to whaling. Historically, the most important island was Terschelling, whose main settlement provided a safe anchorage on the principal shipping lanes into and out of the Zuiderzee. Today, the main concerns of the islanders, apart from the flourishing tourist industry, are to preserve the ecology and environment of these fragile islands.

WEST FRISIAN ISLANDS

Must See

❶ The Waddenzee

Experience More

❷ Noorderhaaks
❸ Den Hoorn
❹ De Koog
❺ Den Burg
❻ De Slufter
❼ Vlieland
❽ Ameland
❾ Griend
❿ Schiermonnikoog
⓫ Rottumerplaat
⓬ Rottumeroog
⓭ Terschelling

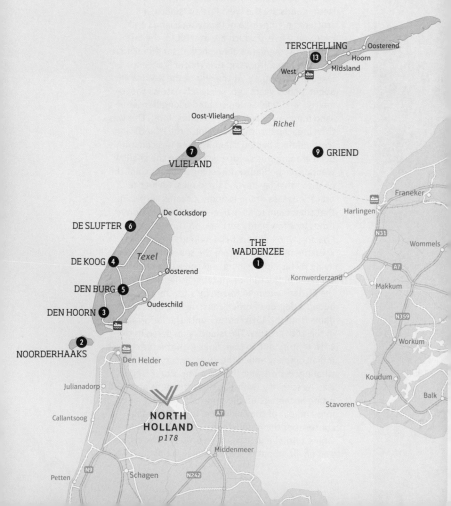

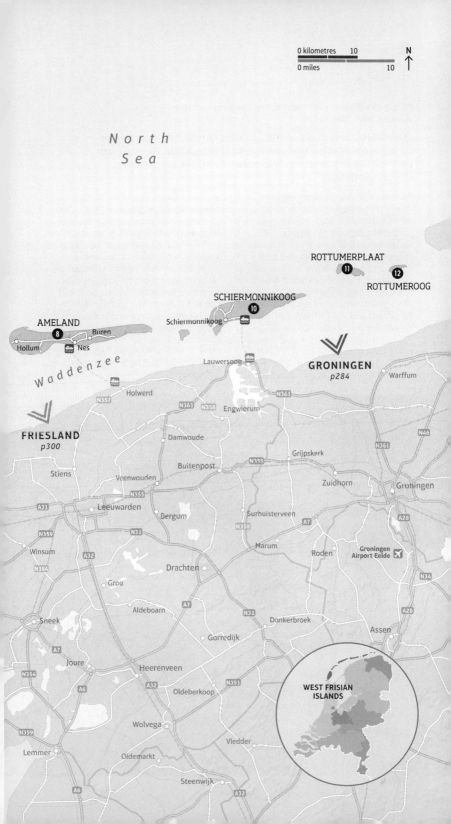

North
Sea

ROTTUMERPLAAT
11

12
ROTTUMEROOG

SCHIERMONNIKOOG
10

Schiermonnikoog

AMELAND
8
Buren
Hollum Nes

W a d d e n z e e

Lauwersoog

GRONINGEN
p284

Warffum

N361

FRIESLAND
p300

Holwerd

N357

N361 N358

Engwierum

N46

Damwoude

N361

Stiens

Buitenpost

Grijpskerk

Veenwouden

N355

Zuidhorn

Groningen

Leeuwarden

N355

Bergum

A31

Surhuisterveen

A7

A28

N359

N31

N358

Winsum

A32

Marum

Roden

Groningen
Airport Eelde

N384

Drachten

N34

Grou

A28

Aldeboarn

A7

N31

Donkerbroek

Sneek

Assen

A7

Gorredijk

Joure

N354

Heerenveen

A6

A32

Oldeberkoop

N351

**WEST FRISIAN
ISLANDS**

N359

Wolvega

Vledder

Lemmer

Oldemarkt

Steenwijk

A6

A32

❶

THE WADDENZEE

🅐 D1-2 🚉 Afsluitdijk Wadden Centre, Kornwerderzand; www.visitwadden.nl

The Waddenzee is a tidal area whose sand or mud flats *(wadden)* are mainly exposed at low tide and disappear at high tide. Together with the West Frisian Islands, the Waddenzee forms the last extensive wild part of Holland.

This entire area has an extremely rich ecosystem because of its ample sources of nourishment. It is a feeding and breeding ground for many species of birds *(p280)*. Bird-watchers flock here, especially in the migratory seasons, and the entire area is dotted with hides. Extensive cockle beds and other underground invertebrates provide food for a variety of wading birds. Dolphins, porpoises, two species of seals, 30 species of fish, shrimp and crabs either live in the Waddenzee or come here to breed.

Because of the diversity of the landscape, with its changing environment (salt water and fresh water, lime-rich soil and lime-poor soil, wet and dry land, sediment-rich marsh and sand dunes), almost 900 plant species grow here, including autumn gentian and creeping willow, as well as black bog rush, fragrant orchid and grass of Parnassus. Sea lavender and sea aster cover the marshes in a haze of purple-blue in late summer.

The Dutch love to walk here, but visitors with no knowledge of the vagaries of the tides need to exercise caution. Seals and dolphins may often be spotted from the ferries operating between the mainland and the West Frisian islands. The VVVs (tourist offices) on the islands offer all kinds of more leisurely sailing trips. Rederij Vooruit *(www.rederij-vooruit.nl)* arranges sailing trips on local boats.

Did You Know?

Stretching all the way up to the Danish coast, this is the largest unbroken intertidal habitat on Earth.

> Dolphins, porpoises, two species of seals, 30 species of fish, shrimp and crabs either live in the Waddenzee or come here to breed.

WALKING THE MUD FLATS

The Dutch revel in *wadlopen* (literally "mud walking"), and the Waddenzee during low tide is perfect for this. It's a strenuous, messy affair, walking at times through thigh-deep mud and waist-high channels of cool seawater. The experience, however, is also exhilarating, as you are surrounded by nothing but sea, sand and the wind. For safety reasons, novices should look for a guided tour, where they can also learn about the flora and fauna of this unusual, highly dynamic environment.

Seals basking on a sandbank exposed by the tide and *(inset)* sea lavender ↑

↑ The tide receding to expose a network of channels at sunset

EXPERIENCE MORE

❷ Noorderhaaks

🇦 C2 ℹ️ Emmalaan 66, Den Burg; 0222-314741

Noorderhaaks, also known as Razende Bol ("raging ball"), is a fairly bleak sandbank west of Den Helder, 2.5 km (1.5 miles) offshore. The sea currents are gradually causing the island to shift eastwards towards Texel. The Dutch air force occasionally uses the island for target practice, but it is not off-limits to visitors. Although rowing and swimming here are risky because of the powerful currents, adventure-seekers regularly visit Noorderhaaks by boat or by helicopter, unable to resist this piece of total wilderness, where mirages are common.

❸ Den Hoorn

🇦 C2 🚌 ℹ️ Emmalaan 66, Den Burg; www.texel.net

Built on boulder clay, Den Hoorn is Texel island's

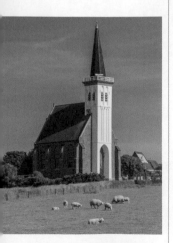

↑ Sheep grazing in front of Den Hoorn's church on Texel island

southernmost village. It has a distinctive Hervormde kerk (Protestant church) with a pointed steeple and churchyard dating from 1425. This exquisitely restored village has protected status.

❹ De Koog

🇦 C2 🚌 ℹ️ Emmalaan 66, Den Burg; www.texel.net

In 1900, the former fishing settlement of De Koog was made up of a church (built in 1415) and a few houses and farms. The first tourist facility was the Badhotel, later the Hotel Prinses Juliana, with a garden overlooking the sea. Today, De Koog has accommodation for 20,000 visitors in hotels, pensions and camp sites. The centre of De Koog is the Dorpsstraat, which has cafés, snack bars and discos. De Koog's visitor attractions are the Calluna waterpark and EcoMare, an information centre for the Waddenzee and the North Sea.

❺ Den Burg

🇦 C2 🚌 ℹ️ Emmalaan 66; www.texel.net

Den Burg is the main town of Texel. Around 1300, the village was fortified by a circular rampart with a moat, now marked by Burgwal and Parkstraat streets. A sheep market was once held in April and May at the Groeneplats, Den Burg's main square, on which stands the town hall. Further on, by the Binnenburg, or inner castle, stands the 15th-century Late Gothic Hervormde kerk (Protestant church). The Kogerstraat runs the length of the Binnenburg. The antiquities museum, the

Oudheidkamer, is located here, set in a picturesque 16th-century building, containing period rooms, a display of artifacts and art in the attic, and a herb garden.

South of Den Burg rises the 15 m (50 ft) Hoge Berg (high mountain), which offers a great view of the island. For a good walk, follow the Skillepaadje from the tomb of the Georgiers (resistance fighters who died in combat against the Germans in 1945) to the fishing village of Oudeschild, past the peat walls and sheep pens.

Oudheidkamer

⊛ 🏠 Kogerstraat 1
🕐 Apr–Oct: 11am–5pm Mon–Fri, 2–4pm Sat
🌐 oudheidkamertexel.nl

❻ De Slufter

🇦 C1 🚌 🕐 All year; northern part closed 1 Mar– 1 Sep ℹ️ Emmalaan 66, Den Burg; www.texel.net

The distinctive natural area of De Slufter, consisting of salt marshes extending over 4.5 sq km (1.7 sq miles), is covered with salt-loving

↑ Looking across the Waddenzee from the Frisian Island of Vlieland

💬 INSIDER TIP
Texel's Beer Brewery

Visitors can tour the award-winning Texelse Bierbrouwerij, near Oudeschild *(texels.nl)*. Tours include tastings of craft beers, made with locally grown hops, wheat and barley.

plants such as sea thrift and sea lavender, and is an important breeding ground for many different bird species. De Slufter, and the neighbouring De Muy, where spoonbills breed, are fantastic areas for rambling.

❼
Vlieland

🅰C1 🚢 ℹHavenweg 10, Oost-Vlieland; 0562-451111

Vlieland is the smallest of the Waddenzee Islands. In some places, less than 1 km (half a mile) separates the North Sea and the Waddenzee. Unlike the other islands, Vlieland consists only of dunes, covered with a purple haze of heather, marram grass and sea buckthorn. In the east, the woods planted just after 1900 provide a bit of variety in the landscape.

In the south is the only village, Oost-Vlieland, where the boat from Harlingen docks. Many old buildings line the main street. One of them, the **Tromp's Huys**, built in 1576, houses a museum with 19th-century paintings.

There is no room for cars here, not even for those of the islanders. The best way to explore Vlieland is by bicycle; the island can be covered in one day. From Oost-Vlieland you can cycle westwards to the Posthuys (post house), where in the 17th century the overseas mail was brought from Amsterdam to be loaded onto ships waiting to sail. Further west is De Vliehors, an area of natural interest which can be explored if no military exercises are taking place. Beware of getting stuck in the drifting sand. This is where the village of West-Vlieland once stood. It was consumed by the waves in 1736.

Tromp's Huys

⊗ 🏠 Dorpsstraat 99, Oost-Vlieland 🕐 Hours vary, check website 🌐trompshuys.nl

EAT

Taveerne De 12 Balcken
Friendly pub with lamb dishes and a fondue made with local cheese.

🅰C2 🏠Weverstraat 20, Den Burg, Texel 🌐12balcken.nl

ⓒⓔⓔ

De Klimop
Excellent vegetarian options and a lovely outdoor terrace.

🅰E1 🏠Johan Hofkerweg 2, Nes, Ameland 🌐deklimopameland.nl

ⓔⓔⓔ

Pura Vida
Healthy breakfast bowls, grilled sandwiches and soups.

🅰D1 🏠Oosterburen 36, Terschelling 🌐puravida terschelling.nl

ⓔⓔⓔ

↑ A flock of oystercatchers in flight over the waters of the Waddenzee

BIRDS OF THE WADDENZEE

The extensive wetlands of the Waddenzee are an important area for breeding and migratory birds. The North Sea coasts of the islands are sandy, with little animal life; the Waddenzee coasts of the islands, however, consist of fine sand and clay that are rich in minerals and nutrients. The innumerable worms, molluscs and crustaceans that live here are an ideal source of food for a huge variety of ducks, seagulls and wading birds. At the peak of the migratory season in August, the number of birds here runs into millions.

PROTECTED SPECIES

The wealth of bird species that occur in the Waddenzee – including diving birds, petrels, cormorants, spoonbills, ducks, birds of prey, waders, scavengers, seagulls, terns, razorbills and songbirds – is a good reason to ensure that the area is carefully protected. These are the only wetlands remaining in the Netherlands, so for many of the birds they are the only breeding grounds in the country. Various parts are closed to visitors, and it is important to observe the regulations in order to help preserve the bird population.

BEAK SHAPES

Many varieties of birds feed on the mud flats, but the different species have managed to avoid competing with one another. The various shapes and lengths of their beaks are suitable for the assorted types of food that can be found in the water and in the sand. Ducks get their food from the surface or dive for it, whereas wading birds get their food from underground. Other species catch fish (spoonbills, cormorants and terns), shellfish (eider ducks) or even other seabirds (the white-tailed eagle), and some steal their food from their neighbours.

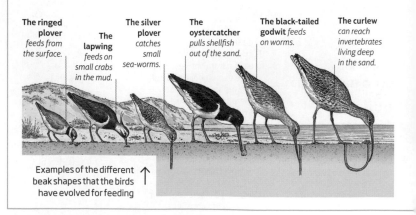

The ringed plover *feeds from the surface.*

The lapwing *feeds on small crabs in the mud.*

The silver plover *catches small sea-worms.*

The oystercatcher *pulls shellfish out of the sand.*

The black-tailed godwit *feeds on worms.*

The curlew *can reach invertebrates living deep in the sand.*

Examples of the different beak shapes that the birds have evolved for feeding ↑

BIRD-WATCHING

The most impressive bird-watching is during the migratory season, but you'll see plenty of species all year round. There are many hides on the mud flats, allowing the birds to be observed without being disturbed. Here are some of the species that you might spot.

Arctic Tern
This extremely rare bird, which breeds in the West Frisian Islands, spends the winter in the Antarctic. This gives it the longest migratory path of all birds.

Avocet
This magnificent wading bird has an upward-curving bill and black-and-white plumage.

Oystercatcher
The oystercatcher is characteristic of the Waddenzee. It forages for cockles and mussels.

Ringed Plover
This is an active bird that rarely breeds here but passes through in large numbers.

Sandwich Tern
This bird has its largest breeding colony in Holland on Griend. Its dwindling numbers means it requires careful protection.

Eider Duck
The eider duck has breeding colonies on Texel, Vlieland and Terschelling. The male is far more impressive in appearance than the brown-coloured female.

Red Knot
This robust bird of passage is always on the move. It stops over sometimes in summer and sometimes in winter.

Tailed Godwit
This wading bird, with fiery red-brown plumage, is a bird of passage but spends the winters and summers in the

Curlew
This is the largest European wading bird and is easily recognizable by its long, curved beak.

Herring Gull
The herring gull is just one of the many varieties of gull that occur here. At more than half a metre (1.5 ft) long, it is an impressive bird.

1 Arctic Tern

2 Avocet

3 Sandwich Tern

4 Red Knot

5 Herring Gull

↑ Cycling along tracks on Ameland - the best way to explore the island

STAY

Hotel Tesselhof
Opt for a suite that includes your own private Finnish sauna at this comfortable hotel.

🄰C2 🄰Kaapstraat 39, De Koog, Texel
Ⓦhoteltesselhof.com

€€€

Hotel Posthuys
This small, out-of-the-way hotel is perfect for a family retreat.

🄰C2 🄰Postweg 4, Vlieland
Ⓦposthuysvlieland.nl

€€€

Hotel Van der Werff
Historic hotel with modern rooms and apartments and vintage details.

🄰E1 🄰Reeweg 2, Schiermonnikoog
Ⓦhotelvanderwerff.nl

€€€

⑧ Ameland

🄰E1 🚢🚌 𝒊Bureweg 2, Nes Ⓦvvvameland.nl

The dunes in the north of this island are dry, with the exception of Het Oerd, a bird reserve in the east. The region is best explored by bicycle; there is a cycle track to a scenic spot on a 24-m (79-ft) dune. In the mud flats in the south there are four villages, one of which is Nes, where the boat from Holwerd calls. Commandeurshuizen (commodores' houses) in the old centre recall the days when many islanders made their living from whaling.

If you want to see the real Ameland, you must visit Hollum, the island's largest village. The Zuiderlaan and Oosterlaan are steeped in the atmosphere of past times. Beyond Hollum lies the **Maritime Center – Abraham Fock**, a museum dedicated to life-saving, where the pride of Ameland, a lifeboat launched by horses, is kept operational.

Maritime Center - Abraham Fock

⊛ 🄰Oranjeweg 18, Hollum
🕒Hours vary, check website
Ⓦamelandermusea.nl

⑨ Griend

🄰D1 𝒊Vereniging Natuurmonumenten Ⓦnatuurmonumenten.nl

Halfway through the boat trip from Harlingen to Terschelling or Vlieland, you will see Griend, abandoned after the St Lucia's flood of 1287. For centuries it seemed about to disappear beneath the waves. In 1988, the Natuurmonumenten trust had a dam built to prevent further erosion. At high tide, the highest part of the island is just 1 m (3 ft) above the water. Access to Griend is granted only to a few bird wardens and biology students. This is Holland's largest breeding ground for great tern.

⑩ Schiermonnikoog

🄰E1 🚢🚌 𝒊Reeweg 5, Schiermonnikoog
Ⓦvvvschiermonnikoog.nl

Schiermonnikoog, or Lytje Pole ("small land"), was a farm belonging to Cistercian monks during the Middle Ages. The village of Schiermonnikoog, which is named after them,

INSIDER TIP

Horse-Drawn Rides

Discover the natural beauty and history of Schiermonnikoog on a guided tour via a covered horse-drawn wagon or tractor ride. Inquire at the local VVV.

has many exquisitely restored houses. The island is a national park. The beach of Schier is one of the widest in Europe. The eastern side of the island in particular makes for wonderful walking, with its varied flora (including many orchids) and bird life.

11 Rottumerplaat

⚑F1 ℹ️ Waddenkust Noord-Groningen, Uithuizen; 0595-434051

Nature has been left to its own devices on the 9-sq-km (3.5-sq-mile) uninhabited island of Rottumerplaat. Outsiders are rarely admitted to the island, a protected nature reserve. Dunes and an impressive salt marsh are its characteristic features.

12 Rottumeroog

⚑F1 ℹ️ Waddenkust Noord-Groningen, Uithuizen; 0595-434051

This easternmost of the West Frisian Islands is due to disappear into the mouth of the Ems soon. Since 1991 it has been left in the hands of nature. Attempts over many years to prevent it from drifting eastwards were

→

The Brandaris lighthouse towering over the village of West on Terschelling island

unsuccessful. In 1998, the northern dunes collapsed, after which the last traces of human settlement were removed. The island is now less than 2.6 sq km (1 sq mile) in size and shrinks with each storm on the north side, though some new land is forming on the south side.

13 Terschelling

⚑D1 🚌🚢 ℹ️ Willem Barentszkade 19a, West-Terschelling
🌐 vvvterschelling.nl

The north of Terschelling consists of dunes, where cattle grazed freely. It is from this practice that the popular Oerol Festival, held each year in June, gets its name ("oerol" means "everywhere").

In Formerum, West and Hoorn, the dunes have been planted with coniferous and deciduous woods. In the south are polders, and beyond the dykes are the salt marshes. There is a nature reserve at either end of the island. West is a real mud-flat village, with a famous lighthouse, the

Brandaris, dating from 1594. **Het Behouden Huys** is a local history museum dedicated to famous islanders such as Willem Barentsz; there is also the educational **Centrum voor Natuur en Landschap**, where you can learn about the ecology of the mud flats.

In the west lies the village of Midsland, surrounded by small hamlets with intriguing names such as Hee, Horp and Kaart, which date back to when the Frisians settled on the islands. The hamlet with the Kerkhof van Striep cemetery is where the first church on the island was built, in the 10th century. Further eastwards is Hoorn, with 13th-century Gothic-Romanesque St Janskerk standing on the site of the original church.

Het Behouden Huys

🏛️♿ ⌂ Commandeurstraat 30 🕐 Hours vary, check website 🌐 behouden-huys.nl

Centrum voor Natuur en Landschap

♿ ⌂ Burg Reedekerstraat 11 🕐 Hours vary, check website 🌐 natuurmuseum terschelling.nl

GRONINGEN

Located in the northeast corner of the country, the province of Groningen is quietly rural, although its capital – also called Groningen – is a busy little town that is home to the region's most popular attraction, the Groninger Museum. The province was settled in prehistoric times, with its first peoples leaving their mark on the land via a multitude of *terpen*, artificial mounds raised high above the surrounding flatlands to keep the encroaching waters at bay. First engulfed by the Frisian kingdom and then by the Frankish empire, the area had become part of the bishopric of Utrecht by the 11th century. By the 13th century, much of the province had been parcelled up between a scattering of large landowners and the town of Groningen had become an important trading centre. The region grew rich during the Middle Ages from agriculture and peat extraction, and the towns of Groningen and Appingedam were given membership of the powerful Hanseatic League. During the 16th century, the province stayed loyal to the Catholic Habsburgs until Dutch Protestants captured it in 1594 and incorporated it into the United Provinces, to which it belonged until the modern state was formed. At the end of World War II, the city of Groningen took a pummelling when the Allied army met stiff resistance from the German army and SS troops recruited from Belgium and the Netherlands. In 1959, the economy of the province received a boost when the vast Groningen natural gas field was discovered. Initially, production proceeded at pace, but the worldwide climate crisis has prompted a rethink and there are now plans to end the production of gas by 2022. The region's other main industry is shipping, and this is expected to drive the economy in the coming years.

WEST FRISIAN ISLANDS
p272

FRIESLAND
p300

GRONINGEN

Must See

① Groningen

Experience More

② Pieterburen
③ Grootegast
④ Leek
⑤ Zoutkamp
⑥ Appingedam
⑦ Lauwersoog
⑧ Fraeylemaborg
⑨ Uithuizen
⑩ Slochteren
⑪ Veendam
⑫ Bourtange
⑬ Ter Apel
⑭ Oude en Nieuwe Pekela
⑮ Winschoten

❶
GRONINGEN

🅰F1 🚗181 km (112 miles) NE of Amsterdam
🚆🚌Stationsplein 🛈Grote Markt 29; www.
visitgroningen.nl

This bustling university city has a number of interesting buildings and museums, among them the maritime Noordelijk Scheepvaartmuseum and the Groninger Museum, with its renowned art collection. The Prinsenhof Garden provides peace in the middle of the city.

①
Grote Markt

The expansive Grote Markt marks the old city centre. Several of the buildings standing on the square were badly damaged near the end of World War II. When the area was rebuilt, the market was enlarged on the northern and eastern sides, and many new modern buildings were added. However, several historic structures still encircle the square, including the impressive Stadhuis, a monumental Neo-Classical building that was completed in 1810. The most famous of the square's buildings is the 97-m (318-ft) **Martinitoren** (St Martin Tower), dating from 1496. Although damaged during the war, the tower remained standing and was later rebuilt. The carillon, whose bells were cast by famous bell-makers the Hemony brothers, has since been enlarged and now has four octaves and 49 bells. If you're willing to tackle over 200 steps, it is possible to climb to the top of the tower, which offers spectacular views over the city.

> ### Did You Know?
> ────
> Martinitoren is called "d'Olle Grieze" (The Old Grey) by locals because of the colour of its sandstone.

Another splendid building found on the Grote Markt is the **Martinikerk** (St Martin's Church). Dating from the 13th century, it still retains traces of the original building: both the northern and the southern façades of the transept and the ornamental brickwork of the windows on the northern side are from the 13th century. During the 15th century, when the city was at the height of its development, the church was extensively remodelled in the Gothic style. The choir features sumptuous murals from 1530 illustrating the life of Christ. The central part of the church became a hall-type church.

An excellent food market is held in the Grote Markt on Tuesdays, Fridays and Saturdays. East of the square you'll find the Poelestraat, which on fine days comes to life with outdoor cafés and restaurants.

Martinitoren

♿🚫 🅰Martinikerkhof 1
🕐Noon–6pm Mon, 10am–6pm Tue–Fri, 10am–5pm Sat, noon–4pm Sun 🌐visit groningen.nl

Martinikerk

🅰Martinikerkhof 3
🕐Hours vary, check website 🌐martinikerk.nl

Aerial view over the university city of Groningen at sunset

picturesque *hofjes*, or court-yards, which are surrounded by almshouses that often belonged to inns. They were once charitable institutions whose aim was to help the poor.

The finest of these are the complex of the 13th-century Heilige Geestgasthuis, or Pelstergasthuis (located in the Pelsterstraat), and St Geertruidshofje, whose Pepergasthuis inn was established in 1405 as a hostel for poor pilgrims. It later became a senior citizens' home. There are two attractive courtyards; the pump in one of these dates from 1829. The first courtyard is bounded by the convent church, the refectory and the warden's chambers, while the second courtyard is surrounded by guest rooms.

②
St Geertruidshofje

🏠 Peperstraat 22
📞 050-312 4082

Groningen is home to a number of wonderfully

③
Gebouw van de Gasunie

◻Concourslaan 17 📞050-521 9111 🚫To the public

The main office of the Dutch Gasunie (gas board) was designed by the Alberts and Van Huut architects on the principles of "organic" architecture, the inspiration of which lies in natural forms. The "organic" nature of the building can be seen at every turn, even in the specially designed furniture. The locals' nickname for the building is the *"apenrots"* (monkey cliff).

④ 🎨 🏛
Noordelijk Scheepvaartmuseum

◻Brugstraat 24 🕐10am-5pm Tue-Sat, 1-5pm Sun 🚫Public hols 🌐noordelijkscheepvaartmuseum.nl

This maritime museum, arranged over two restored medieval houses, deals with the history of navigation in the northern provinces from 1650 to the present. The exhibits, arranged in chronological order, include Utrecht ships, Hanseatic cogs, West Indies merchant ships, peat barges, Baltic merchant ships and Groningen coasters from the 20th century. The pièce de résistance are the scale models of schooners and rigged vessels in all shapes and sizes. A virtual reality video gives an insight into how the city looked in the Middle Ages.

A number of historical workshops, such as a carpenter's shop and a smithy, are located in the attic of the museum. The museum also has an excellent programme of temporary marine-focused exhibitions.

> ### JENEVER: THE GRANDFATHER OF GIN
>
> The predecessor of modern-day gin, *jenever* (or *jenever*) is a Dutch spirit that is flavoured with juniper berries. It made from malt wine that has been distilled alongside different botanicals in a copper still. This easy-drinking liquor comes in two varieties: *jonge jenever* (young) is a clear spirit with a fresh citrus taste, while *oude jenever* (mature) is golden in colour with a richer, maltier taste - but both varieties have hints of juniper. The difference in flavour is based on distilling techniques, not on the actual age of the gin. *Jenever* is served in a goblet-shaped glass or a shot glass filled to the brim.

⑤ 🎨 🏛
Hooghoudt Distillery

◻Hooghoudtstraat 1 🕐8am-5pm Mon-Fri 🌐hooghoudt.nl

Groningen's Hooghoudt Distillery has been producing *jenever* for over 130 years. As well as producing more traditional versions of this national spirit – using receipes that have been passed down over five generations – the distillery also experiments with new blends. Take a tour of the historic family distillery to learn everything about the making of this delicious spirit and then indulge in an illuminating tasting session.

---

⑥
Prinsenhof and Prinsenhoftuin

◻Martinikerkhof 23 🕐Prinsenhoftuin: 10am-6pm daily 🌐prinsenhof.nl

The Prinsenhof originally housed the monastic order of the Broeders des Gemenen Levens. It later became the seat of the first Bishop of Groningen, Johann Knijff, who had the entire complex converted into a magnificent bishop's palace. Until late into the 18th century, the building

← The distinctive Gasunie building, known locally as the "monkey cliff"

↑ The magnificent Prinsenhof, formerly the Stadholder's residence

served as the residence of the Stadholder. Today, it is a hotel with a café and restaurant.

The Prinsenhoftuin (Prinsenhof Garden), laid out as it was in the 18th century, is truly an oasis in the midst of the busy city. Its highlights include a verdant herb garden and a sweet-smelling rose garden. There is also a pretty flowerbed that is arranged into two coats of arms, one with the letter W (for William Frederick, the Stadholder of Friesland), the other with a letter A (for Albertine Agnes, William's wife).

At the side of the entrance is a fine sundial which dates back to 1730. The course of the old city walls of Groningen is still clearly discernible in the Prinsenhoftuin.

Did You Know?

The statue of Ome Loeks' horse at Groningen train station illustrates a famous local folk song.

⑦ 🚲 🐾 🍴 ☕ 🛍️

Hortus Haren

📍 Kerklaan 34, Haren
🕐 Mid-Mar–Nov: 10am–5pm daily; Nov–mid-Mar: 11am–4pm 🚫 1 Jan, 25 Dec
🌐 hortusharen.nl

Around 10 km (6 miles) south of the city is the fashionable town of Haren, where an extensive park, known as the Hortus Haren, is situated.

The park was set up in 1642 by Henricus Munting. Its 20 ha (50 acres) include a large hothouse complex comprising several different greenhouses dedicated to a wide array of climatic zones, including rainforest, desert and tropical.

The Chinese garden ("Het verborgen rijk van Ming", or "The hidden Ming Empire") is also well worth a visit. It is a faithful reconstruction of a real garden owned by a 16th-century high-ranking Chinese official of the Ming Dynasty. It features original Chinese pagodas decorated with carvings of lions and dragons, a waterfall and a tea house where visitors can enjoy refreshments.

Throughout the year, a variety of events are held in the park, including photography and art exhibitions, and scavenger hunts for children.

DRINK

Grand Café Prinsenhof
Sip fine wine or indulge in an afternoon tea out on the lovely terrace, which is surrounded by beautiful gardens.

📍 Martinikerkhof 23 🌐 prinsenhof.nl

Baxbier Brouwerij
An airy tasting room for drinking house-made beer with the locals. You can also take a tour of the brewery to learn how your beverage was made.

📍 Friesestraatweg 201/2a 🌐 baxbier.com

Grand Café De Plantage
Spectacularly set among the Hortus Botanicus Haren gardens, this café makes the perfect place to enjoy a slice of cake and a coffee.

📍 Kerklaan 34, Haren 🌐 hortusharen.nl

8 ⊘ ☐ 🛍

GRONINGER MUSEUM

🏠 Museumeiland 1 🕙 10am–5pm Tue–Sun (Jul & Aug: daily)
🚫 1 Jan, 5 May, 25 Dec 🌐 groningermuseum.nl

Housed in an eye-catching and unmissable modern building, the Groninger Museum is one of the most popular museums in the Netherlands. Its compelling collection showcases archaeological finds, applied arts, early art and cutting-edge modern art.

Standing on an island in the 19th-century Verbindingskanaal, this museum was designed by the internationally renowned Italian architect Alessandro Mendini and opened in 1994. The main focus of the building is the 30-m (98-ft) tower in the middle. Highlights of the museum include a remarkable collection of Chinese and Japanese porcelain, and an impressive collection of works by the Groningen art collective, De Ploeg. Don't miss the section dedicated to the history of the city, which include displays of local crafts and and applied arts.

Illustration of the Groninger Museum ↓

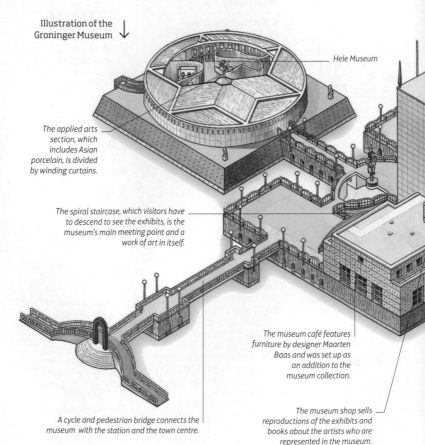

Hele Museum

The applied arts section, which includes Asian porcelain, is divided by winding curtains.

The spiral staircase, which visitors have to descend to see the exhibits, is the museum's main meeting point and a work of art in itself.

The museum café features furniture by designer Maarten Baas and was set up as an addition to the museum collection.

A cycle and pedestrian bridge connects the museum with the station and the town centre.

The museum shop sells reproductions of the exhibits and books about the artists who are represented in the museum.

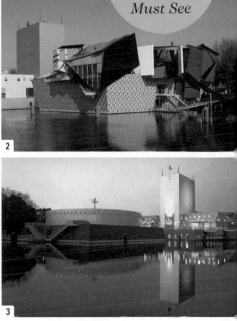

1 An abstract sculpture at the entrance to the Groninger Museum.

2 The impressive Mendini Pavilion is a truly striking example of Deconstructivist architecture.

3 Located on an island, the Groninger Museum is one of the city's most iconic landmarks.

The Mendini Pavilion is easily distinguished by its apparent haphazardness and chaos, and is a good example of Deconstructivism.

Bridge in the Mendini Pavilion

A large concrete staircase in the Mendini Pavilion leads to the upper pavilion, where some of the art is on display.

This wing was designed by Coop Himmelb(l)au Wolfgang Prix and Helmut Swiczinsky.

EXPERIENCE MORE

❷ Pieterburen

🅰 F1 🚍 65, 67, 68
ℹ Waddencentrum, Hoofdstraat 83; 0595-528522

One of the best-known places in Groningen is Pieterburen, which is home to the excellent **Zeehondencentrum**. This seal sanctuary was founded by Lenie 't Hart and others as a reception centre for sick and disabled seals from the nearby Waddenzee.

The **Waddencentrum**, also located in Pieterburen, is an exhibition centre dedicated to the mud flats of the Waddenzee. It also provides useful information on walks and guided tours in the area.

Some 5 km (3 miles) south of Pieterburen, in Saaxum-huizen, take a corn bath, or wander through one of the maize mazes at the **Bloemenboerderij**.

In Leens, 10 km (6 miles) to the southwest of Pieterburen, is the stunning 14th-century *borg* (moated manor house)

Verhildersum, which contains 19th-century furnishings. The castle is surrounded by an impressively wide moat. Its extensive, beautifully manicured formal gardens include an arbour and sculptures. The castle's coach house is regularly used as a venue for exhibitions, while the Schathuis (treasury), set in the castle grounds, is now a lively café and restaurant.

Zeehondencentrum

🏷 🅰 Hoofdstraat 94a
🕙 10am–5pm 🌐 zee hondencentrum.nl

Het Waddencentrum

🏛 🅰 Hoofdstraat 83
📞 0595-528522
🕘 9am–6pm daily

Bloemenboerderij

🏷 🅰 Dikemaweg 10, Saaxumhuizen 🕙 Hours vary, check website
🌐 bloemenboerderij.com

Borg Verhildersum

🏷🏷🏷 🅰 Wierde 40, Leens
🕙 Apr–Oct: 10:30am–5pm Tue–Sun 🌐 verhildersum.nl

💬 INSIDER TIP
Barefoot Walking Path

Remove your shoes and socks and take the Blote Voeten Pad in Opende, near Grootegast, through soft grass, mud and water. It's open all year; you can bring the kids but not the dogs.

❸ Grootegast

🅰 F1 🚍 33, 38, 39, 98, 101, 133 ℹ Nienoord 20, Leek; 0594-512100

The little town of Lutjegast, close to Grootegast, is the birthplace of the 17th-century explorer Abel Tasman. The **Abel Tasman Museum** houses an interesting exhibition about his life, including old sea charts and books.

Abel Tasman Museum

🏷 🅰 Kompasstraat 1, Lutjegast 📞 053-804741
🕙 1:30–4:30pm Thu–Sat

← Borg Verhildersum, built in the 14th century to defend the area around Leens

④
Leek

🅰F1 🚌81, 85, 88, 98, 306, 316 ℹ Nienoord 20; 0594-512100

In the small town of Leek stands the castle of Nienoord, built in approximately 1524 by Wigbold van Ewsum. During the 19th century, things at the castle seemed to be taking a turn for the worse. In 1846, the then owner, Ferdinand Folef Kniphausen, nicknamed "the mad squire", burned all the family portraits in a drunken fit. Later on, the

> In the small town of Leek stands the castle of Nienoord, built in approximately 1524 by Wigbold van Ewsum.

orangery and part of the upper floor were destroyed by fire. In 1950, the municipality bought the castle. Eight years later, the **Museum Nienoord**, exhibiting horse-drawn vehicles, was established here. The complex originally dates from 1524 and contains a unique collection of royal coaches, gigs and hackney carriages.

Museum Nienoord
♦🔲🚶 🅰Nienoord 1
🕐Apr-Oct: 11am-5pm, Tue-Sun; Nov-Mar 1-5pm Fri-Sun 🖱museum nienoord.nl

⑤
Zoutkamp

🅰E1 🚌63, 65, 69, 136, 163, 165 ℹ Inside the Visserijmuseum, Reitdiepskade 11; 0595-401957

The character of the small fishing village of Zoutkamp changed dramatically

STAY

Landgoed
Beautifully renovated farm estate with a romantic touch and an inviting outdoor pool.

🅰G2 🏠Hoofdweg 67, Westerlee 🖱landgoed westerlee.nl

€€€

Hotel Waddenweelde
Spacious, family and pet-friendly suites with breakfast included..

🅰F1 🏠Hoofdstraat 84, Pieterburen 🖱waddenweelde.nl

€€€

after the damming of lake Lauwerszee in 1969. By Zoutkamp's waterside, the area known as Reitdiepskade, there are still a number of traditional warehouses that retain the former charm of the village.

↑ Brightly painted warehouses on the waterside in the fishing village of Zoutkamp

↑ The historic town of Appingedam, with its red-brick buildings and canal bridges

⑦
Lauwersoog

🅰E1 🚌50, 63, 163
ℹ️Reitdiepskade 11, Zoutkamp; 0595-401957

At Lauwersoog, from where the ferry leaves for the island of Schiermonnikoog (p282), is the Lauwersmeer, a 20 sq km (7.7 sq mile) nature reserve. When the Lauwerszee was drained, the land was designated for four purposes: agriculture, recreation, a nature reserve and an army training area.

Lauwersoog is a good base from which to explore the tuff churches that, in the Middle Ages, were built in villages such as Doezum, Bedum and Zuidwolde. They can be recognized by their grey or green porous stone.

⑧ 🏃🎨🎭🍽️🏛️
Fraeylemaborg

🅰F1 🏠Hoofdweg 30, Slochteren ⏰10am-5pm Tue-Fri, 1-5pm Sat, Sun & hols (from 11am Jul-Sep); park open all year
🌐fraeylemaborg.nl

Fraeylemaborg is one of the most imposing castles of Groningen. It dates back to the Middle Ages. Three embrasures in the kitchen and the hall above it bear silent witness to the defensive functions the castle once had. In the 17th century, two side wings were added, and in the 18th century it was given its present form with the addition of the monumental main wing. The castle is surrounded by a double moat.

The extensive wooded park just beyond the castle is an interesting combination of the 18th-century Baroque garden

⑥
Appingedam

🅰F1 🚌40, 45, 78, 140, 178
ℹ️Oude Kerkstraat 1; 0596-620300

A member of the Hanseatic League in the Middle Ages, this town was granted its charter in 1327. Standing at a junction of waterways and favoured with a seaport, it quickly grew into a major international trading centre. The medieval layout of the town has remained largely unchanged. Today, it is known for the so-called "Hangende Keukens" (Hanging Kitchens), visible from the Vlinterbrug bridge, which were constructed in the 16th century.

In the 18th century, Appingendam prospered, as illustrated by the elegant gabled houses of this period, that still line the main street of Solwerdstraat. The town has a preservation order as a place of historical interest, with over 65 listed buildings.

HANGING KITCHENS

If you follow the Damsterdiep canal by boat through the medieval town of Appingedam you'll notice unusual, small white structures jutting out of the side of the red-bricked 16th-century houses. These are the famous Hanging Kitchens, built owing to a lack of space in the main houses, which were actually former warehouses. These kitchens also had another practical function - it was much easier to collect water and dump it back out into the canal below through the kitchen windows.

→

The charming gardens of the attractive Menkemaborg castle in Uithuizen

> **Uithuizen's exceptionally pretty moated castle, the Menkemaborg, dates back to the 14th century.**

style and the 19th-century English landscape gardens and is planted with many unusual and exotic species.

⑨
Uithuizen

ⒶF1 **🚌**41, 61, 62, 641, 662
ℹMennonietenkerkstraat 13; 0595-434051

Uithuizen's exceptionally pretty moated castle, the Menkemaborg, dates back to the 14th century. It acquired its present-day form in around 1700 and its beautifully furnished rooms reflect life in this era. The bedroom features a ceremonial bedstead dating from the early 18th century, when King William III stayed here. The kitchen in the cellar has all the old fittings. The gardens were laid out when the castle was restored in the 18th century. The Schathuis, or treasury, which formerly used to store the food that was brought by the townspeople to the castle, currently houses a restaurant.

Menkemaborg

⊘ 🎫 **Ⓐ**Menkemaweg 2
🚌61 **🕐**Mar-Jun & Sep: 10am-5pm Tue-Sun; Jul-Aug: 10am-5pm daily; Oct-Dec: 10am-4pm Tue-Sun **🚫**Jan-Feb **🌐**menkemaborg.nl

⑩
Slochteren

ⒶF1 **🚌**78, 178
ℹHoofdweg 88a; 06-11024772

When a natural gas field was discovered here in 1959, the village of Slochteren gained overnight national renown. The "Slochteren Dome" appeared to be the largest in the world when it was first discovered, and the revenue it brought in made Holland rich.

The past of this historic town is closely associated with the lords of the castle of Fraeylemaborg. Atmospherically sited on raised ground amid trees, the Reformed Church in Slochteren incorporates the remnants of a 13th-century Romanesque-Gothic cross-naved church. The only part of original church that survives intact is the striking free-standing tower.

The surrounding countryside is excellent for walking or cycling, and includes picturesque nature reserves such as 't Roegwold, with peat lakes, forest and marshland, home to a variety of bird species. There is also a large lake, Schildmeer, bordered by an attractive 14 km (8.7 mile) walking and cycle path.

↑ The Veenkoloniaal Museum, dedicated to the Groningen peatlands

⑪

Veendam

🅰 F2 🚌 71, 73
ℹ Museumplein 5b; 0598-364224

Parkstad Veendam (Veendam Garden City) is so called for the lush greenery in the town. For centuries Veendam was the industrial heart of the Groningen peat colonies. However, at the end of the 19th century, peat-cutting fell into decline. Although shipping grew in importance – Veendam even had its own maritime school – the town retained its character as a peat-cutting centre.

In the heart of the town, the **Veenkoloniaal Museum** (Peat Colony Museum) offers a fascinating permanent exhibition illustrating the history of peat-cutting, navigation, agriculture and industry in the Groningen peatlands.

The most renowned inhabitant of Veendam was Anthony Winkler Prins (1817–1908), who wrote the famous encyclopaedia which is still associated with his name.

Veenkoloniaal Museum
⊘ 🅰 Museumplein 5
🕙 10am–5pm Tue–Fri, 1–5pm Sat–Mon 🚫 Public hols
🌐 veenkoloniaalmuseum.nl

⑫

Bourtange

🅰 G2 🚌 70, 72 ℹ Willem Lodewijkstraat; www.bourtange.nl

Right at the German border is the magnificent fortified town of Bourtange. The town dates back to 1580, when William of Orange ordered that a fortress with five bastions be built here on what had once been swampland. The defence works were continuously upgraded, until the fort gradually lost its defensive functions. It has now been painstakingly restored to its 18th-century appearance. The **Museum "De Baracquen"** exhibits

Did You Know?

Every June, the Battle of Bourtange is recreated at the fort, the largest reenactment in the Netherlands.

> **Bourtange dates back to 1580, when William of Orange ordered that a fortress with five bastions be built here on what had once been swampland.**

artifacts excavated in the fort. The charming town itself lies within a star-shaped labyrinth of moats.

Museum "De Baracquen"

♿ 🏠 Meestraat 3
🕐 Hours vary, check website 🌐 bourtange.nl

13

Ter Apel

🅰 G2 🚌 26, 70, 73
ℹ️ Markt 29; 0599-581277

In Ter Apel, situated between Drenthe and Germany in the Westerwolde region, is a 1465 monastery of the same name. In 1933, the monastery was thoroughly restored and now functions as a museum, the **Museum-klooster Ter Apel**, with permanent and changing exhibitions devoted to ecclesiastic art and religious history and exhibitions of contemporary art. The monastery is set amid a beautiful wooded landscape. The fragrant herb garden located in the monastery cloisters includes a collection of traditional medicinal herbs such as birthwort and common rue.

Museum-klooster Ter Apel

♿😊🕐 🏠 Boslaan 3
🕐 10am–5pm Tue–Sat, 1–5pm Sun & public hols
🌐 kloosterterapel.nl

→

The monument commemorating the Battle of Heiligerlee

14

Oude en Nieuwe Pekela

🅰 G2 🚌 75 ℹ️ Raadhuislaan 8; 0597-617555

The "old" and "new" villages of Pekela are typical ribbon developments with a marked rural, peatland character. In the 18th century, potato flour and straw-board manufacture grew in importance in the region. There are pleasant footpaths along the main canal, ideal for walking and cycling.

15

Winschoten

🅰 G2 🚌 10, 12, 13, 14, 17, 29 ℹ️ Torenstraat 10; 0597-430022

The little town of Winschoten in Oost-Groningen is known primarily for its three mills: Berg, a corn and hulling mill from 1854; Dijkstra, which is 25 m (82 ft) in height and dates from 1862; and Edens, a corn and hulling mill dating from 1761.

The interesting **Museum Stoomgemaal** contains the last surviving steam-powered pump in Groningen. Dating from 1878, it was used to drain the flooded polderland.

DRINK

Eetcafe 't Oal Kroegie

Choose from a selection of coffees, beers, wines and milkshakes at this cosy old pub in the heart of Bourtange.

🅰 G2 🏠 Marktplein 8, Bourtange
🌐 oalkroegie.nl

De Refter

Beer has been brewed by the Monastery Ter Apel since 1465. Sample traditional brews at the on-site café.

🅰 G2 🏠 Boslaan 3, Ter Apel
🌐 kloosterterapel.nl

In Heiligerlee, 3 km (2 miles) northwest of Winschoten, stands a monument to the Battle of Heiligerlee in 1568. This battle, the first Orange victory over the Spanish and marking the start of the Eighty Years' War, is famous for being over in just two hours and for the death of Count Adolf of Nassau. The small **Museum "Slag bij Heiligerlee"** houses an exhibition dedicated to the bloody battle.

Museum Stoomgemaal

♿ 🏠 Oostereinde 4
🕐 Hours vary, check website 🌐 stoom-groningen.nl

Museum "Slag bij Heiligerlee"

♿ 🏠 Provinciale-weg 55, Heiligerlee
🕐 Apr & Oct: 1–5pm Tue–Sun; May–Sep: 10am–5pm Tue–Sat, 1pm–5pm Sun 🌐 museaheiligerlee.nl

An old building on Breedeplaats in Franeker

FRIESLAND

With its elongated coastline, handsome country towns and web of fenlands and waterways, Friesland is one of the most charming provinces in the Netherlands. It takes its name from its earliest known settlers, the Frisians, or Frisii, a Germanic tribe who settled along the North Sea shoreline in the 4th century BC. A century later, they were subdued by the Romans, but re-emerged as the dominant force along much of the same coastline. By about the 4th century AD, these lands were largely abandoned as a result of tribal conflicts and flooding caused by a rise in sea levels. A couple of centuries later, changing environmental and political conditions made the region habitable again, and the coastal regions were repopulated. The Germanic Franks conquered the region after the Battle of the Boarn in 734, but this was just one episode of an ongoing saga in which, over the next eight centuries or so, the Frisians were time and again pitted against more powerful neighbours. The 9th century saw the start of the Freedom of the Frisians, a unique period with an absence of feudalism and serfdom – while feudal lords reigned in the rest of Europe, Friesland had elected *redjeven* (representatives). This came to an end in 1523, when the Habsburgs conquered the region. In 1566, the Frisians joined the Dutch Revolt against the Habsburgs and Friesland was subsequently absorbed into the Verenigde Nederlanden (United Provinces). Despite that, the Frisian language has survived as one of two official languages of the province – the country's only region to have its own language recognized in this way – 94 per cent of the population can understand spoken Frisian, 74 per cent can speak it and 75 per cent can read it. Today, although Friesland remains firmly agricultural, with its famous Frisian cows and horses, it has also started benefiting from a burgeoning tourist industry.

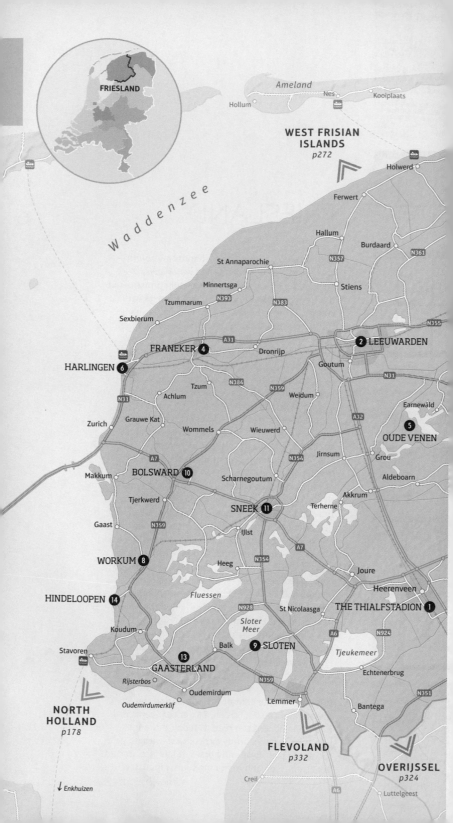

FRIESLAND

Must Sees
① The Thialfstadion

Experience More
② Leeuwarden
③ Dokkum
④ Franeker
⑤ Oude Venen
⑥ Harlingen
⑦ Beetsterzwaag
⑧ Workum
⑨ Sloten
⑩ Bolsward
⑪ Sneek
⑫ Appelscha
⑬ Gaasterland
⑭ Hindeloopen

Schiermonnikoog

Schiermonnikoog

Engelsmanplaat

Lauwersoog

Moddergat

N358

N361

Lauwersmeer

Metslawier

N361

Zoutkamp

N358

Engwierum

③ DOKKUM

Damwâld

Kollum

N355

Grijpskerk

N356

Buitenpost

Feanwâlden

Kootstertille

N358

Burgumer-
Meer

N369

GRONINGEN
p284

Surhuisterveen

Leek

Burgum

N356

Roden

Rottevalle

N31

A7

Groningen
Airport Eelde

Zuidlaren

Oudega

Drachten

A28

N34

Langelo

FRIESLAND

Bakkeveen

Vries

⑦ BEETSTERZWAAG

Norg

N373

Hemrik

N381

Veenhuizen

N392

Donkerbroek

A7

Gorredijk

Hoornsterzwaag

Assen

N371

Oudehorne

Nijeberkoop

Oosterwolde

Rolde

N33

N380

Ravenswoud

N376

Oldeberkoop

N351

APPELSCHA ⑫

DRENTHE
p312

Grolloo

Zorgvlied

N381

Hooghalen

Noordwolde

DRENTHE

N374

Wolvega

A32

Geeuwenbrug

Beilen

Vledder

N381

A28

Westerbork

De Bult

Diever

N371

Dwingeloo

Wijster

Steenwijk

Uffelte

0 kilometres   10

N

Scheerwolde

Giethoorn

A32

0 miles   10

Excitement building in the
crowd before an event in
Thialfstadion's main arena ↑

🅞 ⌗ ⌗ ⌗

THE THIALFSTADION

🄰 E2 🏠 Pim Mulierlaan 1, Heerenveen 🚉 Heerenveen 🕐 Hours vary,
check website 🌐 thialf.nl

Speed-skating is arguably the Netherlands' national sport, and the
high-tech, high-octane Thialf stadium in Heerenveen is the best
place to see the country's top athletes powering across the ice.

The Thialfstadion in Heerenveen is the temple
of Dutch ice-skating and has international
renown. The great hall covers an area of
15,000 m² (17,950 sq yd), with a staggering
70 km (43 miles) of cooling elements under
the rink. It can accommodate 12,500 spectators;
next door is a 4,000-seat ice hockey arena. The
exuberant crowds that converge on the stadium
for international events create a unique
atmosphere. Skating heroes such as Marianne
Timmer, Sven Kramer and Rintje Ritsma have
all experienced emotional highlights in their
sporting careers here. The climax of every
major skating event in the Thialfstadion is the
procession of winners through the stadium
on a special sleigh drawn by a Frisian horse.

↑ Dutch Olympic champion Ireen Wüst
leading the field on the Thialf ice

WHAT ELSE TO DO IN HEERENVEEN

There's more to Heerenveen than ice skating. The city's contemporary art museum, Museum Belvédère *(www. museumbelvedere.nl)* showcases mainly Frisian artists. The building itself is a modern sculpture, houses a collection of 20th-century and modern Dutch paintings in various forms of Impressionism, Expressionism and Realism. The garden park is an extension of the museum, with walkable promenades along the canal.

←
The final of the FIM Ice Speedway Gladiators World Championship, held at Thialf in 2019

💬 INSIDER TIP
Take a Pole

Try your hand at at *fierljeppen* (pole-vaulting across ditches) – it's a favourite extreme sport in Friesland and annual competitions take place throughout the province. Enquire at the VVV (tourist office) in Heerenveen for practice locations *(www. ngoudenplak.nl)*.

↑ The grand plaza marking the entrance to the monumental Thialfstadion

EXPERIENCE MORE

2

Leeuwarden

E1 Achmeatoren, Sophialaan 4; www.visit-leeuwarden.com

The busy Frisian town of Leeuwarden is the provincial capital. It was established in the 13th century, as illustrated by the town park and gardens of the Prinsentuin and Stadhouderlijk Hof which date back to this period.

A cultural hub, Leeuwarden has plenty of museums and galleries, including the fascinating **Fries Museum**. Here you'll find a large collection of ancient items excavated from burial mounds, as well as displays of fashion, art and applied arts. The same building also houses the **Verzetsmuseum Friesland**, dedicated to the Friesland resistance movement of World War II, in which more than 600 Jewish people and nearly 300 members of the resistance were killed. There are chronological exhibitions on World War II and its aftermath, explorations of contemporary wars.

In the town centre, on the street of Oldehoofsterkerkhof, the leaning tower of Oldehove dominates the skyline. When building began in 1529, the church tower was going to be the tallest in the Netherlands. Unfortunately, the foundations began to sink, and so the work stopped just three years later. The tower has remained incomplete ever since. The top of the tower offers an excellent view, reaching as far as the coast on clear days.

The **Het Princessehof** museum, housed in a palace that was formerly the residence of Maria Louise van Hessen-Kassel, contains a unique collection of Asian, European and contemporary ceramics and tiles.

Leeuwarden's old municipal orphanage is now home to the **Natuurmuseum Fryslân** (Natural History Museum), where the popular interactive ride, Underwater Safari, is well worth experiencing.

MATA HARI

Margaretha Geertruida Zelle (1876-1917), who became known to all the world as Mata Hari, grew up in Leeuwarden. Her life came to a tragic end in Vincennes outside Paris, where she was executed by a firing squad after a French tribunal found her guilty of spying for the Germans. Leeuwarden's Fries Museum has exhibits about this legendary woman, who gained international notoriety through films and books about her life. The house where she lived with her parents is at Grote Kerkstraat 212.

Fries Museum
Wilhelminaplein 92 11am-5pm Tue-Sun friesmuseum.nl

Verzetsmuseum
Wilhelminaplein 92 11am-5pm Tue-Sun friesverzetsmuseum.nl

Het Princessehof
Grote Kerkstraat 9 11am-5pm Tue-Sun princessehof.nl

Natuurmuseum Fryslân
Schoenmakersperk 2 10am-5pm Tue-Sun natuurmuseumfryslan.nl

The modern Fries Museum, in the heart of Leeuwarden ↑

❸ Dokkum

🅰E1 🚌 ℹ️Diepswal 27

The trading and garrison town of Dokkum was the headquarters of the Frisian Admiralty between 1596 and 1645. But the town is most well-known as the place where St Boniface was killed by pagan Frisians in AD 754. The local history museum, the **Admiraliteitshuis**, has an exhibition on the life of the saint, with other exhibits including artifacts excavated from burial mounts, costumes, silverware and folk art. Pilgrims travel through the town on a route which takes in Dokkum's church, the Bonifatiuskerk, a park surrounding the chapel and the well of Bonifatiusbron, a natural spring whose waters are believed to have therapeutic qualities.

On the former town walls, now a park, are two 19th-century belt-type mills known as *De Hoop* and *Zeldenrust* (p29).

Admiraliteitshuis

⊛ 🅰Diepswal 27
🕙10–5pm Mon–Sat, 1–5pm Sun 🌐museumdokkum.nl

---

❹ Franeker

🅰D1 🚌🚆 ℹ️Voorstraat 35; 058-2572590

Franeker was a university town from 1585 to 1811. Today, it is the centre of skating in Friesland. In and around the Voorstraat are several monumental buildings, including the 14th-century Cammingahuis, which houses the **Kaatsmuseum** (skating museum). The **Museum Martena**, in a fine 18th-century building, has a collection about the former university. Opposite the Renaissance Stadhuis is the **Planetarium Friesland** dating back to 1781. Beside the Sjûkelân, a sacred place for Frisian skating, is the Bogt fen Guné (16th century), Holland's oldest student café.

Kaatsmuseum

⊛ 🅰Voorstraat 2
🕙Hours vary, check website 🌐keatsmuseum.nl

Museum Martena

⊛⊛ 🅰Voorstraat 35
🕙11am–5pm Tue–Sun
🌐museummartena.nl

Planetarium Friesland

⊛ 🅰Eise Eisingastraat 3
🕙10am–5pm Tue–Sat, 11–5pm Sun 🌐planetarium-friesland.nl

---

❺ Oude Venen

🅰E2 🚌 ℹ️Koaidyk 8a, Earnewâld 🌐np-alde feanen.nl

This region, lying between Earnewâld and Grou, is made up of peat-marshes with reedlands, swampy woodlands and sunken polders. The lakes were formed in the 17th and 18th centuries by peat-cutting and now offer a home to over 100 species of birds and around 400 plant species. Much attention has been paid to water cleanliness, and otters have returned to the area to breed.

Reidplûm Visitors' Centre is a good starting point for hiking and sailing expeditions. Not far from the centre is the Eibertshiem, a breeding place for storks. In winter, the area hosts many skating tours.

Reidplûm Visitors' Centre

🅰Ds v.d Veenweg 7, Earnewâld 📞0511-539410
🕙Mid-Apr–Sep: 1–5pm daily

DRINK

Speciaalbier Café De Markies

Beer-lovers rejoice, as this snug Dutch pub has over 250 bottled beers and 12 rotating brews on tap.

🅰E1 🅰Groot Schavernek 19, Leeuwarden 🌐de-markies.nl

Eetcafé de Winze

Riverside pub with a lovely terrace offering high tea, coffees and good wines.

🅰E1 🅰Wijns 30, Wijns 🌐dewinze.nl.

Grand Café 't Gerecht

Refined café with drinks to match. For parents, there's a supervised kids' club on weekends from 3 to 8pm.

🅰E2 🅰Gemeenteplein 33, Heerenveen 🌐gerecht heerenveen.nl

6
Harlingen

🅰 D1 🚗🚌 ℹ️ Grote
Bredeplaats 12; 0517-
430207

This little port town retains much of its old charm; many houses in the historic centre have been painstakingly restored. A statue of Hans Brinker, a figure from Dutch folklore, stands at the ferry port. Some 9 km (5.5 miles) south of Harlingen is Pingjum, where Menno Simons (1496–1561), the evangelical preacher after whom many Dutch Anabaptists named themselves, began his religious life. Mennonites from all over the world now visit.

←

Harlingen's statue of
Hans Brinker plugging
a dyke with his thumb

7
Beetsterzwaag

🅰 E2 🚌 ℹ️ Kerkepad Oost
33; 06-39677028

This village was once one of the seats of the Frisian landed gentry and so has a number of stately homes and gardens. Fine examples of these are Lauswolt, the Lycklamahuis and the Harinxmastate. Beetsterzwaag is surrounded by varied countryside, with coniferous and deciduous forests, heath and fens, offering ample opportunities for a leisurely afternoon of rambling and cycling.

8
Workum

🅰 D2 🚗🚌 ℹ️ Merk 4; 0515-
541045

The elongated Zuiderzee town of Workum flourished around

1300. Today, the town is known for the fine façades of its houses and its unfinished 16th-century church, the **Grote of Gertrudiskerk**. Beside the lock is the centuries-old wharf of **de Hoop**, where traditional boats are still built. The most popular attraction in Workum is the **Jopie Huisman Museum**, featuring the art of painter and scrap-metal-merchant Jopie Huisman (1922–2000).

WOUDAGEMAAL LEMMER

The 60-m- (197-ft-) tall chimney of the Woudagemaal water pumping station in Lemmer, south of Sloten, is the last remaining steam-powered station of its kind in the world. Built in 1920, it is still used in times of extreme high water. The visitor centre offers tours of the station. You can also view the austere exterior by boat (woudagemaal.nl).

← The attractive canalside buildings of Sloten, Friesland's smallest town

> The most popular attraction in Workum is the Jopie Huisman Museum, featuring the art of painter and scrap-metal-merchant Jopie Huisman (1922-2000).

His drawings and paintings tell the stories of everyday drudgery and toil. The 17th-century weigh house contains the local history museum, the **Museum Warkums Erfskip**.

Jopie Huisman Museum
🏛 ⌂ Noard 6 🕐 Apr-Oct: 10am–5pm Mon-Sat, 1-5pm Sun; Mar & Nov: 1-5pm daily
ⓦ jopiehuismanmuseum.nl

Museum Warkums Erfskip
🏛 ⌂ Merk 4 🕐 Jul-Aug: 10am-5pm Mon-Sat, 1-5pm Sun; Sep-Jun: 1-5pm daily
ⓦ warkumserfskip.nl

---

⑨ Sloten

🅰 E2 🚌 ℹ Museum Stedhûs Sleat, Heerenwal 48; 0514-531541

The smallest town in Friesland, replete with pretty canals, embankments and water-gates, was designed by famous Frisian military engineer Menno van Coehoorn. The old fortress mill at the Lemsterpoort is an octagonal *bovenkruier*-type mill from 1755. The **Museum Stedhûs Sleat** houses the **Laterna Magica** (a museum of magic lanterns), an antique museum and a collection of costumes, hats, fans and bells.

Museum Stedhûs Sleat
🏛 ⌂ Heerenwal 48 🕐 Hours vary, check website
ⓦ museumsloten.nl

---

⑩ Bolsward

🅰 D2 🚌 ℹ Wipstraat 6; 0515-577701

Modest Bolsward first arose in the 11th century as a trading post, enjoying the height of its development in the 15th century. Its Martinikerk, whose tower features a saddleback roof, was built during this period. The Stadhuis, with its local history museum, the Oudheidkamer (closed until 2021 for renovations), is the town's centrepiece.

Local brews can be sampled at the **Us Heit Bierbrouwerij**, the smallest brewery in the country. and guided tours show how the beer is made.

Us Heit Bierbrouwerij
⌂ Snekerstraat 43 🕐 3-6pm Thu & Fri, 10am-6pm Sat
ⓦ www.usheit.com

EAT

't Havenmantsje
Chic restaurant with water views and fine European dishes that resemble works of edible art.

🅰 D1 ⌂ Havenplein 1, Harlingen
ⓦ havenmantsje.nl

€€€

Roast
Modern eatery serving steaks, lamb and big-bowl salads.

🅰 E1 ⌂ Nieuwestad 63, Leeuwarden
ⓦ roastleeuwarden.nl

€€€

Het Witte Huis
Large, casual restaurant amid pretty garden surroundings, cooking up French and Dutch classics.

🅰 E2 ⌂ Van Harinxmaweg 20, Olterterp ⓦ witte huisolterterp.nl

€€€

⑪ Sneek

🄰E2 🚗🚌 𝒊Kleinzand 16;
0515-750678

Sneek's centrepiece is the Waterpoort (water-gate), dating from 1613. The town's "Sneekweek" is a popular sailing event that in early August brings together amateur sailors and partygoers from all over the country. **Fries Scheepvaart Museum** focuses on the Sneek's history of navigation and shipbuilding. Its exhibits include a *skûtsje* deckhouse, the cabin of a *boeier* yacht and some 200 model ships. The *zilverzaal* (silver room) houses one of the country's finest collections of Frisian silver.

The village of Wieuwerd, some 12 km (7 miles) north of Sneek, is known for the human mummies in its 13th-century St Nicholas church (open in summer). They were discovered by chance in 1765 but their origins remain a mystery.

Fries Scheepvaart Museum

♻️🕐 🄰Kleinzand 14
🕐10am–5pm Mon–Sat, noon–5pm Sun 🌐friesscheepvaartmuseum.nl

SKÛTSJE SAILING

Schuitje sailing, or *skûtsjesilen*, is a sport which has gained great popularity in the lakes of Friesland, *skûtje* being the name of the typical local *spritsail* barges. Originally used for carrying goods and as passenger ferries, today these boats are celebrated with *skûtsjesilen* races in Friesland in July and August. Every day, sailing prizes are awarded, and on the last day, in Sneek, the *skûtsje* champion of the year is announced and fêted. The races are held over 11 racing days and three rest days.

---

⑫ Appelscha

🄰F2 🚌 𝒊Boerestreek 23;
0516-431760

The village was created in the 19th century, when the main industry was peat-cutting; it is now on the edge of the Nationaal Park Drents-Friese Wold. The vast coniferous forests, drifting sands and colourful heath and fen areas around Appelscha form stunning surroundings.

A favourite place with visitors is the Kale Duinen area of drifting sands. On the Bosberg – at 26 m (85 ft) above sea level, the highest spot in the area – is a viewing tower and information centre.

A distinctive sight in southeast Friesland is the Klokkenstoel (bell stool). This "poor men's church tower" was a provisional church tower built when funds were low; it was usually situated in the churchyard. In Appelscha you will find a *klokkenstoel* dating from 1453. Some 6 km (4 miles west of Appelscha) Langedijke is home to what is presumed to be the oldest bell in the Netherlands, dating from 1300.

At Ravenswoud, 5 km (3 miles) northeast of Appelsche, an observation tower provides outstanding views of the surrounding countryside.

---

⑬ Gaasterland

🄰D2 🚌 𝒊De Brink 4,
Oudemirdum; 0514-571777

Situated in the southwestern corner of Friesland, this area of fine, rolling woodlands

The beautiful landscape of dunes and heather around the village of Appelscha ↑

offers many opportunities for walking and cycling. The region derives its name from the word *gaast*, which refers to the sandy heights formed here during the last two Ice Ages.

At the edge of Gaasterland are a number of steep cliffs, such as the Rode Klif and the Oudemirdumerklif, formed when the Zuiderzee eroded the coastline. On the Rode Klif at Laaxum is an enormous boulder, set here as a memento of the 1345 Frisian victory over the Dutch.

The Rijsterbos wood, with its abundant bracken, dates from the 17th century and once consisted mainly of oak. The Luts river in Balk, flanked by linden trees, inspired the poem *Mei* by Herman Gorter (1864–1927).

The village of Oudemirdum makes a good base from which to explore the area, with a hostel, shops and the **Informatiecentrum Mar en Klif** (Sea and Cliff Information Centre) which has information about the local geology, flora and fauna.

Informatiecentrum Mar en Klif
🏠 De Brink 4, Oudemirdum
🕐 Apr-Oct: 1-5pm Sun, Mon & hols, 10am-5pm Tue-Sat 🌐 marenklif.nl

↑ Pretty, canalside houses in the little old town of Hindeloopen

14

Hindeloopen

🅐 D2 🚉🚌 *ℹ* Dijkweg 1; 0514-851223

This picturesque old town has its own dialect, costume and style of painting. It is full of little canals with wooden bridges and captains' houses, with characteristic façades. One of the most distinctive spots is the picturesque lock-keeper's house by the port.

In the **Museum Hindeloopen**, the life of the wealthier citizens of Hindeloopen during the 18th century is showcased. Period rooms exhibit the colourful clothes and the painted furniture of the time. A fine exhibition of paintings vividly illustrates the development of painting in Hindeloopen.

The **Eerste Friese Schaatsmuseum** includes a unique collection of old ice skates and a fine exhibition dedicated to Friesland's famous Elfstedentocht ice-skating marathon.

Museum Hindeloopen
🏅 🏠 Dijkweg 1 🕐 Hours vary, check website 🌐 museumhindeloopen.nl

Eerste Friese Schaatsmuseum
🏅 🏠 Kleine Weide 1-3 🕐 10am-6pm Mon-Sat, 1-5pm Sun 🌐 schaats museum.nl

STAY

Hotel It Posthûs
Romantic 17th-century inn with modern rooms, set beside a boat-filled canal.

🅐 E1 🏠 Dominee R.H. Kuipersstraat 1, Burdaard 🌐 itposthus burdaard.nl

€€€

Post Plaza Hotel
Converted century-old post office turned fine hotel where rooms have rain showers. There are also a gym and excellent cafe on site.

🅐 E1
🏠 Tweebaksmarkt 27, Leeuwarden
🌐 post-plaza.nl

€€€

Weidumerhout
Riverside farmhouse hotel with ultra-modern cabins. Bikes and canoes are available to rent here too.

🅐 E2 🏠 Dekemawei 9, Weidum
🌐 weidumerhout.nl

€€€

DRENTHE

Pushing up against the German border, the province of Drenthe is one of the least known and least visited parts of the Netherlands, but, until the Bronze Age, it was one of the region's most densely populated areas. It was colonized by prehistoric peoples, who eked out what must have been a hard and precarious existence along the Hondsrug, low hills that are Drenthe's most distinctive geographical feature. Prehistoric remains can be seen throughout the Hondsrug, most notably a series of megalithic tombs, simple stone structures known as *hunebedden*. In the medieval period, parts of Drenthe were cleared for cultivation by monks, who also established a handful of working monasteries. After long being governed by the bishopric of Utrecht, Drenthe was ceded by Henry of the Palatinate, Prince-Bishop of Utrecht, to Emperor Charles V Habsburg, who incorporated it into the Habsburg Netherlands. In 1581, Drenthe became a part of the Verenigde Nederlanden (United Provinces), although it never gained full provincial status – the region was so poor it was exempt from paying taxes and was denied full representation as a result. Right up until the 19th century, the province was little more than swathes of empty moorland, marshland and peat bog, whose isolation was strategically used by the Nazis during World War II. Before the war, the Dutch government had established Westerbork camp to house German Jewish refugees – it was here, far from prying eyes, that the Nazis set up the country's largest transit camp for the Dutch Jews, including Anne Frank, that they would soon transport to the gas chambers further east. Today, Drenthe remains a sparsely populated area, mainly reliant on agriculture, with pockets of industry among a light scattering of modest little towns.

DRENTHE

Experience

FRIESLAND

FRIESLAND
p300

FRIESLAND
p300

Nationaal Park
Drents-Friese Wold

NORG 1

DIEVER 11

DWINGELOO 9

Nationaal Park
Dwingelderveld

0 kilometres   10

0 miles   10

N

EXPERIENCE

① Norg

⚑ F2 🚍 ℹ Brink 1; 0592-741147

The Romanesque church on the river Brink dates from the 13th century. Sadly, the unique frescoes in the choir have barely survived through the centuries and are in very poor condition.

The area around Norg is steeped in prehistory. Three megalithic tombs (known as *hunnebedden* in Dutch) are to be found there, while in the Noordsche Veld, an area of forest and heathland, are a number of Bronze Age tumuli (burial mounds), the Negen Bergen. Just south of Norg lies an extensive forest of oakwood and holly, one of the oldest forests in the country and a popular gathering point during the Middle Ages.

---

② Assen

⚑ F2 🚍 ℹ Marktstraat 8; 0592 243788

Assen is the capital of Drenthe, although it was only upgraded from a village to a town in 1809. The cloister of the abbey church of Maria in Campis (1258–1600) now forms part of the Rijksarchief (National Adrchive), set on the town green, the Brink. Also here is the **Drents Museum** of local history, which is housed in the abbey church, the Ontvangershuis (1698), the Drostenhuis (1778) and Provinciehuis (1885). The museum contains a wealth of exhibits on prehistoric times and the town's history as well as a "discovery room" for children. There are also collections of local art, including works by landscape painter Bernard Von Dülmen-Krumpelmann (1897–1987).

The controversial finds of Tjerk Vermaning (1929–87), who in the 1960s extended the history of human habitation in Holland by tens of thousands of years, are in a separate display case: disputes on the authenticity of the flint tools he found have not yet been resolved.

Outside the formal gardens of the Drostenhuis is a statue of the the town's trademark, *Bartje*, a little peasant boy from Dutch author Anne de Vries' book (1935) who did not want to pray before his daily meals of brown beans. The main thoroughfares of

> **The area around Norg is steeped in prehistory. Three megalithic tombs (known as *hunnebedden* in Dutch) are to be found there.**

→ Statues scattered among the gardens in front of the Drents Museum in Assen

the Vaart and the Markt sport the characteristic stately white houses of Assen, which were built in the late 18th to the early 19th centuries.

Between Markt and Brink is the commercial centre with its pedestrian precinct and excellent facilities. Modern-day Assen comes to life when the circuit van Assen TT motorcycle racing event is held here each year on the last Saturday in June. Around 100,000 spectators descend on the town, which is home to the only remaining circuit from the championship's inaugural season in 1949. Just south of Assen lies Asserbos, a large public park containing some ancient woodland, and perfect for walking and cycling. There are also several ponds, an open-air theatre and a farm where children can get up close to the animals.

Drents Museum

⊕⊛⊕ 🏛Brink 1 🕐11 am–5pm Tue–Sun (Mon on public hols) 🚫1 Jan, 25 Dec
🌐drentsmuseum.nl

3
Eelde-Paterswolde

🗺F2 🚌52 ℹB Boermalaan 4; 050-3092136

Two villages merge together at Eelde-Paterswolde and are squeezed between the Paterswoldse Meer lake and Groningen Airport, which, despite its name, is actually in Drenthe not Groningen. The lake is a popular place for watersports activities, especially sailing. The airport serves mainly domestic flights (it is a half-hour flight to Schiphol) and amateur flying enthusiasts.

The distinctive modern brick building housing the **Museum De Buitenplaats** (De Buitenplaats museum of figurative art) was designed by the architects Alberts and Van Huut. It is a fine example

↑ The sun setting over the Paterswolde Meer at Eelde-Paterswolde

of their organic architecture. In addition to hosting changing exhibitions, the museum is used as a concert hall. There are also formal and landscaped gardens, the former fronting the 17th-century curator's residence, the Nijsinghuis. Since 1983 the house has been painted by figurative artists and is periodically opened to visitors by prior arrangement.

The Eelde part of town is home to one of the country's more unusual museums. The quirky **International Klompenmuseum** is dedicated to the last two clog-makers to live in the village, and gives an overview of the development of the clog. It displays examples of clogs from around the world – some 2,400 of them. Most visitors, however, come here to see the world's largest clog, which is 6.5 m (21 ft) long.

Museum De Buitenplaats

⊕⊛⊕ 🏛Hoofdweg 76 📞050-3095818 🕐11am–5pm Tue–Sun, Easter Sun & Easter Mon 🚫1 Jan, 25 Dec

International Klompenmuseum

⊕⊛⊕⊕ 🏛Wolfhorn 1a 🕐Apr–Oct: Tue–Sun 2–5pm
🌐klompenmuseum.nl

STAY

Drouwenerzand
Stay in a comfortable treehouse complete with WiFi, kitchen and bathroom.

🗺F2 🏛Gasselterstraat 7, Drouwen
🌐drouwenerzand.nl

€€€

Ky Hotel
Lovingly restored farmhouse with en-suite rooms and room service.

🗺F2 🏛Brink 24, Roden
🌐ky-hotel.nl

€€€

De Jufferen Lunsingh
Country house B&B with spacious rooms overlooking the grazing sheep and cows outside.

🗺F2 🏛Hoofdweg 13, Westervelde
🌐dejufferenlunsingh.nl

€€€

EAT

De Wapser Herberg
Located at the edge of a national park, this hotel restaurant serves traditional Dutch cuisine.

🅰F2 🏠Ten Darperweg 104, Wapse
🆆wapserherberg.nl

€€€

Bij Jaap
Classy award-winning restaurant with creative Dutch dishes and wine to match.

🅰F2 🏠Markt 17, Assen
🆆bij-jaap.nl

€€€

Luning's Restaurant
Family-friendly spot with a tapas menu and Dutch pancakes as their specialities.

🅰F2 🏠Brink 1, Ruinen
🆆restaurantluning.nl

€€€

④ Westerbork

🅰F2 🚌22 🛈BG van Wezelplein 10; 0593-331381

Westerbork's Hoofdstraat (main street) features a Late Gothic 14th-century church, which now houses the Museum van Papierknipkunst (Paper-Cutting Museum), and Saxon farmhouses. However, the town is visited primarily for its more recent history. In World War II, the Westerbork Transit Camp stood here. It was from this camp that 107,000 Jews, among them Anne Frank (p112), Gypsies and resistance fighters were held before being deported to the Nazi concentration camps.Today the **Herinneringscentrum Kamp Westerbork** explores the history of the camp.

Herinneringscentrum Kamp Westerbork
⊛ 🏠Oosthalen 8, Hooghalen 🕐Hours vary, check website
🆆kampwesterbork.nl

⑤ Orvelte

🅰F2 🚌22, 23
🛈Dorpsstraat 1; www.orvelte.net

The whole of Orvelte is in effect an open-air museum. In the restored Saxon farmhouses from the early 19th century, there are exhibits on agriculture and displays of traditional crafts. Cars are banned from the area, but tours in horse-drawn trams or covered wagons are offered. The **Bezoekerscentrum** (Visitors Centre) has information on tours and exhibitions. The more interesting attractions of the town include a tinsmith's shop.

Bezoekerscentrum
⊛🕐🛈🖂 🏠Dorpsstraat 3
☎0593-322335

→ A memorial at Westerbork Camp to the deportees

← Herding a flock of sheep, a common sight in Drenthe

CLOG MAKING IN DRENTHE

Wooden clogs, a typical Dutch icon, were once commonly worn as protective footwear for farmers working with heavy equipment and in muddy fields. Today, you can still see skilled artisans, based in Orvelte and Eelde-Paterswolde, make the clogs in the traditional way, crafted from a single piece of wood and then hollowed out by hand with a special chisel.

6

Hondsrug

⬛F2 ▣ ℹ Hunebedstraat 4a, Borger; www.dehonds rug.nl

Between the Drenthe sand plateau in the west and the Drents-Groningen peat moors in the east lies the Hondsrug ridge, a designated UNESCO Global Geopark. Prehistoric people found it a safe place to settle, leaving behind them numerous megaliths (p322).

The Drentse Aa river basin, the old villages of Gieten, Gasselte, Exloo and Odoorn, the drifting sand areas of the Drouwenerzand and the heathland of Ellertsveld are particularly attractive hiking areas, with plenty of streams in which to cool off.

7

Rolde

⬛F2 ▣ ℹ Onder de Molen (at the base of the windmill), Grote Brink 22; 0592-241502

Rolde was an important town in the late Middle Ages and served as the administrative capital of Drenthe. There are prehistoric tumuli (in the Tumulibos woods), and three megaliths, two of which are on the mound directly behind the church. During the Middle Ages, people were tried at the Ballooërkuil; if guilty they were held prisoner in the 15th-century church, a magnificent Gothic edifice. Forests, peatland and drifting sands surround the village.

→
A mid-19th-century smock mill, dubbed "De Wachter" (Watchman), in Zuidlaren

To the north of Rolde lies the Ballooërveld, a large and beautiful area of heathland grazed by sheep and bearing traces of ancient cart tracks and Celtic field patterns.

8

Zuidlaren

⬛F2 ▣ ℹ Tourist office inside the Brink Hotel, Oostzijde 6; 050-4091261

The Zuidlaren horse market, now the largest in Western Europe, predates even the 13th-century church which stands on the Brink. The market is held on the third Tuesday in October. Zuidlaren is also known for the 17th-century Havezathe Laarwoud, a historic residence (not open to the public) built on the remnants of the fort of the counts of Heiden, who ruled the region in the 14th century.

The Zuidlaardermeer lake offers everything that watersports enthusiasts may require. Children will especially enjoy Zuidlaren's subtropical swimming complex, **Aqualaren**, as well as the **Speelpark Sprookjeshof** recreation centre with playpark; they can be combined on a round tour.

Aqualaren

⊛ ⬛Wilhelminalaan 1, Zuidlaren ▣ aqualaren.nl

Speelpark Sprookjeshof

⊛ ⬛Groningerstraat 10, Zuidlaren ⏱May-Sep: 10am–6pm ▣sprook jeshof.nl

⑨
Dwingeloo

🅰F2 🚌20 ℹBrink 4b; 0521-591000

The first thing that strikes visitors about Dwingeloo is the onion dome of the 14th-century church tower (the Siepelkerk). You can read about the legend behind this oddity on the information board located nearby.

There is some impressive countryside around the town. The Dwingelderveld is a national park and the *krentenbossen* (currant plantations) which flower in April and May – the fruit ripening in July or August – are delightful in every respect: they are pleasant to the eye and to the taste buds. At the edge of the Dwingelose Heide heath is a radio-telescope.

The nearby **Planetron** is an observatory with a planetarium and large-screen cinema, hosts child-friendly exhibits and film screeenings.

Planetron

🐾😊👁 🅳Drift 11b
🕐Hours vary, check website 🔲planetron.nl

⑩
Borger

🅰F2 🚌59 ℹHoofdstraat 25a; 0599-638729

Borger is the capital of the *hunebeddengebeid*, or mega-lith region. There are eight megaliths in and around the town, including the largest in Holland. Nearby is the **Hunebedcentrum**, with a fine exhibition about the Beaker People and a stone casket from the most recently excavated megalith, which was discovered in 1982 in Groningen.

The **Buitencentrum Boomkroonpad** (tree-top walk), 2 km (1 mile) down the "Staatsbossen" turn-off on the Rolde-Borger road, is an interesting attraction. The walk starts at the roots of the trees, with a 23-m (75-ft) tunnel. The trail leads to a 125-m (410-ft) ascent along a boardwalk up to a height of 22.5 m (74 ft), affording a fascinating view of the forest canopy.

Hunebedcentrum

🐾😊 🅳Hunebedstraat 27 🕐10am–5pm Mon–Fri, 11am–5pm Sat & Sun 🚫1 Jan, 25 Dec 🔲hunebed centrum.eu

Buitencentrum Boomkroonpad

🐾😊 🅳Steenhopenweg 4, Drouwen 📞0592-377305 🕐10am–5pm daily 🚫1 Jan

Did You Know?

Borger is home to Holland's largest megalith, which measures 22.5m (74 ft) long.

Hiking through the Dwingelderveld National Park in autumn ↑

⓫
Diever

Ⓐ F2 🚌 20 **ⓘ** Bosweg 2a;
0521-591748

Diever was an important
centre from prehistoric times
to the Middle Ages. Tumuli,
megaliths and remains of the
9th-century wooden found-
ations of the village church
lend it historical importance.
The church features a 12th-
century Romanesque tower of
tufa stone. Diever is in the
middle of the Nationaal Park
Drents-Friese Wold, excellent
for cycling and rambling.

⓬
Coevorden

Ⓐ F3 🚆🚌 **ⓘ** Haven 4; 0524-
525150

The castle here dates from
around 1200. The star-shaped
moat and surviving bastions
and town walls define the
look of the town, while the

façades of the Friesestraat
and Weeshuisstraat are telling
of past centuries. **Stedelijk
Museum Coevorden** high-
lights the town's history.

Stedelijk Museum
Coevorden

♻ 😊 **Ⓐ** Haven 4 **Ⓒ** 9:30-
5pm Tue-Sat, noon-5pm
Sun 🌐 museumcoevorden.nl

⓭
Emmen

Ⓐ G2 🚆🚌 **ⓘ** Hoofdstraat
22; 0591-649712

Emmen is the result of the
amalgamation of several
villages. Eleven megaliths,
including Langgraf op de
Schimmer Es, the urn-fields
and prehistoric farmland in
the vicinity as well as the
12th-century tower on the
Hoofdstraat reflect the district's history. At **Wildlands**
zoo, animals roam freely.
  Roughly 10 km (6 miles)
east of Emmen are the
Amsterdamsche Veld upland
peat marshes, perhaps the
loneliest place in Holland.
In Barger-Compascuum,
Veenpark re-creates the
times when the people of
Drenthe lived in poverty,
cutting peat. In 1883, Vincent
van Gogh stayed at the ferry-
house in Veenoord (Nieuw-
Amsterdam). Now known as
the **Van Gogh House**, this has
been restored to the way it
was when the artist stayed, as
has the café-restaurant below.

Wildlands

♻ 🎡 😊 **Ⓐ** Raadhuisplein
99 **Ⓒ** 10am–5pm daily
🌐 wildlands.nl

Veenpark

♻ 😊 **Ⓐ** Barger-Compascuum
Ⓒ Apr–Nov: 10am–5pm
daily 🌐 veenpark.nl

Van Gogh Huis

🎡 😊 👣 **Ⓐ** Van Goghstraat
1, Nieuw-Amsterdam
Ⓒ 1–5pm Tue-Sun
🌐 vangogh-drenthe.nl

↑ A herd of antelope,
roaming freely at the
Wildlands zoo, Emmen

A DRIVING TOUR
THE MEGALITH ROUTE

Length 130 km (80 miles) **Stopping-off points**
Assen; Diever; Havelt **Terrain** Easy driving along well-signposted roads

Of the 54 prehistoric megaliths in Holland, 52 are in found in Drenthe. Known as *hunebedden*, these ancient landmarks are the remains of tombs built from boulders by the Neolithic Beaker People some 5,000 years ago. According to local folklore, the megaliths were built by the *huynen*, giants of great strength after whom the *hunebedden* are named. Modern historians believe that the boulders were placed with their flat edges on rollers, which allowed the Beaker People to move them to the site of the tomb. Those still standing today are only the frameworks of the tombs, long-hidden beneath sandhills.

This driving tour meanders through the Drenthe countryside, a patchwork of farm- and woodland dotted with ancient tombs, taking in pretty villages and the many major archaeological sights.

*The little hamlet of **Zeijen** has a small tomb signposted from the main road.*

*Begin this drive in **Westervelde**. Here, two passage stones mark the entrance to a small hunebed in a particularly peaceful spot.*

*Admire ancient archaeological finds such as axeheads and beads at Assen's **Drents Museum** (p316).*

↑ Tomb atop a tumulus in Assen; at night, ghostly white women are said to emerge and dance among the stones

Langelo

Norg

Westervelde

START

Zeijen

Assen

Bovensmilde

Smilde

Hooghalen

Hoogersmilde

Beilen

Diever

Dwingeloo

Wijster

Ruinen

Uffelte

FINISH

Havelte

*End this drive at **Havelte**, where two striking megaliths, D53 and D54, are set in a peaceful clearing.*

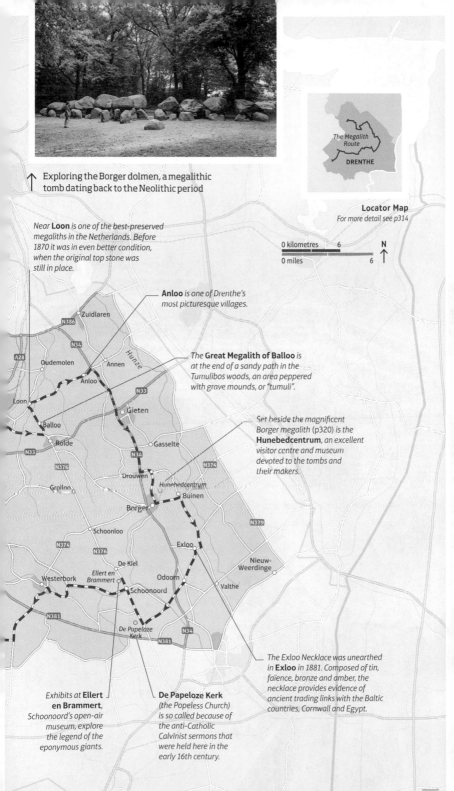

Exploring the Borger dolmen, a megalithic tomb dating back to the Neolithic period

Locator Map
For more detail see p314

The Megalith Route

DRENTHE

Near **Loon** is one of the best-preserved megaliths in the Netherlands. Before 1870 it was in even better condition, when the original top stone was still in place.

Anloo is one of Drenthe's most picturesque villages.

The **Great Megalith of Balloo** is at the end of a sandy path in the Tumulibos woods, an area peppered with grave mounds, or "tumuli".

Set beside the magnificent Borger megalith (p320) is the **Hunebedcentrum**, an excellent visitor centre and museum devoted to the tombs and their makers.

0 kilometres 6

0 miles 6

N

Zuidlaren

N386

N34

Oudemolen

A28

Anloo

Annen

Hunze

Loon

N33

Balloo

Rolde

N376

Gieten

N33

Gasselte

N34

Drouwen

N374

Grollo

Hunebedcentrum

Borger

Büinen

Schoonloo

N374

N376

Exloo

N379

De Kiel

Nieuw-Weerdinge

Westerbork

Ellert en Brammert

Odoorn

Schoonoord

Valthe

N381

De Papeloze Kerk

N34

N381

The Exloo Necklace was unearthed in **Exloo** in 1881. Composed of tin, faïence, bronze and amber, the necklace provides evidence of ancient trading links with the Baltic countries, Cornwall and Egypt.

Exhibits at **Ellert en Brammert**, Schoonoord's open-air museum, explore the legend of the eponymous giants.

De Papeloze Kerk (the Popeless Church) is so called because of the anti-Catholic Calvinist sermons that were held here in the early 16th century.

OVERIJSSEL

On the eastern side of the country, Overijssel is
one of the more diverse of the country's provinces.
Like its immediate neighbours, it had a variety of
overlords during medieval times, albeit within the
ambit of the Holy Roman Empire. Perhaps its most
neglectful rulers were the Prince-Bishops of
Utrecht, who seemed to have done little for the
local population, right from when they took over
in 1347 to when they ceded the region to the
Habsburg emperor Charles V in 1528. Neither did
history favour the provincial capital, Zwolle, which
started life as a 13th-century port at a busy river
junction. The town boomed in the 15th century
on the back of its trade in fish and grain with
the Baltic, which led to it joining the powerful
Hanseatic League, but its success was undermined
two centuries later by the rapid ascendancy of
Amsterdam and the movement of key shipping
and trade routes to the west. This history of
neglect and decline is one of the reasons why
Overijssel seems to have welcomed the occupation
of the Netherlands by French Revolutionary army
in the 1790s and the subsequent creation of the
Napoleonic Batavian Republic (1795–1806), during
which Overijssel became a separate département.
After the French withdrew, however, the province
again became something of a backwater, a sleepy
retreat far from the centres of Dutch power. Today,
Overijssel is experiencing something of a resur-
gence, with tourism and agriculture flourishing,
and light industry coming up in its towns and
cities, and nowhere more so than in the still
charming town of Zwolle.

EXPERIENCE

❶

Zwolle

⚑E3 🚇 ℹ️Grote Kerkplein 13; 038-4218815

In the Middle Ages, Zwolle, capital of the province of Overijssel, was, along with towns such as Deventer, Kampen and Zutphen, a city of the Hanseatic League, a network of trading cities. Its past is evident in the relatively large historical centre. A few dozen metres of the city's ancient fortifications are left standing, along with the fine Sassenpoort gate, dating from 1406, and the Late Gothic 15th-century Pelsertoren tower.

On one side of the Grote Kerkplein is a sculpture by Rodin entitled *Adam*, while on the Grote Markt stands the magnificent building of the Hoofdwacht (Guard house), which dates from 1614.

The Grote Kerk, also known as St Michaelskerk, is worth a visit. The original church, built in 1040, was enlarged in 1370 and again in 1452 to become the present-day three-naved Gothic church.

The **Museum de Fundatie**, is a contemporary art museum housed in a grand Neo-Classical building dating from 1838. The renovated light-filled galleries hold works by the likes of Van Gogh, Picasso and Mondrian.

The Kunstwegen (Art Paths) are outdoor sculpture installations, just to the east of Zwolle, on the country estate of **Landgoed Anningahof**. The 5-ha (9-acre) open-air sculpture park was the creation of art collector Hib Anninga and contains dozens of works, from bright-blue ceramic dogs to giant iron hoops, by around 80 contemporary Dutch sculptors. These works of art are spread across meadows and landscaped gardens, and exploring them makes for a pleasant afternoon's stroll.

Museum de Fundatie
🎨🅰️💷🕐 ⚑Blijmarkt 20 🕐11am–5pm Tue–Sun 🌐museumdefundatie.nl

Landgoed Anningahof
🎨💬 ⚑Hessenweg 9 🕐May–Oct: 1–6pm Wed–Sun 🌐anningahof.nl

> **INSIDER TIP**
> **Cookery Courses at De Librije**
>
> The famed restaurant De Librije in Zwolle offers professional cooking classes, ranging from globally inspired breakfast dishes to desserts *(www.librijesatelier.nl)*.

St Michaelskerk's richly carved pulpit and *(inset)* its Gothic façade ↓

❷ De Weerribben

🅰 E2

De Weerribben is an unspoiled area of wetlands at the northwestern end of Overijssel. This beautiful nature reserve offers plenty for cyclists, walkers and canoeists.

Natuuractiviteiten-centrum De Weerribben
🏠 Hoogeweg 27, Ossenzijl
📞 0561-477272 🕐 Apr–Oct: 10am–5pm daily; Nov–Mar: noon–4pm Thu–Sun

❸ Staphorst

🅰 E3 🚌 40 🏨 Hotel Waanders; 0522-461888

Staphorst is known across Holland as a stronghold of strict Christian beliefs. It was where the Gereformeerde Bond (Reformed Union), one of the strictest embodiments of Protestantism, ruled within the Dutch Reformed Church. Many of the lovely old farmhouses, painted in green and blue, are monumental buildings. Visit the **Museum Staphorst** to see what they once looked like.

The Staphorst townspeople continue to wear traditional dress, a custom that has nearly vanished in Holland. You may see elderly women, wearing traditional blue and black outfits.

Museum Staphorst
♿ 🏠 Gemeenteweg 67
🕐 Hours vary, check website
🌐 museumstaphorst.nl

❹ Vollenhove

🅰 E3 🏨 Boek & Mix shop; 0527-244900

Vollenhove is a picturesque place which was once known as "the town of palaces" owing to the many nobles who once lived here. The aristocratic residences are known as *havezaten* (or manors). The town's large 15th-century church is variously referred to as the Grote Kerk, St Nicolaaskerk or Bovenkerk.

❺ Ommen

🅰 F3 🚂 🏨 Hammerweg 59a; 088-5551480

The district of Ommen lies in stunningly beautiful countryside extending from the town to nearby villages and hamlets. One-third of its total area of 180 sq km (69 sq miles) is covered by nature reserves and forests. To find out more about the nature reserves in Ommen, visit the **Natuurinformatiecentrum Ommen**, which houses a permanent exhibition illustrating the cultural history of the surrounding countryside. Particularly worth seeing are the typical Saxon farmhouses at Beerze, Junne, Stegeren, Besthem and Giethmen.

Natuurinformatiecentrum Ommen
🏠 Hammerweg 59a
📞 088-5551480
🕐 10am–4.30pm Wed–Sun

❻ Giethoorn

🅰 E2 🚌 70, 79
🏨 Eendrachtsplein 2; 0521-360112

If any village were to be given the title "prettiest village in the Netherlands", quaint Giethoorn would be the one. This well-deserved accolade is due to the village's picturesque canals which are flanked by numerous farmhouse-style buildings. A few of these buildings now contain interesting, if small, museums.

EAT & DRINK

De Oale Ste
This picturesque spot offers high tea for kids, which includes a cupcake that they can decorate themselves.

🅰 F3 🏠 Holterweg 116, Nijverdal
🌐 oaleste.nl

€€€

Grand Café De Heeren
Enjoy beer and tasty appetizers on a Friday night while listening to a piano and guitar duo.

🅰 E4 🏠 Brink 72, Deventer 🌐 deheeren opdebrink.nl

€€€

Sluiszicht
Relaxed, lock-side pub and restaurant with hearty Dutch food.

🅰 E3 🏠 Zuiderstraat 2, Blokzijl 🌐 sluiszicht blokzijl.nl

€€€

De Librije
Three-Michelin-starred Dutch restaurant set in a 15th-century former abbey library.

🅰 E3 🏠 Spinhuisplein 1, Zwolle 🌐 librije.com

€€€

De Herderin
Modern Dutch eatery that doubles as a cookery school.

🅰 E3 🏠 Hoogstraat 1, Hasselt 🌐 deherderin.nl.

€€€

❼ Deventer

🅰E4 🚉 𝒊 Brink 56; 0570-710120

The lively centre of the old Hanseatic city of Deventer features numerous medieval houses, including the oldest stone house in Holland today. Buildings worth seeing in particular are those situated on the pleasant Brink (green) and the Bergkerk. In the middle of the Brink stands the impressive Waag (weigh house) from 1528, which contains the VVV and the **Museum De Waag**, with exhibits that illustrate the town's history.

On the first Sunday of August, the town holds the **Deventer Boekenmarkt** (Book Fair), the largest in Europe. It is preceded by a poetry festival.

Museum De Waag

⊛⊛🏛 🅰Brink 56 ⏰11am-5pm Tue-Sun 🚫Public hols 🖥museumdewaag.nl

❽ Enschede

🅰F4 🚉 𝒊Stationsplein 1a; 053-4323200

Enschede is regarded as the capital of Twente, as it is the largest town in Overijssel. It was devastated in 1862 by a fire – little of the old town survived. One of the few historical buildings that can still be seen in the pleasant centre is the Grote Kerk on the Oude Markt. In addition, Enschede has a number of museums, of which the

Cycling through the autumn trees in the pretty village of Delden ↑

Rijksmuseum Twenthe should not be missed. The exhibits here range from manuscripts and paintings to modern, primarily Dutch, art.

Rijksmuseum Twenthe

⊛⊛🎫🏛 🅰Lasondersingel 129-131 ⏰11am-5pm Tue-Sun & hols 🚫1 Jan, 25 Dec 🖥rijksmuseumtwenthe.nl

❾ Delden

🅰F4 🚉 𝒊Langestraat 29; 074-3761363

Delden is a pretty residential village, ideal for walks. This Twente hamlet has a number of interesting attractions, including the **Zoutmuseum** (Salt Museum) and the 12th-century Oude Blasiuskerk. Make sure to visit the lovely gardens of **Tuinen Kasteel Twickel** (Kasteel Twickel Gardens) approximately 2 km (1.2 miles) northeast of Delden.

Zoutmuseum

⊛ 🅰Langestraat 30 ⏰May-Sep: 11am-5pm Mon-Fri, 2-5pm Sat & Sun; Oct-Apr: 2-5pm Tue-Fri & Sun 🖥zoutmuseum.nl

Tuinen Kasteel Twickel (Kasteel Twickel Gardens)

⊛ 🅰Twickelerlaan 7, Ambt Delden ⏰May-Oct: 10am-5pm Wed-Sun 🖥twickel.nl

❿ Nijverdal

🅰F3 🚉 𝒊Willem Alexander Straat 7c; 0540-612729

The impressive beauty of the Sallandse Heuvelrug, with its fine heath and woodland, is especially apparent at Nijverdal. This is the last remaining breeding ground in the Netherlands for black grouse.

An interesting exhibition on the region can be seen at the **Bezoekerscentrum Sallandse Heuvelrug** (Sallandse Heuvelrug visitors' centre). The nearby Avonturenpark Hellendoorn (Hellendoorn Adventure park) is great for children.

Bezoekerscentrum Sallandse Heuvelrug

🅰Grotestraat 281 ⏰10am-5pm daily 🚫1 Jan, 25 & 31 Dec 🖥sallandseheuvelrug.nl

Did You Know?

The Kasteel Twickel Gardens have a *niwaki* bonsai thought to be nearly 250 years old.

Watertoren
Spend the night in a brick water tower from the 1930s.

🅰F3
🅰 Dedemsvaartseweg-Noord 64a, Lutten
🔗 watertorenlutten.nl

€€€

Hotel Huis Vermeer
Historic hotel and restaurant with antique details.

🅰E4 🅰 Grote Kerkhof 9, Deventer
🔗 hotelhuisvermeer.nl

€€€

---

⑪

Kampen

🅰E3 🚆 ℹ️ Oudestraat 41; 038-3313500

Kampen, first mentioned in documents in 1227 and known for its theological university, is a pleasant and lively town encompassing 500 historic buildings. The beauty of this former Hanseatic city is apparent from the IJssel riverfront. The area within the old fortifications features the Dutch Reformed church, St Nicolaaskerk, and the Gotische Huis monument. Particularly noteworthy is the old town hall, or Oude Raadhuis, with its decorated façade, which now houses the **Stedelijk Museum Kampen**, the town's local history museum.

Kampen is also famed for its cigars, so be sure to take a tour of the **Sigarenfabriek de Olifant** cigar factory. A rather more surprising find is the **Ikonenmuseum**, a collection of religious Greek and Russian Icons and the only museum of its kind in the Netherlands. The museum is housed in a former cloister.

Stedelijk Museum Kampen
🅰 Oudestraat 133 🕐 11am-5pm Tue-Sat, 1-5pm Sun
🔗 stedelijkmuseum kampen.nl

Sigarenfabriek De Olifant
🅰 Voorstraat 100-108
🕐 9am-5pm Mon-Sat
🔗 olifant.com

Ikonenmuseum
🅰 Buiten Nieuwstraat 2
🕐 1-5pm Tue & Wed, 10am-5pm Thu-Sat 🔗 ikonen museumkampen.nl

---

⑫

Ootmarsum

🅰G3 🚌 64 from Almelo ℹ️ Markt 9; 0541-291214

The village of Ootmarsum is one of the prettiest places in all of Holland. Places of interest include the 13th-century Roman Catholic church, the only Westphalian hall-type church in Holland, built between 1200 and 1300. Here you can see the burial vaults and some impressive works of art. The Rococo former town hall dates from 1778 and is now the VVV (tourist) office. There are also some interesting old draw-wells. The **Openlucht-museum Ootmarsum** (Open-Air Museum) showing what life was once like in the Twente region, is also worth a visit.

Openluchtmuseum Ootmarsum
♿ 🅰 Commanderieplein 2
🕐 Hours vary, check website 🔗 openlucht museumoot marsum.nl

→
The *Little Onion Girl* statue in Ootmarsum by Berend Seiger

FLEVOLAND

In the whole of Europe, there is nothing quite like Flevoland, the youngest province of the Netherlands. Flevoland's origins are entirely watery, its creation a tribute to the determination of the Dutch to drive the back the seas. After a severe flood in 1916, the government decided to tame the rough, shallow Zuiderzee, which was gouging a great chunk out of the country's northern coastline. The first part of the plan was the construction of the massive Afsluitdijk dam, which, when it was completed in 1932, separated the Zuiderzee from the ocean and turned it into the freshwater IJsselmeer lake. Over the next 40 years, three large chunks of the IJsselmeer – the Noordoostpolder, Oosterlijk Flevoland and Zuidelijk Flevoland – were reclaimed. In 1986, these three new polders officially became a province, named Flevoland after Flevo Lacus, the original name given to the Zuiderzee by Roman historian Pliny nearly 2,000 years ago.

Early on, tweaks were required to be made to the original plan when it became obvious that the reclaimed land was drying out and sinking. A narrow body of water was inserted along the old coast to stabilize the water table, thereby turning all three parts of Flevoland into actual islands, joined to the mainland by a series of bridges. The reclaimed polders also incorporated two old Zuiderzee islands – Urk and Schokland – but these were incidental to the main aims of the scheme, which were to create more farmland and to build new towns to accommodate the overspill population from the crowded cities that lay further to the south and west, such as Amsterdam and Utrecht. Today, the largest of these overspill towns are Almere, the province's fastest growing conurbation, and Lelystad, the capital of Flevoland.

FLEVOLAND

Experience

1. Emmeloord
2. Lelystad
3. Nagele
4. Urk
5. Schokland
6. Swifterbant
7. Batavialand
8. Dronten
9. Knardijk
10. Almere
11. Zeewolde
12. Oostvaardersplassen

EXPERIENCE

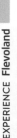

① Emmeloord

ⒶE3 **Ⓐ**Noordoostpolder **▣**
ⓘDe Deel 25a; 0527-
612000

When the oldest polder in
Flevoland was drained,
Emmeloord sprang up as a
pioneer settlement. Over the
years it has developed into a
pleasant place to visit. It is the
main town of the municipality
of Noordoostpolder, encompassing many *groendorps*
(green villages). Emmeloord is
known mainly for its octagonal
Poldertoren, a water tower
topped by a 5-m (16-ft) wind
vane in the shape of an old
merchant ship; the tower is
65-m (214-ft) high and was
built in 1959. Its carillon, one of
Holland's biggest, has 48
chimes. The viewing platform
(open in summer) offers a view
of the polder.

② Lelystad

ⒶD3 **▣▤** **ⓘ**Bataviaplein
60; 0320-292900

Lelystad, the provincial capital,
has a modern centre with a
number of outstanding buildings, such as the Postmodern
Zilverparkkade, a residential
development in the city centre.
East of the town is **Natuurpark
Lelystad**, with animals such as
bison and Przewalski horses. As
well as cycling and pedestrian
paths, the nature park includes
a shipwreck and a reconstructed prehistoric village. The
**Luchtvaartmuseum Avio-
drome**, at Lelystad airport, has
historic aircraft, a cinema and
a reconstruction of Schiphol
Station from 1928.

Natuurpark Lelystad

⊛Ⓣ⊕ **Ⓐ**Vlotgrasweg 11
ⓄSunrise-sunset daily by
appt **ⓦ**flevo-landschap.nl

Luchtvaartmuseum Aviodrome

⊛Ⓣ⊕ **Ⓐ**Pelikaanweg
50, Luchthaven Lelystad
Ⓞ10am-5pm Tue-Sun (Mon
in Jul, Aug & school hols)
Ⓠ25 Dec **ⓦ**aviodrome.nl

③ Nagele

ⒶE3 **▣** **ⓘ**Emmeloord;
0527-612000

This village was built in the
1950s to designs by the De
Acht en de Opbouw, a group
of architects which included
the famous Rietveld, Van Eyck
and Van Eesteren, who represented the Nieuwe Bouwen
movement. The flat-roofed
residential buildings surround
a park-like centre with shops,
schools and churches. The
village is surrounded by a belt
of woodland. **Museum Nagele**
provides information about
the village's architecture
and also stages worthwhile
regular temporary exhibitions
on subjects relating to
architecture and the
visual arts.

Museum Nagele

⊛Ⓣ⊕ **Ⓐ**Ring 23,
Nagele **Ⓞ**1-5pm Thu-Sun
Ⓠ1 Jan, 25, 26 & 31 Dec
ⓦmuseumnagele.nl

The fishing village of Urk,
with its charming alleys
and fishermen's cottages

④ Urk

ⒶD3 **▤▤**From Enkhuizen,
summer only **ⓘ**Wijk 2-3;
0527-684040

The fishing village of Urk
attracts many visitors with its
sloping alleys and charming
fishermen's cottages. Until the
Zuiderzee was drained, Urk
was an island. Some 1,000
years ago, the land mass was
much larger and included five
villages; flooding gradually
reduced its size. The townspeople moved to the highest
point on the island, a hill of
boulder clay. Even after the
polder was drained, Urk

CORNELIS LELY (1854-1929)

Flevoland came into existence thanks
largely to the plans and ambitions of
civil engineer Cornelis Lely. From
1885 to 1891, he was a member of
the Zuiderzeevereniging (Zuiderzee
Society). During his third term as
minister for trade and industry (1913-
18) he oversaw the closing off and
draining of the Zuiderzee. Apart from
the Zuiderzee projects, Lely worked to
improve the Noorzeekanaal. From 1902
to 1905 he was governor of Suriname.
He died in 1929, but his name lives on in
that of Flevoland's capital, Lelystad.

managed to retain its traditional character. Some of the older residents wear the traditional dress, though this is increasingly rare.

Beside the old village centre, the fishing quay, the lighthouse (1844) and the little church (1786) are worth a look. In the **Museum Het Oude Raadhuis**, situated in the old town hall, you can find out about the history of Urk and the fishing industry.

Museum Het Oude Raadhuis
⊛⊛⊡ 🏛 Wijk 2-3 🕐 Apr-Oct: 10am-5pm Mon-Fri; Nov-Mar: 10am-4pm Mon-Sat 🌐 museumopurk.nl

---

5

Schokland
🅰E3 🚌 𝒊 See museum

Like Urk, Schokland was once an island. Archaeological finds show that the site was inhabited in prehistoric times. In 1859, the population had to abandon the island because it was disappearing into the sea. Today the "island" is so tiny that it can barely be seen.

Museum Schokland, consisting of the restored church and reconstructions of fishermen's cottages, is dedicated to geology and local history from the Ice Age up until the land was reclaimed. At the south end of the village are the ruins of a medieval church. In the nearby Schokkerbos forest is the Gesteentetuin, gardens featuring Ice Age boulders.

Museum Schokland
⊛ 🍴 🏛 Middelbuurt 3, Ens 🕐 10am-5pm Tue-Sun (also Mon in Jul & Aug) 🕐 1 Jan, 25 Dec 🌐 museumschokland.nl

---

6

Swifterbant
🅰E3 🚌 𝒊 De Rede 80-82, Dronten; 0321-313802

This young village is known primarily to archaeologists for the flint tools and earthenware of the Swifterbant culture that were unearthed here. The Swifterbant people inhabited the region in the 4th millennium BC. In spring, flower enthusiasts can enjoy the riot of vivid colour in the nearby bulbfields. Nearby, the Swifterbos forest is an excellent spot for cycling and walking.

EAT

Restaurant De Boet
Dine on fresh seafood such as grilled local eel.
🅰D3 🏠 Wijk 1-61, Urk 🌐 restaurantdeboet.nl

€€€

View Almere
Modern Dutch restaurant with a beautiful waterside terrace and city views.
🅰D3 🏠 Bergsmapad 1, Almere 🌐 viewalmere.nl

€€€

Restaurant De Cantine
Family-friendly casual restaurant with a sunny terrace and views of the water.
🅰D3 🏠 Oostvaardersdijk 1-13, Lelystad 🌐 restaurant decantine.nl

€€€

STAY

B&B Morgenster

Located at the edge of the IJsselmeer, right next to the lighthouse, with nautical-inspired rooms.

Ⓐ D3 ⌂ Wijk 3-78, Urk **ⓦ** benbmorgenster.nl

€€€

Buytenplaets Suydersee

Choose from a variety of campsites, cabins, wagons, and tree huts for your overnight stay.

Ⓐ D3 ⌂ Badge 1, Lelystad **ⓦ** buyten plaets-suydersee.nl

€€€

---

❼ 🖊️ 🐾 🖥️ 🛍️

Batavialand

Ⓐ D3 ⌂ Oostvaardersdijk 01-13, Lelystad ⏱ 10am–5pm Mon–Sat, 11am–5pm Sun ⏱ 1 Jan, 25 Dec **ⓦ** batavialand.nl

Take a journey through 7,000 years of Dutch history at this indoor and outdoor museum site. The highlight is the famously splendid replica of the *Batavia*. You can climb on board this VOC East Indiaman ship, as well as learn about the history of Dutch ship-building and ocean-faring through the ages via engaging interactive exhibits. There is also the chance to join workshops in carpentry, sailmaking and blacksmithing.

---

❽

Dronten

Ⓐ D3 🚌 **ℹ** De Rede 80–82; 0321-313802

Dronten is well-endowed with greenery and recreational facilities. The Meerpaal Complex here combines a theatre, cinema and events venue. Outside the town hall stands the Airgunnersmonument, a statue honouring airmen who lost their lives in World War II.

In the countryside around Dronten are many pretty woods and recreational areas that offer opportunities for walking and cycling.

---

❾

Knardijk

Ⓐ D3 **ℹ** Staatsbosbeheer (0320-254585)

The Knardijk marks the border between Oostelijk and Zuidelijk Flevoland (eastern and southern Flevoland). The dyke was built in the 1950s between the island of Lelystad-Haven and Harderwijk to enable the entire area to be placed within a polder at one time. After Oostelijk Flevoland had been dried out, it formed the southwestern ring dyke of this polder. The Knardijk is of great interest to nature lovers, as it offers a fine view of the Oostvaardersplassen lakes. A great many birds live at the foot of the dyke, including hen harriers and marsh harriers. Two bird-watching huts can also be reached along the dyke. The dyke leads southeast along a nature reserve known as the Wilgenreservaat, which has evolved naturally into a mixture of woodland and clearings. Many songbirds, woodland birds, and birds of prey are to be found here, as are deer, foxes, polecats and ermines. Part of the reserve can be seen via a circular path. Nearby is the Knarbos forest, which also boasts a variety of flora and fauna. A 6-km (4-mile) hiking route has been marked out through the trees.

---

❿

Almere

Ⓐ D3 🚌🚆 **ℹ** De Diagonaal 199 **ⓦ** vvvalmere.nl

Almere is the Netherlands' fastest growing town. Its name recalls the 8th-century name for the Zuiderzee but the earliest signs of human settlement date from 65 centuries earlier. Today Almere consists of three centres: Almere-Stad, which is undergoing major renovation and is where all the facilities are; Almere-Buiten, a green suburb; and Almere-Haven, with its lovely marina. If you are interested in modern architecture, visit the districts of Muziewijk, Filmwijk and Stedenwijk in Almere-Stad, and Regenboogbuurt in Almere-Buiten.

> The dyke leads southeast along a nature reserve known as the Wilgenreservaat, which has evolved naturally into a mixture of woodland and clearings.

LANDSCAPE ART

Around Flevoland you will come across unusual works of "landscape art". East of Almere-Haven, for instance, is the *Groene Kathedraal* (Green Cathedral), designed by Marinus Boezem and consisting of 178 Lombardy poplars planted to re-create the outline and pillars of Reims Cathedral, while Piet Slegers' *Aardzee (Earth Sea)*, situated between Zeewolde and Lelystad, consists of a series of artificial ridges resembling waves.

Near Almere are many recreation areas and nature reserves. The Weerwater, the Leegwaterplas lake, and the Beginbos forest afford fantastic walking, cycling and bridleways. The beautiful Kromslootpark, with its polder vegetation, and the lakes of Noorderplassen and Lepelaarsplassen, home to rare wading birds, are popular with bird-watchers and wildlife enthusiasts.

11

Zeewolde

D4 Raadhuis 1; 036-5221405

With its picturesque marina, this village on the Wolderwijd coastal lake is a popular recreational spot. Zeewolde is the youngest town in Flevoland, having officially become a municipality in 1984. Its youth is evident from the imaginative architecture, particularly that of the town hall, library and church.

An enjoyable 7-km (4-mile) walking route has been laid out in and around Zeewolde, with landscape art along the way.

South of Zeewolde extends the Horsterwold, which is the the largest deciduous forest in the Netherlands and is home to many plant species and animals, including wild Konik horses.

12

Oostvaardersplassen

D3 Staatsbosbeheer, Bezoekerscentrum, Kitsweg 1, Lelystad; 0320-254585

Between Lelystad and Almere is internationally renowned marshland covering 6,000 ha (14,825 acres). The nature reserve includes lakes, mud flats, marshes, willow thickets and grasslands and serves as a port of call for hundreds of species of birds, including the hen harrier, great cormorant, great bittern, sacred ibis and grey goose. The marshland is largely off-limits to visitors, but some fine views are to be had from the edge of the swamp, the Oostvaardersdijk and the Knardijk.

The Oostvaarders-plassen marshes and *(inset)* some of waterfowl that live in the reserve ↓

GELDERLAND

The Netherlands' largest province, Gelderland stretches west from the German border to the polders of Flevoland. Its name, in Game of Thrones style, is said to come from "Gelre!", the death rattle of a dragon who met its end at the hands of a local lord. Gelderland has had a complex and often troubled history, with its counts and dukes sometimes loyal to their feudal overlords, sometimes engaged in bitter dispute. Successive counts skilfully expanded their territory to include the Veluwe region to the north, the Betuwe in the southwest and the county of Zutphen. In 1248, when the imperial town of Nijmegen was annexed, the region became a power to be reckoned with. Many of its towns joined the powerful Hanseatic League, and in 1339 the county was promoted to a duchy by the German emperor. The increasing power of the Habsburgs threatened the duchy's independence, and in 1543, it was finally ceded to the Holy Roman Emperor, Charles V. Habsburg control did not last long, however. The region joined the Dutch Revolt in the 1560s, with the rebels defeating the Habsburgs and forming the Verenigde Nederlanden (United Provinces). Gelderland was bound to their cause by the House of Orange – who provided a long line of provincial governors, or stadholders – and gradually became one of the less influential of the Dutch provinces. During World War II, the region's quiet towns suffered heavily, notably Arnhem where an Allied attempt to outflank the Germans and shorten the war ended in disaster – the "Bridge Too Far" of literary and cinematic fame. Today, Gelderland is largely agricultural, but dotted across it are several towns that are successfully reinventing themselves and flourishing as a result.

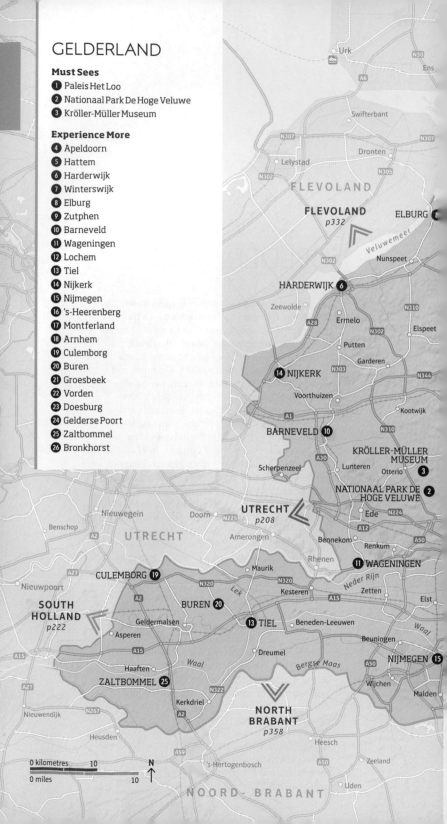

GELDERLAND

Must Sees

1 Paleis Het Loo
2 Nationaal Park De Hoge Veluwe
3 Kröller-Müller Museum

Experience More

4 Apeldoorn
5 Hattem
6 Harderwijk
7 Winterswijk
8 Elburg
9 Zutphen
10 Barneveld
11 Wageningen
12 Lochem
13 Tiel
14 Nijkerk
15 Nijmegen
16 's-Heerenberg
17 Montferland
18 Arnhem
19 Culemborg
20 Buren
21 Groesbeek
22 Vorden
23 Doesburg
24 Gelderse Poort
25 Zaltbommel
26 Bronkhorst

Paleis Het Loo seen from the semicircular colonnade in the Upper Garden ↑

PALEIS HET LOO

⟨A⟩E4 🏛 Koninklijk Park 16 (Amersfoortseweg), Apeldoorn 🚉 Apeldoorn, then bus 10, 102 🕐 Gardens & stables: Apr–Sep 2020: 10am–5pm Tue–Sun & hols, 12 Dec 2020 – 3 Jan 2021 🔒 Palace: closed for renovations until mid-2021; gardens & stables: Oct–Nov 2020, 1 Jan, 4 Jan–mid-2021 🌐 paleishetloo.nl

While the sumptuous palace of Het Loo is closed for a major renovation, its splendid gardens, and the stables containing its famous collection of vintage cars, remain open throughout the spring and summer.

The Stadholder William III built the elegant Paleis Het Loo in 1692 as a hunting lodge. For generations, the Orange family used it as a summer residence. Its pomp and splendour led to Het Loo being dubbed the "Versailles of the Netherlands". Its main architect was Jacob Roman (1640–1716); the interior and the gardens were designed by Daniel Marot (1661–1752). The severe Classical façade belies the opulence of the lavish interior.

Het Loo was last used as a royal residence in 1975; after intensive restoration work, the palace opened as a state museum in 1982. In 2018, it closed for substantial refurbishment due to finish in 2021 (check website for regular updates). However, the magnificent formal gardens and collection of royal carriages and vintage cars housed in the stables easily make for a fine day out in themselves. A bonus during the restoration programme is that the palace roof is open to visitors, with views of the new building works and of the garden.

> The magnificent formal gardens and collection of royal carriages and vintage cars housed in the stables easily make for a fine day out in themselves.

45

blue delftware vases are scattered around the gardens.

THE FORMAL GARDENS

When the formal gardens on the grounds behind the palace were reconstructed, the garden designers were inspired by old illustrations, prints, plans and documents. In the 18th century, the original ornamental gardens had been grassed over. In 1983, the intricate patterns of the original gardens were restored and planting began. The gardens of Paleis Het Loo are typical of the formal landscaping of the late 17th century, in which plantings were rigidly patterned and manicured and teamed with Classical statuary to achieve an ideal harmony between the worlds of art and nature.

1 The Fountain of Venus stands in front the colonnade in the Upper Garden.

2 The Koningssprong (King's Leap), a 13-m (42-ft) tall fountain in the Upper Garden, was Europe's highest at the time when it was built.

3 Paleis Het Loo's elegant exterior will remained unchanged after the renovation, which will create new visitor facilities underground.

2 🗺️ 🍴 🖥️ 🛍️

NATIONAAL PARK DE HOGE VELUWE

🅰️ E4 📍 Houtkampweg 9, Otterlo 🚌 Ede, Apeldoorn 🕐 Hours vary, check website 🌐 hogeveluwe.nl

The De Hoge Veluwe national park, the largest nature reserve in the Netherlands, and the Kröller-Müller Museum at its heart, are the product of a Dutch couple's remarkable vision.

Helene and Anton Kröller-Müller collected plots of unused land in the Veluwe hills until they possessed one single tract of natural land. They even bought, in 1914, the public road between Otterlo and Hoenderlo. In total, 5,500 ha (13,600 acres) of protected woodland, marshland, heath and drifting sand extend southwards from the Kröller-Müller residence, the splendid Jachthuis Sint Hubertus.

The park is a treasure trove for all kinds of wildlife: rare birds, butterflies, plants and fungi. Red deer, roe deer and moufflon sheep still live freely here. If you are lucky, you may catch a glimpse of a wild boar or a stag. Cycle and pedestrian paths have been laid out everywhere, and at the main visitor centre you can borrow a white bicycle free of charge.

Underneath the visitor centre is the world's first underground museum, the Museonder, giving visitors an idea of what life is like below the earth's surface. You can see the roots of a 140-year-old beech tree, experience a re-created earthquake and drink Veluwe groundwater. The park has three restaurants, with other options nearby.

JACHTHUIS SINT HUBERTUS

This architectural masterpiece by H P Berlage from 1914 was inspired by English country manors and included a library, a smoking room, and a billiards room. Berlage not only designed the building with its 31-m (101-ft) tower, but also the interior, the furnishings, and the surrounding gardens. Tours must be booked, at the visitor centre.

1 The park's bicycles are free to use within the park.

2 Jachthuis Sint Hubertus is named for the patron saint of hunting.

3 Foraging families of wild boar can be seen in the park.

Did You Know?

Wolves, absent from the Netherlands for 140 years, have been spotted in the park recently.

EAT

Park Paviljoen
Savour coffee and a sandwich on the pine-shaded terrace of the park's pleasant visitors' centre café.

⬛E4 🏠Houtkampweg 9B, Otterlo
🌐hogeveluwe.nl

€€€

Restaurant Cèpes
With a focus on local and organic ingredients, the French and Italian-inspired set menus here are well worth splashing out on.

⬛E4
🏠Houtkampweg 1, Otterlo 🌐cepes.nl

€€€

←
A red deer stag, a shy creature despite its proud appearance

📷 PICTURE PERFECT
Stay Focused

The contrast between the natural surroundings and Jean Dubuffet's *Jardin d'Email* – bright white with jagged black lines – makes for starkly interesting images.

↑ Jean Dubuffet's *Jardin d'Email* (1974), one of the garden's most distinctive sculptures

3

KRÖLLER-MÜLLER MUSEUM

E4 **Houtkampweg 6, Otterlo** **Ede, Apeldoorn** **Museum: 10am–5pm Tue–Sun & public hols; sculpture garden: 10am–4:30pm** **1 Jan** **krollermuller.nl**

The highlight of the Nationaal Park De Hoge Veluwe, the Kröller-Müller Museum, with its world-famous art and its sculpture garden, gives expression to the notion that nature, architecture and art should be combined to form a whole.

The museum owes its existence above all to one person: Helene Kröller-Müller (1869–1939). In 1908, with the support of her industrialist husband Anton Kröller, Helene started to collect modern art. In 1935, she donated her entire collection to the state, and a special museum was built to house it.

At the heart of the museum is the world's second-largest collection of works by Vincent van Gogh, with almost 90 paintings and over 180 drawings; these include *Café Terrace at Night* (1888) and one of the six versions of *Portrait of Joseph Roulin* (1889). The Kröller-Müller also has a major collection of 19th- and 20th-century French paintings alongside old Flemish masters and a dozen abstract paintings by Piet Mondriaan.

As well as its large collection of modern art, the museum is famed for its 25-ha (62-acre) open-air sculpture garden, the Beeldentuin, which provides a backdrop for works by sculptors such as Rodin, Moore and Hepworth.

← Oswald Wenckebach's *Statue of Monsieur Jacques* (1955) and Mark di Suvero's *K-piece* (1972)

Artworks from the museum's lauded ↓ Van Gogh collection

20,000
The number of artworks owned by the Kröller-Müller Museum.

←
Saint Andrew's Church rising above the charming market square in Hattem

Church) is particularly remarkable, its oldest part dating from 1176. The **Anton Pieck Museum** is dedicated to the Dutch painter and graphic artist Anton Pieck (1895–1987); it is in the same complex as the **Voerman Museum**, which showcases the IJssel painter Jan Voerman and his son, who illustrated the famous Verkade card albums.

Anton Pieck Museum/ Voerman Museum

🎨🏛 ⬛Achterstraat 46–48 & Noordwal 31 ⏰10am–5pm Tue–Sat, 1–5pm Sun (Jul & Aug also 1–5pm Mon) 🌐voermanmuseum hattem.nl

EXPERIENCE MORE

④ Apeldoorn

🅐E4 🚌🚆 ℹDeventer-straat 18; 526-0200

Apeldoorn is first mentioned as Appoldro in 793, and for centuries it was a small rural town in the Veluwe. This was changed by William III in 1692 when he built his hunting lodge Het Loo (p338) here. Many wealthy burghers followed William's example and set themselves up in Apeldoorn. The engaging **CODA Museum** gives a good overview of the area's history.

The **Apenheul Primate Park** is a zoo situated in the Berg en Bos nature park, where more than 30 species of primate run free among the visitors. The gorillas live on wooded islands that separate them from both the other primates and visitors.

CODA Museum
🎨 ⬛Vosselmanstraat 299 🌐coda-apeldoorn.nl

Apenheul Primate Park
🎨🍴📷 ⬛JC Wilslaan 21 ⏰Apr–Oct: 10am–5pm daily; Jul–Aug: 9am–6pm daily 🌐apenheul.com

⑤ Hattem

🅐E3 🚌

The picturesque town of Hattem (first mentioned in 891) was granted its town charter as early as 1299, joining the Hanseatic League in the 15th century. Its monumental buildings, such as the house of Herman Willem Daendals, later the governor-general of the Dutch Indies, bear witness to Hattem's eventful and prosperous past. St Andreaskerk (St Andrew's

←
A ring-tailed lemur in the Apenheul Primate Park, where animals roam freely

⑥ Harderwijk

🅐E4 🚌🚆 ℹAcademiestraat 5; 085-2733575

The eel-smoking frames may have disappeared from the streets, but the Zuiderzee town of Harderwijk is still a pleasant place to wander around. The town has an interesting history. In the 13th century it had become so important through fishing and the trade in dyes that in 1221 Count Otto II of Gelre granted it a town charter and ordered fortifications to be built. Remnants of the old

> **In the 13th century Harderwijk had become so important through fishing and the trade in dyes that in 1221 Count Otto II of Gelre granted it a town charter.**

fortifications are still intact in places. Between 1647 and 1811 Harderwijk even had a university, from which the Swedish scholar Linnaeus graduated in 1735. The Paling Museum (Eel Museum), pays homage to the town's heritage as a centre of eel fishing, with exhibits on the life cycle of the fish and traditional smoking methods.

8
Winterswijk

⌖F4 🚆 **ℹ️ Mevr, Kuipers Rietbergplein 1; 0543-512302**

The 20th century was not kind to the town of Winterswijk and the grand railway station bears witness to better times. Its main draw is the **Villa Mondriaan,** a museum located in Piet Mondriaan's former family home, which tells the story of the famous painter's early life and displays prints by Pieter Mondriaan Senior.

↓ The main square in the well-preserved old town of Elburg

Villa Mondriaan

⊛⊛⊜⊜ **⌂ Zonnebrink 4** **🕐 Mar-Oct: 11am-5pm Tue-Sun; Nov-Feb: 11am-5pm Fri-Sun** **🌐 villamondriaan.nl**

9
Elburg

⌖E3 🚌 **ℹ️ Jufferenstraat 8; 0525-681341**

Elburg is the best-preserved fortified town on the former Zuiderzee. Its prosperity is evident in the 14th-century St Nicolaaskerk. From the 38-m (125-ft) tower you can clearly make out the medieval rectangular street pattern.

Beside the Vischpoort (fish gate), is the oldest ropemaker's workshop in Holland. Elburg was once much nearer the coast, but in the late 14th century the flood-plagued town was moved well away from the sea. The interesting local history museum, the **Museum Elburg**, is in a 15th-century monastery.

Museum Elburg

⊛⊛ **⌂ Jufferenstraat 6-0** **🕐 11am-5pm Tue-Sat** **🌐 museumelburg.nl**

9
Zutphen

🄰E4 🚉 𝑖 Houtmarkt 75;
0575-844538

This hanseatic town is one of the Netherlands' oldest historical towns. One of the most distinctive features of the town, first mentioned in 1030, is the preserved medieval street layout. Among the main sights are Walburgiskerk, the church square and the remains of the fortifications.

DRINK

Café Hart van de Betuwe
Vist this busy local pub on Thursdays for "shopping evening" specials on drinks and meals.

🄰D5 🄰Markt 2, Tiel
🅆 hartvande
betuwetiel.nl

Café Camelot
Located in the historic centre of Zutphen, this friendly pub has an excellent selection of beers.

🄰E4 🄰 Groenmarkt 34,
Zutphen
🅆 camelotzutphen.nl

Café Onder de Linden
Historic brew pub that gets lively with locals on weekends.

🄰E4 🄰 Haagsteeg 16,
Wageningen
🅆 onderdelinden
wageningen.nl

→

An open-air cafe on St Walburgiskerk's square at the heart of Zutphen

---

Zutphen has a number of interesting museums, including the informative **Stedelijk Museum** (local history museum) and the **Henriette Polak Museum** (modern art museum), which is highly recommended.

Definitely worth visiting is the reading room of the unique **Librije** (library) of the **St Walburgiskerk**. All of the 750 books in it date from before 1750 and include 80 incunabula printed before 1500. The books in the library, which was built in 1564, are chained to the desks. This is because it was a public library, which was unsupervised at the time. There are only four other libraries of this kind in the world: two are in England and two are in northern Italy.

Stedelijk Museum and Henriette Polak Museum
⊛ 🄰 Kerkhof Gravenhof 4
🄲 11am-5pm daily
🅆 museazutphen.nl

St Walburgskerk and Librije
⊛ 🄰 Kerkhof 3
🄲 11am-3pm Tue-Sat
🅆 walburgiskerk.nl

10
Barneveld

🄰D4 🄰🚌 𝑖 Langestraat
85a; 0342-420555

Barneveld owes its place in history books to one individual: Jan van Schaffelaar, commander-in-chief of the armed forces, who on 16 July 1482 chose suicide rather than surrender and leapt from the tower of today's Nederlands Hervormde kerk (Reformed church). The Nairac museum of local history devotes considerable attention to this event. Today Barneveld is known as a poultry centre. The local **Pluimveemuseum** (poultry museum) shows how this industry has developed here.

Pluimveemuseum
⊛ 🄰 Hessenweg 2a
🄲 10am-5pm Tue-Sat
🅆 pluimveemuseum.nl

11
Wageningen

🄰E4 🚉

Wageningen, at the southwestern edge of the Veluwe region, is a pleasant

↑ The handsome Oldenaller Castle, set in idyllic surroundings

town that is home to the highly regarded Wageningen University and Research Centre (specializing in agriculture and food). Its botanical gardens are open to the public. The town played an important role at the end of World War II; the Germans signed the official surrender in the **Hotel de Wereld**.

Hotel De Wereld

🏠 5 Mei Plein 1 📞 0317-460444 ⏰ Call ahead to book

---

⑫ Lochem

🏠 F4 🚉 ℹ️ Markt 2; 0573-251898

One of the oldest villages in the Achterhoek to have its own parish church, Lochem was granted its town charter in 1233. During the Dutch War of Independence, the town was often besieged. It was razed to the ground in 1615. Only the Grote kerk, also known as St Gudulakerk, with its 56-m (185-ft) steeple, was spared. This 14th-century hall-type church has fine murals dating from Catholic times (it is now a Reformed Church). The handsome Stadhuis (town hall), across from the church, dates from 1615.

⑬ Tiel

🏠 D5 🚉🚌 ℹ️ Rechtbank straat 1; 0344-636060

Tiel, situated on the Waal, is an ancient town that flourished during the Middle Ages because of its strategic location on the trading routes to and from Cologne. One of the best-preserved monuments from this time is the Ambtmanshuis, dating back to 1525. The town also has the oldest elm tree in the country. The local history museum, De Groote Sociëteit on the Plein, is worth a visit. Tiel is the centre of fruit farming in the Betuwe region. On the second Saturday in September of each year, it hosts the Fruitcorso (p60), in which a procession of floats decorated with fruit winds through the streets of the town. Tiel is also renowned for its tinsmith industry.

Nearby Asperen is a peaceful little town on the River Linge. On the Lingedijk is Fort Asperen, which was part of the Nieuwe Hollandse Waterlinie. Farther upstream is the little town of Acquoy, with its crooked 15th-century tower. A Lady Pisa is buried in the town's churchyard (no connection to the Leaning Tower in Italy).

⑭ Nijkerk

🏠 D4 🚉🚌 ℹ️ Verlaat 13; 055-5260200

Nijkerk is a pleasant old town with many shops, restaurants and open air cafés. The tobacco industry made the town rich in the 18th century. The Grote Kerk features the tomb of Kiliaen van Renselaer, one of the founders of New York. Just outside Nijkerk, is the **Stoomgemaal Arkemheen**, a paddle-wheeled steam pumping-station, the last functioning one of its kind in Europe.

On the road east to Putten is the Oldenaller estate with a castle from 1655. The grounds are open to the public.

Stoomgemaal Arkemheen

♿🚻 🏠 Zeedijk 6 🌐 stoom gemaal-arkemheen.nl

💬 INSIDER TIP
Betuwe Blossom Tour

Spring is the best time to cycle through the Betuwe orchards, when the trees are filled with blossom. Pick up a bike in Tiel (bimbimbikes.com) and pedal through the countryside to Buren.

15
Nijmegen

AE5 🚉 **i** Keizer Karelplein
32; 0481-366250

Nijmegen, occupying a
strategic position on the river
Waal, is one of the oldest
towns in Holland. Archae-
ological remains show that
the Batavians were settled
here even before the first
millennium BC, while the
Romans had a fort here from
12 BC. The most important
sights include the **Museum
Het Valkof**, which stands on
the spot where the fort of the
Batavians and, later, one of
Charlemagne's palaces stood.
All that remains of the palace
is the St Maartenskapel from
1155 and the St Nicolaaskapel,
one of the earliest stone
buildings in all of Holland,
part of which dates back to
1030; it is a rare example of
Byzantine architecture in
northern Europe.

A fascinating insight into
the Dutch national obsession
with all things two-wheeled
can be found at **Velorama**,
the bike museum, which
includes examples from the
entire history of cycling, from
the earliest "hobby horse"-
style bikes dating from 1817
to ultra-modern shiny racers.

Nijmegen is perhaps best
known for its annual four-day
rambling meet in July, the

Vierdaagse, accompanied
by de-Affaire, a week-long
music festival.

Museum Het Valkhof
⊘ ⊘ ⊕ **A** Kelfkensbos 59
🕙 11am–5pm Tue–Sun
museumhetvalkhof.nl

**Velorama National
Bicycle Museum**
⊘ ⊘ **A** Waalkade 107
📞 024-3225851 🕙 10am–
5pm daily, 11am–5pm Sun

16
's-Heerenberg

AF5 🚌 24
i Emmerikseweg 17;
0316-291404

The old castle
town of
's-Heerenberg
and the area
surrounding it
are among the

---

prettiest corners of
Achterhoek. The little town,
which was granted its charter
in 1379, retains its historical
centre, with buildings from
the 15th and 16th centuries.
Kasteel Huis Bergh is one of
Holland's finest castles and
houses the art collection of
textile magnate J H van Heek.

Kasteel Huis Bergh
⊘ ⊘ ⊕ **i** Hof van Bergh 8
🕙 Hours vary, check website
🌐 huisbergh.nl

17
Montferland

AE5 **i** Emmerikseweg 17,
's-Heerenberg; 0316-
291404

Montferland,
one of the few
hilly regions in
the country, is

Splendid Kasteel Huis
Berghe in the town
of 's-Heerenberg ↑

exceptionally picturesque. Apart from 's-Heerenberg, there are a number of other attractions, such as Zeddam, Beek and nature reserves where you can walk, cycle and swim. The natural spring in Beek, "het Peeske", and the historic farmhouses along the Langeboomseweg in Velthuizen, are worth seeing.

18

Arnhem

🅰E4 🚆🚌 *i* Stationsplein 158c; 0481-366250

In September 1944, Arnhem, the capital of the province of Gelderland, suffered serious damage in the Battle of Arnhem, one of the most notorious battles of World War II. All of the townspeople were forced to abandon their homes and were not able to return until 1945. Arnhem rose again from the ashes and rebuilt itself rapidly. The monuments that have been restored include the Eusebiuskerk from 1560. The tower, at 93 m (305 ft), is now taller than it ever was and has a glass lift which affords visitors a stunning view of the Rhine valley. The Duivelshuis, built in 1545

by Maarten van Rossum (*p357*), is an outstanding example of Dutch Renaissance architecture. Arnhem is also known for its monumental parks, such as the Sonsbeek, a romantic landscape park, and Zypendaal. It is also worth visiting the **Openluchtmuseum** (Open-Air Museum), where the staff, dressed up in traditional costume, illustrate rural handicrafts and industry of the 19th century.

Openluchtmuseum

🚭🚼🚶 🏠 Hoeferlaan 4
🕐 Apr-Oct: 10am-5pm daily
🅦 openluchtmuseum.nl

19

Culemborg

🅰D4 🚆🚌 *i* Camping de Hogekuil, Achterweg 4; 0345-515701

Culemborg is picturesquely situated on the River Lek and is a great place to wander around. If you enter the former fortress through the old Binnenpoort gate, you'll reach the Markt with its Stadhuis (town hall), built by Flemish masterbuilder Rombout Keldermans for Vrouwe Elisabeth van Culemborg (1475–1555). Her estate was sufficient to finance the **Elisabeth Weeshuis Museum** (1560),

now a historical museum. Other well-preserved buildings include the house where Jan van Riebeeck, who founded Cape Town, was born. The large clock in the Grote Kerk was a gift from South Africa.

Elisabeth Weeshuis Museum

🚭🚼 🏠 Herenstraat 29
🕐 11am-5pm Tue-Sun
🅦 weehuismuseum.nl

20

Buren

🅰D5 🚌 *i* Markt 1; 0344-571922

The little town of Buren is known for its historic links with the House of Orange, and the entire town has been listed. One of the town's most beautiful houses is the Koninklijk Weeshuis (Royal Orphanage), which was built in 1613 by Maria of Orange. Buren's impressive Late Gothic Lambertuskerk is also worth seeing.

21 Groesbeek

🅰E5 🚌 ℹ️ Dorpsplein 1a; 024-3977118

Set beside a stream in a wooded valley, the town of Groesbeek and its surrounds make an attractive place for cyclists and hikers. The route of the four-day annual hike (*Vierdaagse*) follows the Zevenheuvelenweg from Groesbeek to Berg and Dal, past the Canadian war cemetery. Groesbeek was subjected to heavy bombardment at the end of World War II. The **Vrijheids Museum** (liberation museum) illustrates the development of Operation Market Garden (1944), and Operation Veritable (1945), which brought about the final liberation of Holland.

EAT

Brasserie Dudok
Try the famous apple pie at this modern café.
🅰E4 🏠 Koningstraat 40, Arnhem 🌐 dudok.nl

€€€

Pannenkoekenhuis Den Strooper
This lovely café serves Dutch pancakes all day.
🅰E4 🏠 Koningsweg 18, Arnhem 🌐 denstrooper.nl

€€€

De Kromme Dissel
A Michelin-starred restaurant set in a Saxon farmhouse.
🅰E4 🏠 Klein Zwitserlandlaan 5, Heelsum 🌐 krommedissel.nl

€€€

Vrijheids Museum

⊗ 🏠 Wylerbaan 4 🕐 10am–5pm Mon–Sat, noon–5pm Sun & hols 🚫 25 Dec, 1 Jan 🌐 vrijheidsmuseum.nl

---

22 Vorden

🅰F4 🚉 ℹ️ Kerkstraat 1b; 0575-553222

There is mention of a Huis Vorden (Vorden house) as early as 1208; the first record of the family dates from 1315. The Nederlands Hervormde Kerk, which dates from around 1300, is well worth a visit. The best-known figure to come from Vorden is the poet of Achterhoek A C W Staring (1767–1840), who lived in De Wildenborch castle from 1791 until his death.

Around Vorden are eight castles in very picturesque settings. A bicycle trip of the area, passing farms and country estates, is definitely worth the effort.

---

23 Doesburg

🅰E4 🚌 27/29 Arnhem and 26/28 Dieren ℹ️ Gasthuisstraat 13; 0313-479088

Doesburg is a snug Hanseatic town on the IJssel. Granted its town charter in 1237, this small town's well-preserved old centre has had listed status since 1974.

Doesburg contains at least 150 national monuments, including a Late Gothic town hall. Also of note are the Martinuskerk, a Late Gothic basilica with a 97-m (320-ft) tower and the local museum of Doesburg's history and culture, the **Streekmuseum Roode Tooren**.

Streekmuseum Roode Tooren

🏠 Roggestraat 9-13 📞 0313-474265 🕐 11am–5pm Tue–Fri, 1–5pm Sat & Sun

Wild Konik horses in the unspoilt woodlands of the Gelderse Poort →

24 Gelderse Poort

🅰E5 ℹ️ De Bastei, Waalkade 83, Nijmegen; 024-3297070

At the point where the Rhine meets the Waal, the IJssel and the Lower Rhine is the Gelderse Poort, a protected area where the flora and fauna have been allowed to flourish freely. At the heart of this region is the Millingerwaard, an area of marshy woodland which regularly floods at high water. The riverbanks, woodlands and marshes provide ideal breeding grounds for endangered birds such as corncrakes and penduline tits.

---

25 Zaltbommel

🅰D5 🚉🚌 ℹ️ Markt 10; 0418-648774

Bommel, as its inhabitants call it, is more than 1,000 years

old. During the Eighty Years' War (p64), it was an important mainstay of the Republiek der Zeven Verenigde Nederlanden (Republic of the Seven United Netherlands). The town is surrounded by two well-preserved sets of walls, which are now part of a park. Within the town walls is the 15th-century St Maartenskerk, an impressive example of late Gothic architecture, whose low towers give the town its distinctive skyline. The church interior, with its medieval vault paintings, is worth a look.

Another worthwhile stop is at the house of the Gelderland commander-in-chief Maarten van Rossum (1478–1555), who is known for plundering The Hague in 1528. The house, the **Stadskasteel Zaltbommel**, is now an intimate museum with a large collection of drawings and prints from the region.

Stadskasteel Zaltbommel
♿🌐🕐 🅐 Nonnenstraat 5
🕐 1–5pm Tue–Sun 🌐 stads kasteelzaltbommel.nl

㉖

Bronkhorst

🅰 F4 🚌 52 from Zutphen train station

Bronkhorst is one of the smallest towns in the country, with just 160 inhabitants. The lords of Bronkhorst were granted a town charter in 1482. A rural collection of farmsteads and restored farmhouses, Bronkhorst retains its quiet traditional character, with strict conservation rules forbidding new

↓ Traditional thatched cottages in the tiny village of Bronkhorst

development. Motor vehicles are prohibited, and must be left in a car park outside the town. All that remains of the once-mighty castle of the Lords of Bronkhorst, which had fallen into disrepair by the 17th century, is the *kasteelheuvel* (castle hill).

📷 PICTURE PERFECT
Bronkhorst

The tiny medieval village of Bronkhorst offers photogenic vistas at every turn with its quaint cobblestoned streets, pretty little chapel, and tidy red-bricked and thatch-roofed houses.

NORTH BRABANT

The Celts, who settled In this region in the 7th century BC, were defeated by Julius Caesar, who described them as the "Belgae" in his writings. When the Romans left, the Franks took control of Toxandria, as the region was known then. The Frankish empire was followed by the Holy Roman Empire, and under Charlemagne the region grew in importance as new towns flourished along trade routes. In 1183, the Duchy of Brabant was established, becoming an important part of the empire. Its heyday – at least for its ruling clique – came in the 14th century when the burgeoning cities they controlled, including 's-Hertogenbosch, Breda and Brussels, produced handsome tax revenues. All seemed to be going well until Mary of Burgundy, the Duchess of Brabant, died in a riding accident in 1482 and her lands passed to her Habsburg husband, Maximilian. At a stroke, Brabant lost its independence. When the Dutch rebelled against their Habsburg rulers in the 1550s, Brabant was on the front line, its citizens subject to the atrocities of both the Protestant and Catholic armies. When peace finally came, the southern part of Brabant was retained by the Habsburgs – and is now part of Belgium – while the northern part went to the Netherlands as North Brabant. It's no wonder, then, that the irregular shape of the region doesn't make much geographic sense: indeed, agreement has proved so elusive that the frontier does not actually form a contiguous line, but leaves out a handful of tiny crossborder enclaves, such as Baarle-Nassau. Today, North Brabant is one of the most prosperous regions of the country, its economy sustained by tourism and both light and heavy industry.

NORTH BRABANT

Must See

1 's-Hertogenbosch

Experience More

2 Heusden
3 Breda
4 Tilburg
5 Willemstad
6 Oudenbosch
7 Eindhoven
8 Nuenen
9 Bergen op Zoom
10 Helmond
11 Deurne
12 Gemert
13 Heeze

❶ 'S-HERTOGENBOSCH

🅰D5 **🚗88 km (55 miles) south of Amsterdam** **🚆's-Hertogenbosch CS, 's-Hertogenbosh Oost** **🚌Stationsplein** **ℹ️Markt 77; www.bezoekdenbosch.nl**

In 1185, Henry I of Brabant founded the town of 's-Hertogenbosch. The strategically positioned town – usually called Den Bosch – grew rapidly. From the 16th century, however, its prosperity waned, when the States General ignored Brabant and chose to favour other regions. Its prestige rose again after 1815, when it became the capital of North Brabant. Today, it is a vibrant, lively town.

① 🖥️ De Moriaan

🏠Markt 77
🕐10am–5pm Mon–Sat, 11am–3pm Sun
🌐bezoekdenbosch.nl

Right in the heart of the city stands De Moriaan, an imposing structure with stepped gables, dating back to 1220. It was originally built as a fortified castle for a local aristocratic family and is one of the oldest brick buildings in the country. De Moriaan has seen many transformations, including serving as a church, a residence for a bishop, a concert venue, military barracks and a warehouse.

Today it is a national monument and houses the office of the local tourist information center for the city, the VVV, and they are happy to provide further information about the building and its long history. There's also a late-night bar in the basement, called P79.

② ⚐ Ⓜ️ Binnendieze

🏠Molenstraat 15a
🕐Apr–Oct: tours daily
🌐dagjedenbosch.com

The city's inner canal, called the Binnendieze, was part of an important waterway network used by merchants centuries ago. It also served as a water supply, was used for fishing, and as a place for waste and washing clothes. A few kilometres of the original stretch remains and can be

→
Statue of Hieronymus Bosch, the city's most renowned figure

← Traditional buildings on a typical Den Bosch street, dotted with bicycles

toured by boat with a guide. The narrow canal alleys are lined with medieval fortifications, intriguing buildings and monuments, beautiful brick arches, and dark tunnels. Private tours can be arranged at sunset as well.

③ ⊗ ⊗

Museum Het Zwanenbroedershuis

⌂ Hinthamerstraat 94
🕐 2–3:30pm Tue-Thu & Sun, by guided tour only
🌐 zwanenbroedershuis.nl

The Lady Brotherhood, founded in 1318 in Den Bosch and of which Hieronymus

> 💬 **INSIDER TIP**
> **Delicious Treat**
>
> When visiting Den Bosch be sure to try a *Bossche bol,* also called a *chocoladebol* – a giant cream puff covered in chocolate. The best are found at Banketbakkerij Jan de Groot, a bakery on Stationsweg 24.

Bosch (or, Jeroen Bosch) and William of Orange (Willem van Oranje) were both members, was a religious society known for its charitable work. The brotherhood occupied a building here since 1483. The Neo-Gothic structure that can be seen today was built on the same site much later, in 1847.

Today the building is a fine but modest museum that displays artifacts from the brotherhood, including paintings by Bosch, medieval books and a drinking cup belonging to William of Orange.

④ ⊗ ⊗ ⊡ ⊡

Noordbrabants Museum

⌂ Verwersstraat 41
🕐 11am-5pm Tue-Sun
🌐 hetnoordbrabants museum.nl

The Noordbrabants Museum displays art by renowned artists, Including Pieter Brueghel and Teniers, as well as modern artists such as Van Gogh, Mondriaan and Sluyters. The museum also features exhibits on the history of the province of North Brabant, from prehistoric times to the present. The building itself is worth a visit, originally built in 1615 as a Jesuit monastery. It was renovated in the 1760s

EAT

Restaurant Fabuleux
Choose from two separate dining rooms, one business-like, one romantic, at this fine-dining French restaurant.

⌂ Verwersstraat 23
🕐 Sun & Mon 🌐 rest aurantfabuleux.nl

€€€

Het Warenhuis
Modern and airy brasserie with a heated terrace for colder days, right in the city's main square.

⌂ Markt 2
🌐 hetwarenhuisden bosch.nl

€€€

adding the sandstone facade in a classical Louis XIV style, and then used for local governmental purposes. The notable pastel-coloured museum café is the former government state hall and can be visited without a museum ticket.

⑤

SINT JAN

🏠 Torenstraat 16 🕐 9am–5pm daily but restrictions apply during church services 🌐 sint-jan.nl

The St John's Cathedral (Sint Jan) dominates the skyline of the old town of 's-Hertogenbosch, and is one of the largest and most impressive Gothic churches in The Netherlands.

There was a church of Sint Jan in Den Bosch as early as the beginning of the 13th century, although nothing of the original Romanesque church exists today. The present-day majestic Gothic church was built from the late 14th to the 16th century, surviving the Iconoclastic Riots of 1566 (p64) and a devastating fire in 1584. The church was restored in Neo-Gothic style during the 19th century and a great deal was changed, including the lively and colour-ful stained-glass windows. The revolving baldachin in the middle of the cathedral is ascribed to Alart Duhameel – the all-seeing eye looks down from the vaults. The Chapel of St Anthony contains a spectacular Passion altar made by a studio in Antwerp.

→

Illustration of Sint Jan

The great organ (1617) has been restored to its original state.

The gargoyles are designed to channel rainwater pouring off the roof. Here, the drain pipes are encased by the head of mythical animals.

Flying buttresses are designed to strengthen the structure of the building. They are richly ornamented with saints, angels and other figures.

The ornamental south portal is dedicated to Saint John the Evangelist.

↑ Sint Jan Cathedral, a stunning architectural centrepiece in the town of 's-Hertogenbosch

🔍 HIDDEN GEM
Statue of St Mary

Concealed within the Lady Chapel is a figure of Our Good Lady of Den Bosch, the 13th-century miracle worker. For centuries the statue was kept in Brussels, but it was returned to Sint Jan in 1853.

The revolving baldachin in the middle of the cathedral is ascribed to Alart Duhameel.

The cathedral tower, and *(inset)* Neo-Gothic style stained glass windows, restored in the 19th century ↑

The stained-glass window frame depicts the woman and the dragon from The Book of Revelation.

The sanctuary was built from 1380 to 1425 by Willem van Kessel. The vaults are painted with a variety of religious scenes.

The Chapel of St Anthony contains a spectacular Passion altar made by a studio in Antwerp.

The seven radiating chapels around the choir form an elegant crown.

CARNIVAL

Every year in February, in the week before Ash Wednesday, carnival breaks out in the towns south of the great rivers. A festive mood abounds everywhere, with the best-known celebrations being held in Den Bosch, Bergen op Zoom and Maastricht. For days on end, there is drinking, singing and dancing all over Brabant and Limburg.

HISTORIC TRADITION

The carnival season officially starts on 11 November, the "day of fools". This is when the Raad van Elf (Council of Eleven) - the central office of the local carnival organization - names the Prince of the Carnival, who will hold power in the municipality on the days of the festival. From then on, the municipalities are busy with preparations, and on the Sunday (in many places now on the Friday) before Ash Wednesday, the festivities begin. Wild celebrations are held throughout North Brabant and Limburg, and most public institutions are closed. Long processions with floats parade through the towns. People dress up festively; in earlier times it was customary to put on masks, whereas today the trend is to wear as unusual an outfit as possible. "Dansmarietjes" (dancing girls) accompany the floats in their colourful costumes, and the mood everywhere is upbeat. All the merriment comes to an end after Shrove Tuesday, the climax of the carnival.

↑ A carnival celebrant dressed in an exuberant outfit that is typical of the colourful costumes on show

The Prince of the Carnival riding
a float with a *carnavalsstokken*
(carnival rod) in his hand

MUSIC

Music plays an important role at carnival
time. Every year, the associations choose
the official carnival anthem that will be played
over and over again. The Zaate Herremienekes of
Maastricht are among the better-known bands.
Dozens of its members march through the streets
blaring out enthusiastically; what their music
may lack in elegance is made up for by their verve.

FLOATS

At carnival time, long processions with
extravagantly decorated floats wind their way
through the main streets of towns and villages.
Months of preparation often go into creating
the floats, and secrecy prevails during their
preparation. The decoration of the float is usually
on an upbeat and amusing theme, but current
affairs are sometimes illustrated in imaginative
ways. When leading politicians are featured,
they are more often than not caricatured mer-
cilessly, and social ills are exposed, often using
costumed participants in *tableaux vivants*.

**Months of preparation
often go into creating
the floats, and secrecy
prevails during their
preparation.**

↑ Revellers participating
in a lively carnival parade
through Maastricht

CATHOLICISM IN
THE SOUTH

While people in the south of
the country celebrate the long-
standing tradition of carnival,
life goes on as usual in the north.
One of the main reasons for this
difference is the marked
presence of Catholicism in the
southern provinces of Holland,
even in these secular times.
Religious imagery is a common
sight here, particularly statues
of the Madonna and Child. There
are also several notable Catholic
churches in the region, including
the Basiliek van de HH Agatha en
Barbara in Oudenbosch *(p369)*,
the Onder de Linden Chapel near
Thorn *(p387)*, and the Maria
Magdalena Chapel in Gemert.
The latter is also known as the
Spijkerkapelleke ("nail chapel")
because people historically made
offerings of nails here in the
hopes of having their skin
disorders cured.

← A pedestrianized street in picturesque Heusden, much restored in recent years

been extensively restored in the centuries since.

At the Spanjaardsgat water-gate, near the castle, Kasteel van Breda, legend has it that in the 16th century, during the Eighty Years' War of independence from Spain, Adriaen van Bergen tricked his way past the Spanish with a peat barge full of soldiers and liberated the town.

Located in one of the oldest buildings in the city (dating back to the 13th century) is the **Stedelijk Museum Breda**, focusing on visual arts, film, design, architecture, science, and history of the area.

Stedelijk Museum Breda

 ☐ Boschstraat 22 🕐 11am–5pm Tue–Sun 🌐 stedelijkmuseumbreda.nl

EXPERIENCE MORE

❷ Heusden

🅰 D5 🚌 ℹ Pelsestraat 17; 0416-662100

After a refurbishment that started in 1968 and lasted for decades, the picturesque ancient fortified town of Heusden on the River Maas has been restored to its former glory. That Heusden fell victim to the redevelopment craze of the 1960s matters little. Walls, houses, moats, the Veerpoort (ferry gate) and the Waterpoort have all been restored in the old style. As advertising is

Did You Know?

In 1680 Heusden Castle was destroyed by a vast explosion as lightning struck the castle munitions.

banned in Heusden, it is easy to imagine that time has stood still here, save for the fact that motor vehicles are allowed into the fortress.

❸ Breda

🅰 C5 🚇🚌 ℹ Stadserf 2; 0900-5222444

The Old Bastion of Breda was built at the confluence of the rivers Aa and Mark around, the Kasteel van Breda, the town's fortress, now the home of the Koninklijke Militaire Academie (royal military academy). Breda was granted its town charter in 1252.

A walk through the old centre will take you to the Grote Kerk, also known as the Onze Lieve Vrouwe Kerk (Church of Our Lady). It stands prominently on the Grote Markt and cannot be missed. Construction of this magnif-icent Brabant Gothic-style church began in 1410; it has

❹ Tilburg

🅰 D5 🚉🚌 ℹ Spoorlaan 434a; 013-5323720

Tilburg, the sixth-largest town in Holland, once had a flour-ishing textile industry. The interesting **Textielmuseum**, housed in a former textile mill, illustrates the history of the country's textile industry and how textiles were produced.

The kermis van Tilburg (Tilburg fair), held each year at the end of July, is the biggest fair in Holland, attracting visi-tors from across the country.

Kaatsheuvel, some 15 km (9 miles) to the north of Tilburg, is home to the popular fantasy theme park of **De Efteling**, where all kinds of fairytale personalities come to life.

Textielmuseum

 ☐ Goirkestraat 96 🕐 10am–5pm Tue–Fri, noon–5pm Sat & Sun 🌐 textiel museum.nl

De Efteling
Europalaan 1, 5171 KW Kaatsheuvel 11am-6pm daily efteling.com

5

Willemstad

C5 Hofstraat 1; 0168-755211

The Bastions of Willemstad were built in 1583 by William of Orange. The Mauritshuis (1623), the former hunting lodge of Maurice, Prince of Orange, is today a visitor centre with an exhibition on the history of the town. The influence of the Oranges in Willemstad can also been seen in the white Oranjemolen mill (1734). There is a pleasant harbour to explore and a tree-lined "Wedding Walk", which leads to a domed church, the Koepeikerk, built in 1607.

Between 1860 and 1870, Oudenbosch was the point from which the Zouaves set out on their journey to Rome to defend the pope against Garibaldi.

6

Oudenbosch

C5 Stationsstraat 7; 0165-786530

Between 1860 and 1870, Oudenbosch was the point from which the Zouaves set out on their journey to Rome to defend the pope against Garibaldi. Upon their return to Oudenbosch, they had the renowned architect P J H Cuypers *(p386)* build a miniature replica of St Peter's basilica in Rome, the Basiliek van de HH Agatha en Barbara (Basilica of SS Agatha and Barbara) which was completed in 1892.

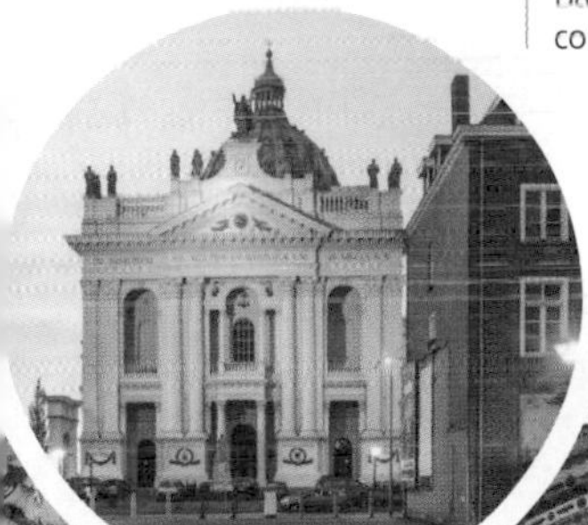

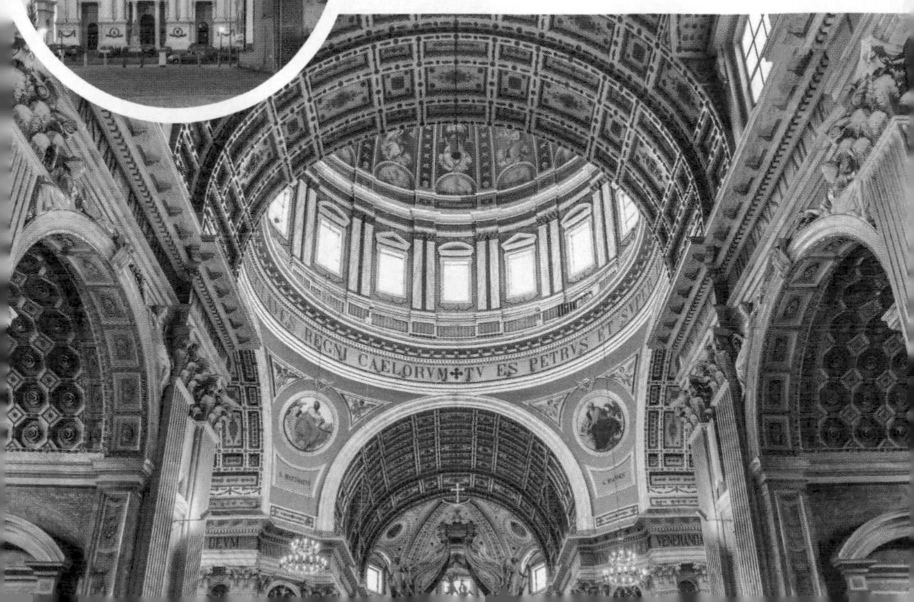

The interior of the Basilica of SS Agatha and Barbara, and *(inset)* its grand columned façade

DRINK

't Hart van Breda
Lively pub known for its nachos and large fishbowl cocktails, perfect for sharing.

C5 Grote Markt 4-6, Breda hartvanbreda.nl

Burgemeester Jansen
Choose from over 200 speciality beers at this traditional pub.

D5 Piushaven 22, Tilburg burgemeesterjansen.nl

Mauritz Willemstad
Sample fine European wines on the lovely garden terrace at this relaxed hotel bar.

C5 Landpoortstraat 24, Willemstad mauritzwillemstad.nl

7

Eindhoven

Δ D6 🚉💻 **ℹ Stationsplein 17; 040-2979115**

The old market town of Eindhoven was merged with the villages of Strijp, Woensel, Tongelre, Stratum and Gestel in the 19th century. The municipality of Eindhoven grew enormously in the last century when Philips, the electronics company, sited its factory there. Philips's best-known building, the highly distinctive Witte Dame (White Lady) was built in 1928 by architect Dirk Roosenberg; it has now been sold and con-verted into a design college, library and centre for artists. The former Philips complex, Strijp-S, is also being devel-oped and turned into a residential area with shops, restaurants and theatres.

The city centre was heavily bombed in World War II and as a result very few old build-ings have survived. In their place a clutch of striking modern buildings have been constructed, including the great concrete Stadhuis designed by Dutch architect Jan van der Laan, an imposing structure, surrounded by a large empty space, the Stadhuis Plein. Nearby is the more appealing train station with its slender tower and glassy frontage.

The **Philips Museum**, in the city centre, holds a fascinating collection of electrical objects dating back to the earliest days of the company. On display are dozens of the very first light bulbs dating from the 19th century, beautiful bakelite radios and hulking cabinets going right back to the birth of broadcasting. Visitors can learn about the history of light-bulb making, from handmade to mass-produced, and how the light bulb transformed Eindhoven from a small town into an industrial giant.

A rather more surprising find in the centre of this very industrial city is the **PreHistorisch Dorp**. This open-air museum, located in the middle of the Genneper Park, contains reconstructions of an Iron Age village, a Viking settlement and a medieval town. Actors in costume people the scene, and are on hand to answer questions. There's also a restaurant where visitors can eat meals based on ancient recipes, such as grain stew and lentil pâté.

Looming over the railway station is the ultramodern, space-age **Philips Stadion**, home of the PSV Eindhoven football team. The stadium, although ultra-modern these days, still stands on the spot where the first pitch was laid out for the team in 1913. Guided tours, for which booking is essential, allow

Did You Know?

Eindhoven is known as the "City of Light" for its history as a centre of match and light bulb production.

visitors to enter the players' changing rooms and to walk down the tunnel onto the pitch.

The most important sight in Eindhoven, however, is the **Van Abbemuseum**, which is devoted to modern and contemporary art and holds more than 3,000 artworks, including paintings, sculpture and video installations. The museum was founded by Henri van Abbe, a Dutch industrialist and art collector. The original building was designed in 1936 by A J Kropholler and has been described as a "brick castle". In the 1990s, architect Abel Cahen was commissioned to expand the museum. Cleverly integrating the existing building into a large new wing, he quadrupled the exhibition space and added a restaurant and multimedia centre. Queen Beatrix opened the museum in January 2003. The collection contains works by Chagall, Dufy and Joseph Beuys, and is particularly known for Picasso's Cubist-style *Femme en Verte (Woman in Green)*, painted in

1909. It also has one of the largest collections in the world of works by Russian artist El Lissitzky.

Philips Museum
⊘⊜⊜ 🄰Emmasingel 31 🄲11am–5pm Tue–Sun 🅆philips.nl

PreHistorisch Dorp
⊘⊜⊜ 🄰Boutenslaan 161b 🄲Apr–Oct: 10am–5pm Tue–Sun 🅆prehistorischdorp.nl

Philips Stadion
⊘⊛⊛ 🄰Frederiklaan 10a 🄲Hours vary depending on event 🅆philipsstadion events.nl

Van Abbemuseum
⊘⊛⊜⊜ 🄰Bilderdijklaan 10 🄲11am–5pm Tue–Sun 🅆vanabbemuseum.nl

> The most important sight in Eindhoven, however, is the Van Abbemuseum, which is devoted to modern and contemporary art and holds more than 3,000 artworks.

STAY

Hotel Lumière
A stylish boutique hotel with modern rooms that feature hardwood floors and large windows with expansive city views.

🄰D6 🄰Hooghuisstraat 31a, Eindhoven 🅆hotellumiere.nl

€€€

Kapellerput
Large, modern hotel in the middle of a nature reserve. There are a chic bar and restaurant, gardens and original artwork throughout.

🄰D6 🄰Somerenseweg 100, Heeze 🅆kapellerput.nl

€€€

Bed and Breakast Fort Bakkerskil
Choose between a room in the sickbay or in the powder magazine at this converted fort, part of the 19th-century New Dutch Water Line.

🄰C5 🄰Kildijk 143, Nieuwendijk 🅆fortbakkerskil.nl

€€€

← The white Philips factory juxtaposed with futuristic architecture

8

Nuenen

🅰D6 🚌 ℹ️ Berg 29; 040-2839615

Nuenen, northeast of Eindhoven *(p370)*, is the village where Vincent van Gogh lived from 1883 to 1885. The Van Gogh Village is an outdoor and indoor museum. You can see the locations that inspired some of the artist's paintings and visit the **Vincentre**, where you can find out more about Van Gogh's time in Nuenen.

Vincentre
⊕ 🅰Berg 29 🕐10am-5pm Tue-Sun (Mon in summer only) some public hols
🌐 vangoghvillagenuenen.nl

9

Bergen op Zoom

🅰B6 🚉🚌
ℹ️ Steenbergsestraat 6; 0164-277482

The old town of Bergen op Zoom grew up around a chapel that was dedicated to St Gertrude. In 1260, Bergen op Zoom was granted its town charter, after which it enjoyed a period of prosperity. The 15th-century St Geertruids-kerk, with its striking tower, stands on the site of the original chapel. The lords of Bergen op Zoom built the **Markiezenhof**, which was finally completed in 1511. The castle is today a museum, with period rooms and an unusual collection of fairground items.

Markiezenhof
⊕⊖ 🅰Steenbergsestraat 8 🕐11am-5pm Tue-Sun
🌐 markiezenhof.nl

10

Helmond

🅰E6 🚉🚌
ℹ️ Watermolenwal 11; 0492-522220

The most outstanding feature of Helmond is the castle dating from 1402, today one of the two buildings making up the **Museum Helmond**. The castle itself has many historical artifacts, while the modern annexe hosts a fine collection of modern art.

Museum Helmond
⊕⊖⊕ 🅰Kasteelplein 1 & FJ van Thielpark 7 🕐10am-5pm Tue-Fri, noon-5pm Sat & Sun 🌐 museumhelmond.nl

← A statue of Vincent van Gogh by Klaas van Rosmalen in the park in Nuenen

← The entrance to graceful Kasteel Heeze, set amid verdant countryside

11

Deurne

🅰E6 🏛🚌 𝑖 Markt 1; 0493-323655

The little town of Deurne is an artistic hub. The house (1922) of the extravagant doctor and painter Henrik Wiedersma, who used to make house calls on his motorcycle, is now the **Museum De Wieger**, which displays expressionist works by the doctor and his avant-garde friends, including Ossip Zadkine, who often stayed with him. Poets such as Roland Holst, were also regular visitors to the house.

Museum De Wieger

🎨🚻 🏛 Oude Liesselseweg 29 🕐 Noon–5pm Wed–Sun 🚫 Mon, Tue & most public hols 🌐 dewieger.nl

12

Gemert

🅰E5 🚌 𝑖 Ridderplein 49; 0492-366606

Gemert is a town of historical importance; its nickname was once "Heerlijkheid Gemert" ("glorious Gemert"). Until 1794 it was ruled by the Catholic group, the Knights of the Teutonic Order: their castle still stands and is now used as a monastery.

The Boerenbondmuseum (agricultural museum) is in a farmhouse dating from the beginning of the 20th century; the displays portray what rural life was like at that time.

13

Heeze

🅰D6 🏛🚌 𝑖 Schoolstraat 2; 040-2260644

The 17th-century castle of **Kasteel Heeze** is the centre-piece of this small Brabant town, just outside of Eindhoven. Designed by Pieter Post, it stands amid lovely streams, woods and water meadows. Among the many exhibits set out in the castle's 30 halls are valuable Gobelin tapestries.

Kasteel Heeze

🎨🚻 🏛 Kapelstraat 25 🕐 May–Sep: 2pm Wed, 2 & 3pm Sun (Jul & Aug: also 3pm Wed) 🌐 kasteelheeze.nl

---

VAN GOGH IN BRABANT

Vincent van Gogh was born in 1853 in Zundert, south of Breda. In 1883, he moved to Nuenen, where his father was rector. He stayed there until 1885, when he moved on to Antwerp. Van Gogh's Nuenen period was a particularly prolific time for the artist. He drew great inspiration from rural life in Brabant; it was during this period that he painted farms and labourers in the blue and brown tones that are so characteristic of his Nuenen work. It is here that he produced his masterpiece *The Potato Eaters*.

Bookshop in a former 13th-century Dominican church, Maastricht

LIMBURG

Hanging off the edge of the country like a giant ear ring, with Belgium on one side and Germany on the other, Limburg is the southernmost province of the Netherlands. From a geological point of view, Limburg is much older than the rest of Holland, sitting on coal deposits that are around 270 million years old. The Maas river valley has been attractive to settlers since the last Ice Age. There is evidence of early nomads, followed by the remains of successive sedentary societies. Politically, the region has long been strategically important and has suffered as a consequence, beginning with an onslaught by Julius Caesar, who, in 53 BC, annihilated the Eburones, the Gallic-German clan who lived here. The Romans stayed for around 400 years, colonizing the southern parts of the region, including Maastricht, which is now the province's capital and its most interesting town. In the medieval period, Limburg was passed from ruler to ruler, alternately part of the duchies of Brabant and Gelderland and even seized for a time by the Prince-Bishop of Cologne. Although its various rulers all owed fealty to the Holy Roman Emperor, this rarely prevented them from warring amongst themselves. In the 16th century, during the Dutch Revolt, Catholic Limburg sided with the Habsburgs, but was still sequestered into the Verenigde Nederlanden (United Provinces). Its strategic vulnerability was again exploited in 1673, when Louis XIV besieged Maastricht and laid waste to the surrounding countryside. The final shape of Dutch Limburg – and the course of its international border with Belgian Limburg – was finally decided by the Treaty of London in 1839. Since then, thanks to its location on major trade routes, the province has prospered as a logistics and technology hub.

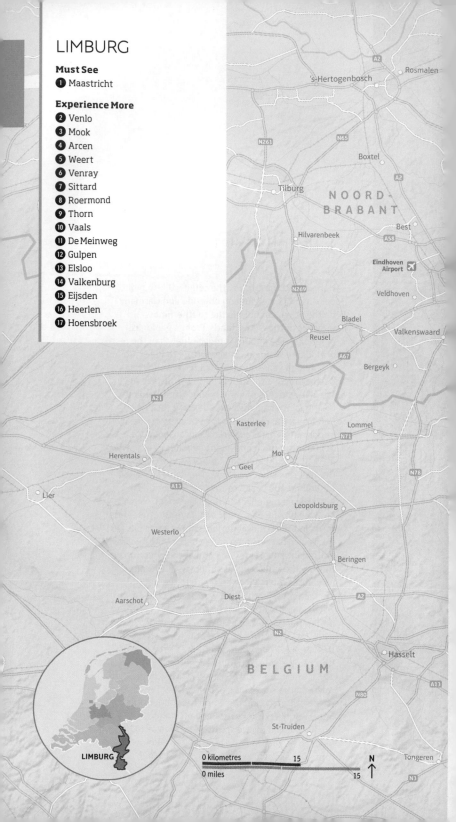

LIMBURG

Must See

❶ Maastricht

Experience More

❷ Venlo
❸ Mook
❹ Arcen
❺ Weert
❻ Venray
❼ Sittard
❽ Roermond
❾ Thorn
❿ Vaals
⓫ De Meinweg
⓬ Gulpen
⓭ Elsloo
⓮ Valkenburg
⓯ Eijsden
⓰ Heerlen
⓱ Hoensbroek

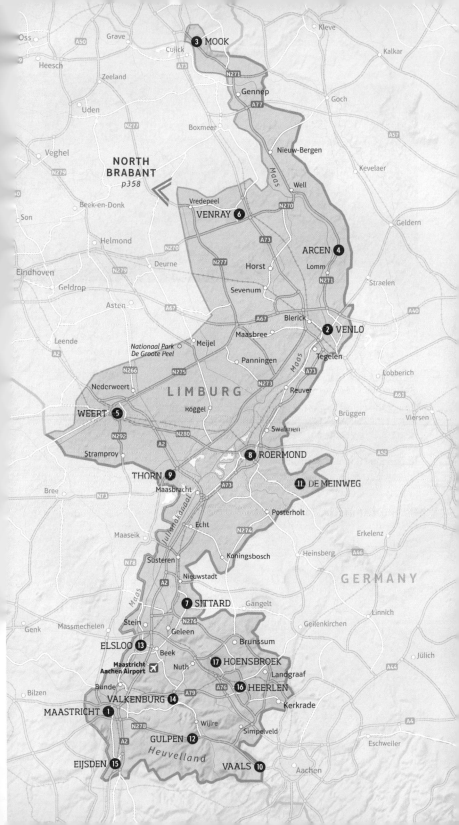

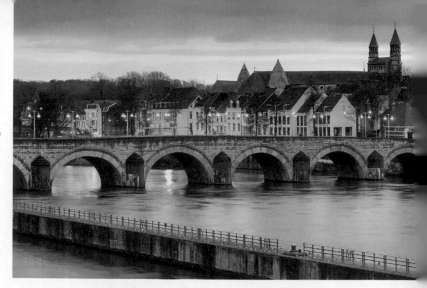

① MAASTRICHT

🅰E7 🚉213 km (132 miles) southeast of Amsterdam 🚊🚌 Stationsplein ℹ️Kleine Staat 1; 043-3252121

One of the oldest towns in Holland, Maastricht was the seat of the country's first bishopric and an impressive fortress. It has some outstanding Romanesque basilicas and Gothic churches, and a great deal remains of the original Roman fortifications.

① 🖼️🖥️ Natuurhistorisch Museum

🏠De Bosquetplein 7 🕐11am-5pm Tue-Fri, 1-5pm Sat & Sun 🚫Some public hols 🌐nhmmaastricht.nl

This attractive natural history museum features the natural history of the south of Limburg through the ages. Highlights of the museum include the remains of the enormous mosasaur and giant tortoises found in the limestone strata of St Pietersberg.

---

② Roman Foundations of the Tower

🏠OL Vrouweplein 7 📞043-3213854 🕐8:30-5pm daily

In the courtyard of the Onze-Lieve-Vrouwebasiliek you can see the foundations of a Roman tower that was once part of the Roman *castellum*. The fortress stood on the banks of the River Maas, just south of the St Servaasbrug bridge, where the Romans settled in 50 BC and where the district of Stokstraat, with its medieval and 17th-century buildings, now lies. The pavement of Op de Thermen, a small and peaceful square in this district where the original Roman fort once was, has been marked with the outlines of the old Roman baths. The first medieval wall around Maastricht dates from around 1229. Of these, the Onze-Lieve-Vrouwewal – which has cannons standing in front of it – and the Jekertoren tower can still be seen.

---

③ 🖼️ Helpoort

🏠St Bernardusstraat 24b 📞043-3212586 🕐Easter Day-Oct: 1-4:30pm daily voluntary donation

The rough-cut-stone Helpoort gateway, dating from the early

Did You Know?

Fictionalized in Dumas' *The Three Musketeers*, the Count of d'Artagnan died during the Siege of Maastricht in 1673.

INSIDER TIP
Bake a Pie

Learn to bake a traditional Limburg fruit pie *(vlaai)* at De Bisschopsmolen *(bisschopsmolen.nl)*. This bakery is at the site of an operational 7th-century water mill.

↑ Maastricht at dusk, laid out along the river with the Basilica of Our Lady rising behind

EAT

't Kläöske

Try the bouillabaisse (fish soup) or the freshly steamed mussels at this casual French bistro.

⌂ Plankstraat 20
ⓦ klaoske.nl

€€€

Wijnrestaurant Mes Amis

Looking for Dutch wine? This place is ideal for perfectly matching reds and whites with a meal.

⌂ Tongersestraat 5
⏰ Tue ⓦ mesamis.nl

€€€

Tout à Fait

Modern Michelin-starred French restaurant with beautifully plated food.

⌂ Sint Bernardusstraat 18 ⏰ Mon & Tue
ⓦ toutafait.nl

€€€

13th century, also forms part of the early medieval town fortifications. It stood at the southern end of the town and is the oldest surviving town gate in Holland, and the only one still standing in Maastricht. You can look inside but the main charm is the southern exterior, a red box-window sitting above a tunnel-passage.

Other structures from this period can be seen across the River Maas in Wyck: the Waterpoortje gate, the Stenen Wal (wall) along the river, and the Maaspunttoren. Built around 1350, the second medieval fortifications were made necessary by the rapid growth of the city. Of these, the Pater Vinktoren near the Helpoort gate, the romantic embankment wall, and the semicircular towers known as De Vijf Koppen and Haet ende Nijt, continue to survive to this day.

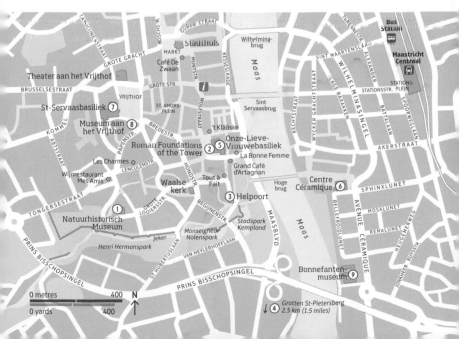

↑ The caves of Sint Pietersberg, which conceal a warren of beautifully inscribed walls

INSIDER TIP
Secret Spaces

Discover the hidden corners of Maastricht on a Hidden Places, Secret Spaces walking tour. This two-hour tour is in both English and Dutch and takes place on Mondays and Thursdays throughout the year, starting at 1:30pm *(visitmaastricht.com)*.

④ ⊗ Ⓜ 🍴 ☕

Grotten St-Pietersberg

🏠 Luikerweg ⏰ For tours, check website 🌐 explore maastricht.nl

The famous St Peter's caves were created when limestone was quarried through the centuries. Eventually a maze of over 20,000 passageways came into being. Some of the inscriptions on the walls are very old, and reveal artistic skills of the miners.

⑤

Onze-Lieve-Vrouwebasiliek

🏠 O-L-Vrouweplein 7 📞 Treasury: 043-3213854 ⏰ Hours vary, call ahead; church closed during services

Construction of Onze-Lieve-Vrouwebasiliek began around 1000. The oldest part of the basilica is the imposing west façade. Once this was completed, work began on the nave and transept. The chancel followed in the 12th century, built over an 11th-century crypt. The apse pillars, made from limestone, are crowned with lavishly sculpted capitals, such as the renowned Heimokapiteel.

⑥ ☕ 🏠

Centre Céramique

🏠 Avenue Céramique 50 ⏰ Noon-6pm Tue-Fri, 1-5pm Sat & Sun 🌐 centreceramique.nl

For a more in depth look at Maastricht and Limburg's history and culture, this multi-functional building provides a wealth of information for visitors and it is free to visit. It houses the city's library and has exhibit spaces for archaeological finds, including pottery, glassworks and a coin collection from the 1st century BC. The centre also organizes temporary exhibits, often with a focus on fine art. Two casual cafés are onsite as well, which offer breakfast and lunch.

⑦ ⊗ Ⓜ

St-Servaasbasiliek

🏠 Keizer Karelplein 6 📞 043-4335062 ⏰ 10am-5pm Mon-Sat, 12:30-5pm Sun 🚫 1 Jan, Carnival, 25 Dec

Construction on St Servatius Basilica began around the year 1000 on the spot where the saint was buried (upon which stood an earlier church). The nave, the crypt, the transept and the chancel are the oldest parts of the basilica, dating

THE RELIQUARY OF ST SERVATIUS

The restored reliquary is a monumental shrine containing the relics of St Servatius and St Martin of Tongeren. It is made of wood covered with embossed gilded copper plate in the shape of a house. Dating from about 1160, it was built by artists from the Maasland region. The front depicts Christ, with the 12 apostles along the sides, and St Servatius surrounded by angels on the back. The roof of the house shows scenes from the Last Judgement.

back to the 11th century. The apse and the chancel towers were built in the following century. The western end also dates from the 12th century. The southern Bergportaal gate dates from the early 13th century, and is one of the earliest Gothic buildings in the Maasland region. This portal is dedicated to St Mary, with representations of her life, death and Assumption in the arch. The side chapels and the Gothic transept date from approximately 1475.

Highlights of the basilica's treasury are the 12th-century reliquary containing the relics of St Servatius and St Martin of Tongeren, and the golden bust of St Servatius. The latter was donated to the town by the Duke of Parma when Maastricht was captured by the Spaniards in 1579.

During the 19th century, thorough restoration works were undertaken by Pierre Cuypers. He restored the western end to its original Romanesque splendour, as well as commissioning new murals and ceiling paintings. These were repainted during a subsequent restoration, which was completed in 1990.

→
Homage to Humanity photos by Jimmy Nelson at the Museum aan het Vrijthof

(8) (image) (image) (image)

Museum aan het Vrijthof

Vrijthof 18 10am-5:30pm Tue-Sun Public hols museumaanhetvrijthof.nl

The Museum aan het Vrijthof is located at the heart of the city in one of the oldest buildings in Maastricht, the former retreat of Charles V. This young photography museum faces the city's main square and was extensively renovated in 2012. Each year it organizes several temporary exhibitions showcasing local modern art and antiques. The museum has a cosy café located in a pretty covered courtyard and serves a nice selection of pastries and drinks. Tour packages are available that include snacks at the café. It is recommended to book tours at least two weeks in advance.

↓ St-Servaasbasiliek's exterior flanked by two 12th-century towers

STAY

Les Charmes
Boutique hotel with spacious, modern rooms.

Lencuenstraat 18
charmes.nl

€€€

DRINK

La Bonne Femme
Classic brown café with a large terrace.

Graanmarkt 1
labonnefemme.nl

Café De Zwaan
Beer has flowed from the taps of this friendly local pub since 1901.

Markt 68 dezwaanmaastricht.nl

Grand Café d'Artagnan
This historic pub is housed in an old brewery dating from the 17th century.

Graanmarkt 3
cafedartagnan.nl

⑨ ⬨ 🍴 🖥 🛍

BONNEFANTEN MUSEUM

🏠 Avenue Céramique 250 🚌 🕐 11am–5pm Tue–Sun & public hol Mon 🚫 1 Jan, Carnival, 25 Dec 🌐 bonnefanten.nl

The Bonnefantenmuseum is one of Maastricht's most prominent landmarks, on the right bank of the Maas in a distinctive building designed by the Italian architect Aldo Rossi. The museum's exhibits include old masters, painting and sculpture from the medieval period to 1650, and a celebrated international collection of modern art.

For sheer variety, this museum is hard to beat. Its noteworthy modern-art installations include Bonnefantopia; in 2002, the Rotterdam group of artists Atelier van Lieshout created this huge installation, featuring stylized polyester bodies hanging, squatting and lying down throughout the structure. Another fascinating piece is *La Natura è l'Arte del Numero*, designed by Mario Merz and consisting of tables covered with glass, branches, stones, vegetables and numbers fashioned out of fluorescent tubes. A major highlight of the museum is the magnificent medieval wood carving collection. Notable artwork includes *Cimon and Pero*, where Peter Paul Rubens (1577–1640) depicts Pero feeding her starving father Cimon while he awaited execution in prison.

The Cupola tower by Aldo Rossi houses a restaurant and an exhibition hall.

The fine collection of medieval wood carvings includes St Anna-te-Drieën, a walnut sculpture by Jan van Steffeswert (1470–1525).

Terrace

Plattegronden by René Daniels (b. 1950) is a simplified re-creation of a museum hall. Daniels painted yellow rectangles over the red flat paintings, which are out of sync with the perspective of the hall, creating a disorienting effect.

← A medieval wood carving on display at the Bonnefantenmuseum

The unique domed tower on
the banks of the Mass, and
(inset) staircase leading to
the exhibition spaces

← Illustration of the
Bonnefanten-
museum

Entrance

Inner Tower

*The monumental staircase runs through
the middle of the museum and leads into
the different wings and floors.*

 INSIDER TIP
**Boekhandel
Dominicanen**

For more medieval
marvels head to this
lovely nearby book-
shop, set within a 13th-
century church *(www.
libris.nl/dominicanen).*

EXPERIENCE MORE

② Venlo

AE6 **🚌** **ℹ** Klaasstraat 17; 077-3543800

The combined city of Venlo/Blerick began as a Roman settlement on the river Meuse. In the Middle Ages it grew rich on trade. The 15th-century St Martinuskerk, a Gothic hall-type church, and Ald Weishoes, a Latin school built in the Gelderland Renaissance style dating from 1611, are among the few historical buildings to have survived World War II. The town hall was designed between 1597 and 1600 by Willem van Bommel. The local **Museum Van Bommel-Van Dam** features modern art, while the **Limburgs Museum** is dedicated to archaeological finds from the prehistoric era up to more recent times.

Museum Van Bommel-Van Dam

⊘ ⊗ **🏠** Keulsepoort 1
🕐 11am-5pm Thu-Sun
🚫 Mon, 1 Jan, Carnival, 25 Dec
w vanbommelvandam.nl

Limburgs Museum

⊘ ⊘ **🏠** Keulsepoort 5
🕐 11am-5pm Tue-Sun
🚫 1 Jan, Carnival, 25 Dec
w limburgsmuseum.nl

③ Mook

AE5 **🚌**83 **ℹ** Witteweg 10, Plasmolen; 024-6961762

The village of Mook is on the River Maas in the very north of Limburg. On 14 April 1574, the Prince of Orange's army was routed on the nearby Mookerhei by the Spanish. The star-shaped fortifications of the Heumense Schans from the Eighty Years' War stand atop a 43-m (141-ft) ridge from the Saalian Ice Age. It offers a fantastic vantage point from which to view the Maas valley.

A little south of Mook lies the recreation area of the Mookerplas lake, which is ideal for canoeing and other watersports activities, and also the fine estate of Sint Jansberg, where the Bovenste Plasmolen, an ancient water-mill, has been restored.

> **💬 INSIDER TIP**
> **Rose Festival, Arcen Castle**
>
> Visit the Arcen Castle gardens during the Rose Festival in the last week of June for a spectacular sight of over 8,000 blooming rose bushes in more than 100 stunning varieties.

④ Arcen

AE6 **🚌**83

The main attraction of Arcen, picturesquely located on the Maas, is the finely restored 17th-century Arcen Castle with its **Kasteeltuinen** (castle gardens). They incorporate a rose garden, subtropical gardens, Eastern gardens, a pine forest and a golf course. You can also take the waters at the Thermaalbad Arcen spa; its mineral-rich water is extracted from 900 m (2,955 ft) underground. Other local delights include special Arcen beer, asparagus (with an

→ An attractive pedestrianized street, lined with outdoor cafés, in Venlo

↑ The lofty interior of the glorious Late-Gothic St Martinuskerk in Weert

asparagus market held on Ascension Day), and the liqueur distilled by the Branderij De IJsvogel, which is located in the attractive 17th-century Wijmarsche water mill.

Kasteeltuinen

⊕⊕⊕ 🅰 Lingsforterweg 26 🗓 Apr-Oct: 10am-6pm daily 🗓 Sep-Mar 🔲 kasteel tuinen.nl

5

Weert

🅰 E6 🚇 🗓 Markt 11; 0495-534211

The jewel of Weert is the St Martinuskerk, one of the few Late Gothic hall-type churches in the Netherlands (in hall-type churches, the side aisles are equal in height and width to the nave). When restoration works were carried out around 1975, paintings from the 15th and 16th centuries were discovered beneath the layers of whitewash on the vaulted ceilings. Before the high altar (1790), by Italians Moretti and Spinetti, lies the tomb of the lord of Weert, beheaded in 1568 on the order of Alva in Brussels. Not far from the church is the Ursulinenhof, an example of a new building successfully integrated into a historical centre.

Nearby is the Nationaal Park De Groote Peel, an area of unspoilt peat moors. The reserve is rich in bird life and rare plant species. Walkboards over the marshy ground have been laid out to make it more accessible for visitors.

DRINK

Bosbrasserie In de Sluis

The terrace at this casual canalside restaurant offers great views of the surrounding water and forest.

🅰 E5 🅰 Bosserheide 3e, Well 🔲 bosbrasserie indesluis.nl

Brasserie Alt Arce

Sip tea, coffee, or beer by the fireplace or out on the pleasant terrace at this modern waterside pub.

🅰 E6 🅰 Raadhuisplein 16, Arcen 🔲 altarce.nl

In den Dorstigen Haen

The heated terrace at this traditional pub has lovely views of Venlo's historic town hall. The whisky selection is pretty good, too.

🅰 E6 🅰 Markt 26, Venlo 🔲 dehaen.nl

6

Venray

🅰 E6 🚌 27, 29, 30, 39 🗓 M Goumansplein 1; 0478-510505

Venray was largely destroyed during World War II, when Noord Limburg was the scene of heavy fighting; the Oorlogs-en Verzetsmuseum (War and Resistance Museum) in nearby Overloon, explores this period of history. A highlight of the town, which was completely rebuilt after the war, is the 15th-century basilica of St Petrus Banden. The church features a magnificent interior, and was given a new 80-m (262-ft) tower in restoration works.

↑ Sittard's market square, with its Baroque St Michielskerk

7
Sittard

🅰E7 🚉 ℹ️Rosmolenstraat 2; 0900-5559798

In the 13th century, Sittard was granted its town charter and built its defensive walls, of which considerable sections remain intact, including Fort Sanderbout. The Grote Kerk, or St Petruskerk, built around 1300, is worth a visit. Its 80-m (262-ft) tower, flanked by turrets, is the highest in Limberg. The church is built of layers of alternating brick and limestone blocks, a technique known as *"speklagen"* (bacon layers). In the Markt is the 17th-century Baroque St Michielskerk; Our Lady of the Sacred Heart basilica stands in the Oude Markt. The oldest house in Sittard is the half-timbered house built in 1530 on the corner of the Markt and the Gats and containing the Tapperie De Gats gastro-pub. The steeply gabled Jacob Kritzraedthuis, a patrician house, was built in 1620 in Maasland Renaissance style.

8
Roermond

🅰E6 🚉 ℹ️Markt 17; 0475-335847

The oldest church in Roermond is the 13th-century Late Romanesque, Early Gothic Onze-Lieve-Vrouwemunster-kerk (Minster Church of Our Lady), originally the church of a Cistercian abbey. The St Christoffelkathedraal, a Gothic cruciform basilica with a gilded statue of St Christopher on the tower, dates from the early 15th century. Roermond is by the Maasplassen lakes, one of the country's largest

areas for watersports. The lakes cover more than 300 ha (740 acres) and have a length of approximately 25 km (15 miles). The Maasplassen were created through large-scale gravel quarrying in the Maas valley.

9
Thorn

🅰E6 🚌72, 73, 76
ℹ️Wijngaard 8; 0475-561085

The little town of Thorn, with its picturesque narrow streets and houses, historical farm

DR P J H CUYPERS (1827-1921)

Architect Pierre Cuypers was born in Roermond in 1827. He lived and worked both in his hometown and in Amsterdam. One of Cuypers' sons and one of his nephews also became renowned architects. Considered one of the prime representatives of the Netherlands Neo-Gothic, Cuypers designed the Central Station and the Rijksmuseum in Amsterdam, and De Haar castle in Haarzuilens. He was also the architect and restorer of countless churches, including the Munsterkerk (minster church) in Roermond.

INSIDER TIP
Take the Waters

Take a cooling dip in the Maasplassen, just south of Thorn. This network of man-made lakes (former gravel quarries) lined with little beaches is perfect for swimming and water sports like surfing and canoeing.

buildings and Abbey Church, looks almost like an open-air museum. For some 800 years, until 1794, Thorn was the capital of an autonomous secular foundation headed by an abbess. The Wijngaard, the village square, is surrounded by whitewashed houses where the noble ladies of the foundation once lived. The 14th-century abbey church with its 18th-century interior was restored at the end of the 19th century by renowned architect Pierre Cuypers, who also added a splendid Gothic tower. A canoness of the foundation established the Kapel van O-L-Vrouwe onder de Linden (Chapel of Our Lady under the Linden) north of the town in 1673.

⑩
Vaals

🅐 E7 🚌 50 ℹ️ Landal Maastrichterlaan 73a; 0900-5559798

Vaals' wooded countryside is known for the Drielandenpunt, from which three countries are visible. At 322 m (1,058 ft), it is also the highest point in Holland. Worth visiting are Kasteel Vaalsbroek (now a hotel) and the Von Clermonthuis; both date from the 18th century. De Kopermolen, once a church, is now the town hall.

⑪
De Meinweg

🅐 E6 🚌 78, 79 ℹ️ Bezoekerscentrum, Meinweg 2, Herkenbosch; 0475-528500

The national park of De Meinweg, an area of wooded valleys, heathland and streams, has a unique natural beauty. Nine hiking routes have been laid out here. You can also tour the park by horse-drawn cart, with expert guides.

STAY

La Vie en Rose
Modern bed and breakfast set in a former brewery from 1880. Enjoy afternoon tea in the lush gardens or relax at the side of the heated pool.

🅐 E6 🏠 Markt 8, Lottum 🌐 residence lavieenrose.nl

€€€

___

Kasteel Daelenbroeck
A romantic 14th-century castle on a large estate with luxurious rooms, some with private saunas, and an excellent restaurant serving a range of dishes.

🅐 E6 🏠 Kasteellaan 2, Herkenbosch 🌐 daelenbroeck.nl

€€€

↑ Purple heather growing in the national park of De Meinweg

12 Gulpen

▲E7 **🚌150** **🛈Dorpsstraat 27; 0900-5559798**

Located at the confluence of the Gulp and Geul rivers, Gulpen is surrounded by beautiful countryside, peppered with half-timbered houses, water mills and orchards. There are hiking routes marked throughout the area. A striking sight is the town's 17th-century Kasteel Neubourg, built on the site of a Roman temple from 2,000 years ago. Beside the castle (which is privately owned) is the Neubourgermolen mill, with a fish ladder for trout. The Gulpen brewery, **De Vrije Brouwer**, which offers tours and tastings, is worth a visit.

De Vrije Brouwer
🏠Rijksweg 16, 6271 AE Gulpen 🕐By guided tour, check website 🌐gulpener.nl

13 Elsloo

▲E7 **🚲🚌93** **🛈Rosmolen straat 2, Sittard; 0900-5559798**

Artifacts from the prehistoric pottery culture found at Elsloo are on display in the **Streek Museum**, the local history museum. In the Waterstaatskerk, dating from 1848, is the 16th-century St-Anna-te-Drieën by the Master of Elsloo. Remnants of Elsloo's earliest castle can be identified in the river at low water. Of the later Kasteel Elsloo, only one tower survives.

Streek Museum
🏠Op de Berg 4-6 🕐1-4pm Tue-Thu, 1-4pm, 2-5pm Sun 🌐streekmuseumelsloo.nl

14 Valkenburg

▲E7 **🚲🚌36, 47, 63** **🛈Th Dorrenplein 5; 0900-5559798**

The old fortified town of Valkenburg, situated in an area dotted with historic castles, is popular with visitors. In addition to sights such as a 13th-century Romanesque church and the ruins of a 12th-century castle, there are many other attractions, such as the catacombs, **Gemeentegrot** (a Roman quarry and cave complex), a cable car and the Steenkolenmijn (coal mine).

15 Eijsden

▲E7 **🚲🚌58, 59** **🛈Breusterstraat 27; 0900-5559798**

Eijsden, the southernmost town in the Netherlands, is a protected rural area. There is a pleasant walk to be had here along the quiet Maas quay. Kasteel Eijsden was built in 1636 in the Maasland Renaissance style on the foundations of an earlier stronghold. The castle itself is not open to the public, but the park makes for a pleasant stroll.

VINEYARDS IN SOUTHERN LIMBURG

The Netherlands might not be synonymous with wine, but there are in fact over 170 vineyards across the land producing some impressive reds and whites. Most are located in southern Limburg, where the temperatures are just a little higher than in the rest of the country. The oldest vineyard in the country is the Wijngaard Apostelhoeve, though only dating back to 1971.

← The ruined castle of Valkenberg, overlooking the town below

16
Heerlen

AE7 **R** **i**Bongerd 19; 0900-5559798

The Roman town of Coriovallum has been discovered beneath Heerlen. The **Thermenmuseum** contains the foundations of the ancient thermae and many everyday items from Roman times. Romanesque St Pancratiuskerk dates back to the 12th century. In the 20th century, until 1974, Heerlen was the centre of coal mining in Limburg. F P J Peutz built the town hall and former Schunck department store (known as the Glaspaleis, or crystal-glass palace) in the 1930s.

Thermenmuseum
ACoriovallumstraat 9 **C**045-5605100 **O**10am–5pm Tue-Fri, noon–5pm Sat, Sun & public hols **Q**1 Jan, Carnival, 24 & 25 Dec

17
Hoensbroek

AE7 **R** **i**Hoofdstraat 26; 0900-5559798

Before the state-run Emma mine was opened here in 1908, Hoensbroek was a sleepy farming town. It subsequently grew into the centre of the Dutch coal mining industry. Its industrial importance waned with the closing of the mines.

Kasteel Hoensbroek was built in the Middle Ages. All that remains of the original castle is the round corner-tower. The wings and towers around the rectangular inner courtyard date from the 17th and 18th centuries. It is now a cultural centre and museum.

Kasteel Hoensbroek
AKlinkertstraat 17 **O**10am–5pm daily **W**kasteelhoensbroek.nl

↑ An 18th-century Rococo-style salon in Kasteel Hoensbroek

A DRIVING TOUR
HEUVELLAND

Length 80 km (50 miles) **Stopping-off points** There are especially good viewpoints at Noorbeek, Slenaken and Epen **Terrain** Some hilly areas with narrow roads along the route

In the Zuid Limburg region of Heuvelland, the hills and the river valleys are covered with fertile loess soil, which occurs nowhere else in Holland. In the peaceful rolling countryside, with its stunning views, is a region of wooded banks, orchards and fields, dotted with picturesque villages and castles, and criss-crossed by narrow roads passing through cuttings with roadside shrines and field chapels. Here in Holland's most southerly region, there are even vineyards; in the 18th century, this was a substantial wine-making region. With its rich and varied agricultural heritage, Heuvelland just may be one of the prettiest parts of Holland.

The most famous of the vineyards that can still be found in the region is **Apostelhoeve.** *Here, above the de Jeker river, white wine is made from Müller-Thürgau, Riesling, Auxerrois and Pinot Gris grapes grown on the valley slopes.*

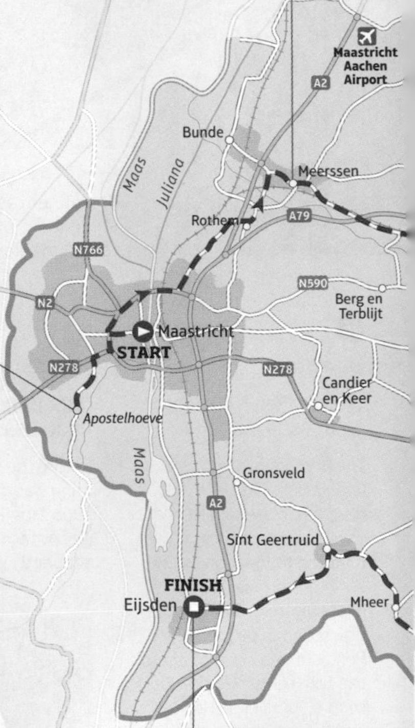

The Basilica of the Holy Sacrament *in Meerssen, built in late 14th century Maasland Gothic style, is one of the most elegant churches in Holland.*

0 kilometres — 5
0 miles — 5

N ↑

Bunde

Meerssen

Rothem

A79

N766

N590

Berg en Terblijt

N2

Maastricht
START

N278

N278

Candier en Keer

Apostelhoeve

Gronsveld

A2

Sint Geertruid

FINISH
Eijsden

Mheer

The imposing **Kasteel Eijsden,** *a moated manor house, was built in the Maasland Renaissance style in 1636. You can walk its parkland for free.*

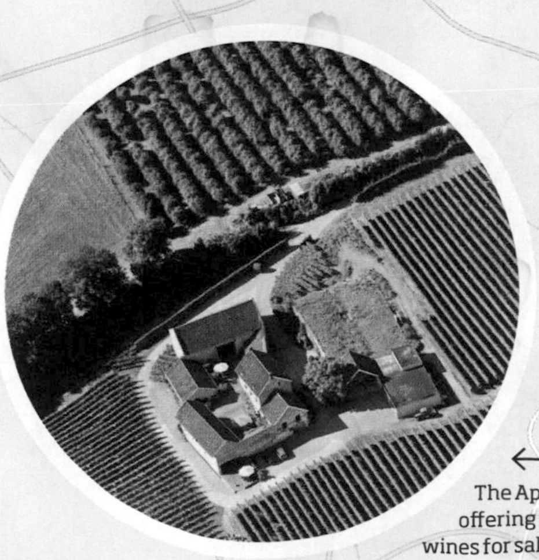

← The Apostelhoeve vineyard, offering its well-respected wines for sale at the cellar door

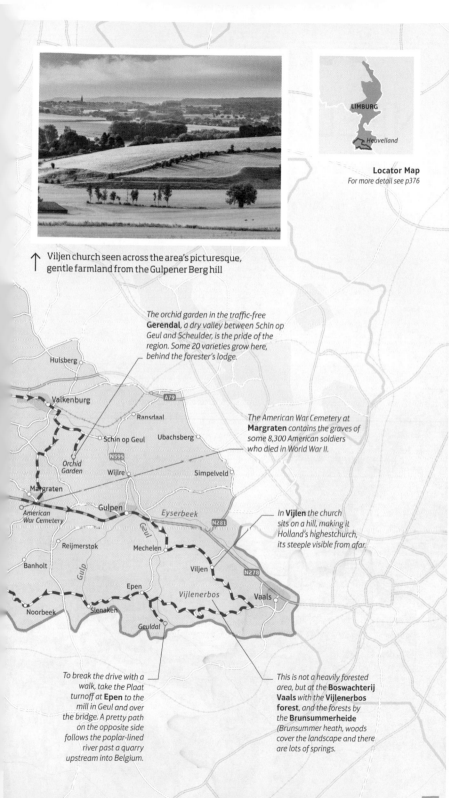

↑ Viljen church seen across the area's picturesque, gentle farmland from the Gulpener Berg hill

Locator Map
For more detail see p376

LIMBURG

Heuvelland

The orchid garden in the traffic-free **Gerendal**, *a dry valley between Schin op Geul and Scheulder, is the pride of the region. Some 20 varieties grow here, behind the forester's lodge.*

The American War Cemetery at **Margraten** *contains the graves of some 8,300 American soldiers who died in World War II.*

In **Vijlen** *the church sits on a hill, making it Holland's highest church, its steeple visible from afar.*

Hulsberg

Valkenburg

A79

Ransdaal

Schin op Geul   Ubachsberg

N595

Orchid
Garden   Wijlre   Simpelveld

Margraten

Eyserbeek   N281

American
War Cemetery   Gulpen

Reijmerstok   Mechelen

Banholt   Viljen   N278

Epen   *Vijlenerbos*

Noorbeek   Slenaken   Vaals

Geuldal

To break the drive with a walk, take the Plaat turnoff at **Epen** *to the mill in Geul and over the bridge. A pretty path on the opposite side follows the poplar-lined river past a quarry upstream into Belgium.*

This is not a heavily forested area, but at the **Boswachterij Vaals** with the **Vijlenerbos forest**, *and the forests by the* **Brunsummerheide** *(Brunsummer heath, woods cover the landscape and there are lots of springs.*

NEED TO KNOW

Bicycles on Amsterdam's snowy canal side

BEFORE YOU GO

Forward planning is essential to any successful trip. Be prepared for all eventualities by considering the following points before you travel.

AT A GLANCE

CURRENCY
Euro (EUR)

AVERAGE DAILY SPEND

SAVE	SPEND	SPLURGE
€80	€170	€300

BOTTLED WATER	COFFEE	BEER	DINNER FOR TWO
€1.00	€3.00	€5.00	€65

ESSENTIAL PHRASES

Hello	Hallo
Goodbye	Tot ziens
Please	Alstublieft
Thank you	Dank u
Do you speak English?	Spreekt u Engels?
I don't understand	Ik begrijp het niet

ELECTRICITY SUPPLY

Power sockets are type C and F, fitting two-pronged plugs. Standard voltage is 220–230v.

Passports and visas

EU and EEA nationals, plus citizens of Australia, New Zealand, Canada and the USA, do not need a visa to enter the Netherlands if staying for 90 days or less, but they do need a valid passport. Travellers from most other countries need a passport and a tourist visa for visits of less than 90 days. For more information, check the **Netherlands and You** website or contact the nearest Dutch embassy.
Netherlands and You
🅦 netherlandsandyou.nl

Travel Safety Advice

Visitors can get up-to-date travel safety information from the **UK Foreign and Commonwealth Office**, the **US Department of State** and the **Australian Department of Foreign Affairs and Trade**.
Australia
🅦 smartraveller.gov.au
UK
🅦 gov.uk/foreign-travel-advice
US
🅦 travel.state.gov

Customs Information

An individual is permitted to carry the following within the EU for personal use:
Tobacco products 800 cigarettes, 400 cigarillos, 200 cigars or 1kg of smoking tobacco.
Alcohol 10 litres of alcoholic beverages above 22 per cent strength, 20 litres of alcoholic beverages below 22 per cent strength, 90 litres of wine (60 litres of which can be sparkling) and 110 litres of beer.
Cash If you plan to enter or leave the EU with €10,000 or more in cash (or the equivalent in other currencies) you must declare it to the customs authorities.

Insurance

It is wise to take out an insurance policy covering theft, loss of belongings, medical problems,

repatriation costs, cancellations and delays. EU/EEA citizens are eligible for free or discounted medical treatment within the Dutch public healthcare system, but may be asked to produce documentation proving eligibility, such as a valid **EHIC** (European Health Insurance Card) and a current passport. Non-EU/EEA nationals are not entitled to free or discounted treatment, although some countries, such as Australia, do have limited mutual healthcare agreements with the Netherlands.

EHIC

W gov.uk/european-health-insurance-card

Vaccinations

No inoculations are needed for the Netherlands.

Money

Major credit, debit and prepaid currency cards are accepted in most hotels, shops and restaurants. Contactless payments are widely accepted, even on public transport. However, it is always wise to carry some cash, as some smaller establishments and street markets won't accept card payments.

Booking Accommodation

The Netherlands offers a wide variety of accommodation, from family-run B&Bs and budget hostels to luxury five-star hotels. Amsterdam is busy all year round and its prices are a good deal higher than elsewhere. Algorithms dominate hotel websites, with prices varying enormously according to demand. In the rest of the country, the busiest period is usually the summer holidays. It's wise to book ahead at any time of the year, especially if you are catching a ferry to one of the islands.

Travellers with Specific Needs

In Amsterdam and other major cities, the most obvious difficulty you'll encounter is in handling the cobbled streets and narrow pavements of the older districts, where key sights tend to be located. Provision for travellers with specific needs on the country's urban public transport is only average, although improving – many new buses, for instance, are wheelchair-accessible.

Places that are certified wheelchair-accessible now display the International Accessibility Symbol (IAS). If you intending to use the Dutch train network and would like platform assistance, phone the **Bureau Assistentieverlening Gehandicapten** (Disabled Assistance Office) at least 24 hours before your train departs, and there will be someone to help you at the station. **NS** (Nederlandse Spoorwegen), the main train company, publishes information about train travel for travellers with specific needs on its website, and **Visit Holland** is another a good source of information.

Bureau Assistentieverlening Gehandicapten

C 030 235 7822

NS

W ns.nl

Visit Holland

W holland.com

Language

Dutch is the official language, but English is widely understood, particularly in Amsterdam and the big cities of the Randstad.

Closures

Mondays Some smaller shops and businesses are closed on Monday mornings; many museums are closed for the entire day.

Sundays Many shops and stores are closed, except in the larger cities where most open from 11am/noon to 5pm.

Public holidays Public services, shops, museums and attractions are mostly closed.

PUBLIC HOLIDAYS	
1 Jan	New Year's Day
Mar/Apr	Good Friday
Mar/Apr	Easter Sunday
Mar/Apr	Easter Monday
27 Apr	King's Day
5 May	Liberation Day
May	Ascension Day (40 days after Easter)
May/Jun	Whit Sunday and Monday
25 & 26 Dec	Christmas
31 Dec	New Year's Eve

GETTING AROUND

Whether you are visiting for a short city break or rural retreat, discover how best to reach your destination and travel like a pro.

PUBLIC TRANSPORT COSTS

AMSTERDAM

€3.20

Single ticket
Metro, tram, bus

ROTTERDAM

€4.00

Single ticket
Metro, tram, bus

DEN HAAG

€4.00

Single ticket
Tram, bus

TOP TIP
OV-chipkaart offers good savings on normal price tickets across the country.

SPEED LIMIT

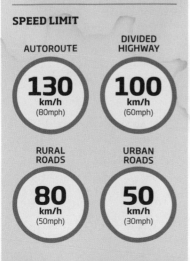

AUTOROUTE

130 km/h (80mph)

DIVIDED HIGHWAY

100 km/h (60mph)

RURAL ROADS

80 km/h (50mph)

URBAN ROADS

50 km/h (30mph)

Arriving by Air

Amsterdam Schiphol, the country's main international hub, is one of Europe's busiest airports. It offers flights to all major European cities as well as to airports around the world, including many in the United States.

Schiphol is well connected to Amsterdam's city centre by train, bus and taxi. **Connexxion Schiphol Hotel Shuttle** is a privately run minibus service that will transport you to and from almost every hotel in Amsterdam. Trains from Schiphol Station connect to all large cities in the Netherlands. In addition, the airport has good bus connections with many towns.

There are direct international flights between Rotterdam and Eindhoven and Manchester and London, and between Maastricht and Munich, Berlin and London. Rotterdam, Eindhoven, Maastricht and Groningen are all also served by domestic flights.

Amsterdam Schiphol
w schiphol.nl
Connexxion Schiphol Hotel Shuttle
w schipholhotelshuttle.nl

Train travel

International Train Travel
Regular international trains connect the major cities of the Netherlands with all neighbouring countries via three high-speed trains – **Thalys**, **InterCityExpress (ICE)**, operated by NS, and **Eurostar**. Most services require advance bookings and seat reservations. Eurail and Interrail sell passes (to European non-residents and residents respectively) for rail travel to and within the Netherlands. The rules for these two passes are complex, but the **Rail Europe** website has information and details.

Eurostar
w eurostar.com
InterCityExpress (ICE)
w nsinternational.nl
Rail Europe
w raileurope.com
Thalys
w thalys.com

GETTING TO AND FROM AMSTERDAM SCHIPHOL AIRPORT

Transport	Journey Time	Average Fare
Bus 397	30 mins	€6.50
Connexxion Schiphol Hotel Shuttle	from 40 mins	€18
Schiphol Travel Taxi	from 40 mins	€32
Taxi	from 40 mins	€40-60
Train (Sprinter or Intercity)	15-20 mins	€4.50

RAIL JOURNEY PLANNER

This map is intended as a handy reference for travel by rail within the Netherlands. Journey times given below are for the fastest available service on each route.

Leeuwarden
Groningen
Zwolle
Amsterdam
Utrecht
Den Haag
Arnhem
Rotterdam
's-Hertogenbosch

••• Train routes

Maastricht

Amsterdam to Den Haag	50 mins	Rotterdam to Den Haag	30 mins
Amsterdam to Leeuwarden	2 hrs 10 mins	Rotterdam to Utrecht	40 mins
Leeuwarden to Groningen	50 mins	Zwolle to Arnhem	1 hr
Maastricht to Arnhem	2.5 hrs	Zwolle to Groningen	1 hr
Maastricht to Utrecht	2 hrs	Zwolle to Leeuwarden	1 hr

Domestic Train Travel

Easily the best way of travelling round the Netherlands is by train. The system is operated by **NS** (Nederlandse Spoorwegen), and trains are fast, frequent and generally reliable. NS domestic trains come in two types: Intercity for speedy city-to-city connections and Sprinter on local routes with multiple stops.

Ordinary train fares are calculated by the kilometre with the rate diminishing the further you travel. Same-day return tickets can provide substantial discounts on the ordinary fare, as can weekend deals, but normally a return ticket is simply double the price of a single. Tickets are sold at the ticket office at every station and at multilingual ticket machines on every station concourse. Rather confusingly, there are two sorts of ticketing machines – one with the NS logo for buying an individual ticket; the other for passengers using a plastic **OV-chipkaart**, a plastic, rechargeable smart card that is checked against an electronic reader when you use any part of the public transport network. If you are staying in the country for a week or two, it's worth investing in an OV-chipkaart as these offer significant savings on the normal price.
NS
w ns.nl
OV-chipkaart
w ov-chipkaart.nl

Long-Distance Buses

For travellers from many European countries, the cheapest way to reach the Netherlands is by bus. A dense network of services includes regular buses to all major Dutch cities from many European capitals, but Amsterdam is especially well served. One of the biggest operators is **Eurolines**, who, for example, run a daily service from London to Amsterdam (12 hours) and Den Haag (10 hours). **Flixbus** also offers a variety of routes to Amsterdam from other European cities. Almost all these long-distance buses have toilets and make regular stops.

Within the Netherlands, a patchwork of different bus companies supplements the train network, reaching almost every rural bolthole. Conveniently, most local bus services are either routed through or begin at the nearest train station. Tickets can be bought direct from the driver, but in remoter spots some bus services only operate after passengers have made an advance booking; timetables indicate where this is the case. Regional bus timetables are sold at some train station bookshops, but it is easier to go online.
Eurolines
w eurolines.eu
Flixbus
w flixbus.co.uk

Boats and Ferries

Three companies operate car ferries from the UK to the Netherlands. **DFDS Seaways has services** from Newcastle (North Shields) to Ijmuiden, near Amsterdam (16 hours); **P&O Ferries** from Hull to the Europoort, 40 km (25 miles) west of Rotterdam (12 hours); and **Stena Line** from Harwich to the Hook of Holland (8–9 hours). Tariffs vary considerably, depending on how long you stay, when you leave, if you're taking a car, what size it is and how many passengers are in it. As a sample fare, a weekend excursion from Hull to the Europoort for two adults, a car and a cabin could cost €240 return.
DFDS Seaways
w dfdsseaways.co.uk
P&O Ferries
w poferries.com
Stena Line
w stenaline.co.uk

Public Transport

Buses and Trams
In Amsterdam, Rotterdam, Utrecht and Den Haag, buses and trams are the core of the public transport system, operating in tandem. Tickets can be bought direct from the driver, although there are savings to be made if you buy ahead of time – there are multilingual ticket machines at most urban tram stops. Visit **9292**'s website for local bus and tram timetables and journey planning resources.
9292
w 9292.nl

Water Taxis and Boats
In several major cities, water taxis supplement the public transport system and are an inexpensive and often scenic way to traverse rivers and canals. Amsterdam is famous for its canal cruises – a tourist favourite – but the city also operates free passenger ferries across the River IJ to its up-and-coming northern districts.

Taxis
Official taxis are readily recognized by the "taxi" sign on the roof and blue number plates. If you need a taxi, head for the nearest taxi stand – there are plenty of them. It is less common to hail a taxi in the street, although it can be done. Begin by asking the approximate fare of the ride before you set off. Taxis currently have a start rate of €7.50, which includes the first 2 km (1 mile) for a maximum of four persons. The final fare consists of the start rate plus the distance and duration of the trip. The rate per additional kilometre can be as much as €2.20. Waiting time is fixed at €33 per hour. A taxi driver is also

allowed to offer you a fixed fare, including a small surcharge for additional services, for example carrying suitcases; passengers must agree on the fixed fare and surcharges before the taxi ride commences.

Driving

Driving laws are usually well observed and the Netherlands is one of the safest places to drive in Europe. Driving rules and regulations are weighted in the favour of cyclists, reflecting the country's love of cycling.

Driving to the Netherlands

To get to the Netherlands by car from the UK, you can either take a ferry or the **Eurotunnel** shuttle train from Folkestone to Calais; advance booking is advised. From the Eurotunnel exit in Calais, Rotterdam is roughly 200 km (124 miles) away, Arnhem 260 km (162 miles) away and Amsterdam 370 km (230 miles) away. The capital is about 210 km (130 miles) away from Brussels and 270 km (168 miles) away from Cologne.

To take your own foreign-registered car into and around the Netherlands, you will need to carry the vehicle's registration and insurance documents, have a full and valid driving licence, and carry a valid passport or national ID at all times. EU driving licences are valid. If visiting from outside the EU, you may need to carry an International Driving Permit (IDP).

Eurotunnel
ⓦ eurotunnel.com

Driving in the Netherlands

Generally speaking, driving in the Netherlands is easy. The country has a good to excellent road network, signage is clear and most of the major towns are linked by some kind of motorway. That said, once you actually get into any of the major cities, one-way systems and narrow streets can make driving challenging. Park-and-ride facilities, available on the outskirts of cities, are much cheaper and less stressful than parking in city centres. The **ANWB** (the Royal Dutch Touring Club) provides breakdown services for members of foreign motoring organizations. A non-member can pay for the ANWB's services, or beome a temporary member for the duration of their stay.

ANWB
ⓦ anwb.nl

Car Rental

Every major international car rental agency is represented in the Netherlands. To rent a car, you must be over 21, have held a valid driver's licence for at least a year and have a credit card. Rental charges are fairly high, beginning around €280 per week for unlimited mileage in the smallest vehicle, but include collision damage waiver and vehicle (though not personal) insurance. Satnavs are rarely included in the basic price and cost about €7 per day extra. Watch for special deals offered by the bigger companies. If you break down in a rented car, you'll get roadside assistance from the particular repair company the rental firm has contracted.

Rules of the Road

Rules of the road are standard: drive on the right; drivers and front-seat passengers are required by law to wear seat belts; penalties for drunk driving are severe; and the use of mobile phones while driving is prohibited, with the exception of hands-free systems. The Dutch strictly enforce speed limits (p396) and use traffic enforcement cameras in urban areas and radar guns on motorways.

Cycling

The Netherlands is, of course, famously flat, which makes cycling a great way to explore the country. The short distances involved make it possible to see most sights with relative ease by utilizing the nationwide system of clearly signed cycle paths and numbered junctions: a circular blue sign with a white bicycle on it indicates an obligatory cycle lane, separate from vehicular traffic. Red lettering on signposts gives distances for fairly direct routes; lettering In green denotes a more scenic (and lengthy) route. Long-distance (LF) routes thread through the cities and countryside, often linking up with local loops and scenic trails.

For longer journeys, you can take your bike onto the train – bike carriages have a clear cycle symbol on the outside. You'll need to buy a flat-rate ticket (€6.90) for your bike, which is valid for the whole day, but space can be limited and on most routes bikes are not allowed during the morning and evening rush hours.

Bike Hire

There are lots of bike rental outlets in all the major cities. A standard, single-speed city bike will cost you about €8–10 a day, plus a deposit of up to €150. More sophisticated bikes are commonly available, but prices mount with the model. All the major train stations have bike rental outlets. In all cases, you'll need ID, and advance reservations are advised. Most train stations have cheap and secure bike storage. **Holland-Cycling** and **Nederland Fietsland** cover everything you need to know about cycling in the Netherlands.

Holland-Cycling
ⓦ holland-cycling.com
Nederland Fietsland
ⓦ nederlandfietsland.nl

PRACTICAL
INFORMATION

A little local know-how goes a long way in the Netherlands. Here you will find all the essential advice and information you will need during your stay.

EMERGENCY NUMBERS

GENERAL EMERGENCY

112

TIME ZONE
CET/CEST. Central European Summer Time (CEST) runs from the last Sunday in March to the last Sunday in October.

TAP WATER
Unless stated otherwise, tap water in the Netherlands is safe to drink.

TIPPING

Waiter	5-10 per cent
Hotel Porter	€1-2
Housekeeping	Not expected
Taxi Driver	Round up
Tour Guide	€4

Personal Security

The Netherlands is generally a safe country and most visits are trouble-free. However, when travelling late at night, avoid waiting around at train and bus stations. Note that Amsterdam's Red Light District can feel a little unpredictable; under no circumstances should you take a photo of a woman in a "window brothel" – if you do, be prepared for some harassment.

Beware of pickpockets in major tourist areas, and in all the larger cities be vigilant after dark. If you are cycling, always lock your cycle when you leave it.

If anything is stolen, report it as soon as possible to the nearest police station, and take ID with you. Get a copy of the crime report in order to claim on your insurance. Contact your embassy if you have your passport stolen.

Health

If you fall sick during your visit, pharmacies (*apotheek*) are an excellent source of advice – pharmacists can diagnose minor ailments and suggest appropriate treatment. If the pharmacy is closed, details of the nearest 24-hour service will be posted in the window. In general, health-care in the Netherlands is of a high standard and only rarely will English speakers encounter language problems – most doctors and nurses can speak at least a modicum of English, while many are fluent.

Under reciprocal health arrangements, EU/EEA citizens are entitled to free or discounted medical treatment in the Dutch public health-care system, but may be asked to provide proof of eligibility, such as a valid **EHIC** *(p395)* and a current passport. Non-EU/EEA nationals should ensure that they have medical insurance. EU/EEA citizens may also want to consider health insurance for items not covered by the EU/EEA scheme, such as repatriation. If you have health insurance, you can seek treatment in either the public or private health sectors. If you plan to stay in the Netherlands for more than three months, be advised that everyone is required by law to take out private health insurance.

Smoking, Alcohol and Drugs

Smoking tobacco is prohibited inside all public buildings, including train and bus stations, as well as in restaurants, clubs, bars and cafés. Curiously, it is also banned in cannabis-smoking coffee shops; there are still outside smoking areas on train station platforms. All hard drugs are illegal in the Netherlands, but cannabis use is essentially decriminalized for personal use and in small quantities; coffee shops are allowed to sell cannabis (in several forms) in quantities of up to 5g per person per day. The Netherlands has strict drink-driving laws with a limit of 0.5 mg BAC (blood alcohol content) for drivers.

ID

Every Dutch citizen over the age of 14 is legally required to carry ID and show it to police or other officials on request. Visitors are expected to follow suit by carrying ID at all times – a driving licence or a photocopy of your passport will suffice. If you don't have any documentation with you when requested, the police may escort you to wherever your documentation is kept.

Visiting Churches and Cathedrals

Entrance to most churches is free, although there may be entry fees at more famous monuments. Dress respectfully in places of worship.

Mobile Phones and Wi-Fi

The Netherlands has excellent mobile phone coverage at GSM 900/1800, the band common to the rest of Europe, Australia and New Zealand. Mobile phones bought in North America will need to be able to adjust to this GSM band. Before departure, check foreign tariffs with your phone supplier, but note that visitors on EU/EEA tariffs are able to use their devices without being affected by data roaming charges.

Post

The Dutch postal system is operated by **PostNL**. Since privatization, many former post offices have closed down and been replaced with counters in stores and supermarkets, although these can be difficult to track down. Stamps (*postzegels*) are sold at a wide range of outlets, including shops, newsagents, tabacconists and hotels, and post boxes are ubiquitous.
PostNL
w postnl.nl

Taxes and Refunds

Non-EU residents can reclaim the VAT they pay on certain goods and purchases over €50. The Dutch acronym for VAT is BTW. The rules and regulations are complex – but look out for the Global Refund Tax-Free sign when you make the purchase. VAT is currently fixed at 21 per cent in the Netherlands. **Global Blue** has information on tax-free shopping.
Global Blue
w globalblue.com/tax-free-shopping

Discount Cards

Several cities, including Amsterdam, sell city cards that entitle visitors to discounts on a range of attractions and free public transport for one, two or three days. The **Museumkaart** (Museum Card) gives free entry to over 400 museums and galleries nationwide for a year. Most major museums are in the scheme and the card can be purchased either online or at any participating museum.
Museumkaart
w museumkaart.nl

WEBSITES AND APPS

Holland.com
   holland.com is the Netherlands' official tourism website.
I Amsterdam
   www.iamsterdam.com is the official tourism website for the capital.
Instabridge
   Accessable offline, this app directs you to free Wi-Fi hotspots in Amsterdam.
VaarWater
   This app has information on boating routes, timetables and mooring spots.
NS Reisplanner
   The official app of the NS (Nederlandse Spoorwegen).

INDEX

Page numbers in **bold** refer to main entries.

PHRASE BOOK

IN EMERGENCY

Help!	**Help!**	*Help*
Stop!	**Stop!**	*Stop*
Call a doctor	**Haal een dokter**	*Haal uhn dok-tur*
Call an ambulance	**Bel een ambulance**	*Bell uhn ahm-bew-luhns-uh*
Call the police	**Roep de politie**	*Roop duh poe-leet-see*
Call the fire brigade	**Roep de brandweer**	*Roop duh brahnt-vheer*
Where is the nearest telephone?	**Waar is de dichtstbijzijnde telefoon?**	*Vhaar iss duh dikhst-baiy-zaiyn-duh tay-luh-foan*
Where is the nearest hospital?	**Waar is het dichtstbijzijnde ziekenhuis?**	*Vhaar iss het dikhst-baiy-zaiyn-duh zee-kuh-houws*

COMMUNICATION ESSENTIALS

Yes	**Ja**	*Yaa*
No	**Nee**	*Nay*
Please	**Alstublieft**	*Ahls-tew-bleeft*
Thank you	**Dank u**	*Dahnk-ew*
Excuse me	**Pardon**	*Pahr-don*
Hello	**Hallo**	*Hallo*
Goodbye	**Dag**	*Dahgh*
Good night	**Slaap lekker**	*Slaap lek-kah*
morning	**Morgen**	*Mor-ghuh*
afternoon	**Middag**	*Mid-dahgh*
evening	**Avond**	*Ah-vohnd*
yesterday	**Gisteren**	*Ghis-tern*
today	**Vandaag**	*Vohn-daagh*
tomorrow	**Morgen**	*Mor-ghuh*
here	**Hier**	*Heer*
there	**Daar**	*Daar*
What?	**Wat?**	*Vhat*
When?	**Wanneer?**	*Vhan-eer*
Why?	**Waarom?**	*Vhaar-om*
Where?	**Waar?**	*Vhaar*
How?	**Hoe?**	*Hoo*

USEFUL PHRASES

How are you?	**Hoe gaat het ermee?**	*Hoo ghaat het er-may*
Very well, thank you	**Heel goed, dank u**	*Hayl ghoot, dahnk ew*
How do you do?	**Hoe maakt u het?**	*Hoo maakt ew het*
See you soon	**Tot ziens**	*Tot zeens*
That's fine	**Prima**	*Pree-mah*
Where is/are?	**Waar is/zijn...**	*Vhaar iss/zayn...*
How far is it to...?	**Hoe ver is het naar...?**	*Hoo vehr iss het naar...*
How do I get to...?	**Hoe kom ik naar...?**	*Hoo kom ik naar...*
Do you speak English?	**Spreekt u engels?**	*Spraykt ew eng-uhls*
I don't understand	**Ik snap het niet**	*Ik snahp het neet*
Could you speak slowly?	**Kunt u langzamer praten?**	*Kuhnt ew lahng-zahmer praa-tuh*
I'm sorry	**Sorry**	*Sorry*

USEFUL WORDS

big	**groot**	*ghrooht*
small	**klein**	*klaiyn*
hot	**warm**	*vharm*
cold	**koud**	*khowt*
good	**goed**	*ghoot*
bad	**slecht**	*slekht*
enough	**genoeg**	*ghuh-noohkh*
well	**goed**	*ghoot*
open	**open**	*open*
closed	**gesloten**	*ghuh-slow-tuh*
left	**links**	*links*
right	**rechts**	*rekhts*
straight on	**rechtdoor**	*rehkht dohr*
near	**dichtbij**	*dikht baiy*
far	**ver weg**	*vehr vhekh*
up	**omhoog**	*om-hoakh*
down	**naar beneden**	*naar buh-nay-duh*
early	**vroeg**	*vroohkh*
late	**laat**	*laat*
entrance	**ingang**	*in-ghahng*
exit	**uitgang**	*ouht-ghang*
toilet	**wc**	*vhay say*
occupied	**bezet**	*buh-zett*
free (unoccupied)	**vrij**	*vraiy*
free (no charge)	**gratis**	*ghraah-tiss*

MAKING A TELEPHONE CALL

I'd like to place a long-distance call	**Ik wil graag interlokaal telefoneren**	*Ik vhil ghraakh inter-loh-kaahl tay-luh-foe-neh-ruh*
I'd like to call collect	**Ik wil "collect call" bellen**	*Ik vhil "collect call" bel-luh*
I'll try again later	**Ik probeer het later nog wel eens**	*Ik pro-beer het laater nokh vhel ayns*
Can I leave a message?	**Kunt u een boodschap doorgeven?**	*Kuhnt ew uhn boat-skhahp dohr-ghay-vuh*
Could you speak up a little please?	**Wilt u wat harder praten?**	*Vhilt ew vhat hahr-der praah-tuh*
Local call	**Lokaal gesprek**	*Low-kaahl ghuh-sprek*

SHOPPING

How much does this cost?	**Hoeveel kost dit?**	*Hoo-vayl kost dit*
I would like	**Ik wil graag**	*Ik vhil ghraakh*
Do you have...?	**Heeft u...?**	*Hayft ew...*
I'm just looking	**Ik kijk alleen even**	*Ik kaiyk alleyn ay-vuh*
Do you take credit cards?	**Neemt u credit cards aan?**	*Naymt ew credit cards aan*
Do you take traveller's cheques?	**Neemt u reischeques aan?**	*Naymt ew raiys-sheks aan*
What time do you open?	**Hoe laat gaat u open?**	*Hoo laat ghaat ew opuh*
What time do you close?	**Hoe laat gaat u dicht?**	*Hoo laat ghaat ew diklıt*
This one	**Deze**	*Day-zuh*
That one	**Die**	*Dee*
expensive	**duur**	*dewr*
cheap	**goedkoop**	*ghoot-koap*
size	**maat**	*maat*
white	**wit**	*vhit*
black	**zwart**	*zvhahrt*
red	**rood**	*roat*
yellow	**geel**	*ghayl*
green	**groen**	*ghroon*
blue	**blauw**	*blah-ew*

TYPES OF SHOPS

antique shop	**antiekwinkel**	*ahn-teek-vhin-kul*
bakery	**bakker**	*bah-ker*
bank	**bank**	*bahnk*
bookshop	**boekwinkel**	*book-vhin-kul*
butcher	**slager**	*slaakh-er*
cake shop	**banketbakkerij**	*bahnk-et-bahk-er-aiy*
cheese shop	**kaaswinkel**	*kaas-vhin-kul*
chip shop	**patatzaak**	*pah-taht-zaak*
chemist (dispensing)	**apotheek**	*ah-poe-tayk*
delicatessen	**delicatessen**	*daylee-kah-tes-suh*
department store	**warenhuis**	*vhaar-uh-houws*
fishmonger	**viswinkel**	*viss-vhin-kul*
greengrocer	**groenteboer**	*ghroon-tuh-boor*
hairdresser	**kapper**	*kah-per*
market	**markt**	*mahrkt*
newsagent	**krantenwinkel**	*krahn-tuh-vhin-kul*
post office	**postkantoor**	*pohst-kahn-tor*
shoe shop	**schoenenwinkel**	*sghoo-nuh-vhin-kul*
supermarket	**supermarkt**	*sew-per-mahrkt*
tobacconist	**sigarenwinkel**	*see-ghaa-ruh-vhin-kul*
travel agent	**reisburo**	*raiys-bew-roa*

SIGHTSEEING

art gallery	**gallerie**	*ghaller-ee*
bus station	**busstation**	*buhs-stah-shown*
bus ticket	**strippenkaart**	*strip-puh-kaart*
cathedral	**kathedraal**	*kah-tuh-draal*
church	**kerk**	*kehrk*
closed on public holidays	**op feestdagen gesloten**	*op fayst-daa-ghuh ghuh-slow-tuh*
day return	**dagretour**	*dahgh-ruh-tour*
garden	**tuin**	*touwn*
library	**bibliotheek**	*bee-bee-yo-tayk*
museum	**museum**	*mew-zay-uhm*
railway station	**station**	*stah-shown*
return ticket	**retourtje**	*ruh-tour-tyuh*
single journey	**enkeltje**	*eng-kuhl-tyuh*
tourist information	**VVV**	*fay fay fay*
town hall	**stadhuis**	*staht-houws*
train	**trein**	*traiyn*

STAYING IN A HOTEL

Do you have a vacant room?	**Zijn er nog kamers vrij?**	*Zaiyn er nokh kaa-mers vray*
double room with double bed	**een twees persoonskamer met een twee persoonsbed**	*uhn tvhay-per soans-kaa-mer met uhn tvhay-per-soans beht*
twin room	**een kamer met een lits-jumeaux**	*uhn kaa-mer met uhn lee-zjoo-moh*
single room	**eenpersoons-kamer**	*ayn-per-soans-kaa-mer*
room with a bath	**kamer met bad**	*kaa-mer met baht*
shower	**douche**	*doosh*
porter	**kruier**	*krouw-yuh*
I have a reservation	**Ik heb gereserveerd**	*Ik hehp ghuh-ray-sehr-veert*

EATING OUT

Have you got a table?	**Is er een tafel vrij?**	*Iss ehr uhn tah-fuhl vraiy*
I want to reserve a table	**Ik wil een tafel reserveren**	*Ik vhil uhn tah-fuhl ray-sehr-veer-uh*
The bill, please	**Mag ik afrekenen**	*Mukh ik ahf-ray-kuh-nuh*
I am a vegetarian	**Ik ben vegetariër**	*Ik ben fay-ghuh-taahr-ee-er*
waitress/waiter	**serveerster/ober**	*Sehr-veer-ster/oh-ber*
menu	**de kaart**	*duh kaahrt*
cover charge	**het couvert**	*het koo-vehr*
wine list	**de wijnkaart**	*duh vhaiyn-kaart*
glass	**het glas**	*het ghlahss*
bottle	**de fles**	*duh fless*
knife	**het mes**	*het mess*
fork	**de vork**	*duh fork*
spoon	**de lepel**	*duh lay-pul*
breakfast	**het ontbijt**	*het ont-baiyt*
lunch	**de lunch**	*duh lernsh*
dinner	**het diner**	*het dee-nay*
main course	**het hoofdgerecht**	*het hoaft-ghuh-rekht*
starter, first course	**het voorgerecht**	*het vohr-ghuh-rekht*
dessert	**het nagerecht**	*het naa-ghuh-rekht*
dish of the day	**het dagmenu**	*het dahgh munh cw*
bar	**het cafe**	*het kaa-fay*
café	**het eetcafe**	*het ayt-kaa-fay*
rare	**rare**	*'rare'*
medium	**medium**	*'medium'*
well done	**doorbakken**	*dohr-bah-kuh*

MENU DECODER

aardappels	**aard-uppuhls**	*potatoes*
azijn	**aah-zaiyn**	*vinegar*
biefstuk	**beef-stuhk**	*steak*
bier, pils	**beer, pilss**	*beer*
boter	**boater**	*butter*
brood/broodje	**broat/broat-yuh**	*bread/roll*
cake, taart, gebak	**"cake", taahrt, ghuh-bahk**	*cake, pastry*
carbonade	**kahr-bow-naa-duh**	*pork chop*
chocola	**show-coa-laa**	*chocolate*
citroen	**see-troon**	*lemon*
cocktail	**cocktail**	*cocktail*
droog	**droakh**	*dry*
eend	**aynt**	*duck*
ei	**aiy**	*egg*
garnalen	**ghahr-naah-luh**	*prawns*
gebakken	**ghuh-bah-ken**	*fried*
gegrild	**ghuh-ghrillt**	*grilled*
gekookt	**ghuh-koakt**	*boiled*
gepocheerd	**ghuh-posh-eert**	*poached*
gerookt	**ghuh roakt**	*smoked*
geroosterd brood	**ghuh-roas-tert broat**	*toast*
groenten	**ghroon-tuh**	*vegetables*
ham	**hahm**	*ham*
haring	**haa-ring**	*herring*
hutspot	**huht-spot**	*hot pot*
ijs	**aiyss**	*ice, ice cream*
jenever	**yuh-nay-vhur**	*gin*
kaas	**kaas**	*cheese*
kabeljauw	**kah-buhl-youw**	*cod*
kip	**kip**	*chicken*
knoflook	**knoff-loak**	*garlic*
koffie	**coffee**	*coffee*
kool, rode of witte	**coal, roe-duh off vhit-uh**	*cabbage, red or white*
kreeft	**krayft**	*lobster*
kroket	**crow-ket**	*ragout in bread-crumbs, deep fried*

lamsvlees	**lahms-flayss**	*lamb*
lekkerbekje	**lek-kah-bek-yuh**	*fried fillet of haddock*
mineraalwater	**meener-aahl-vhaater**	*mineral water*
mosterd	**moss-tehrt**	*mustard*
niet scherp	**neet skehrp**	*mild*
olie	**oh-lee**	*oil*
paling	**paa-ling**	*eel*
pannekoek	**pah-nuh-kook**	*pancake*
patat frites	**pah-taht freet**	*chips*
peper	**pay-per**	*pepper*
poffertjes	**poffer-tyuhs**	*tiny buckwheat pancakes*
rijst	**raiyst**	*rice*
rijsttafel	**raiys-tah-ful**	*Indonesian meal*
rode wijn	**roe-duh vhaiyn**	*red wine*
rookworst	**roak-vhorst**	*smoked sausage*
rundvlees	**ruhnt-flayss**	*beef*
saus	**souwss**	*sauce*
schaaldieren	**skaahl-deeh-ruh**	*shellfish*
scherp	**skehrp**	*hot (spicy)*
schol	**sghol**	*plaice*
soep	**soup**	*soup*
stamppot	**stahm-pot**	*sausage stew*
suiker	**souw-ker**	*sugar*
thee	**tay**	*tea*
tosti	**toss-tee**	*cheese on toast*
uien	**ouw-yuh**	*onions*
uitsmijter	**ouht-smaiy ter**	*fried egg on bread with ham*
varkensvlees	**vahr-kuhns-flayss**	*pork*
vers fruit	**fehrss frouwt**	*fresh fruit*
verse jus	**vehr-suh zjhew**	*fresh orange juice*
vis	**fiss**	*fish/seafood*
vlees	**flayss**	*meat*
water	**vhaa-ter**	*water*
witte wijn	**vhih-tuh vhaiyn**	*white wine*
worst	**vhorst**	*sausage*
zout	**zouwt**	*salt*

NUMBERS

1	**een**	*ayn*
2	**twee**	*tvhay*
3	**drie**	*dree*
4	**vier**	*feer*
5	**vijf**	*faiyf*
6	**zes**	*zess*
7	**zeven**	*zay-vuh*
8	**acht**	*ahkht*
9	**negen**	*nay-guh*
10	**tien**	*teen*
11	**elf**	*elf*
12	**twaalf**	*tvhaalf*
13	**dertien**	*dehr-teen*
14	**veertien**	*feer-teen*
15	**vijftien**	*faiyf-teen*
16	**zestien**	*zess-teen*
17	**zeventien**	*zayvuh-teen*
18	**achtien**	*ahkh-teen*
19	**negentien**	*nay-ghuh-teen*
20	**twintig**	*tvhin-tukh*
21	**eenentwintig**	*aynuh-tvhin-tukh*
30	**dertig**	*dehr-tukh*
40	**veertig**	*feer-tukh*
50	**vijftig**	*faiyf-tukh*
60	**zestig**	*zess-tukh*
70	**zeventig**	*zay-vuh-tukh*
80	**tachtig**	*tahkh-tukh*
90	**negentig**	*nayguh-tukh*
100	**honderd**	*hohn-durt*
1000	**duizend**	*douw-zuhnt*
1,000,000	**miljoen**	*mill-yoon*

TIME

one minute	**een minuut**	*uhn meen-ewt*
one hour	**een uur**	*uhn ewr*
half an hour	**een half uur**	*uhn hahlf ewr*
half past one	**half twee**	*hahlf tvhay*
a day	**een dag**	*uhn dahgh*
a week	**een week**	*uhn vhayk*
a month	**een maand**	*uhn maant*
a year	**een jaar**	*uhn jaar*
Monday	**maandag**	*maan-dahgh*
Tuesday	**dinsdag**	*dins-dahgh*
Wednesday	**woensdag**	*vhoons-dahgh*
Thursday	**donderdag**	*donder-dahgh*
Friday	**vrijdag**	*vraiy-dahgh*
Saturday	**zaterdag**	*zaater-dahgh*
Sunday	**zondag**	*zon-dahgh*

ACKNOWLEDGMENTS

The publisher would like to thank the following for their kind permission to reproduce their photographs:

Key: a-above; b-below/bottom; c-centre; f-far; l-left; r-right; t-top

123RF.com: bloodua 230-1t; ekinyalgin 165tl; giuseppemasci 246tr; keleny 252b; mediagram 140-1b; Carlos Edgar Soares Neto 8cla; William Perry 105tr, 122bl; skyfish555 231bl; Dennis van de Water 148bc; Rudmer Zwerver 322b.

4Corners: Francesco Carovillano 378-9t; Reinhard Schmid 216-7b.

500px: Bart van Dijk 74bl, 152-3.

A'DAM Toren: Martijn Kort 170b.

Alamy Stock Photo: Lee Adamson 247br; Joost Adriaanse 385tl; AGAMI Photo Agency / Marc Guyt 387b; age fotostock / César Lucas Abreu 186bl, / Historical Views 119cra; Alto Vintage Images 65cra; Archivart 64-5t; Archive Images 64tl; Arterra Picture Library / Voorspoels Kurt 281br; Artokoloro Quint Lox Limited 63crb, 202bl, 243cra; Peter Barritt 56bl; Henry Beeker 189br; Ger Beekes 32tr, 372-3t; René van den Berg 299bc; Bildagentur-online / Schoening 24crb; Blickwinkel / Agami / E. Tempelaar 353t, / C. Wermter 19tl, 272-3, / B. Zoller 281cra; Ger Bosma 28bl; Buiten-Beeld / Els Branderhorst 43cla, / Hendrik van Kampen 47crb; Magdalena Bujak 226-7t; cascoly / Collection Nationaal Museum van Wereldcultuern. Coll. no. TM-4551-28 66cla; Chronicle 66bc; Tim Clark 21cb, 324-5; Ian G Dagnall 52-3t; devi 392-3; Yury Dmitrienko 125br; Maria Douwma 305tr; Dutch Cities 214-5t, 293tr, 319br, 362br; Everett Collection Inc 63rt, 66tl, 66-7t; Peter van Evert 183bl; eye35 13t, 129t; eye35 stock 101bl; eye35.pix 76-7; Stuart Forster 49tr; Karen Fuller 187; Nick Gammon 54-5b; David Gee 123br; Manfred Gottschalk 238-9t, 244bl; Granger Historical Picture Archive / NYC 62bc, 64br; Renato Granieri 46b, 365t; John Green 249tl; Robbert Frank Hagens 51tr; Rik Hamilton 174tr; HelloWorld Images 89bc; hemis.fr / Maurizio Borgese 132tl, / Ludovic Maisant 248bl, / René Mattes 53br, 94rb, 114b, 167tl; Heritage Image Partnership Ltd / © Fine Art Images 186cra; The History Collection 382bl; Robert van 't Hoenderdaal 102bl; Peter Horree 20t, 32-3ca, 131t, 147tr, 173tl, 291t, 300-1, 336br; imageBROKER / Barbara Boensch 196bl, / Hans Blossey 67tr, / Günter Lenz 191tr, / Karl F. Schöfmann 389br, / Jochen Tack 308-9t, / Hans Zaglitsch 73tl, 92-3, 117br; incamerastock / ICP 65bl; INTERFOTO / Personalities 64clb; Zairon Jacobs 60cl; James Mundy, Nature's Ark Photography 281crb; Jon Arnold Images Ltd 253tr; Kim Kaminski / Let Me be by Myself © Kobra / DACS, London 2020 175b; Daan Kloeg 36t, 368tl; ton koene 60cr, 167br, 255br, 373br; ton koene / Statue from Memorial Center Camp Westerbork 318br; Sergey Kolesnikov 190clb (Crocus); Olga Kolos 67crb; Andriy Kravchenko 191br; Douglas Lander 126tr; Lanmas 64cr; Lebrecht Music & Arts 65cb; frans lemmens 12cl, 33tr, 38tl, 40-1b, 44-5t, 46-7t, 89tl, 123tl, 182clb, 188, 198tl, 268cra, 277cra (lavender), 330-1t, 356-7t, 380tl, 390bl, 391tr; Chon Kit Leong 227ca; Yadid Levy 24bl; David Lichtneker 48tl, 59c; Eddie Linssen 367tr; Iain Masterton 139ca; mauritius images GmbH / Hans Blossey 206b; McPhoto / Rolf Mueller 281cr; Roel Meijer 321tr; Iryna Melnyk 61br; MI News & Sport / Mark Fletcher / Ian Charles 305clb; Daryl Mulvihill 171tr; Perry van Munster 383t; Orange Pictures vof 305br; Painters 62crb; Panther Media GmbH 357br; Picture Partners 39clb; The Picture Art Collection 62t, 63cra, 66cr; PjrWindows 365cra; Premium Stock Photography GmbH / Willi Rolfes 346-7b; Prisma by Dukas Presseagentur GmbH / Van der Meer Rene 35tl, 264b, 297b, 350tl; Mieneke Andeweg-van Rijn 240tl; Olha Rohulya 310-1b; Joern Sackermann 17bl, 42-3t, 208-9, 260-1b, 352br; Maurice Savage 217tr; Scott Hortop Images 266tl; Lourens Smak 261crb; Pim Smit 128tl, 130tl; Richard Sowersby 243tl; SPK 41crb; Gunnar Freyr Steinsson 350bl; Steve Allen Travel Photography 388-9t; StfW 190clb; Bettina Strenske 61cr; Jochen Tack 366cra, 366-7b; Tasfoto 202cra; E.D. Torial 263cra; Universal Art Archive 65tr; Urbanmyth 383cra; Peter van Evert / Hendrick Petrus Berlage sculpture by Hildo Krop © DACS 2020 173br; Ivan Vdovin 186cl; S. Vincent 126tl, 242-3b; Lilyana Vinogradova 99br; W.Wiskerke 130tr; Monica Wells 41cl; WENN Rights Ltd 61cl; Don White 10ca; Wild Places Photography / Chris Howes 323tr; chris willemsen 48-9b; Sara Winter 184tr; Wiskerke 172-3b, 204b, 308bl; wonderful-Earth.net 281tr; World History Archive 139tr; Ernst Wrba 58tr; Bartek Wrzesniowski 269tl; Rudmer Zwerver 317tr.

Amsterdam Museum: 7cra, 97cla, 97cr; caro bonink 96-7b; Rene S Gerritsen 97crb; Monique Vermeulen 97br, 164-5b.

Anne Frank House: Cris Toala Olivares 113tl, 113tr, 113cla.

AWL Images: Peter Adams 50-1t; Alan Copson 198-9b; Jason Langley 163bl.

Black Bikes: 47ca.

Bridgeman Images: 63bl.

Collection Kröller-Müller Museum, Otterlo, The Netherlands: Jardin d' email by Jean Dubuffet © ADAGP, Paris and DACS, London 2020 348; Cary Markerink 349br, / Monsieur Jacques statue by Oswald Wenckebach © DACS 2020 and K-Piece, 1972 by Mark di Suvero, Collection of Kröller-Müller Museum, Otterlo, The Netherlands. © Mark di Suvero. Courtesy of the Artist and Spacetime C.C. 349cla.

Collection of the Gemeentemuseum Den Haag: Gerrit Schreurs 235t.

Collection Stedelijk Museum Amsterdam: 144-5b; Le violoniste (1912-13) by Marc Chagall Collection Cultural Heritage Agency of the Netherlands. Long-term loan Stedelijk, Museum Amsterdam. c/o Pictoright Amsterdam Chagall ® / © ADAGP, Paris and DACS, London 2020 145tl.

De Hoge Veluwe National Park: 347cra; Jurjen Drenth 347t; Ruben Drenth 347cla; Robbert Maas 51b.

Deltapark Neeltje Jans: 261br.

Depositphotos Inc: sakhanphotography 306-7b.

Doesburg Mustard and Vinegar factory: 36bl/

Dorling Kindersley: Clive Streeter 33tl.

Dreamstime.com: Evgeniya Alferova 191clb; Amoklv 370-1b, 386t; Andreykr 88bl, 138-9b; Antonfrolov 81br; Peter Apers 32tl; Asiantraveler 182bl; Atosan 96tr, 277tl; Anthony Baggett 13br; Benkrut 328cl; Izabela Beretka 166bl; Rene Van Den Berg 63tl; Frans Blok 2-3; Artur Bogacki 87bl, 116bl; Boris Breytman 149 185b, 364bl; Marcello Celli 362t; Denniskoomen 60crb; Devy 182bc; Digikhmer 102-3t, 235br; Dutchscenery 13cr, 21tl, 311tr, 312-3; Serban Enache 73c, 108-9; Inna Felker 90-1t; Harmen Goedhart 74t, 134-5; Goldilock Project 339cr; Tom Goossens 58-9b; Hansenn 36cr, 60cra, 331bc; Peter Hoeks 150tr, 372bl; Hpbfotos 220-1b, 262bl, 328b, 351b; J P 158cla; Ronald Jansen 316b; Ronald Jansen / Glass by Jaap Drupsteen, architecture by Neutelings Riedijk 207tr; Jjfarq 140t; Joophoek 128tr; Jorisvo 11br, 254-5t; Pavel Kavalenkau 148t; Peter De Kievith 36cl; Kisamarkiza 233bl, 234b; Kloeg008 320-1b; Georgios Kollidas 66clb; Jan Kranendonk 100t, 107br, 120t; Bogdan Lazar 106cla; Ethan Le 75, 151bl, 168-9; Lenazajchikova 190crb;

Chon Kit Leong 229t; Lornet 26cr; Madrabothair 296tl; Marcelmaaktfotoos 10clb; Mikhail Markovskiy 236-7t; Sander Meertins 11t; Minacarson 55cl; Napa735 31tl; Neirfy 232t; Nicknickko 205t; Olgacov 91br; Chris Rinckes 278-9t; Olha Rohulya 190-1t; Dmitry Rukhlenko 52br; Tatiana Savvateeva 127t; Siraanamwong 176-7, 369clb; Claire Slingerland 45cl; Alfred Georg Sonsalla 81cra; TasFoto 11cr, 17t, 178-9, 218b, 219tl, 226bl; Alexander Tolstykh 142-3; Tomas1111 16c, 70-1, 104-5b, 116-7t, 118-9t; Georgios Tsichlis 30-1ca; VanderWolfImages 244-5t, 354-5b; Venemama 35tr, 278bl, 298t, 380-1b; Dennis Van De Water 12-3b, 132tr, 144cla, 146-7b; Hilda Weges 22bl, 340-1; Tosca Weijers 219br; Ivonne Wierink 295bl; Sara Winter 8cl, 262-3t, 283br; Björn Wylezich 34tl; Kuan Leong Yong 240br; Rudmer Zwerver 18bl, 256-7, 277cra, 280t, 288-9t, 290bl, 294-5t.

Dries van den Berg: Ronald Bonestroo fotografie 39tr.

Efteling: 42bl.

Foam Museum: 121br.

Fries Museum: Ruben van Vliet 34-5ca.

Fruitcorso Tiel: Jan Bouwhuis 60clb.

Gemeente Gouda: 10-1b, 250cra, 250-1b, 251cl.

Getty Images: AFP / Lex Van Lieshout 213tr; AWL Images / Peter Adams 4; Corbis Documentary / Atlantide Phototravel 24cr; EyeEm / Fokke Baarssen 336-7t, / Guy Daems 268-9b; Moment / Daniel Bosma 22t, 276-7b, 332-3, / Hollandluchtfoto 12t; NurPhoto / Romy Arroyo Fernandez 61clb; Paris Match Archive / Michou Simon 67bc; Premium Archive / Anne Frank Fonds Basel 109hr; Soccrates Images 304br; Universal Images Group / Prisma by Dukas 202-3t, 318t.

Golden Consulting (IEFAF): Loraine Bodewes 61tl.

Groninger Museum: Marten de Leeuw 293tl; Ralph Richter 293cra.

Heinen Delfts Blauw: 49crb.

Museum Willet-Holthuysen: Caro Bonink 114cra; Monique Vermeulen 114cr.

Hortus botanicus Leiden: Wim Sanius 31tl.

House of Sports: MNO Photo / Menno van der Veen 304-5t.

iStockphoto.com: 35007 246-7b; ahavelaar 86t; bluejayphoto 270-1t; Peter-Braakmann 369b; csfotoimages 23tl, 358-9; Deejpilot 124-5t; DreamyHarry 61tr; E+ / Brzozowska 30tl, / Focus_on_Nature 50br, / republica 196-7t; espiegle 133t; freeskyline 26crb; georgeclerk 251tr; HildaWeges 19cb, 284-5; iStock Editorial / JJFarquitectos 18t, 222-3; Arie J. Jager 24t; justhavealook 98bl, 384-5b; Lorado 60cla; Madzia71 82clb; mila103 80bl; nantonov 247clb; Nettedotca 242cra; photonaj 338-9b; pidjoe 26bl, 158-9b; Prasit Rodphan 142cb; Siempreverde22 189crb; Sloot 265ct, 266-7b; TasfotoNL 212t, 282t; Vetta / IlonaBudzbon 8-9b; VLIET 28t; sara_winter 194-5t; YinYang 190fcrb.

Joods Historisch Museum: 26t, 82clb, 82br; Ardon Bar-Hama 82bc.

Kasteeltuinen Arcen (Castle Gardens Arcen): Joyfotografie.com 40-1t.

Manoir Restaurant Inter Scaldes: © 2016, Adriaan Van Looy 39br.

Markthall: 38-9b.

Mary Evans Picture Library: Sueddeutsche Zeitung Photo 306tr.

Mauritshuis, The Hague: 56-7t, 236br; Margaret Svensson 237cl; Ronald Tilleman 237br; Frank van der Burg Galerij / Prins Willem V 234cr.

MIESMEDIA: 30tr.

Museum aan het Vrijthof: 381tr.

Museum Het Rembrandthuis: 84, 85cr; Mike Bink 85bl; Gerhard Taatgen 57cla.

Museum Het Schip: Marcel Westhoff 53ca.

Museum Ons' Lieve Heer op Solder: 99bc.

Museum Prinsenhof Delft: 239cra, 241t.

The National Jenevermuseum Schiedam -Today's specials : Belinda Speijer 55tr.

National Maritime Museum Amsterdam (Het Scheepvaartmuseum): Marjo van Rooyen 159ca; Twycer / Igor Roelofsen 159tr, 159cra.

NEMO Science Museum: DigiDaan 161t, 161cla.

Nijntje Museum: mercis bv / Jan-Kees Steenman 43bl.

Olivier Utrecht: Michele Giebing 28cl.

Op Het Dak: Marlissa Hilkmann 45b.

Oude Kerk, Amsterdam: Gert Jan van Rooij 81tr, / Installation at Oude Kerk, Amsterdam 24 November 2017 - 29 Arpil 2018 NA-Christian Boltanski © AGADP, Paris and DACS, London 2020 81tl.

Paleis Het Loos: 345crb, 345bl; Hesmerg 345clb.

Picfair.com: Frans Blok 23cb, 374-5; Johannes Türme 139tl.

Rijksmuseum Amsterdam: 141cra; Carola van Wijk 141cla.

Rijksmuseum Boerhaave: 228br.

Rijksmuseum van Oudheden: Mike Bink 227tl.

Rijksmuseum, Amsterdam: 57br, 141bc.

Robert Harding Picture Library: Michael Jenner 112bl.

Shutterstock: Fokke Baarssen 6-7; Fotografiecor.nl 344-5t; Natalia Paklina 51cla.

Spoorwegmuseum: 28cr.

Stephen and Penelope: Mel Whelan 49cl.

SuperStock: imageBROKER 162t.

Tropenmuseum: Collection Nationaal Museum van Wereldculturen. Coll.no. TM-A-1389 157br, / TM-A-2357-77 157bl; Rob van Esch 156; Jakob van Vliet 157cra.

Van Gogh Museum, Amsterdam (Vincent van Gogh Foundation): The Bedroom, (October 1888) by Vincent van Gogh 142bl.

We Are Public: Annegien van Doorn 44bl.

Wetlands Safari: 58tl.

Wijnhoeve de Kleine Schorre: 54tr.

Wini Communicatie: Lucas Kemper 34tr.

Zuiderzeemuseum: Frank Bedijs 193cla; Erik en Petra Hesmerg 193tl; Heliante Moningka 192clb; Maria Stijger 193tr.

Front flap images:
Alamy Stock Photo: frans lemmens t, br ; David Lichtneker cra; **Dreamstime.com:** Napa735 cla; Tomas1111 c; **House of Sports:** MNO Photo / Menno van der Veen bl.

Cover images:
Front and spine: Windmills set along the Lek river in the village of Kinderdijk, South Holland. **AWL Images:** Francesco Iacobelli.
Back: **Alamy Stock Photo:** Ian G Dagnall tr; Don White c; **AWL Images:** Francesco Iacobelli b; **Dreamstime.com:** Andreykr cla.

For further information see: www.dkimages.com

The information in this DK Eyewitness Travel Guide is checked regularly.
Every effort has been made to ensure that this book is as up-to-date as possible at the time of going to press. Some details, however, such as telephone numbers, opening hours, prices, gallery hanging arrangements and travel information, are liable to change. The publishers cannot accept responsibility for any consequences arising from the use of this book, nor for any material on third party websites, and cannot guarantee that any website address in this book will be a suitable source of travel information. We value the views and suggestions of our readers very highly. Please write to: Publisher, DK Eyewitness Travel Guides, Dorling Kindersley, 80 Strand, London, WC2R 0RL, UK, or email: travelguides@dk.com

Penguin Random House

Main Contributors Phil Lee, Mike MacEacheran, Lisa Voormeij, Gerard van Vuuren, Robin Gauldie, Gerard M L Harmans

Senior Editor Ankita Awasthi Tröger

Senior Designer Sarah Snelling

Project Editor Amy Braddon

Designers Bharti Karakoti, Bhagyashree Nayak, Chhaya Sajwan, Stuti Tiwari Bhatia, Priyanka Thakur

Factchecker Lisa Voormeij

Editors Louise Abbott, Elspeth Beidas, Rebecca Flynn, Emma Grundy Haigh, Rachel Laidler, Sarah MacLeod, Ruth Reisenberger, Lucy Sara-Kelly, Lucy Sienkowska, Jackie Staddon, Brana Vladisavljevic, Danielle Watt

Proofreader Clare Rudd-Jones, Christine Stroyan

Indexer Helen Peters

Senior Picture Researcher Ellen Root

Picture Research Marta Bescos, Flora Spens, Sumita Khatwani, Rituraj Singh, Manpreet Kaur

Illustrators Hilbert Bolland, Jan Egas, Gieb van Enckevort, Nick Gibbard, Mark Jurriëns, Maltings Partnership, Derrick Stone, Khoobie Verwer, Martin Woodward

Senior Cartographic Editor Casper Morris

Cartography Rajesh Chhibber, Zafar ul-Islam Khan, Jane Hanson, Armand Haye

Jacket Designers Sarah Snelling, Maxine Pedliham

Jacket Picture Research Susie Watters

Senior DTP Designer Jason Little

DTP Designer Rohit Rojal

Producer Kariss Ainsworth

Managing Editor Hollie Teague

Managing Art Editor Bess Daly

Art Director Maxine Pedliham

Publishing Director Georgina Dee

First edition 2003

Published in Great Britain by Dorling Kindersley Limited, 80 Strand, London, WC2R 0RL

Published in the United States by DK Publishing, 1450 Broadway, Suite 801, New York, NY 10018

Copyright © 2003, 2020 Dorling Kindersley Limited
A Penguin Random House Company
20 21 22 23 10 9 8 7 6 5 4 3 2 1

A CIP catalog record for this book is available from the British Library.

A catalog record for this book is available from the Library of Congress.

ISSN: 1542 1554
ISBN: 978 0 2414 0937 4

Printed and bound in China.

www.dk.com